Francis Bacon
and his
Secret Society

Francis Bacon
and his
Secret Society

By
Mrs Henry Pott

Athens ‡ Manchester

Francis Bacon and his Secret Society

Published by: Old Book Publishing Ltd

Book Cover Design: Old Book Publishing Ltd

Copyright © 2012 Old Book Publishing Ltd
All rights reserved.

Title of original: Francis Bacon and his Secret Society

Originally published in 1891, Chicago, Francis J. Schulte &
Company

ISBN–10: 1-78107-152-7
ISBN–13: 978-1-78107-152-6

EDITOR'S NOTE

FRANCIS BACON AND HIS SECRET SOCIETY.

AN ATTEMPT TO COLLECT AND UNITE THE LOST LINKS
OF A LONG AND STRONG CHAIN.

BY MRS. HENRY POTT.

"Commend it, or amend it."

CHICAGO:
FRANCIS J. SCHULTE & COMPANY.
1891.

"Go. litel Booke, GODDE send thee good passage,
And specialie lette this be thy praier,
Unto them alle that thee wil rede or heare:
Wher thou art wrong, after their help to calle
Thee to corecte in anie parte atte alle."
—*Chaucer.*

CONTENTS.

FRANCIS BACON AND HIS SECRET SOCIETY.

CHAPTER I.

INTRODUCTORY.

" Read, not to contradict and confute, nor to believe and take for granted, nor to find talk and discourse; but to weigh and consider."

THE object with which this book has been written is to invite attention and help in clearing some obscurities, and answering some difficult questions, which have lately presented themselves, in the course of a close investigation into the works and aims of Francis Bacon and his friends.

Although, for the sake of brevity, propositions are here stated rather than argued, it must not be thought that such statements are dogmatic, or that the conclusions drawn by the writer are intended to be forced upon others.

So far as is possible, facts have been distinguished from conjectures, suggestions, or inferences. Nevertheless, since, to most minds, it is helpful to learn what general conclusions have resulted from certain disconnected items of evidence, such conclusions as have been reached are frankly offered, and will readily be withdrawn, if proof or stronger evidence should be forthcoming on the contrary side.

Let those who peruse these pages regard them only as the faint rays of a lamp of inquiry, which may guide others, stronger and more capable, to come forward and work, till this mine of truth shall be thoroughly explored, and its treasures brought to the surface.

The chain of argument which has been formed is of the following kind:

1. There is a mystery about the life, aims, and actual work of Francis Bacon. Ben Jonson (whose accuracy is never questioned) acknowledges this in his verses to Bacon:

"Thou stand'st *as though a mystery thou didst.*"

And Jonson's testimony to Bacon's immense and *poetic* genius, " filling up *all numbers,*" etc., would be unintelligible if we were to maintain that all is known which could be known about Bacon and his works.

The more we study these, the more we weigh his utterances, his fragmentary papers, his letters, his ambiguous or enigmatic notes, his wills, and the dedications and prefaces to many of his acknowledged or suspected works,— the more closely we compare the opinions expressed on any of these subjects, so much the more clearly do we perceive *the mystery,* the apparent contradictions which exist in his life and writings, and which embroil and confuse the statements of his innumerable critics and biographers. The *apparent* " contraries of good and evil " are, in Bacon's case, so many and so strong, that there is hardly an opinion expressed concerning him by one " great authority" which is not absolutely contradicted by another equally great.

2. In spite of Bacon's distinct and repeated statements as to the deep and prevailing darkness, the ignorant grossness of his own era; —in spite of his catalogue of the " *deficiencies*" of learning, deficiencies which, commencing with lack of words, extend through some forty distinct departments of learning; and not only to " knowledges," but to everything requisite to form a fine and polished style, or to express noble thoughts: — in spite of all this, we are taught to believe in an outburst of literary genius and of " giant minds," simultaneously all over the world, during the age in which he lived. Yet we are compelled to confess that Bacon's statements have never been challenged or refuted.

Philology shows a marvellous correspondence in the English literature of the Elizabethan and Jacobean period. True, some works are superior to others, as are the first efforts of a clever boy to the compositions of his mature manhood—still, a very decided resemblance in thought, opinion, knowledge, and diction is perceptible, when the works of the time are exhaustively compared.

This likeness extends even to foreign works, especially when they are divested of their Latin, French, German, Italian, or Spanish mantles, and appear as " translations" in very Baconian diction. In many cases the translations appear to be the originals.

3. It is manifestly impossible that any one man, however gigantic his power, could have performed, single-handed, all that we believe to have been done and written by Francis Bacon. But many entries in his private notes, many hints in his letters and acknowledged works, indicate his faith in the efficacy of united efforts, and that, besides the mystery which surrounded himself, there was also a mystery concerning many of his nearest relations and friends, who seemed to have worked for the same ends as he did, and perfectly to have understood the ambiguous language in which he expressed himself. Secret societies were common in the Middle Ages, and Bacon, we believe, was the centre of a secret league for the advancement of learning. This revival of learning was the " New Birth of Time"—the " Renaissance."

4. Examination into the history of the secret societies of the Middle Ages shows the Rosicrucian fraternity as the one of all others which would have been best fitted to promote Bacon's lofty aims; its very constitution and mode of procedure seeming to be the result of his own scheme or " method."

5. It further appears that no sharply defined line could be drawn between the method and objects of the Rosicrucians and those of the Freemasons; and that, in fact, although the prophetic imagination of Bacon carried him into the highest flights of poetic and religious aspiration, and into the sublimest regions whither the Rosicrucian brethren strove to follow him, yet he was observant and practical enough to see that there were things in heaven and earth unheard of in ordinary philosophy; that only

a few in his own times would be able to comprehend them, and that, even in the ages to come, such things must be " caviare to the general," and quite beyond the reaches of their souls.

Consequently, whoso would set about a " universal reformation of the whole wide world," such as the Rosicrucians dreamed of, must begin in a very humble way, and on the *low level*, but the *very broad basis*, which is the first stage or platform of Freemasonry.

6. A secret society implies and involves secret means of communication and mutual recognition—ciphers or secret writing. Mr. Donnelly's great discovery of cipher in the Shakespeare Folio of 1623 has been the cause of much investigation, not only into the typography of old books, but also into the art of cryptography, which, in and after Bacon's time, forms an important element of education in the higher schools of learning, especially in the seminaries and Jesuits' colleges on the Continent. " Every prince has his cipher."[1] It is certain that, in those dark and dangerous days, no correspondence of importance was conducted without the use of some secret writing or cipher.

So numerous are the works on cryptography published in the sixteenth and seventeenth centuries, that they form a small bibliography of themselves. The most important of these is a large octavo volume, published with a pseudonym (and under the auspices of the Duke of Brunswick, who is said to have patronized Shakespeare and his company) at Luneberg in 1623 (1624 New Style)—in the same year, namely, as that of the publication of Bacon's *De Augmentis*, in which his own cipher is described, and of the Shakespeare Folio, in which Mr. Donnelly has found a cipher narrative.

7. Inquiry as to cipher systems and their wide-spread use, and immensely varied forms, led to the observation that the use of stenography, or short-hand, though used as a method of " swift" writing, is, in some of the old books, found to be intimately connected with cryptography. The results of this research, so far as it goes, tend to show Bacon again as the introducer and great

---

1 Promus.

encourager of this short-hand cipher. It even appears probable that he taught it to his young assistants and secretaries, and that by this means a great deal of his wonderful conversation, and the contents of many small treatises, tracts, sermons, etc., were taken from his lips, such discourses being at leisure written out, sometimes revised by himself, and published at various places and under various names, when the opportunity arose or when the time seemed ripe.

8. With regard to the peculiar typography and the "typographical errors" which were tabulated from the Shakespeare Folio of 1623, it is found that the same peculiarities, the same "errors," the same variations in type, exist throughout the whole circle of Baconian (or "Rosicrucian") publications of a certain period. Such errors and peculiarities predominate in the most important works, especially in the head-lines, prefaces, indexes, tables of contents; and "accidents" in printing, when very frequent in such places, or in the pagination of the book, are, as a rule, not to be found in the text of the book itself. Usually one edition only contains these "errors and accidents;" often this is the "*second edition, carefully revised and augmented.*" Such books have every condition requisite for cipher.

9. In books where there are other distinct signs of Baconian origin, the wood-cuts are found to have a strange connection and affinity. The collation of a large number of tracings and photographs from a certain class of books reveals a complete chain-work, linking one book to another. This chain invariably leads up to Francis Bacon and his friends, as the authors, "producers," or patrons of those works.

10. The same system of mutual connection is found to be kept up by "water-marks," or paper-marks, in these same books. These paper-marks are extremely numerous and vary very much. From three to twenty-four different patterns have been found in one volume.

11. The tooling of the binding forms another chain of connection amongst these books.

12. Further examination discloses other secret marks, chiefly made, we think, to take the place of paper-marks, and inserted

during the last stage of perfecting the book. They tally with each other, and also form a complete chain of evidence as to the workings of a secret society. Say that they are printers' marks; yet they are *secret* marks produced with cunning, skill, and forethought, and not without expense as well as trouble.

13. All these secret signs are traceable, variously modified, and ingeniously introduced to suit the exigencies of modern printing and publishing, from the time of Bacon to the present day. The chain of connection seems to be complete. Inquiries amongst notable printing-firms and printers, and researches into books, supposed authorities on the subject, fail to produce definite information; but *the facts are not denied nor these statements refuted.* The impossibility of getting a straightforward answer to the questions, " Are these things true ? " or " Are these things untrue ? " confirms the long-growing conviction that the same system which was set going in the time of Bacon is at the present time in full working order; and that the Freemasons form the Arts and Crafts, the later-established and lower degrees of the society which, at the eighteenth degree, rises into the literary and religious society of " Rose Croix," or the " *Rosicrucians,*" as they were called by Andreas.

14. The Rosicrucians and the Freemasons speak in their books of the necessity for a " universal language. " This language is to be partly by signs, but also largely by symbols or emblems. It is the language of the " Renaissance. " A collation of passages shows that all the metaphors, similes, symbols, and emblems of the Rosicrucians and Masons, and of all the works which we connect with them, *are included in the works of Bacon.* The greater contains the less, and the language is his. No one has since improved upon it, although many have paraphrased and diluted his words, as well as his original thoughts.

15. Bacon's most intimate friends, relations, and correspondents seem to have been all either Rosicrucians, Freemasons, or *Illuminati,* as, in Italy and parts of Germany, they were sometimes called. Their names continually appear in connection with the works produced under the auspices of these societies; their portraits often include the recognized marks of distinction;

their very graves comply with the rules of the section of the society to which they belonged.

16. It is not concluded, from the evidence which has been collected, that Bacon *originated* secret societies, or that there were no religious fraternities or trade guilds, before his time, possessing secrets which they kept for mutual help and protection.

On the contrary, all evidence goes to show that *such institutions did exist*, in a rude and inefficient condition; that in all probability Sir Nicholas Bacon and others had conceived a thought of attempting to consolidate or erect some such society, for the purpose of reviving learning, and of promoting unity in religion. But it remained for the genius, energy, and untiring devotion of Francis Bacon to accomplish these things, and he seems to have been peculiarly educated for the purpose.

Throwing the whole weight of his gigantic intellect and the enthusiasm of " that great heart of his "[1] into the work of methodising and perfecting previous weak and disjointed schemes, he built up, step by step, stone by stone, the great fabric of learning, the " Solomon's House " which his descendants have kept in repair, and to which the " future ages " have made additions in some departments.

It was Bacon who designed the exquisite machinery or " engine " which still exists for the reception, arrangement, digestion, and wide-spread distribution of knowledge. It was he who, finding the new truth in vain trying to struggle up in a thankless soil, and the learning of the ancients smothered and buried in the dust of oblivion, set himself the task of raking and digging up and setting it forth again, polished and glorified with all the lustre of his radiant mind. The organisation or " method of transmission " which he established was such as to ensure that never again, so long as the world endured, should the lamp of tradition, the light of truth, be darkened or extinguished; but that, continually trimmed and replenished with the oil of learning, it should be kept alight, a little candle in a

---

[1] Dr. Rawley's Life of Bacon.

dark place, or a beacon set on a hill, burning with undimmed and perpetual brightness.

Many questions arise in the course of the inquiries with which the following pages are concerned — doubts and knotty points which cannot yet be definitely settled, but which must be considered open questions, fair subjects for discussion and further research. Present knowledge is not equal to the task of solving many such enigmas, and doubtless these will for a while continue to obtrude themselves. But we say "*present knowledge,*" speaking in regard to the world and readers in general. There is little room for doubt that the difficulties and obstacles which we have met with, and the obscurity which enshrouds so much of the history of Bacon and his friends, are neither dark nor difficult to a certain clique of learned men, still representing the brethren of the Rosie Cross. As to the lower degrees of Masonry, the Arts and *Crafts* (or the mysteries of handiworks), there are, doubtless, a limited number of personages, presiding over some of the Freemason lodges, to whom all these details are perfectly well understood.

It is by no means so sure that even the high initiates in any branch of the society are informed of *all* or of *the same* particulars. Probably the supreme head, or Imperator, and two or three of his subordinates, are acquainted with the whole history of the society, and with every detail of its method and present work. But with regard to the lower orders of the fraternity, it does not appear, from the evidence we have collected, that they possess any true knowledge or idea of their origin. Perhaps they believe the fictitious histories which we shall presently have occasion to glance at. But, at all events, so far as observation and inquiry have enabled us to ascertain, every craft or mechanical art, connected with Freemasonry, still keeps up the old secret signs, which, though now perhaps useless anachronisms, were, at the time of their invention and institution, excellent and ready means for the transmission of information and mutual intelligence, not only from man to man, in a living generation, but from man to posterity, and to " the future ages."

Masons mark the stones they chisel with marks which they do

not understand; but the architect who decorates his building, externally and internally, with the symbolic ornamentation of the Renaissance, is a Freemason of higher rank, and we do not suppose, from the specimens which we see of recent workmanship, that he, like the mechanics in his employ, works or designs in mere " base imitation " of his predecessors. The very nature, position, or circumstances of the buildings thus decorated prohibit the belief that their ornaments are casually or aimlessly applied.

In like manner, craftsmen, employed in the arts and trades of paper-making, printing, engraving, and book-binding, continue to reproduce, under certain circumstances, not only the old secret marks, but the old hieroglyphic or symbolic pictures, modified to suit modern requirements.

Here, again, it is plain that the simple craftsman is the mere tool, obediently performing, he knows not precisely what, or wherefore. But who orders and guides that workman? Who dictates the style of the peculiar designs which we see repeating the same story, handing down the same lamp of tradition which was lighted in the days of Queen Elizabeth? Whosoever he may be who dictates or designs, he is not, like the workman, ignorant of the what or the wherefore. When you meet with him and question him, he will not tell you that he " *does not know;* " he will reply that he " *cannot tell.* " To this is often added some suggestion as to the improbability of such a method being now in existence: " *Is it likely* that this system should continue ? Of what use could it be at the present time? " To the latter question we can only reply that, if this system was established in connection with a society bound by repeated vows of secrecy and constancy to continue it from one generation to another, we cannot see at what point they could ever break it off, except by discovery. It is precisely because of its apparent *inutility* in the present day, and because it seems that such secresy now hinders and confounds knowledge (without any compensating advantages), that we desire to aid in lifting that curtain which Bacon intended should be one day raised; and which we have good reason for knowing that many of his

2

followers desire to see withdrawn, though they may not move one finger for the purpose.

At the present hour it does indeed appear as if such marks and symbols were practically useless—anachronisms, in free England at least. Yet neither can we truly say that they are totally valueless, seeing that, little as we understand their purport, we have been able to use them as guides through a strange and unmapped region.

The very nature of the case makes it impossible to be accurate in describing these occult signs. Many of them, doubtless, are mere blinds, the puzzling dust of which we shall read, cast in our eyes with intent to deceive and mislead us. This is right, and as it should be; for it would be but a poor secret which could easily be discovered; and from Bacon, and in anything which he devised, we should expect the utmost ingenuity and subtlety combined with the greatest power and the wisest forethought ; — a scheme planned by Prospero, with mischievous improvements by Puck, and carried out by him in conjunction with Ariel.

We are armed and well prepared for a volley of perhaps good-natured abuse and derision from those, on the one hand, who wish to discourage others from following up the lines of research which are here indicated; on the other hand, from that very numerous class which so often attracted Bacon's notice — those, namely, who, never having studied a subject, are the more positive, either that it is a delusion, or that it is not worthy of study. His remarks on such critics are so satisfactory and exhaustive, that this prospect in no way troubles us.

There is yet a third class which has been before us throughout the process of collecting the particulars included in the following pages—students not too easily satisfied, but willing to take some personal trouble to reach the bottom of things, and to get at *the truth*. To these we need not say, as to the former class of readers:

"Before you judge, be pleased to understand."

But we do entreat that, accepting nothing at second-hand, taking nothing for granted, they will contribute some personal help in testing, disproving, or confirming the statements and suggestions made in this book, for, the sooner error is confuted and truth established, the better for all.

If these statements be incorrect, *those especially connected with trades and crafts*, it must be easy for those at the head of great houses connected with such crafts plainly and unreservedly to confute them. Men are not usually found to be backward in contradicting other men's assertions when they consider their own knowledge superior. And to the simple question, " *Am I wrong?* " the answer " *Yes* " would be at once conclusive and satisfactory, if delivered by a competent authority and an honorable man.

Such an answer has hitherto been withheld, and it cannot be thought unreasonable if for the present we continue in the faith that the statements and theories here set forth are approximately correct. When those who have it in their power absolutely to confirm or refute our observations will do neither the one nor the other; when published books are found invariably to stop short at the point where full information is required, and which *must* be in the possession of those who, having written up to that point, know so well where to stop and what to omit, then we are assured that the questions remain unanswered, the books incomplete, because those who have in their possession the information which we need are bound by vows to withhold it. In Freemasons' language, they " *cannot tell* "—an expression which recurs with remarkable frequency in correspondence on these subjects, and which is judiciously or graciously varied and paraphrased: " I regret to be unable to give you the information you seek " — " I am sorry that I can tell you nothing which will assist your researches "—" These inquiries are most interesting — I wish it were in my power to help you, " etc.

In vain have we endeavored to extract the answer, " *I do not know.* " Such a phrase does not seem to exist amongst the formulæ of Freemason or Rosicrucian language.

It has been our effort, throughout this work, to keep each subject distinct from every other; at the same time showing how all are inseparably linked and bound together; how every clue pursued in this argument leads to the same point; how all lines converge to the centre.

In attempting this, all effort at a pleasing composition in our book has had to be renounced, for it is better to be understood than applauded; and frequent repetitions are needful in order to spare the reader from puzzling and from the worry of perpetual foot-notes or references. He may often be disappointed at the slight and sketchy treatment which very interesting and important matters have received. But since the present object it to rouse inquiry, rather than to clinch any argument, or to silence objectors, it seems the wisest plan first to state and suggest, not stopping at every turn in order to prove each statement.

This appears to be especially desirable since it is notorious that, in such matters as are here brought forward, judgment will and must be delivered according to each man's light and knowledge. Those who know most will understand most, inquire most, and be the most interested and sympathetic. But we cannot " go beyond Aristotle in the light of Aristotle."

And surely our sympathies should rather be with those " who seek to make doubtful things certain" than with those others " who labor to make certain things doubtful." If so, let us beware of forming opinions positive and stereotyped upon matters of which we have but little knowledge, and which are only now beginning to be duly weighed and sifted. It is in vain to assume a knowledge if we have it not; and judgments delivered under the wig of Folly are sure to be soon reversed. Bacon underwent such mock trials in his own life-time, and he has told us how lightly he regarded them. " We decline," he says, " to be judged by a tribunal which is itself upon its trial."

To the end that this investigation may be the more easily and swiftly performed, we append a few notes, but for brevity's sake (and to avoid the deterring appearance of erudition which, to some minds, is produced by an array of quotations and references) these have been curtailed to a minimum. They will not satisfy the real lover of truth, but such a one will pursue the subject for himself, and dig to the very roots of matters which can be here merely noted or pointed out.

Before concluding these preliminary remarks, we would ask leave to say a few words respecting an idea which has lately become the fashion. This idea finds expression in the statement that it is impossible to credit the Baconian theories because they are *contrary to common sense.*

Common sense, we are assured, tells, or should tell us, that the notion is absurd that a great secret society exists in the present day; that there are ciphers introduced into many Baconian books; that Bacon wrote all that philology declares him to have written; or that he inaugurated the vast amount of works of all kinds which evidence seems to show that he did inaugurate. On the whole no one with any common sense can suppose that things are true which the speaker (whose common sense is always excellent) does not understand.

Such remarks, from those who have never studied the matter in question, invariably suggest the inquiry, — What is this omniscient common sense, which is supposed capable of deciding without effort, and by some mysterious short cut, many hard and knotty points which have cost the investigator so much pains and labor?

Surely common sense is not, as many seem to imagine, a kind of intuitive genius, or even a penetrative insight. Rather it should be defined as *the power of reasoning upon experience.*

For example, suppose a man never to have seen or heard of an egg; could any amount of sense, common or uncommon, lead him to expect that some day the shell would be cracked from within, and that a living ball of fluff and feathers would step forth? Yet, having seen one such egg, and the chicken which issued from it, the man would, on finding another egg, expect a like result. If, after watching a hen roost for many days or weeks, seeing the same phenomenon frequently repeated, he still remains doubtful as to what might come out of an egg, thinking it equally probable that, instead of a chicken, a mouse, a frog, or a swarm of bees might appear, we should consider him a fool, entirely without common sense, incapable of reasoning by analogy or experience. And so with all cases in which common sense is exercised.

Now, it is plain that things which are entirely new to us,
things of which we have never had any previous experience, are
not matters upon which we can successfully decide by common
sense. On the contrary, we must use some sense out of the common if we would attain to the knowledge and comprehension of
totally new sciences or branches of learning; and to learn new
things, as *Shakespeare* tells us, is the end of study:

Biron.   What is the end of study? Let me know.
Long.   Why, that to know which else we should not know.
Biron.   *Things hid and barr'd, you know, from common sense.*
King.   Aye, that is study's glorious recompense.

Those who, without any experience in the questions involved,
pronounce that Bacon could not have written *Shakespeare*, or
that there is no cipher in the Plays, or that Bacon did not found
Freemasonry and Rosicrucianism, or that, although the former
society exists, the latter does not, are going in direct opposition
to common sense, or to reason based upon experience.

For experience has shown that the philology, science, ethics,
and many other particulars in the Plays prove them, by internal evidence, to be the products of Bacon's heart, brain, and hand;
and hundreds of other pieces of evidence, connected with the
circumstances of their publication, confirm the doctrines which
are founded upon internal evidence. The evidence is precisely
of the same kind as that which has been held good in examining
the claims of many authors to their accredited works; and the
same rules of criticism which are employed in one case should
hold good in another, where the same similarities are seen in
infinitely greater numbers.

From the *Promus* [1] we gather the elements of a new
phraseology, newly coined words, turns of expression, metaphors, proverbial sayings, and quotations from five or six
languages; from the *Natural History* and the *History of Life and
Death,* a mass of scientific facts, new and curious in the days
when they were recorded and published. From the *Novum
Organum* and the *Advancement of Learning,* a mass of new

---

1 Bacon's private MS. notes, in the Harleian collection, British Museum.

ideas, theories, aphorisms, and philosophical reflections. From the *Wisdom of the Ancients,* parables " new " and " deep, " and mythological interpretations different from any previously offered.

Now, when all these things are seen reflected in the poetry of *Shakespeare* and other supposed authors, in days when we have the authority of the great Verulam himself for pronouncing knowledge " deficient " in nearly every branch of polite learning, common sense tells us that the author who wrote the notes, and the author who used them in his prose and poetry, was one and the same.

Again, when we find *Shakespeare* writing in many different styles; when we find his styles so varied that his warmest admirers differ and wrangle over them, and assign bits of his plays first to one author, and then to another, calling some plays " spurious, " others " doubtful; " when we find some of his poetry very prosy, and some of his prose to be finest poetry; and then, when the same observations recur with Bacon's acknowledged works, Ben Jonson praising both authors in the same words, but saying that *Bacon alone filled all numbers;* when we find the analogies between the two groups of works made patent by thousands of extracts and passages, on all conceivable subjects, and notably by a harmony of about forty thousand metaphors and similes, common sense is forced to declare that here again the author is one and the same.

When experience shows that Freemasonry exists, exercising the same functions, rules, and system as it did nearly three hundred years ago, reason tells us that what is a fact concerning the *lower* grades of a society is likely to be equally a fact concerning the *upper* grades of the same society; and when we see the Freemasons exhibiting and proclaiming themselves, in their meetings, dresses, and ceremonials, much as they did at their first institution, we find it contrary to common sense to maintain that the retiring and silent Rosicrucians, whose rules from the first enforced concealment and silence, *cannot now be in existence, because they are not seen or generally recognised.*

With regard to the use of ciphers, it is true that modern society has little or no experience of their use; but since the art of cryptography constituted in Bacon's time an important part of a learned education, it is contrary to common sense to say that the introduction of ciphers into printed books is either impossible or improbable; or that, though the societies which used them may still exist, working on their original lines, yet it is absurd to suppose that they know of the ciphers or use them still. If the society exists, its ciphers exist also.

There are some drawbacks to the delight of pursuing these many and various questions. One is the conviction which presses upon us, that all the information which we seek is perfectly well known to certain living persons; that the particulars which, with painful slowness, we rake for and sift from the dust of time, from books whose titles are generally forgotten, from manuscripts whose very existence is generally unknown, are all formally recorded, or have been verbally transmitted to those certain few; so that, in the endeavors now made toward reaching absolute truth in these particulars, we are doing what Bacon would call *actum agere* — doing the deed done — a process always unsatisfactory, and one from which we seek to deliver others who may follow in our footsteps.

It is, moreover, disheartening to know that this book must be, of its very nature, imperfect. It must go forth unfledged, "flying," as Bacon says, "out of its feathers." Hardly will it have flown, when the "dogs," Bacon's cynics, and his critics, the "birds of prey," will be after it, and hunt it down, and peck it to pieces. Yet if, perchance, it may be fortunate enough to attract the attention of some dozen students in our great libraries, *workers* in any department of knowledge, this little work will have fulfilled its mission. Perhaps some fresh streams of information may flow in to assist the subsequent portions of this book. At all events, even common criticism, hostile though it may be, will, we trust, lend further aid to the clearing-up of errors or misapprehensions, and to the "finding out Truth, though she be hid indeed within the center."

CHAPTER II.

FRANCIS BACON: SOME DOUBTS CONNECTED WITH HIS PERSONAL HISTORY, AND ACTUAL WORKS AND AIMS.

"I have been induced to think that if there were a beam of knowledge derived from God upon any man in these modern times, it was upon him."
—*Dr. Rawley.*

IT is certain that, although much is known about Francis Bacon in some parts or phases of his chequered life, yet there is a great deal more which is obscure, or very inadequately treated of by his biographers.

So little has, until recently, been generally thought about him, that the doubts and discrepancies, and even the blanks which are to be found in all the narratives which concern him, have usually passed unnoticed, or have been accepted as matters of course. Yet there are points which it would be well to inquire into.

For instance, what was he doing or where was he travelling during certain unchronicled years? Why do we hear so little in modern books of that beloved brother Anthony, who was his "comfort," and his "second self"? And where was Anthony when he died? Where was he buried? And why are no particulars of his eventful life, his last illness, death, or burial, recorded in ordinary books?

Where is the correspondence which passed for years between the brothers? Sixteen folio volumes at Lambeth inclose a large portion of Anthony's correspondence. Letters important, and apparently unimportant, have been carefully preserved, but amongst them hardly one from Francis. And where is any correspondence of the same kind either from or to him—letters, that is, full of cipher, and containing secret communications, information concerning persons and politics, such as Anthony was engaged in collecting for his especial use? The letters to Anthony are preserved. Where are those from him? Then, again, of his chief friends and confidants—why do his published letters and biographies pass over lightly, or entirely ignore, his intimate acquaintance with many remarkable men; as, for instance, with Michel de Montaigne, John Florio, Father Fulgentius, and Pierre DuMoulin, with John Beaumont and Edward Alleyn, with Giordano Bruno, Theodore Beza and Ben Jonson?

Or, turning to more general inquiries, how came there to be such an outburst of learning and wit in the immediate society of the very man who repeatedly pronounced learning and true literary power to be deficient? How was it that, although from the first moment when he began to publish all authors adopted his words, his expressions and his ideas; though they continually echoed, paraphrased, or curtailed his utterances, and set up his judgment as a standard, working, thenceforward, on his lines, his NAME was seldom mentioned, and that, even to this day, the tremendous debts owed to him by the whole civilized world are practically ignored? Seeing the prodigious difficulty which now meets any attempt to eradicate an old error, or to gain acceptance for a new idea, why, we would ask, did Bacon contrive so to impress, not only his new diction, but his new ideas, upon the literature and upon the very life of whole nations?

In the process of collecting material for a harmony between the scientific works of Bacon, *Shakespeare,* and others, it became apparent that many of Bacon's works, especially the fragmentary works, *Valerius Terminus, Thema Cœli,* the *Histories of Dense and Rare,* or *Salt, Sulphur and Mercury,* etc., still more notably the *Sylva Sylvarum,* the *New Atlantis,* and the *History of Life and Death* (published together, after Bacon's death, by his secretary, Dr. Rawley), as well as the *Praise of the Queen* (for the publication of which Bacon left special instructions), *were not that alone which they pretended to be.* They *profess* to be works on science or history; they prove, when more closely examined and collated with the rest of Bacon's acknowledged works, to be *parables,* or figurative pieces, conveying a double meaning to those who had knowledge enough to receive it.

These works (like the *Shakespeare* sonnets) are all more or less obscure and incomprehensible in aim or form. They are, apparently, full of allusions to other parts of his works, where similar expressions are applied to quite different purposes. Sometimes they are to outward appearance fragmentary, imperfect, manifestly inaccurate or incomplete, in matters with which Bacon was acquainted, yet permitted, nay, ordered, by him to be so published.

It is well known that Bacon's great desire was to be clear, perspicuous, and easily understood. Obscurity in his writing was, therefore, not caused by disregard of the limited comprehensions of his readers, or by inadvertence in the choice of words, for he was an absolute master of language and could write or speak in any style or to any pitch, high or low, which suited his subject. The obscurity, then, was, we are sure, *intentional.* He admits as much in many places, where he confesses that he finds it desirable " to keep some *state* " concerning himself and his works, and where he, over and over again, commends the use of reserve, secresy, ambiguous or parabolic language, of allegory, metaphor, simile, and allusion, which are (as he says in the preface to the *Wisdom of the Ancients*) a veil to hide from the eyes of the vulgar things too deep and difficult for their comprehension. It is desirable that this system or method, of Bacon, should be clearly recognised and understood; it forms a very important element in the matters which are presently to be discussed, and since there are many persons ready to enter into arguments connected with Bacon, but who have never read his works, no apology is needed for reproducing passages from various places where he speaks for himself and in no uncertain tones:

" *Parabolic poesy is of a higher character than others (narrative or dramatic),* and appears to be something sacred and venerable; especially as religion itself commonly uses its aid as a means of communication between divinity and humanity. But this, too, is corrupted by the levity and idleness of wit in dealing with allegory. It is of double use and serves for contrary purposes; for it serves for an infoldment, and it likewise serves for illustration. In the latter case, the object is a certain method of teaching; in the former, an artifice for concealment. Now, this method of teaching, used for illustration, was very much in use in the ancient times. For, the inventions and conclusions of human reason (even those that are now common and trite) being then new and strange, the minds of men were hardly subtle enough to conceive them, unless they were brought nearer to the sense by this kind of resemblances and examples. And hence the ancient times are full of all kinds of fables, parables, enigmas, and similitudes; as may appear by the numbers of Pythagoras, the enigmas of the Sphinx, the fables of Æsop, and the like. The apophthegms, too, of the ancient sages, commonly explained the matter by similitudes. Thus Menenius Agrippa, among the Romans (a nation at that time by no means learned), quelled a sedition by a fable. In a word, as hieroglyphics were before letters, so parables were before arguments. And even now, and at all times, the force of parables is and has been excellent; because arguments cannot be made so perspicuous, nor true examples so apt.

"But there remains yet another use of poesy parabolical, opposite to the former; wherein it serves (as I said) for an infoldment; for such things, I mean, the dignity whereof requires that they should be seen, as it were, through a veil; that is, when the secrets and mysteries of religion, policy, and philosophy are involved in fables or parables. *Now, whether any mystic meaning be concealed beneath the fables of the ancient poets is a matter of some doubt. For my own part I must confess that I am inclined to think that a mystery is involved in no small number of them. Nor does the fact that they are commonly left to boys and grammarians, and held in slight repute, make me despise them;* but rather, since it is evident that the writings in which these fables are related are, next to sacred story, the most ancient of human writings, and the fables themselves still more ancient, I take them to be a kind of breath, from the traditions of more ancient nations, which fell into the pipes of the Greeks. *But since that which has hitherto been done in the interpretation of these parables, being the work of unskillful men, not learned beyond commonplaces, does not by any means satisfy me,* I think to set down Philosophy according to the ancient parables among the *desiderata,* of which work I will subjoin one or two examples; not so much, perhaps, for the value of the thing, as for the sake of *carrying out my principle, which is this: whenever I set down a work among the* desiderata *(if there be anything obscure about it) I intend always to set forth either instructions for the execution of it, or an example of the thing;* else it might be thought that it was merely some light notion that had glanced through my mind; or that I am like an augur measuring countries in thought, without knowing the way to enter them."

He then gives three examples (to which we will by and by return), " one taken from things natural, one from things political, and one from things moral."

From this notable passage we learn, (1) that Bacon regarded parabolic poetry as a means of communication between Divinity and Humanity, consequently as of greater importance than any other; (2) of double use, for infoldment and illustration; (3) that the use of parables was sanctioned by religion and Divinity itself; (4) that it was largely employed in the philosophy of the ancients, and that, although this was a matter of doubt with others, there was no doubt in the mind of Bacon that the philosophical interpretation of the ancient myths was *deficient*, left to boys and incapable persons; and that (5) according to his custom, he was prepared to set forth instructions for the purpose of meeting this deficiency.

The examples given in the *Advancement of Learning* are but solitary instances. In the *Wisdom of the Ancients* (now too little read), thirty-one essays disclose to us the matured opinions of Bacon on this subject. The preface to that delightful book repeats at greater length, and in more poetic language, the sentiments expressed in the *Advancement of Learning*, that " parables serve as well to instruct and illustrate as to wrap up and envelope, and every man of learning must readily allow that this method is grave, sober, or exceedingly useful, and sometimes *necessary in the sciences*, as it opens an easy and familiar passage to the human understanding in all discoveries that are abstruse and out of the road of vulgar opinions. Hence, in the first ages, when such inventions and conclusions of the human reason as are now trite and common were new and little known, *all things*[1] abounded with fables, parables, similes, comparisons, and illustrations, which are not intended to conceal, but to inform and teach, whilst the minds of men continued rude

---

[1] "For there's *figures in all things.*" (Henry V. iv. 7.)

and unpractised in matters of subtlety and speculation, or were impatient, and in a manner incapable, of receiving such things as did not directly fall under and strike the senses. *And even to this day,* if any man would let new light in upon the human understanding, and conquer prejudice, without raising contests, animosities, opposition, or disturbance, *he must still go on in the same path, and have recourse to the like method of allegory,* metaphor, and allusion." Bacon had said in the *Advancement of Learning* — and he repeated in the *De Augmentis* in 1623 — that such parabolic teaching and method of interpretation was *deficient,* and that he was about to set forth examples for the instruction of others. His assertions and conclusions were never challenged or contradicted. On the contrary, his contemporaries tacitly acquiesced in his statements, and posterity has endorsed the estimate given by the great men of his time as to his vast and profound learning and his excellent judgment. When, therefore, we meet with other works of his time, *not published under his name,* but abounding in "the like method" and use of allegory, metaphor, and allusion, we may with reason question the origin of such works; we may even consider it to be a matter of considerable doubt. In any case we shall be prepared to find Bacon's own works abounding with metaphors and similes, and his new and subtle ideas and theories " *wrapped or delivered* " in a veil of parable, and allegory, and symbolic language.

Having regard to such considerations as the foregoing, it was thought necessary to test the matter by forming a kind of dictionary or harmony of the metaphors, similes, and figurative expressions in the acknowledged works of Bacon and in *Shakespeare.* About forty thousand of such figurative passages have been brought together from the two groups of works, and it is thus made clear that the metaphors and figures used are to a marvellous extent the same. They exhibit everywhere the same knowledge, the same opinions and tastes, and often the same choice of words; they mutually elucidate and interchange ideas; they are found to be connected by innumerable small links and chains with certain fixed ideas which reappear throughout the whole of Bacon's works, and which are indissolubly bound up with the system or method by which he was endeavoring to educate and reform the world. It will be observed that Bacon bases his teaching, in the first instance, upon the figures used in the Bible and by the ancient philosophers, but that he beautifies and expands every symbol, transmuting stones into gold, and making dry bones live. It is impossible to follow up the many questions which grow out of this subject without perceiving that Bacon must in his early youth have deeply studied and mastered the philosophy, not only of the Greeks and Romans (with whom he often compares himself), but also of the learned men of Asia and Africa. The works of Claudius Galen, Porphyry, Diogenes of Babylon, Constantinus Porphyrogenitus, and Confucius seem to have been as well known to him as those of the Africans, Origen, Diophantus, Athenæus, Athanasius, Euclid, St. Augustine, or Mohammed Rhazi. Many of the allegories and fanciful symbols or emblems which Bacon introduces into his writings, and which are also abundant in *Shakespeare,* seem derivable from such studies.

We shall presently have to consider the use which Bacon intended to make of this symbolic language and the manner in which it may be interpreted. Let it be said, in passing, that, although Bacon seems to have made an unwearied and exhaustive research into all the ancient philosophies attainable in his time, and although, in his early youth, he seems to have been strongly attracted by the study, extracting from it many beautiful and poetic ideas, yet there is in his works no trace of his mind having undergone the upsetting which is perceptible in so many modern students who have " puzzled their intellects" over the origin of religion. There is no indication of his having ever tried to persuade himself, or others, that Paganism or Buddhism itself was the pure and primitive form of religion from which Christianity derives all that is most good and elevating in its teaching or doctrine.

He observes the errors and corruptions of these old cults, although at the same time appreciating all that is worthy of praise; and in his effort to mingle heaven and earth, metaphys-

ics and science, the abstract and the concrete, he never indulges
in the ecstasies of mysticism or occultism, which modern students of these subjects, following the questionable guidance of
the mediæval orientalists and mystics, have allowed themselves.
The symbols which these ancient religions are said to have
adopted were in many cases connected with ideas and ceremonies gross and repulsive, the natural product of coarse and
ignorant minds. And these seem to have grown even more
coarse and injurious when the world—no longer in its infancy,
but assuming the airs and speaking with the authority of manhood—proceeded, several hundred years after the death of
Christ, to erect an elaborate fabric of philosophy upon the
original rough-hewn foundations; endeavoring to blend the
pure morality of Christianity, and the most sublime attributes
of Christ Himself, with the worship of Buddha, and then to
make it appear that the " Light of the World" is but a reflected
light from the " Light of Asia."

There is no trace of such a result from Bacon's researches into
the philosophies of antiquity, and it will be seen that, even in
adopting the emblems and symbols of the ancient religions, he
modified them, refined them, and separated from the dross of
base matter all that was pure, good, and bright, for the use of
man.

Doubts as to authorship, though intensified by examination of
the metaphors, etc., were not satisfied, and quickly gave rise to
others.

An attempt was next made to trace the notes of Bacon's
Promus, as well as his figures and peculiar terms of speech,
his opinions, scientific statements, and philosophic aphorisms,
into other works *not Shakespeare.* So few *Promus* notes of
this kind were found, when compared with the multitude of
them which are easily perceptible in *Shakespeare,* that, at the
time of the publication of the *Promus,* we were disposed to reject
as non-Baconian most of the Elizabethan dramatists excepting
" *Marlowe,*" in whose works at least five hundred points of sim-
ilarity to Baconian notes and diction are to be found. A closer

(or perhaps a more enlightened) study obliges us to modify these views. For it is observed that, although, in many of these works, the *Promus* notes are scarce, and the entries in certain folios of that collection altogether absent, yet, *wherever any Promus notes are discovered in the works of Bacon's time, or for some years later, there also will almost surely be found a number of metaphors of the same kind as those mentioned above.* The majority of these will be found traceable to the ancient philosophers and to the Bible, and are always used in the same characteristic and graphic manner in Bacon's works; the form of the metaphor being modified to suit the style and subject of the piece in which it is set.

This perceptible connection between the metaphors, the *Promus* notes, and the use of texts from the Bible, throughout the works of Bacon, and the school which he seems to have created, strengthened still further the growing conviction that he was the centre of a powerful and learned secret society, and that the whole of the literature contemporaneous with him was bound together by chains and links, cords and threads, forged, woven, and spun *by himself.*

With regard to the *Promus*, edited with passages from *Shakespeare*, and published in 1883, we would say that further study has thrown new light upon many of the entries. Some, which appeared very obscure, seem to be intimately connected with Bacon's plans for the establishment of his secret society. There are also many errors in the arrangement of the notes, some being divided which should have been treated as a whole, and the sheets themselves, as arranged in the Harleian collection, are not, in the editor's opinion, correctly placed. We make no apologies for deficiencies in carrying out a work which was, in the then stage of knowledge, a much more difficult business than it now appears. Ill health must have its share of blame, the editor being rendered incapable of revising proofs with the manuscript at the British Museum. A future edition shall be much more perfect.

Still prosecuting the work of comparative philology and science, the present writer was irresistibly drawn to the con-

3

clusion that the works actually written by Bacon himself are far
in excess of those ascribed to him by the majority even of his
most enthusiastic admirers. It became evident that it would
have been beyond human power for any single individual to
have observed, experimented, travelled, read, written, to the
extent which we find Bacon to have done, unless he had been
aided in the mechanical parts of his work by an army of
amanuenses, transcribers, collators, translators, and publishers,
and even by powerful friends in high places, and by the control
of the leading printing-presses.

An examination into Bacon's own repeated statements as to
the ignorance, incapacity, and miseries of the age in which he
lived, shows him pointing out, amongst other things, the
" poverty " of language, the lack of words, the necessity for a
mutual exchange of words through many countries, in order to
perform that noble and much needed work of building up a fine
model of language. He notes the absence of graceful forms of
speech; of commencements, continuations, and conclusions of
sentences; of a scientific grammar of philology, in default of
which he has been obliged to make " a kind of " grammar for
himself. He shows that there were, in his time, no good collections of antitheta, sophisms, and arguments, and that the
good sayings of the ancients were lost, or choked in the dust of
ages; also the ancient and scriptural use of parables, figures,
metaphors, similes, and so forth, was extinct; the sciences were
" weak things " weakly handled; the learning had become
" words, not matter;" " the muses were barren virgins;" poetry
and the theatre at the lowest level.

So Bacon found things when he conceived his magnificent idea
of the " Universal Reformation of the whole wide world." He
was at that time a lad of fifteen, and there is reason to believe that he had already written, or was in process of writing,
poetry and other works which passed then, and at later periods,
as the productions of men of mature years, " authors " of an
earlier or later date than is generally ascribed to the works of
Francis Bacon.

And, as in his boyhood he found the world of science and literature, not in this country only, but also on the continent *(for he makes no exceptions or qualifications to his statement as to the general ignorance which prevailed)*, so, excluding his own work from the inquiry, he found it still, when, in his old age, he for the last time summed up the wants and deficiencies of the world in all these matters. In youth, enthusiasm had led him to hope and believe in a speedy regeneration and quickening of the minds and spirits of men. In old age he had learned that "the dull ass will not mend his pace," and that such advance could only be by slow degrees, and in the future ages. "*Of myself*," he says, "*I am silent*," but he repeats his former opinions and statements with undiminished emphasis in 1623.

In the face of such facts as these, it appears monstrous to believe that there could really have been in Bacon's time that "galaxy of wits," that extraordinary blaze and outburst of light from many suns, and from a heaven full of stars of the first magnitude, such as we have been taught in our childhood not only to discern, but to distinguish. It is more reasonable to suppose that one sun, one supreme spirit, the great natural magician and natural philosopher, like Prospero, with many "meaner ministers" to do his biddings, should have planned and carried out, by a method to be transmitted through the whole century, that Great Reformation of the whole world which had been his boyish dream, his fixed idea at the age of fifteen. Bacon's chief biographer lays stress upon this fact, and as it is one which is intimately connected with the history of the Secret Society which is the subject of the following pages, it is desirable that it should be firmly established. Again, therefore, we draw attention to the eloquent and beautiful chapter with which Mr. Spedding opens his "Letters and Life of Bacon." After telling of the brilliant career of the youthful Francis at Trinity College, Cambridge, of the disappointment which he experienced in that university where he hoped to have learned all that men knew, but where, as he declared, they taught "words, not matter," Mr. Spedding says: "It was then a thought struck him, the date of which deserves to be recorded, not for anything extraordinary in the thought itself, but for its influence upon his after life. If our study of nature be thus barren, he thought, our method of study must be wrong ; might not a better method be found ? In him the gift of seeing in prophetic vision what might be, and ought to be, was united with the practical talent of devising means and handling minute details. He could at once imagine like a poet, and execute like a clerk of the works. Upon the conviction, This may be done, followed at once the question, How can it be done ? Upon that question followed the resolution to try and do it."

Of the degrees by which the suggestion ripened into a project, the project into an undertaking, and the undertaking unfolded itself into distinct propositions and the full grandeur of its total dimensions, I can say nothing. But that the thought first occurred to him during his residence at Cambridge, therefore *before he had completed his fifteenth year,* we know on the best authority — his own statement and that of Dr. Rawley. " I believe," says Mr. Spedding, " that it ought to be regarded as the most important event of his life ; the event which had a greater influence than any other upon his character and future course. From that moment there was awakened within his breast the appetite which cannot be satiated, and the passion which cannot commit excess. From that moment he had a vocation which employed and stimulated all the energies of his mind, gave a value to every vacant interval of time, an interest and significance to every random thought and casual accession of knowledge ; an object to live for, as wide as humanity, as immortal as the human race ; an idea to live in, vast and lofty enough to fill the soul forever with religious and heroic aspirations. From that moment, though still subject to interruptions, disappointments, errors, regrets, he never could be without either work, or hope, or consolation."

The biographer then shows how the circumstances of Bacon's early life tended to enlist him on the side of reform, religious, scientific, literary, and philanthropic, and to nourish in him high and loyal aspirations.

" Assuming, then," continues he, " that a deep interest in these three great causes — the cause of reformed religion, of his

native country, and of the human race through all their generations — was thus early implanted in that vigorous and virgin
soil, we must leave it to struggle up as it may, according to the
accidents of time and weather. . . . Of Bacon's life I am persuaded that no man will ever form a correct idea, unless he bear
in mind that from very early youth his heart was divided by
these three objects, distinct but not discordant." [1]

In the preface to the *De Interpretatione Naturæ Præmium*
(*circa* 1603) Spedding describes that paper as of " peculiar
interest for us, on account of the passage in which Bacon
explains the plans and purposes of his life, and the estimate he
had formed of his own character and abilities; a passage which
was replaced in the days of his greatness by a simple *De nobis
ipsis silemus.* It is *the only piece of autobiography in which he
ever indulged,* [2] and deserves on several accounts to be carefully
considered. The biographer goes on to say that Bacon's own
account, written when he was between forty and fifty, of the
plan upon which his life had been laid out, the objects which he
mainly aimed at, and the motives which guided him, will be
found, when compared with the courses which he actually
followed in his varied life, to present a very remarkable example
of constancy to an original design. He began by conceiving
that a wiser method of studying nature would give man the key
to all her secrets, but the work would be long and arduous, and
the event remote; in the meanwhile, he would not neglect the
immediate and peculiar services which, *as an Englishman, he
owed* to his country and his religion. With regard to the last
two he found, as life wore away, that the means and opportunities which he had hoped for did not present themselves; and he
resolved to fall back upon the first, as an enterprise which
depended upon himself alone."

Perhaps it may be found that Bacon's reason for throwing his
chief weight into the work which none could execute except
himself, was that *he did find means and opportunities, through*

---

[1] Spedding, Letters and Life of Bacon, i. 4, 5.

[2] This observation will, we think, require modification. " It is the only
piece of autobiography which he acknowledges."

others, to advance not only politics and statesmanship, but religion and the cause of the church. It will, however, be easily
seen that if Bacon would carry forward such work, in times so
" dark and dangerous," he must do it secretly, and by the aid
of powerful friends and assistants. We, therefore, find ourselves
engaged in tracing the workings of a great secret society;
and since, so far as we have discovered, that work depended
mainly upon Bacon himself, it is necessary to regard his life and
actions from a totally new point of view, and to acknowledge at
the outset that, excepting in the capacity of lawyer, which he
disliked and shrank from; of courtier, for which he felt himself
" *unapt;*" and of statesman, for which he pronounced himself
to be " *least fit,*" very little is really known about Francis Bacon.

This lack of satisfactory information has probably led modern
writers too much to copy from each other, without duly weigh-
ing and examining statements made hastily, to turn a phrase,
or of malice prepense. It is usual, in other cases, to lay great
store by the evidence of respectable contemporary authority.
(Need we remind any one of the eagerness with which such pieces
of evidence, even the weakest, have been snatched at and en-
shrined as gems of priceless value, when they seemed to affect William Shakspere?)   But, with Francis Bacon, the case is altered.
Evidence of contemporary writers, such as Ben Jonson, or Dr.
Sprat, president of the Royal Society, or of Bacon's secretary,
afterwards the Queen's chaplain, Dr. Rawley, or of his intimate
friend and life-long correspondent, Sir Tobie Matthew, is waived
aside, when they pour out, in eloquent language, their witness as
to his greatness, his genius, his sweetness, and devoutness of
disposition and mind.   Aubrey is " a gossip " when he echoes
the tale, and says, emphasising the words, that " all who were
good and great loved him." The rest were " prejudiced, " or
" partial, " or did not mean what they said.

Why are such records of Bacon's closest friends, secretaries,
coadjutors, and contemporaries, as well as those of his most
painstaking biographers, and of his most appreciative disciples
and followers, to be rejected in favor of two lines of poetry
penned more than a hundred years after his death, and of a hos-

tile review of Basil Montagu's edition of Bacon's works? For many years those two lines of Pope, and that review of Macaulay, together with Lord Campbell's odious little " Life of Bacon" (based upon Macaulay's essay), were nearly all that the English public read with regard to " Francis Bacon, the glory of his age and nation, the adorner and ornament of learning, " " the most prodigious wit" that the world has seen, " the benefactor of the human race in all ages. "

Let us forget the foolish and cruel things which modern ignorance and prejudice have said of him, things which must be excused and partly justified by our theory that he was, throughout his life, a " *concealed man*"—not only a " concealed poet, " but a concealed theologian and religious reformer or revivalist ; and that, by the very rules of his own secret society, not only was he bound, in these capacities, to efface himself, to allow himself to be, to any extent, maligned and disgraced, rather than declare his real vocation and aims, but, also (and this is very important), *his own friends must ignore him, as he must likewise ignore them,* in all relations excepting those which he " professed "—as a public character and a philosopher.

In the following chapters we shall not attempt to give a " life" of Bacon in his accepted characters of statesman, lawyer, or scientist, all of which has been faithfully, and, perhaps, exhaustively, treated of by Spedding and others. Our efforts will be directed to selecting, from the writings of his contemporaries and later biographers and critics, some passages which seem to throw light upon the obscure or private recesses of his life— passages which are sometimes introduced in such a manner as to favour the belief that they were intended to be passed over by the general reader, whilst, to the initiated· observer, they were full of suggestion and information.

CHAPTER III.

" I prefer to keep state in these matters."
" Be kind to concealed poets."

THE more closely we peer into Bacon's history, the more particularly we follow up inquiries about him,—his private life,
his habits, his travels, his friends, his will, his death,—the more
mysterious a personage does he appear. His public or superficial life seems easy enough to understand, but whenever we
endeavour to go beyond this we find ourselves continually con-
fronted with puzzles and enigmas, and we feel that Ben Jonson
was justified in saying, in his ode on Bacon's birthday,—

" Thou stand'st as though a mystery thou didst."

This mystery is felt in many ways. Several times we find him
writing with locked doors, the subject of his labours not known,
his friends offended by his secresy and reticence. We find collections of his letters, distinctly his, and with nothing in them which
could apparently injure the writer, or any one else, published
with names and dates cancelled, and with everything possible
done to conceal their aim or their author. We find him writing
in ambiguous terms (which only knowledge derived from other
sources enables us to interpret), and using feigned names, initials, and pass-words in his private letters. The cipher which
he invented when he was eighteen or nineteen years old, he has
used and tested, and finds to be superior to all others, when he
is sixty-two. How, when, and wherefore, did he use or require
this extensive knowledge and use of ciphers? And, in describing the ciphers, he speaks of other concealed means of com-

munication, of short-hand writing, of hieroglyphic pictures and designs. Since he tells us that what he recommends he always endeavours to practice or achieve, we seek for these things in his own books, *and find them there.*

He enumerates the thirty or forty great deficiencies of learning in his time, and shows how he has endeavoured to supply them; we take much pains to master these, to understand them thoroughly, and to trace them in his works. Thus armed and well prepared, we set forth to mark their deficiency, or to compare their use in works by other contemporary authors. We are almost appalled to meet with them there, too, sometimes fewer in number, but the same in nature and quality. What is to be thought of this? That Bacon did not know what he was talking about? or that there was a general conspiracy of the wits of his age to gull the public as to the authorship of these works? If they were Bacon's works, why did he not acknowledge them? Yet, if they were not his, how could he persist that all the chief flowers of language were uncultivated, when the works in question were overrun by them?

There are many knotty points connected with this branch of the subject. Why, for instance, did Bacon, notably so kind, so large-hearted, so just in acknowledging merit in others, and in " giving authors their due, as he gave Time his due, which is to discover Truth " — why, we say, did he ignore the existence of nearly every great contemporary author? How came it that this bright man, who so pre-eminently shone in his power of drawing out the best parts of those with whom he conversed, who delighted, when quoting from others, to set an additional sparkle on their words, and to make them appear cleverer or more learned than they really were — how did such a man contrive to avoid all allusion to the mass of great literature of all kinds which was poured out unremittingly during nearly fifty years of his life, and which continued for some years after his death?

Bacon spoke of parabolic poetry as *deficient,* and the use of it lost or misunderstood; and he ignores the *Arcadia,* the *Faerie Queene,* and the *Shepherd's Calendar.*

In 1623 he mourns the degradation of the theatre, and the contempt with which the noble arts of rhetoric and stage playing were treated, ignoring the *Shakespeare* plays, which had at that time been played upon the stage for a quarter of a century, and of which the first collected edition had just been (almost simultaneously with the publication of the *De Augmentis*) published, heralded into the world with a great flourish of trumpets by Ben Jonson. He equally ignores Ben Jonson, although *Every Man in his Humour* was acted at the Blackfriar's Theatre in 1598 (two or three years after the first appearance of the *Shakespeare* plays), and although, too, William Shakspere acted on this occasion.

It is remarkable that it should have ever been, for an instant, credited that Francis Bacon never saw the *Shakespeare* plays performed, or even that he should not have known all about the plays, and the man who was passing with the public as their author. For thirty years Shakspere lived in London. During those years Bacon was continually assisting, and promoting, and joyfully witnessing the performances of these and other plays, at Gray's Inn and Whitehall, and at the private houses of his friends the Earls of Leicester, Pembroke, Montgomery, and others. Why did he never, in any acknowledged work, allude to *Shakespeare* or to *Ben Jonson*, who, as has been shown, was at one time resident in his house ?

Essays were a new form of writing, and the very word "essay," Bacon tells us, was *new*. One would suppose that in saying this he would allude to the "Essays of Montaigne," published long before Bacon's "Moral Essays." All the more he might be expected to allude to Montaigne, because, at the time of the publication of the first edition of *Montaigne's Essays*, Francis and Anthony Bacon were living in the South of France, and on very intimate terms with the good mayor, "the kind patron of learned men," as we learn from Anthony Bacon's correspondence. But, although the friendship between these men continued to the end of Montaigne's life, and although the old man made a pilgrimage to Verulam to visit his younger friend, yet Bacon, in his enumeration of deficiencies, makes no allusion to him as the author of essays which were in their day most famous, and which ran through a surprising number of editions within a few years.

John Florio is supposed to have translated these French essays into English. Now, we have documentary evidence that Florio translated *" all the works of Bacon "* into foreign languages (we suppose French and Italian), and *"published them beyond the seas."* Bacon, then, must have been intimately acquainted with Florio. Yet he never mentions him. James I. gave Florio an annuity of £50 per annum, because he had " translated the King's work, and *all the works of Viscount St. Albans."* So James, also, was deeply interested in Bacon's proceedings. It might have been supposed that the circumstance of his having pensioned Florio because the latter translated Bacon's works, would have been noted by Bacon's biographers, and that more inquiries would have been made concerning Florio and some remarkable works in English which are attributed to him. But no; the whole matter seems to have been studiously kept in the background. The documents which record the fact of the translation and subsequent pensioning have been printed by the Historical Manuscripts Commission. But, although the editors and publishers must know of them, their purport lies unheeded, uncommented on. A paragraph inserted in *Notes and Queries,* in which the inquiry was made as to any book or books of Bacon's known to have been translated by Florio, and published on the continent, has never been answered. Yet, amongst the transcribers, editors, and publishers of the " Pembroke Papers " by the Historical Commission, there must have been men who are acquainted with the current history of Bacon, and who must have seen something strange in the fact that James I. granted an annuity to the supposed translator of *Montaigne's Essays, on the ground of his being the translator of all Bacon's works.*

Then, again, the sixteen folio volumes of Anthony Bacon's correspondence which rest under the dust of oblivion on the shelves of the library at Lambeth Palace —how comes it that these, too, have been so much kept in the background that, on tracing a letter of Nicholas Faunt to Anthony Bacon, which is the first alluded to by Mr. Spedding (and this in a foot-note), we find it to be one of a large and important collection which throws great light upon the position and aims of the Bacons? Two or three references are all that can be found to this voluminous correspondence.

The sense of mystery is again perceptible in the explanations given by Bacon's biographers of his system of philosophy, or " methods," which are, of course, treated of as applying merely to the science which is their ostensible aim. This evident and intentional obscurity has been rightly attributed to two causes. First, he hoped, by his method of teaching by means of parables, similitudes, and analogies, to avoid all occasion of dispute and controversy, things always abhorrent to his nature. Next, his doctrine was to be veiled in an abrupt and obscure style, such as, to use his own expression, would " choose its reader "—that is, would remain unread excepting by worthy recipients of its hidden meaning. This affected obscurity appears in the *De Interpretatione Naturæ Præmium*, where he speaks of his peculiar method as a thing *not to be published, but to be communicated orally to certain persons*. The same veil of mystic language is thrown over *Valerius Terminus*, the *Temporis Partus Masculus*, and, as we now know, over the *New Atlantis*. The whole of the notes in the *Sylva Sylvarum*, the *Histories of Dense and Rare*, of *Sulphur, Mercury, and Salt*, of *Principles and Origins* according to the Tables of Cupid and Cœlam, and even, we believe, the *Thema Cœli*, the *History of the Winds*, the *Interpretation of Nature*, the *History of Life and Death*, the *New Atlantis*, are written with a double meaning and for a double purpose, and the same ambiguity pervades the collections of letters to and from Anthony Bacon and Francis himself.

There are upwards of sixty letters from Anthony Standen to Anthony Bacon *previous* to the one from which Spedding extracts his first quotation; and there are other correspondents whose letters will, undoubtedly, at some future date, be held of great value and interest. The drift of these letters must have been understood by the compilers of the printed catalogue of

the Tenison manuscripts, and by biographers who have quoted
from some of these letters. What satisfactory reason can be
given for the fact that a hint of the existence of this correspondence is here and there given, and letters are published
which bear directly upon politics or the passing history of the
day, but that the true purport of the collective correspondence
is everywhere concealed? For these letters, taken collectively,
have a distinct and harmonious aim and drift. They teach us that
Francis Bacon was the recognised head of a secret society bound
together to advance learning and to uphold religion, and that
Anthony Bacon was his brother's propagandist and corresponding manager on the continent.

It seems very probable that future research will prove Anthony
Bacon to have been "a concealed poet," as well as his
brother. If this was not the case, then Anthony must have been
another of the many masks behind which Francis screened his own
personality; but the former seems to be the more probable conjecture. Amongst the " Tenison manuscripts " at Lambeth Palace,
there is a large sheet covered on three sides with French verses,
headed " Au Seigneur Antoine Bacon — Elegie," and signed La
Tessée. These verses described " Bacon " as *the flower of
Englishmen, the honour of the nine Muses*, who, without his aid,
wandered sad and confused in the wilderness, without guide,
support, or voice. The writer laments the want of more
Mecenases who should value the favourites of Phœbus, Mercury,
and Themis, and " lend a shoulder " to help poets; in future, he
trusts that the number of these will be glorified not less beyond
the seas than in these islands, remembering a time " when our
swans surpassed those of the Thames "—alluding to the loss of
Bonsard, Garnier, Aurat, Bayf, and Saluste. Himself, the surviving poet, sees a new Age of Iron after their Age of Gold. He
alludes to " Bacon " as " a brilliant star seen in tranquil nights
as through a thick veil;" so a man of honour, virtue, and wit
shines amongst these " milords," and so does " Bacon," the
" oracle of his isle," one whom to praise is an honour.

Such a man, continues the poet, is the hope and ornament of
his country. To him Themis, the wise (by the messenger Mer-

cury, who expounds her message), entreats heaven, earth, and the
infernal regions to forward his steps. To him " devout Piety,
the pillar of the church, offers her most precious gifts, that he
may rank with immortal heroes," for " so rare a spirit, continually bent upon safely steering the helm of the state in the
stormiest times, is not unworthy that the state should care for his
interests. Baccon [*sic*], the eye of wisdom, in whom goodness
abounds, raises men above themselves and above the world. He
retires into himself — a perfect and holy place — his soul wrapped
in his reason, and his reason wrapped in God."

Surely, though the poetry is poor, the matter of these verses
is sufficiently remarkable for them to have been commented
upon by some biographer or antiquarian ? We note, then, as a
remarkable fact, that these verses (numbered folio 175, in vol.
xv. 661) are *not included in the printed catalogue.* Nos. 174 and
176 are duly registered, but *175 is omitted.* Could this omission be accidental ?

In the Harleian MSS. there is the collection of notes described
as the " *Promus* of Formularies and Elegancies." These papers
consist of fifty sheets, numbered from 83 to 132, and the collection is marked No. 7017. *It is omitted in the catalogue.*[1] Yet,
within the last few years, these MSS. have been frequently seen
and studied by various inquirers.

By and by there will be occasion to return to these questions ; they involve a great many others which we must not, at
present, stop to consider. But the list of inquiries in other
directions is still a long one, and should incline those who
heartily desire to get at the pith and truth of these matters, to
be very humble as to their own knowledge, very cautious about
adopting ready-made opinions or assertions, which, when tested,
are found incapable of supporting themselves.

What was the cause of Bacon's *great poverty* at times when he
was living very quietly, and at small personal expense ? Why
did his elder brother Anthony never remonstrate or disapprove

---

[1] Rather it was omitted until June, 1890, when a gentleman, who became
aware of the omission. requested that the MSS. No. 7017 should be duly registered in the catalogue.

of his unexplained expenditure, or of the straits to which he himself was sometimes put, in order to meet the claims upon Francis? Did the brothers' money go chiefly in publishing? And again we say, what share did Anthony Bacon take in his brother's works? If, as Dr. Rawley declared, his learning was not so profound, but his wit was as high as Francis's, did he, perhaps, frame the plots of many of the plays which Francis polished and finished? Where did Anthony die? Where is he buried? The absence of knowledge on this point draws our attention to the number of " great writers" and personal friends of Francis Bacon who died and were buried without notice or epitaph ; a plain slab sometimes marking the grave, but no mention being made of any works of which they were the authors. Yet " monuments of brass and stone" were then, as now, the rule, rather than the exception. On comparing the tombs of Bacon's friends, certain singular resemblances strike the eye, and are peculiar (so we think) to them and to their descendants.

Such coincidences ought, one would think, to be easily explained where such a man is concerned; but search the records of the time which are, up to the present date, published, and see how far you can enlighten yourselves as to any particulars of Bacon's domestic life. It becomes, after long search, impossible to resist the idea that Bacon had some great purpose to serve by keeping himself always in the background — behind the curtain. Whenever you catch a glimpse of him " he goes away in a cloud."

It likewise seems that the whole of his most dear and loving friends combined to conceal his true personality, to assist him to enact the part of Proteus, and to ensure that when he should appear here, there, and everywhere, he should be able to pass unrecognised. Amongst Anthony's correspondents, he is rarely mentioned, but often alluded to as " the Hermit," the character which perhaps he himself undertook in the *Gesta Grayorum.* There are also some short poems, especially one adorned with a device of a hermit spurning a globe, which seem to apply to Francis Bacon, and to have been written by him.

When the French ambassador, the Marquis Fiat, visited him during an illness, he said that his lordship had ever been to him like the angels, of whom he had often heard and read, but never seen. "After which visit they contracted an intimate acquaintance, and the Marquis did so much revere him, that besides his frequent visits [of which history tells us nothing] they wrote letters under the appellations of father and son." [1]

With regard to Bacon's life, it is impossible to study it with any degree of care, without observing how often in his biographies we come upon questions or doubts such as these: "*Was he the author of Notes on the present state of Christendom?*" [2] "*Reasons for suspecting him to be author of a 'Letter of Advice to the Queen.*'" [3] "*This alleged authorship* of 'A Discourse touching the Low Countries, etc.*'"[4] "*Resemblance between Bacon's style and that of* writings imputed to Essex," [5] etc.

We read of his reluctance to devote himself to the practice of a lawyer, and of the difficulty of understanding what else he proposed to himself, or to what course he actually betook himself in the year 1595-6. [6] "I do not find," says his biographer, any letter of his that can be assigned to the winter of 1596, nor have I met, among his brother's papers, with anything which indicates what he was about. I presume, however, that he betook himself to his studies." He then gives a list of a few fragments written at this time. "But there are," he continues, "some other compositions with which (*though they do not pass under his name*) there is reason to believe he had something to do, and which, *considering the possibility that they are entirely his work, and the probability that they have some of his work in them*, and their intrinsic value, I have determined to lay before the reader in this chapter." [7] The biographer then enumerates the contents of a box of letters and other papers which dated from this time, and which were in charge of Dr. Tenison in 1682. Amongst these, one of the most important was "The Earl of Essex's advice to the Earl of Rut-

1 Rawley's Life of Bacon.   2 Let. Life, i. 16, 17.   3 *Ib.* 43, 56, etc.
4 *Ib.* 67.   5 *Ib.* 391.   6 *Ib.* ii. 1.   7 *Ib.* ii. 2.

land on his journey," of which three versions seem to exist,[1] and which Spedding shows to be written so much in Bacon's style as to be undistinguishable from it. "If Essex wrote a letter of grave advice to a young relative going on his travels, it would, no doubt, have a good deal of Bacon in it; if Bacon drew up a letter for Essex to sign, it would be such a one as Essex might naturally have written. Still, there is a character in language as in handwriting, which it is hardly possible to disguise. Little tricks of thought, like tricks of the hand,— peculiarities of which the writer is unconscious,—are perceptible to the reader." [2] Presently a similar question of authorship arises with regard to a " Letter of advice from the Earl of Essex to Foulke Greville;" [3] and again the true author seems to be Bacon.

Then we find a " Letter of advice to the Earl of Essex," which, *" like several others we shall meet with,* has been preserved through two independent channels, and in two different forms; one in the collection kept by himself, and printed by Rawley in the *Resuscitatio,* the other in a collection made, *we do not know by whom, and printed very incorrectly in the 'Remains'* (1648), *and afterward in the ' Cabala'* (1654)." [4]

There is a mystery about Sir Tobie Matthew's collection of letters to and from Bacon. These letters are, as a rule, not only without a date, but likewise they appear to have been " stripped of all particulars that might serve to fit the occasion" for which they were penned; sometimes, even, the person to whom they were addressed. One of these letters, " Desiring a friend to do him a service," is remarkable, as showing that, although the matter which it concerns was of some importance, and might bring serious consequences to Bacon (he says that it will probably " fall and seize on" him), yet it had been put out of his mind by some great *" invention"* or work of imagination,

---

[1] One is in the Harleian MSS. (6265, p. 428). Sped. Let. Life, i. 4.

[2] *Ib.* 5.

[3] *Ib.* 21.

[4] Spedding, Let. Life, ii. 94. This letter is suspected of cipher and should be examined.

which at the time wholly engrossed him. What was the particular occasion upon which this letter was written, it is, says Spedding, "probably impossible to guess," but it was as follows:

"SIR:—*The report of this act, which I hope may prove the last of this business, will, probably, by the weight it carries, fall on and seize me. And, therefore, not at will, but upon necessity, it will become me to call to mind what passed; and, my head being then wholly employed upon invention, I may the worse put things upon the account of mine own memory.* I shall take physic to-day, upon this change of weather and vantage of leisure; and I pray you not to allow yourself so much business, but that you may have time to bring me your friendly aid before night," etc. [1]

Another letter, dateless, but which has been referred to 1605–6, is all written in a tone of mystery and double entente — there seems to be no good reason why Bacon should plainly mention by name one work which he had accomplished, and carefully omit the name of another, or others, in which it is clear that his friend was interested:

"SIR:—I perceive you have some time when you can be content to think of your friends, from whom, since you have borrowed yourself, you do well, not paying the principal, to send the interest at six months day. The relation which here I send you inclosed carries the truth of that which is public; and though my little leisure might have required a briefer, yet the matter would have endured and asked a larger.

"*I have now at last taught that child to go, at the swadling whereof you were.* My work touching the *Advancement of Learning* I have put into two books; whereof the former, which you saw, I count but as a page to the latter," etc. [2]

In another ambiguous letter to Sir Tobie Matthew (*circa* 1609), Bacon says: "I have sent you some copies of the Advancement which you desired; and a little work of my recreation, which you desired not. My *Instauration* I reserve for our conference — it

---

[1] See Sir Tobie Matthew's collection of letters, p. 20, or Spedding, Let. and Life, iii. 216.

[2] Spedding, iii. 255; Sir T. M.'s coll. p. 11.

sleeps not. *Those works of the alphabet are in my opinion of less use to you where you are now, than at Paris, and therefore I conceived that you had sent me a kind of tacit countermand of your former request. But, in regard that some friends of yours have still insisted here, I send them to you; and for my part I value your reading more than your publishing them to others. Thus, in extreme haste, I have scribbled to you I know not what,"* etc.[1]

" What these works of the alphabet may have been, I cannot guess," says Spedding, in commenting upon this letter, " unless they related to Bacon's cipher, in which, by means of two alphabets, one having only two letters, the other having two forms for each of the twenty-four letters, any words you please may be so written as to signify any other words, provided only that the open writing contains at least five times as many letters as the concealed."[2]

In the *Promus*, the mysterious letter has been connected with an entry in which Bacon seems to connect *the plays* with an alphabet: *Ijsdem e'literis efficitur tragædia et comedia (Tragedies and comedies are made of one alphabet)*,[3] and the first impression conveyed by this entry was that the *alphabet* was a secret term to express *the comedies and tragedies*, since Bacon quotes Aristotle to the effect that " *Words* are the images of cogitations, and letters are the images of words." The recent discoveries of Mr. Donnelly and others seem to enhance the probability that the entry in question refers to the *plays containing a cipher*, the word *alphabet* bearing in this case a bifold allusion to the nature of the tragedies and comedies, and a double fitness.

And how are we to interpret the following passage from a letter of March 27, 1621-2, to Mr. Tobie Matthew? " If upon your repair to the court (whereof I am right glad) you have any speech with the Marquis [*of Buckingham*] of me, *I pray p'ace the alphabet, as you can do it right well, in a frame,* to express my love, faithful and ardent, to him."

---

1 Spedding, i. 134, and Sir T. M. p. 14.

2 Let. Life, iv. 134.

3 *Promus*, 516. The Latin quotation from Erasmus' *Adagia*, 725.

It has been suggested that this was a proposal (not carried out) that Sir Tobie should collect and edit the plays, and fit them to be presented as a tribute to the Marquis. Or it is possible that the mysterious words express a wish that some message should be introduced in the alphabet cipher, which the Marquis would, supposing him to be a member of the secret society, be able to interpret. If so, this letter gives a hint of the system which the present writer believes to have been pursued with regard to nearly all these cipher notes or narratives, namely, that Bacon provided the materials or substance of the information to be conveyed, but that his " sons," or disciples, did the mechanical work of fitting type, and other particulars, for the reception of the matter.

We turn to a consideration of Bacon's character, his motives and aims in life, about which one would suppose that at this hour there could be no difficulty in arriving at a definite conclusion. How many distinguished pens have been busy with lives, treatises, and essays on Francis Bacon! Here, at least, it may be expected that the mists of doubt and darkness shall have been cleared away, and that we may rest upon positive authority. We are prepared to receive many shocks to our feelings, to find flaws in the character which we would wish to be an entire and perfect chrysolite ; still, it will be at least satisfactory to know that the whole truth is laid out before us, even if the contraries of good and evil must appear in this as in all things human.

But here the confusion is worse than ever; the contradictions, the divergencies of opinion, are as extraordinary amongst those who have read much or something about Bacon as they are amongst those who have read little or nothing. Who has been more admired, more shamed, more spitefully or conscientiously abused, more revered and loved than Francis Bacon? A strange and wonderful man surely, who can be the subject of so many opposed opinions ! Somebody is right and somebody is wrong, that is clear, and we proceed to relieve the oppression produced by this cloud of witnesses, by putting down on paper the verdicts delivered by the numerous self-constituted judges

who are the great authorities of the present day. To these we
will add the utterances of Bacon's friends and contemporaries,
who surely have an equal right to be heard.

The startling result is this: That it is hardly possible to produce a single statement concerning Bacon's character, disposition, motives or aims, made by one " great authority," which is
not contradicted by another authority, equally great. The following are specimens of this kind of comparison — they might
be trebled in volume — but they are enough to show that in
this, as in other particulars, there is a mystery, and a want of
accurate knowledge concerning our great subject.

THE CHARACTER AND GENIUS OF FRANCIS BACON AS DESCRIBED BY GREAT AUTHORITIES.

He was mean, narrow, and wanting in moral courage.

" The wisest, brightest, *meanest* of mankind." (Pope, Essay
on Man.)

" A serenity bordering on *meanness* . . . his fault was *meanness of spirit.* The mind of Waller coincided with that of
Bacon . . . a *narrowness to the lowest degree,* an *abjectness* and
want of courage to support him in any virtuous undertaking.
. . . Sir Anthony Weldon . . . is likely enough to have exaggerated *the meanness of Bacon.*" (Macaulay.)

" *He was anything rather than mean.*"

" On the other hand, he was generous, open-hearted, affectionate, peculiarly sensitive to kindness, and equally forgetful of
injuries. The epithet of ' great,' which has been so ungrudgingly
accorded to him as a writer, might, without any singular impro-
priety, be applied to him as a man." (Prof. Fowler's Bacon, p. 28.)

" Greatness he could not want." (Ben Jonson, Discoveries.)

" A man splendid in his expenses." (Sir Tobie Matthew.)

" Weighted by the magnificence of his character." (Dr. Abbott's introduction to Bacon's Essays.)

Servile—A flatterer, fawning on the great—A courtier by choice.

" Fearful to a fault of offending the powerful, . . . his sup-
plications almost *servile.* . . . A servile advocate, that he might
be a corrupt judge. . . . He excused himself in terms which
. . . must be considered as shamefully servile." (Macaulay.)

" Mixed up with servile entreaties for place." (Sortaine, Life
of Lord Bacon, 40, etc. Followed by Lord Campbell, pp. 3,
12, 26, etc.)

" For his want of leisure he was himself to blame, because he
deliberately preferred the life of a courtier and a politician to
the life of a seeker after truth." (Abbott, Francis Bacon, 413.
See *infra.*)

Neither servile nor a flatterer.

" He must have been most of all *a stranger amid the alien servility* imposed upon him by the court of James 1. . . . He was
altogether too vast and grand for an easy flatterer." (Dr. Abbott, introduction to the Essays.)

Bacon seems to have been several times in disgrace with his
relations and others for *not sufficiently cultivating the courtly sub-
servience* which was required in those days. See his letter to
his uncle and aunt, Lord and Lady Burghley, who have
reproached him with this. (Spedding, L. L. i. 12–59, and Spedding's Evenings with a Reviewer, 1. 69.)

*Intriguing, selfish, money-loving — Hunting after place and
power from vanity and ambition.*

" The boldest and most useful of innovators . . . the most obsti-
nate champion of the foulest abuses . . . a heart set on things
which no man ought to suffer to be necessary to his happiness,
on things which can be obtained only by the sacrifice of integrity and honour. . . . All availed him nothing, while some quib-
bling special pleader was promoted before him to the bench,
while some heavy country gentleman took precedence of him,
by virtue of a purchased coronet, . . . could obtain a more cordial salute from Buckingham; or while some buffoon, versed in all
the latest scandal of the court, could draw a louder laugh from

James." (Macaulay, 336, 317, 429; Campbell, pp. 3, 5, 25, etc.; Sortaine, 93, etc.)

Generous, open-hearted — Regardless of money, place or pomp, for their own sakes.

" I will hereafter write to your lordship what I think of that supply; to the end that you may, as you have begun, to your great honour, *despise money* where it crosseth reason of state or virtue." (Francis Bacon to Villiers, Nov. 29, 1616.) [1]

" Money is like muck — not good except it be spread." (Essay of Seditions. See Essays, Riches, Expense, etc.)

" To his easy liberality in the spending, was added a carelessness in the keeping, which would be hardly credible," etc. (See Spedding, L. L. vii. 563, etc.)

Basil Montagu, Prof. Fowler, Hepworth Dixon, Storr, all bear the same witness.

" He was most desirous to obtain a provision which might enable him to devote himself to literature and politics. . . . His wishes were moderate." (Macaulay, 298.)

He strove for money, position, etc., that by their means he might advance learning, science, and religion. (Anthony Bacon's correspondence. Dr. Rawley, Basil Montagu, Spedding, Fowler, Craik, Abbott, Wigston, etc.)

" Having all the thoughts of that large heart of his set upon adorning the age in which he lives, and benefiting, as far as possible, the whole human race." (Sir T. Matthew's preface to an Italian translation of the Essays.)

He was successful in his endeavours after wealth and place.

" During a long course of years Bacon's unworthy ambition was crowned with success. . . . He was elated if not intoxicated by greatness." (Macaulay, 336, 347, etc.) " Bacon deliberately sat down to build his fortunes . . . and, as we shall see, succeeded." The truth is, admiration for place and power had dazzled his intellect and confounded his judgment. (Dr. Abbott's introduction to Essays.)

---

[1] Compare Coriolanus, ii. 2.   Money or wealth "the *muck* of the world."

*He was singularly unsuccessful — There must have been some
unexplained cause which kept him back.*

" He stood long at a stay in the days of his mistress Elizabeth." (Dr. Rawley, Life.) " But though Bacon's reputation
rose, his fortunes were still depressed. He was still in great
pecuniary difficulties." (Macaulay, 309.) " Countenance, encourage and advance men in all kinds, degrees and professions,
for in the time of the Cecils, the father and the son, able men
were, by design, and of purpose, suppressed." (Letter from
Bacon to Villiers ; see, also, Dr. Church's Bacon, pp. 33, 58–9,
100.)

He married for money.

".He made a bold attempt to restore his position by matri-
mony. Instead of offering incense to Venus he was considering
a scheme to make his pot boil." (Campbell, Bacon, p. 40.)
" He had some thoughts of making his fortune by marriage. . . .
Bacon was disposed to overlook her faults for the sake of her
ample fortune." (Macaulay, 310.) " Just at this period he was
offering his heart to the daughter of a rich alderman." (Devey's
ed. of Essays, introduction, xix.)

*He married a lady on whom he settled double the amount of her
dowry.*

(See Carleton to Chamberlain, May 11, 1606 ; Spedding's L.
L. i. 8 ; Hepworth Dixon's Story of Bacon's Life, pp. 218, 219,
and same in Personal Life ; Bacon's Will, Dec. 19th, 1624.)

*His patient, conciliating, pliable nature blamed as weakness
and servility.*

" He bore with a patience and serenity which, we fear, *bor-
dered on meanness*, the morose humours of his uncle . . . the
sneering reflections . . . cast on him " [as a " speculative "
man]. (Macaulay, p. 301.)

" There was in Bacon an invariable pliancy, in the presence of
great persons, which disqualified him for the task of giving wise
and effectual counsel. In part this obsequiousness arose from his

mental and moral constitution, in part it was a habit deliberately adopted, as one among many means by which a man may make his way in the world . . . that he must 'avoid repulse.' " (Abbott, Life of Bacon, p. 21. Compare the passage quoted before on Bacon as " no flatterer " from the same author's introduction to the Essays.)

His patient, conciliating, pliable nature praised as excellent and admirable.

" A man most sweet in his conversation and ways; an enemy to no man." (Sir Tobie Matthew's character of Bacon.)

" He was no dashing man, . . . but ever a countenancer and fosterer of other men's parts. . . . He contemned no man's observations, but would light his candle at every man's torch. " (Dr. Rawley's character of Bacon.)

" Retiring, nervous, sensitive, unconventional, modest, " etc. (Spedding, L. L. vii. 567–8.)

" The habit of self-assertion was not at his command. . . . When a man who is naturally modest attempts to put on the air of audacity, he only makes himself offensive. The pliancy or submissive attitude toward his official superiors . . . is generally blamed in him as an unworthy condescension, . . . but I am not so sure that he would have acknowledged it as a fault. As the world was in Bacon's time, and as it still is, if you want a man to help you in your work, you must beware of affronting him, and must show him the respect to which he thinks himself entitled." (*Ib.* 368-9.)

His faith in his own cause, his self-confidence, and his sanguine, hopeful spirit, blamed as arrogance and pride.

" To an application to his uncle, Lord Burleigh, to entitle him to come within bars, " " he received a churlish answer; the old Lord taking the opportunity to read Francis a sharp lecture on his *' arrogancy and overweening.'* " (Campbell, 15; and Macaulay, 301.)

Campbell, throughout his " Life of Bacon," clings to the " evil opinion of them that do misaffect " Bacon, and treats his natural gentleness as mere hyprocrisy. " A touch of *vanity*, even, is to be found in this composition — a quality *he hardly ever betrays* elsewhere, although he had an inward consciousness of his extraordinary powers. *Boasting* of his great influence, etc., . . . in three days Bacon was obliged *hypocritically* to write," etc. . . . " The following is Bacon's *boastful* account," etc. (Campbell's Bacon, pp. 111, 152.)

" Bacon's overweening self-confidence," etc. (Storr, Essays, introd.)

His self-confidence, fixed purposes, and hopeful spirit praised.

" I find that such persons as are of nature bashful as myself is . . . are often mistaken for proud. But I know well . . . that arrogancy and overweening is so far from my nature, as if I think well of myself in anything, it is this, that I am free from that vice." (Reply by F. B. to Ld. B.'s letter.)

" A hopeful, sensitive, bashful, amiable boy . . . glowing with noble aspirations." (Spedding, L. L. i. 6.)

" Even as a philosopher . . . he thought that he had struck into the right path by accident, and that his merit lay in endeavouring to keep in it. The qualities for which he gave himself credit were only patience and faith, and love of truth, *carrying with it* confidence in the power of truth. . . . Bacon had by nature a large faculty of hope; but it was hope from things that lay out of and beyond himself; . . . he attached little importance to himself except as an instrument for their accomplishment. No correct notion can be formed of Bacon's character till this suspicion of self-conceit is scattered to the winds." (Abbott, introduction to Essays, xxxvi.) (*Ib.* vii. 568.)

Averse to details.

" A nature indifferent to details." (Abbott, int. to Essays, xix.)

" Lord Macaulay speaks in admiration of the versatility of Bacon's mind as equally well adapted for exploring the heights of philosophy, or for the minute inspection of the pettiest detail. But he has been imposed upon by Bacon's *parade of detail*," etc. (*Ib.* lxxxvii.)

Careful about details.

" The secret of Bacon's proficiency was that, *in the smallest matters*, no less than in the greatest, he took a great deal of pains." (Spedding, Works, vii. 197.)   See the evidence of this in Bacon's Promus of Formularies and Elegancies, his collections of Proverbs and Quotations, the Sylva Sylvarum, the History of Winds, and other collections of minute particulars and jottings. See, also, an excellent page in Macaulay's Essay, 417.

Without elevation of sentiment—His philosophy low and utilitarian.

" The moral qualities of Bacon were not of a high order.   We do not say that he was a bad man; . . . his faults were . . . coldness of heart, and meanness of spirit.   He seems to have been incapable of feeling strong affection, of facing great dangers, of making great sacrifices.   His desires were set on things below," etc. (Macaulay, pp. 320–327, etc.)

" There is nothing that savours of the divine in Bacon's philosophy; . . . it began in observation, and ending in arts; . . . a low object." (See *Ib.* 373–396.)

Lofty in sentiment — Truly great.

" Greatness he could not want." (Ben Jonson, *Dominus Verulamius.*)

" That mind lofty and discursive . . . as a politician no less grand and lofty in theory, than as a philosopher." (Dr. Abbott, int. to Essays.)

" In his magnificent day-dreams there was nothing wild; . . . he loved to picture to himself the world.   . . . Cowley, in one of his finest poems, compared Bacon to Moses standing on Mount Pisgah, . . . the great lawgiver looking round from his lonely elevation on an infinite expanse," etc. (Macaulay, 423, 429.)

Commenting on Bacon's observation that " assuredly the very contemplation of things . . . is more worthy than the fruits of inventions," etc. (Nov. Org. i. 129), Spedding says, in a footnote to the Latin edition: " This is one of the passages which show how far Bacon was from what is now called a utilitarian." (Spedding's Works, i. 222.)

His statements about himself not to be credited.

" We have this account only from himself, and it is to be regarded with great suspicion." (Campbell, p. 53.)

His statements, even against himself, always candid and accurate.

" Never was a man franker in committing to paper his defects and infirmities." (Abbott, Francis Bacon, p. 317.) Dr. Abbott enters at some length into Bacon's " habit of thinking with a pen in his hand," and reviews the Essays as being documentary evidence of Bacon's own mental experiences. " Perhaps no man ever made such a confidant of paper as he did," and, *note,* he compares him to Montaigne. (See Essays, pp. xvii–xxi.)

He was cold, calculating, without any strong affections or feelings.

" His fault . . . coldness of heart . . . not malignant, but wanted warmth of affection and elevation of sentiment." (Macaulay, p. 321.) " It was as the ministers or tools of science that Bacon regarded his friends ; . . . it was an affection of a subdued kind, kept well under control, and duly subordinated to the interests of the Kingdom of Man. Bacon could not easily love friends or hate enemies, though he himself was loved by many of his inferiors with the true love of friendship. . . . He liked almost everybody with whom he was brought into close intercourse, . . . *but he loved and could love no one.*" (Abbott's int. to Essays, xxviii.) " Instinct and emotion were in him unduly subordinated to reason. . . . No one of ordinary moral instinct would accept Bacon's oft-repeated precept of Bias — ' Love as if you were sometime to hate, and hate as if you were sometime to love.' " (Abbott's Francis Bacon, 326.)

Affectionate — A firm friend — Peculiarly sensitive to kindnesses.

" But little do men perceive what solitude is, and how far it extendeth; for a crowd is not company, and faces are but a gallery of pictures, and talk but a tinkling cymbal where there is no love; . . . it is a mere and miserable solitude to want true friends, without which the world is but a wilderness. . . . Whosoever, in the frame of his nature and affections, is unfit for friendship, he taketh it of the beast, and not from humanity. . . . It was a sparing speech of the ancients to say that *a friend is another himself*, for that a friend is far more than himself," etc. (Bacon's Ess. of Friendship.)   Bacon places the love of friends, or true sympathy of souls, far above the mere love or passion of " the Ancient Cupid." The " more close sympathy of the younger Cupid" . . . depends upon deeper, more necessitating and more uncontrollable principles, as if they proceeded from the Ancient Cupid, on whom all exquisite sympathies depend." (Wisdom of the Ancient Cupid.)   " A very sensitive man, who felt acutely both kindness and unkindness."   (Spedding, L. L. vii. 567.)

A faithless, time-serving friend — Ungrateful. (Chiefly regarding Essex.)

" The person on whom, during the decline of [Essex's] influence, he chiefly depended, to whom he confided his perplexities, . . . whose intercession he employed, was his friend Bacon. . . . This friend, so loved, so trusted, bore a principal part in ruining the Earl's fortunes, in shedding his blood, and in blackening his memory. But let us be just to Bacon; . . . to the last he had no wish to injure Essex. Nay, we believe that he sincerely exerted himself to save Essex, *as long as he thought that he could serve Essex without injuring himself*," etc. (Macaulay, p. 311.)   This miserable view, exhibiting Francis Bacon as an utterly selfish creature, is repeated by Campbell and others.

" No one who reads his anxious letters about preferment and the Queen's favour, about his disappointed hopes, about his straitened means and distress for money, . . . can doubt that the question was between his own prospects and his friend; and that to his own interest he sacrificed his friend and his own honour."   (Dr. Church, Bacon, p. 57.)

See also Dr. Abbott's Francis Bacon, p. 277, of Yelverton's trial : " Bacon's behaviour was peculiarly cold-blooded and ungrateful."

" *A friend unalterable to his friends.*"   (Sir Tobie Matthew's
character of Bacon.)

No man knew better, or felt more deeply, the duties of friendship. (Basil Montagu.)

See also the whole subject argued in Spedding's *Evenings with
a Reviewer*, vol. i., and Letters and Life, i. 104–106, 250–254,
295, 370–375; ii. 69–105, 123–102, 105, 367.

" The fictitious biography paints him as bound by the sacred
ties of gratitude and affection to the Earl of Essex, who, after
striving, in the most disinterested spirit, to procure for him a
great office and a wealthy wife, had, failing in these efforts, gen-
erously bestowed upon him Twickenham Park; as helping and
advising that Earl, so long as he could do it safely and with
profit, but as going over to his enemies when the hour of danger
came; and when the Earl's rash enterprise gave those enemies a
legal advantage over him, as straining his utmost skill as an
advocate and a writer, to take away the life and to damn the
memory of a noble and confiding friend. A plain story of the
times will show that the connexion of Bacon with Essex was
one of politics and business; that this connexion was in the highest degree injurious to Bacon and to Bacon's family; that Essex
caused him to lose for fourteen years the post of Solicitor; that
Twickenham Park had never been the property of Essex, and
was not given by him to Bacon; that the connexion between
them ceased with Essex's own acts; . . . that ' the rash enterprise'
for which Essex suffered on the block was treason of so black a
shade, — so odious in the conception, so revolting in the details,
as to arm against him every honest man; . . . that, while Essex
was yet free from overt and unpardonable crimes, Bacon went
beyond the extremest bounds of chivalry to save him. That in
acting against Essex, when Essex had stained his hands with
blood and his soul with treason, Bacon did no more than he was
bound to do as a public man; that, though he could not save
the guilty chief, he strove, and not in vain, to rescue from the
gallows his misled accomplices; finally, that to the generous
suppressions of the State Paper, which he drew up under her
Majesty's command, was due the fact that Essex's name should

be pronounced without a curse, and that his son could one day be restored in blood." (Hepworth Dixon, Story, i. 6. See the same book, pp. 46–186.)

Unloved as he was unloving, he had but few friends and was little reverenced.

This is the impression conveyed by most of Bacon's antipathetic biographers — a view of his character which Dr. Abbott tries hard to reconcile with " the spirit of genuine affection which breathes " through the records of his friends and contemporaries, and, we may add, through all the letters which refer to him, written to him or of him, where his personal relations with intimate friends and acquaintances are touched upon. (See *infra.*) It is difficult, sometimes, to decide whether to place the criticisms upon Bacon's character on the side of the goats or of the sheep. They are often so self-contradictory and neutralising that the writers appear to be writing against their own convictions — rejecting the evidence patent and unchallenged of eye-witnesses, in favour of theories and personal antipathies found long after their great subject had passed away. As to forming a judgment upon detached expressions, notes or sentiments, culled from Bacon's works with a special purpose, and with special glosses attached, to suit certain theories, we protest that no author's private character can be rightly so judged; and with regard to Bacon, in particular, passages to prove the exact opposite to everything so advanced could be produced.

" *All who were good and great loved and honoured him.*" (John Aubrey.)

" My conceit of his person was never increased towards him by his place or honours; but I have and do reverence him for the greatness that was only proper to himself, in that he seemed to me ever, by his work, one of the greatest of men, and most worthy of admiration, that hath been in many ages. In his adversity I ever prayed God would give him strength, for greatness he could not want. Neither could I condole a word or syllable for him, as knowing no accident can happen to virtue, but rather help to make it manifest." (Ben Jonson, *Dominus Verulamius*.)

The same is echoed by Dr. Rawley, Osborne, Peter Böener, and Sir Tobie Matthew, all personal friends. (See Spedding, L. L. vii. 576; Hepworth Dixon, Story, 482, etc.)

The following rather grinding version is from a usually hostile critic of Francis Bacon: "Bacon's better traits have to be inferred from the brief testimony of one or two of his most intimate friends, whose disinterested eulogies, after his disgrace and death, prove that, to them, at least, he seemed not only genial, kindly, and affectionate, but also a bright example of lofty virtue. There seems something in the nature of a problem in the contradiction between Bacon as he appeared to his friends, and Bacon as he appears to us. [1] We have noted already the spirit of genuine affection which breathes through the short memoir of him written by his chaplain, Rawley. His domestic apothecary and secretary, Peter Böener, expresses a wish that a statue of him may be erected, not for his learning and researches, but 'as a memorable example to all of virtue, kindness, peacefulness, and patience.' Ben Jonson speaks in the same strain of his 'virtue.' . . . To the same effect writes Sir Tobie Matthew, one of his most intimate friends, who was in the secret of his philosophic projects, and to whom he dedicated his *Essay on Friendship*. 'It is not his greatness that I admire, but his virtue. It is not the favours that I have received of him that have enthralled and enchained my heart, but his whole life and character; which are such that, if he were of an inferior condition, I could not honour him the less, and if he were mine enemy, I could not the less love, and endeavour to serve him.' With all his faults . . . neither his formal works nor his private letters convey more than a fraction of the singular charm with which his suavity of manner and gracious dignity fascinated his contemporaries and riveted the affections of some

[1] This must depend upon who the "us," the modern reporter and critic, may be. The "us" at present writing sees nothing inharmonious in the character of Bacon, but "we" do perceive that, as a rule, very little is known of his real life and character, and that accounts of him have been intentionally "*disguised* and *veiled*."

whom it must have been hardest to deceive. . . . His enthusiasm for truth in Nature ennobled his intercourse with his associates, and placed them on a footing of such cordial fellowship with his brother workers that he really loved them. At least it is certain that he made them love him." (Abbott, Francis Bacon, 319, 33, etc.)

His cruelty — Want of feeling for animals — Vivisection.

" He seems to have no liking for birds or beasts, wild or tame. The torture of a long-billed fowl by a *waggish* Christian, who called down on himself the resentment of the Turks by his cruelty, inspires him with no deeper feeling than amusement." (See the passage quoted below, of which this is the exposition, in the introduction to Dr. Abbott's edition of the Essays.)

" The restrictions on aviaries have been treated as an indication that Bacon had a strong love for animals; but it would seem he did not object to cages, *provided the want of 'nestling'* and *'foulness'* do not *obtrude themselves on the spectator.*" (Abbott, notes to Ess. of Gardens.)

" While condemning vivisection of men, he assumes its lawfulness when applied to animals, without restriction or justification." (Abbott, notes to Ess. of Goodness.)

Macaulay, Campbell, and others, charge Bacon with aiding and abetting the torturing of Peacham.

His kindness and tenderness of heart—Love of animals, flowers—Vivisection.

Bacon is showing that " The inclination to goodness is imprinted deeply in the nature of man; insomuch that, if it issue not towards men, it will take unto other living creatures: as it is seen in the Turks, a cruel people, who nevertheless are kind to beasts, and give alms to dogs and birds; insomuch, as Busbechius reporteth, a Christian boy in Constantinople had like to have been stoned for gagging, in a waggishness, a long-billed fowl." (Essay of Goodness and Goodness of Nature.)

" I love the birds as the French king doth." (Spedding, L. L. v. 444. Bacon's Notes.)

5

" In his face a thought for the bird on the tree, the insect on the stream, . . . he pursued his studies, sniffing at a flower or listening to a bird. In the bright country air, among his books, fish, flowers, collections, and experiments, with his horse, his dog, Bacon slowly regained some part of his lost health."

" Sure, yet subtle, were the tests by which Bacon judged of men. Seeing Winwood strike a dog for having leaped upon a stool, he very justly set him down as of ungentle nature. 'Every gentleman,' he said loudly, 'loves a dog.'" (H. Dixon, Story, pp. 23, 29, 331.)

" And now," in Bacon's account, " we see the lover of birds and fowls:

" To the washerwoman for sending after the crane that flew into the Thames, five shillings.

" The Lord Chancellor was as fond of birds as of dress, and he built in the gardens of York House a magnificent aviary at a cost of three hundred pounds. From this aviary the poor crane had flown into the Thames," etc. (*Ib.* p. 355.)

" Then, again, the accounts make visible, as he lived in the flesh, the tender and compassionate man." (*Ib.* 355–357.)

" He was not inhuman or tyrannical." (Macaulay, 320.)

" For aviaries, *I like them not, except they be of that largeness as they may be turfed, and have living plants and bushes set in them, that the birds may have more scope and natural nestling, and that no foulness appear on the floor of the aviary.*" (Ess. of Gardens.)

In the *New Atlantis* the Father of Solomon's House (who had " an aspect *as though he pitied men*") is explaining the " preparations and instruments" for study and experiment at the " House." " We have," he says, " also parks and inclosures for all sorts of beasts and birds ; which we use not only for view or rareness, but likewise for dissections and trials, that thereby we may take light what may be wrought upon the body of man ; wherein we find many strange effects : as continuing life in them, though divers parts which you account vital be perished and taken forth ; resuscitating of some that seem dead in appearance, and the like. We try also poisons and other medicines upon them, as well as surgery and physic." (*New Atlantis.*)

" Of that other defect in anatomy, that it has not been practised on human bodies, what need to speak? *For it is a thing hateful and inhuman, and has been justly reproved by Celsus. . . . Wherefore, that utility may be considered, as well as humanity, the anatomy of the living subject . . . may well be discharged by beasts alive,*" etc. (*De Aug.* iv. 2.)

Montagu, Spedding, Abbott, Anton, and others, show that Bacon was in no way responsible for the torturing of Peacham.

He did not study human nature.

" Human nature and the human passions were not sciences in which Bacon was versed. He wanted that pliancy and congenial feeling which identifies itself with the pains and pleasures, the cares and solicitudes, the frailties and imperfections, whims and caprices, sympathies, passions, emotions, and affections which variously agitate and disturb, rouse and irritate, terrify and calm, enrapture, moderate, suspend, and enchain all the faculties of our nature, and all the cravings and desires of the human heart — for it is only in the delineation of the heart and its affections that we can expect to discover the soul and spirit of poetry." (Ess. by S. N. Carvalho, in New York *Herald*, Oct. 5, 1874.)

He was a profound student of human nature.

" So, then, the first article of this knowledge is to set down sound and true distributions and descriptions of the several characters and tempers of men's natures and dispositions, specially having regard to those differences which are most radical in being the fountains and causes of the rest," etc. " I cannot sufficiently marvel that this part of knowledge, touching the several characters of natures and dispositions, should be omitted both in morality and policy, considering it is of so great ministery and suppeditation to them both. (*Advancement of Learning*, ii.; Spedding, Works, iii. pp. 432–473.) See, also, *De Augmentis*, viii. 2 — " of procuring information of persons; their natures, their desires and ends, their customs and fashions, their helps and advantages," etc., etc. (Spedding, Works, v. pp. 59–78.)

See " The Essays," which, Bacon says, " of all my other works have been most current; for that, as it seems, they come home to men's business and bosoms." They are all, more or less, *studies of human nature and character.*

See, also, " Experiments touching the impressions which the passions of the mind make upon the body." (*Sylva Sylvarum*, cent. viii. 713–722), and of the effect of mind on body, and body on mind, etc.

" His style, . . . for the most part, describes men's minds as well as pictures do their bodies: so it did *his* above all men living. The course of it is vigorous and majestical . . . in all expressing a soul equally skilled in men and nature."

(See A Character of the Lord Bacon—Dr. Sprat's History of the Royal Society, part I. sec. 16, pages 35–36.)

See, also, Cowley's poem on Bacon, addressed to the Royal Society, for evidence that Bacon painted human nature " to the life."

Wanting in boldness and independence of character.

" He had no political back-bone, no power of adhering to his convictions and pressing them on unwilling ears."

" Young or old, from twenty to sixty, he was always the same; . . . from the beginning to the end of his career his wiser counsels were neglected, and he was little better than an instrument in the hands of the unwise." (Abbott, Francis Bacon, p. 22.)

" He had no moral courage, and no power of self-sacrifice or self-denial." (Campbell, Bacon, p. 220.)

A patriot — Politically bold and independent in matters which he esteemed important.

" It is creditable alike to his statesmanship and to his independence of character that, at a time when all deviations from the forms of the prayer-book were known to be distasteful to the Queen, Bacon should have pleaded for elasticity, and that 'the contentious retention of custom is a turbulent thing.' " (Abbott, Francis Bacon, p. 26.)

" Bacon, who now sat for Middlesex, *barred his own path* by a speech in the House of Commons . . . upon subsidies, which he considered too burdensome for a people overlaid with taxes. . . . It was, therefore, in entire good faith that Bacon protested against the subsidies, declaring that the gentlemen must sell their plate and the farmers their brass pots before this should be paid. The House was unanimously against him. . . . But the speech, though made in manifest sincerity, did not, on that account, conciliate the Queen; and *Bacon's conscientious opposition* brought on him the penalty of exclusion from the royal presence." (*Ib.* p. 35.)

" Bacon's fame as a patriot was fixed in these transactions. The breadth of his views, the comprehensiveness of his politics, the solidity of his understanding were observed by his contemporaries." (Hepworth Dixon, Story, p. 37.)

" The House had not sat a week . . . before he hinted at his scheme for amending the whole body of English law. . . . Reform the code! Bacon tells a House full of Queen's serjeants and utter barristers that laws are made to guard the rights of the people, not to feed the lawyers. . . . So runs his speech . . . a noble thought . . . a plan developed in his maxims of the law . . . universally read . . . the Code Napoleon is the sole embodiment of Bacon's thought. Ten days later he gave a check to the government, which brought down on his head the censures of Burghley and Puckering, which are said to have represented the personal anger of the Queen. . . . Burghley asked the Peers to confer on a grant of money for the Queen's service, and Cecil reported to the Commons that the Peers had decided for them what they were to give. . . . Who rose to warn the minister of this grave mistake? . . . Bacon stood up. A few clear words declared that . . . to give was the prerogative of the people — to dictate what they should give was *not the duty of* the Peers." ⟨*Ib.* 65–66.⟩

Bacon compared unfavourably with Coke.

Bacon as Attorney-General " holding up to posterity for ever the contrast between his courtier-like servility, and Coke's manly independence." (Abbott, int. to Essays, lvi.)

Bacon compared favourably with Coke.

" Some of the judges, and amongst them Egerton, wished to make Bacon Attorney-General, for the great common-lawyer, if a giant in legal erudition, had the manners of a bully, and the spirit of a slave. In the long succession of English judges, it is doubtful whether any one has left on the bench so distinct an impression of having been a cold, harsh, brawling, ungenerous man as Coke," etc., etc. (Hepworth Dixon, 79–80.)

" Wanting the warmth of heart, the large round of sympathies, which enabled his rival at the bar to see into political questions with the eye of a poet and a statesman, Coke could only treat a constituted court as a thing of words, dates, readings, and decisions, not as a living fact in close relation to other living facts, and having in itself the germs of growth and change." (*Ib.* 231.) See Spedding, Let. and Life, i. 232.

An inequitable judge — His judgments questioned.

" Unhappily he was employed in perverting laws to the vilest purposes of tyranny." (Macaulay, 330.)

" He did worse than nothing in politics. He degraded himself, he injured his country and posterity by tarnishing the honourable traditions of the bench." (Abbott, int. to Essays, xcvi. And see, by the same, " Francis Bacon," pp. xx, xxi, xxix.)

An equitable judge — His judgments neither questioned nor reversed.

" His favourites took bribes, but his Lordship always gave judgment *secundum æquum et bonum.* His decrees in chancery stand firme; there are fewer of his decrees reverst than of any other Chancellor." (John Aubrey, Sped. L. L. vii. 557.)

" A most indefatigable servant to the King, and a most earnest lover of the public." (Sir Tobie Matthew.)

" Bacon was the first of a new order of public men. . . . Bad men kill offices and good men found them." (See Hepworth Dixon's Story, p. 210, etc. See also Lord Chief Justice Hale on the Jurisdiction of the Lords' House, 1716.)

Apologises abjectly to the Queen about his speech on the subsidy.

" The young patriot *condescended to make the most abject apologies; . . . he bemoaned himself to the Lord Keeper, in a letter which may keep* in countenance the most unmanly of the epistles which Cicero wrote during his banishment. The lesson was not thrown away. *Bacon never offended in the same manner again.*" (Macaulay, Essays, pp. 303–4.)

" The Queen was deeply incensed, and desired it to be intimated to the delinquent . . . that he must never look to her for favour or promotion. An eloquent eulogist says that 'he heard them with the calmness of a philosopher,' *but his answers show that he was struck with repentance and remorse, and that, in the hope of obtaining pardon, he plainly intimated that he should never repeat the offence.*" (Campbell, p. 23.)

" *His compunction for his opposition to the subsidy.*" (*Ib.* 24.)

Does not offer any apology to the Queen about his speech on the subsidy.

The letter is extant and contains not a word of apology.

" *This letter is a justification and no apology.*" (Spedding, L. L. i. 233.)

" It is worthy of note that, among the many expressions of regret at the royal displeasure, *there is no record of any apology* tendered by Bacon for his speech." (Abbott, int. to Essays, i. xxix.)

See also the polite but independent letter which Bacon wrote not long afterwards to the Queen herself, ignoring the obnoxious matter of the speech, and applying directly to be employed in the Queen's service. (Spedding, L. L. i. p. 240.)

His speech charging Essex, and his connection with the trial, condemned as perfidious and unpardonable.

" The lamentable truth must be told. *This friend, so loved, so trusted, bore a principal part in ruining the Earl's fortunes, in shedding his blood, and in blackening his character,*" etc. (Macaulay's Essay.)

"*To deprive him of all chance of mercy* . . . Bacon compared him to the Duke of Guise. . . . The Queen wished a pamphlet to be written to prove that Essex was properly put to death, and she selected Francis Bacon to write it. *He, without hesitation, undertook the task. . . . No honourable man would purchase Bacon's subsequent elevation at the price of being the author of this publication,*" etc. (Campbell, p. 64.)

His speech charging Essex commended as lenient — His conducting of the trial explained as being obligatory; an official duty, etc.

Basil Montagu. Spedding, ii. 367.

" Bacon closed the case in *an eloquent and memorable speech.* His own relations with the Earl of Essex, he said, were at an end. Yet, in spite of this avowal, *he spoke as the Earl's advocate*, rather than as the Queen's ; charging him with hasty expressions, but distinctly freeing him from the charge of disloyalty. *Bacon's speech at York House saved Essex in his fortunes and his fame.*" (Hepworth Dixon's Story of Bacon, p. 162, quoting from Chamberlain to Carleton, July 1–26, 1600, Record Office ; Confessions of D. Hayward, July 11, 1600, R. O. ; Abstract of Evidence against Essex, July 22, 1600; Examination of Thos. Wright, July 24, 1600, R. O. ; Moryson, pt. ii. 68; Sydney Papers, ii. 200 ; and see Personal Life.)

" Yet, even when it was made thus sternly and just by the Queen, the ' Declaration of the practises and treasons attempted committed by Robt. Devereux, late Earl of Essex, and his complices,' was, *perhaps, the most gentle and moderate state paper ever published in any kingdom,*" etc. (Hepworth Dixon's Story, pp. 186–7 ; see, also, Prof. Fowler's Bacon, pp. 8, 9.)

He incurred the indignation and contempt of his contemporaries on account of the part which he took in Essex's trial.

" The base ingratitude and the slavish meanness manifested by Bacon on this occasion called forth the indignation of his contemporaries. . . . For some time after Essex's execution, Bacon was looked upon with aversion," etc. (Campbell, pp. 66, 68.)

" It is certain that his conduct excited great and general disapprobation." (Macaulay, p. 323.)

" The multitude loudly condemned him." (*Ib.* 325 and 326.)

No indignation was exhibited against him on account of the part which he took in Essex's trial. He was now honoured more highly than before.

" That the lofty and gentle course which Bacon pursued through these memorable events commanded the admiration of all his contemporaries, save a faction of the defeated band, is a fact of which the proofs are incontestible. . . . If he were thought of with aversion, here were the means, the opportunities for condign revenge. . . . Did the friends of Lord Essex rise on his adversaries? Was the . . . stone flung at Bacon? Just the reverse. (Hepworth Dixon, " Story," p. 183.)

" The world had not been with the rebellious Earl, either in his treason at Temple Bar or in his suffering at Tower Hill, and those who had struck down the Papist plot were foremost in the ranks of the new Parliament. Four years ago Bacon had been chosen to represent Ipswich, and the chief town of Suffolk again ratified its choice. But his public acts now won for him a second constituency in St. Albans. Such a double return, always rare in the House of Commons, was the highest compliment that could be paid to his political life." (Hep. Dixon, " Story," p. 183. See 184-5, of the Queen revising Bacon's " Declaration" as being too lenient to Essex; and notes, part iii. 149.)

Struck to the earth by the discovery of his corruption — Confessing the truth of the charges brought against him — Treated as a degraded man.

" Overwhelmed with shame and remorse." (Macaulay, p. 353.)

Lord Campbell quotes passages from Bacon's letter to the King and Buckingham (where Bacon expresses his resolution to indulge in no excuses if he has " partaken of the abuses of the times ") as a clear *negative pregnant*, admitting that the bribes had been received. (See Campbell's Bacon, p. 172.)

See also his straightforward, modest appeal to the King, repudiating the idea that he had " the troubled fountain of a corrupt

heart in a depraved habit of taking rewards to pervert justice,
... howsoever I be frail and partake of the abuses of the times."
Resolving to defend nothing in himself, and praying God that
" no hardness of heart steal upon me under show of more neatness
of conscience than is cause." (Montagu, Spedding, and others.)

*Overwhelmed with horror and surprise at the charges brought
against him — Acknowledges carelessness — Utterly repudiates
the charge of bribery — Never shows any remorse for guilt, but
even in his "prayer" regrets that he had wasted and misspent
his life in trying to follow the profession of the law and the
pursuits of a politician, for which by nature he was least fit—
Not treated as degraded, but as one who would return to power.*

" The law of nature teaches me to speak in my own defence.
With respect to this charge of bribery I am as innocent as any
born upon St. Innocents' day. I never had bribe or reward in
my eye or thought when pronouncing sentence or order." (B.
Montagu, Works, v. 549.)

Montagu, xii. 457–459; xvi. part ii. 426. See also Spedding's
Evenings with a Reviewer, vol. ii. Abbott, Francis Bacon, pp.
306, 320. Hepworth Dixon, " Story," pp. 410–411, 412–447, 466,
482; and " Personal Life." Council Registers, Dec. 30, 1617;
Mar. 17–27, 1618; June 19, 1619; Jan. 20, 1620. Bacon Memo-
randa, Lambeth MSS., 936, fol. 146.

Without a sense of humour — Never made a pun or a quibble.

" What is said by Dr. Rawley [see below] of Bacon's avoid-
ance of all mere verbal conceits is true, and the fact merits
especial attention as notably discriminating the wit of Bacon
from that of every other English writer eminent for that quality
in his age. Probably nothing resembling a pun, or any quibble of that class, is to be found in all that he has written."
(Craik, i. 30.)

" The idea of robbing the world of Shakespeare for such a stiff,
legal-headed old jack-ass as Bacon, is a modern invention of
fools." (Essay on " The Humbug of Bacon," signed B. J. A., in
the New York *Herald*, Oct. 5, 1874.) This extract is given as a

good specimen of the kind of knowledge and criticism displayed
by the press articles of this date.

*The most prodigious wit that ever lived — Fond of quibbles —
Could not pass by a jest.*

" His speech, when he could pass by a jest, was nobly censo-
rious." (Ben Jonson, *Dominus Verulamius.*)

Bacon's paradoxical manner of turning a sentence so as to
read two ways has been the frequent subject of comment. A
large number of puns and quibbles are to be found even in his
graver works, and Ben Jonson's remark shows that, however
much he might try to exclude these plays upon words from
his writings, the habit of punning was so confirmed in him as to
be, in Jonson's opinion, a disfigurement to his oratory.

" The most prodigious wit that ever I knew . . . is of your
Lordship's name, albeit he is known by another." (Sir Tobie
Matthew, letter to Bacon.)

Want of imagination of the higher type.

" Of looks conversing with the skies, of beauty born of mur-
muring sound that passes into the face, he takes no account. It
is the exclusion of the higher type that leads him to doubt
whether beauty is a hindrance or a help in running the race of
life." (Storr of Ess. of Beauty.)

" There is hardly a trace in Bacon of that transfusing and
transforming imagination which creates a new heaven and a
new earth; which reveals the elemental secrets of things, and
thrills us with a shock of surprise and delight as a new revelation. . . . There is more of poetry in Browne's Hydriotaphia
than of poetry in Bacon's collected works. Yet of poetry, in all
but the strictest and highest sense of the word, Bacon is full."
(Storr, int. lxxxiii. See below.)

Imagination of the highest type.

" Bacon, whose vast contemplative ends embraced the image
of the universal world." (Storr.)

" His life of mind was never exceeded, perhaps never equalled.
The extent of his views was immense. . . . His powers were

varied and in great perfection, his senses exquisitely acute. . . .
His imagination was most vivid and fruitful," etc., etc. (Basil
Montagu, vol. xvi. 451–463.)

" He was a man of strong, clear, and powerful imaginations.
His genius was searching and inimitable, and of this I need give
no other proof than his style itself, which, as for the most part
it describes men's minds as well as pictures do their bodies:
so it did *his* above all men living. The course of it is vigorous
and majestical: the wit bold and familiar. The comparisons
fetched out of the way, and yet the most easy : in all expressing
a soul equally skilled in men and nature. . . . He seems to take
all that comes, and to heap together rather than to register.
But I hope this accusation of mine can be no great injury to his
memory; seeing at the same time that I say he had not the
strength of a thousand men. I do also allow him to have had
as much as twenty." (See Character of Lord Bacon, by Dr.
Sprat; History of the Royal Society, part I. sec. 16, pp. 35–36.)

*Highly poetical—Possessing every faculty and gift of the true
    poet.*

" It is he that filled up all numbers, and performed that which
may be compared or preferred to insolent Greece or haughty
Rome." (Ben Jonson.)

" His Lordship was a good poet, but *concealed*, as appears by
his letters." (John Aubrey.)

The author of " The Great Assises Holden in Parnassus"
ranks Lord Verulam next to Apollo.

" The poetic faculty was strong in Bacon's mind. No imagination was ever at once so strong and so subjugated. In
truth, much of Bacon's life was passed in a visionary world
. . . magnificent day-dreams . . . analogies of all sorts," etc.,
etc. (Macaulay.)

" Few poets deal in finer imagery than is to be found in Bacon.
. . . His prose is poetry." (Campbell.)

" The varieties and sprightliness of Bacon's imagination, an
imagination piercing almost into futurity, conjectures improv-
ing even to prophecy. . . . The greatest felicity of expression,

and the most splendid imagery," etc., etc.   (Basil Montagu.)

" The Wisdom of the Ancients, .   . a kind of parabolical poetry.   The fables abounding with the deepest thought and beauty. . . . To the Advancement of Learning he brings every species of poetry by which imagination can elevate the mind from the dungeon of the body to the enjoying of its own essence. . . . Metaphors, similitudes, and analogies make up a great part of his reasoning. . . . Ingenuity, poetic fancy, and the highest imagination and fertility cannot be denied him."   (Craik.)

" The creative fancy of a Dante or Milton never called up more gorgeous images than those suggested by Bacon, and we question much whether their worlds surpass his in affording scope for the imagination.   His extended over all time.   His mind brooded over all nature, . . . unfolding to the gaze of the spectator the order of the universe as exhibited to angelic intelligences."   (Devey.)

" The tendency of Bacon to see analogies . . . is characteristic of him, the result of . . . that mind not truly philosophic, but truly poetic, which will find similitudes everywhere in heaven and earth."   (Dr. Abbott.)

" He had the liveliest fancy and most active imagination. But that he wanted the sense of poetic fitness and melody, he might be almost supposed, with his reach and play of thought, to have been capable, as is maintained in some eccentric modern theories, of writing Shakespeare's plays. No man ever had a more imaginative power of illustration drawn from the most remote and most unlikely analogies ; analogies often of the quaintest and most unexpected kind, but often, also, not only felicitous in application, but profound and true."   (Church, pp. 21, 22; see, also, pp. 19, 24, 173, 197, 200, 204, 217, 171, 201 ; and note that Dr. Church here gives Bacon every attribute of the poet excepting the power to write poetry.)

" Gentle and susceptible in genius. . . . A mind susceptible of all impressions. . . . Trott, a lover of poetry and wit, advanced him money. . . . As a bencher Bacon became the light and genius . . . of Gray's Inn; . . . dressed the dumb show, led

off the dances, invented the masques; a genial and original
nature." (Hepworth Dixon, Story, 21, 23, 33, etc.)

"I infer from this sample that Bacon had all the natural
faculties which a poet wants : a fine ear for metre, a fine feeling
for imaginative effect in words, and a vein of poetic passion.
. . . The truth is that Bacon was not without the 'fine phrensy'
of a poet," etc. (Spedding, Works, vii. 267–272.)

Sir Francis Bacon is also enumerated, by Edmund Howes,
amongst a list of "Our modern and present excellent poets,
which worthily flourish in their owne works; and who, according to their priorities as neere as I could, I have orderly set
downe." In this curious list Bacon stands eighth and Shakespeare fifteenth in order.

See, also, Sir Tobie Matthew's account of Bacon's "sprouting invention;" his "ravishing way of words, metaphors, and
allusions as perhaps the world hath not seen since it was a
world;" his pre-eminence as the "Genius of England."

See Halliwell Phillips's Outlines, p. 512.

Dr. Fischer, of Heidelberg, endorses these opinions in his work
on Bacon.

He had little or no religion.

"Bacon's zeal against persecution and intolerance arose probably in no small measure from vagueness, uncertainty, or indifference in his own religious beliefs." (Fowler's Bacon, p. 185,
and see p. 182.)

"He was guarded by every sentinel but those of virtue and
God's favour. . . . May we not humbly, but urgently, say,
'Remember Lord Bacon' . . . whenever any effort or combination of human faculties awakes your admiration and
applause. . . . Let such qualities be found in union with 'repentance toward God, and faith in our Lord Jesus Christ.' We
cannot but believe that all that was low, . . . degrading, . . .
treacherous, . . . subservient, . . . and dishonest . . . in
the life of Lord Bacon could never have blotted his noble
escutcheon if he had walked humbly with his God, . . . with a

confidence in God as a Father; . . . a jealousy for the honour of
his Saviour, and an hourly reference . . . to the guidance of
the Holy Ghost," etc. (Life of Bacon, by the Rev. J.
Sortain, 1790.)

It is science that makes him in any sense a religious man —
non-religious in conduct, etc. (Abbott, introd'n. to Essays,
p. xl.) Many other writers and critics have adopted such views.

He was truly religious.

" This lord was religious; for though the world be apt to suspect and prejudge great wits and politiques to have somewhat
of the atheist, yet *he was conversant with God*, as appeareth
throughout the whole current of his writings. . . . No man will
deny him . . . to have been a deep philosopher. And not only
so, but he was able *to render a reason for the hope* which was in
him, which that writing of his of the *Confession of Faith* doth
abundantly testify. He repaired frequently (when his health
would permit him) to the services of the church to hear sermons,
to the administration of the sacrament of the blessed body and
blood of Christ; and died in the true faith, established in the
Church of England." (Dr. Rawley's Life of Bacon, 1670.)

His toleration in religious matters blamed.

Bacon's toleration showed a fatal want of religious enthusiasm.
(Storr, intn. to Essays.)

His toleration applauded.

We do not pretend that he ever became a *violent partisan*
against the Church of Rome; . . . neither, on the other hand,
was he an exclusive advocate for the Church of England in
opposition to the Puritans. . . . In the whole range of ecclesiastical history we can recall no one whose mind looked down
upon church controversies with more *anxious concern. His
was not the latitudinarianism of indifference*. . . . We should
feel that we were performing a high duty to the Church of
Christ, at the present times, to transcribe the whole of

Bacon's enlarged view of church controversies. . . . In thus stating *his comprehensiveness of charity,* we must again add that *it was most remote from indifferentism."* (Rev. J. Sortain.) This is the same author who shows in the same book (*Life of Francis Bacon*) that Bacon's weak point was want of religion and earnest faith.

AMONGST the many proofs of the intense admiration and affection, esteem and reverence, which Francis Bacon inspired in those who were personally intimate with him, none are more satisfactory than those contained in the voluminous, but still unpublished, correspondence of Anthony Bacon, in the library at Lambeth Palace.

Here we find him spoken of as "Monsieur le Doux," and "Signor Dolce;" his extreme kindness, sweetness of disposition and heavenly-mindedness being continual subjects of comment. His followers and disciples vow fidelity to him from simple love of him and his cause; they are willing to go through the greatest perils and sufferings, as indeed we find them doing, in order to aid in the objects and plans which are most dear to him— the propagation of Christian truth and of a wide-spread and liberal education. [1]

"For my name and memory, I leave it to men's charitable speeches, and to foreign nations and the next ages;" or, as in another copy of his will, "*and to mine own countrymen, after some time be past.*"

These prophetic words seem now to be in process of fulfilment. Englishmen must regret that with "foreign nations" lies the honour of *first* and fully appreciating the genius of Francis Bacon, and of being *the first* willing or eager to hear, and to investigate the claims which have been brought forward with regard to his authorship of the "Shakespeare Plays." What Dr. Rawley said in 1657 is true even now: "His fame is greater and sounds louder in foreign parts abroad, than at home in his own nation; thereby verifying that divine

---

[1] The following is reprinted from a little pamphlet published by the present writer in 1884.

sentence, A prophet is not without honour, save in his own country and in his own house." Yet Bacon had a just confidence "in that old arbitrator, Time," and in the verdict of the "next ages." He had assured himself, long before he made his will, that "the monuments of wit and learning are more durable than the monuments of power, or of the hands;" that learning, "by which man ascendeth to the heavens, is immortal," for "the images of men's wits and knowledges remain in books, exempted from the wrong of time, and capable of perpetual renovation."

We appeal to those into whose hands this outline of a great and wonderful life may fall, to lay aside prejudice acquired at second hand, and to study for themselves the life and character of Francis Bacon, as displayed, not in any one or two questionable transactions, not from a few picked passages of his voluminous works, or in a few letters written under exceptional circumstances, but as the characters and lives of other great men are studied, and as we humbler individuals would wish posterity to study and to judge our own. Let Bacon be judged by the whole general tenour of his life, and works, and letters; and by their influence on his contemporaries and on posterity for good or for evil.

It has unhappily become habitual to Englishmen to criticise and represent this "glory of his age and nation" in such a manner that the few blemishes which dim that glory are magnified and intensified so as to obscure the picture itself. The result is that, perhaps, no other great man has been so much talked of, and so little generally known or understood, as Bacon. Probably, also, there are few men of any kind of whom, whilst contemporary biographers agree in recording so much that is great and good, writers of 150 years later date have delighted in ignoring the good, and in bringing to the front and dwelling upon every circumstance, or action, or word, which can admit of a base or evil interpretation. Rather let us consider *first* his many great virtues, his amiability, gentleness, sweetness of temper, and consideration for others, his readiness to forgive injuries and to acknowledge any error in himself, his generosity and liberality as soon as he had any means at his disposal, his magna-

6

nimity and fortitude under calamity, his ardour in pursuit of truth, his endless perseverance and patience, (an acquired virtue. since he felt that by nature he was impatient and over-zealous), his bright, hopeful spirit and large-hearted toleration, his modesty, and absence of self-importance or self-assertion. This last virtue has been held by his biographers to have been almost a weakness, and in some respects a disadvantage to him, as well as to the world at large, since the pliancy of his disposition and the submissive attitude which he maintained toward his official superiors, and which were part of his nature, have been brought against him as proofs of " cringing " and " servility." Let us also remember the threefold aims which he had set before him as the object of his life — " an object to live for as wide as humanity and as immortal as the human race; an idea vast and lofty enough to fill the soul for ever with religious and heroic aspirations. . . . Of Bacon's life no man will ever form a correct idea unless he bear in mind that, from very early youth, his heart was divided between these *three* objects, distinct but not discordant — the cause of reformed religion, the cause of his Queen and country, and of the human race through all their generations." [1]

If we also bear in mind that not only was he profoundly learned, laboriously hard-working, and painstaking in search of truth, but that he was intensely sensitive and highly imaginative; his mind, as he said, " nimble and versatile, quick to perceive analogies " (the poet's faculty), and ingenious in their application, we shall acknowledge that such a character is not one to be harshly judged in the portion of his carreer for which he repeatedly confesses himself " *unfit,* " as a lawyer and a chancellor. For our own sakes, for justice' sake, let us first contemplate and know him at his best, as " the pioneer of truth," the " patriot born," the poet-philosopher, the man who wished to spend and be spent for the advancement of learning and the benefit of the human race.

Theobald, in the preface to his edition of " Shakespeare," says kindly: " The genius that gives us the greatest pleasure

---

1 Condensed from Spedding, L. L. i. 5.

sometimes stands in need of our indulgence. Whenever this happens with regard to Shakespeare, I would willingly impute it to *a vice in his times.*"

So said Bacon of himself (though it was never his manner to excuse himself): "This is all I can say for the present concerning my charge. . . I do not fly to say that *these things are vitia temporis, and not vitia hominis.*" But may not the same indulgence which has been accorded to "Shakespeare" be accorded equally to Bacon?

Of Shakespeare we know nothing creditable; he was vulgar, jovial, and money-loving. Of Bacon we have the testimony of contemporaries whose opinion is above all suspicion of interested motives, and we know that those who saw him nearest, and those who knew him longest, give him the best character.

Sir Tobie Matthew, writing (1618) to the Grand Duke of Tuscany, gives some account of his career and position, and a description of his immense intellectual powers. He goes on to say that the praise applies not only to the qualities of the intellect, but as well to those " which are rather of the heart, the will, and the moral virtue; being a man most sweet in his conversation and ways, grave in his judgments, invariable in his fortunes, splendid in his expenses; a friend unalterable to his friends; an enemy to no man; a most hearty and indefatigable servant to the King, and a most earnest lover of the public — having all the thoughts of that large heart of his set upon adorning the age in which he lives, and benefiting, as far as possible, the whole human race."

" And I can truly say," he adds, " having had the honour to know him for many years, as well when he was in his lesser fortunes as now that he stands at the top and in the full flower of his greatness, that I never yet saw any trace in him of a vindictive mind, whatever injury were done him, nor ever heard him utter a word to any man's disadvantage which seemed to proceed from personal feeling against the man, but only (and that too very seldom) from judgment made of him in cold blood. It is not his greatness that I admire, *but his virtue:* it is not the favours I have received from him (infinite though they be) that have thus

enthralled and enchained my heart, *but his whole life and char-*
acter; which are such that if he were of an inferior condition I
could not honour him the less, and if he were mine enemy I
should not the less love and endeavour to serve him."

Dr. Rawley's short *Life of Bacon* deals more with his circumstances and works than with his character, yet his opinion is
the same as Sir Tobie's. During his residence in Gray's Inn,
Bacon " carried himself," says Dr. Rawley, " with such sweetness, comity, and generosity, that he was much revered and
loved by the Readers and Gentlemen of the House " (or Inn).
Again, " When his office called him, as he was the King's Council Learned, to charge any offenders, . . . he was never insulting
or domineering over them, but always tender-hearted, and carrying himself decently towards the parties (though it was his
duty to charge them home), as one that looked upon the example
with the eye of severity, but upon the person with the eye of
pity and compassion. And in civil business, as he was Councillor
of State, he had the best way of advising, . . . the King giving
him this testimony, 'That he ever dealt in business *suavibus modis,*
which was the way that was most according to his heart.'"
Having borne testimony to his "prime and observable parts,
. . . abilities which commonly go singly in other men, but
which in him were conjoined "—sharpness of wit, memory,
judgment, and elocution, together with extraordinary celerity
in writing, facility in inventing and " caution in venting the
imagination or fancy of his brain "— Dr. Rawley records his
industry, his anxiety to write so as to be easily understood, the
charm of his conversation, and his power of " drawing a man on
so as to lure him to speak on such a subject as wherein he was
peculiarly skilful, and would delight to speak, contemning no
man's observation, but lighting his torch at every man's candle·
. . . His opinions and assertions were, for the most part, binding, and not contradicted by any. . . . As he was a good servant to his master" (being never in nineteen years' service
rebuked by the King for anything), " so he was a good master to
his servants, . . . and if he were abused by any of them in their
places, it was not only the error of the goodness of his nature,

but the badge of their indiscretions and intemperances." After speaking of Bacon as a "religious" man, able to give a reason of the hope which was in him," and observant of the services and sacraments of the Church of England, Dr. Rawley continues: "This is most true. He was free from malice, no revenger of injuries, which, if he had minded, he had both opportunity and high place enough to have done it. He was no bearer of men out of their places.   He was no defamer of any man to his Prince, . . . which I reckon not among his moral but his Christian virtues."

John Aubrey, in his MS. notes, jotting down several pleasant anecdotes of Bacon and his friends, adds: "In short, all that were *great and good* loved and honoured him [the italics are Aubrey's own]; his favourites took bribes, but his Lordship always gave judgment *secundem æquum et bonum.* His decrees in Chancery stand firm: there are fewer of his decrees reversed than of any other Chancellor."

The tributes to Bacon's personal worth by his physician, Peter Boëner and by Sir Thomas Meautys, have already been noticed. We conclude this brief sketch with the last clause in the posthumous record which Ben Jonson wrote, under the title of *Dominus Verulamius,* in his notes on " Discoveries upon Men and Matter ":

"My conceit of his person was never increased toward him by his place, or honours; but I have and do reverence him for the greatness that was only proper to himself, in that he seemed to me ever, by his work, one of the greatest men, and most worthy of admiration, that had been in many ages. In his adversity I ever prayed that God would give him strength; for greatness he could not want, neither could I condole in a word or syllable for him, as knowing no accident could do harm to virtue, but rather help to make it manifest."

If, as we have been told, such heartfelt words as these are merely the effusions of personal attachment, or of " partial " and " admiring " friendship, what can any of us desire better ourselves than that we may so live as to win such admiration and to attach and retain such devoted friends? And yet the friendship of those who lived in the presence of Bacon, who

worked with and for him, who knew him in his struggles and in
his triumphs, in his greatness and in his fall, is not the only
friendship which he has secured. Those still revere and love
him best who, like Basil Montagu, James Spedding, and Hepworth Dixon, have devoted years of their lives to the study of
his works and the contemplation of his life and character.

Lord Macaulay, who wrote one essay on Bacon, is astonished at
the enthusiasm with which a prolonged intimacy with the works
and life of that great man had inspired his biographer, Basil
Montagu. "The writer," says Macaulay, "is enamoured of his
subject. It constantly overflows from his lips and his pen."
But this is the impression made upon most thoughtful persons
who read and read again (without previous prejudice or the aid
of a commentator) the works and letters of Bacon, until they
come to know not only the matter, but the man himself.

There can, we think, be but one issue to such a study:
admiration deepening into esteem, sympathy, and a feeling of
personal friendship, which no hostile or piecemeal criticism will
avail to shake.

The admiring warmth with which "Shakespeare" scholars
have justly extolled the character of their ideal author is precisely
that which creeps over and possesses the soul of the earnest
disciple of the "myriad-minded" Bacon. We may be incapable
of following, even in imagination, "the vast contemplative
ends" which he proposed to himself, and to the accomplishment
of which his life was actually consecrated. But no one who can
apprehend, however dimly, the plan and purpose of such a life,
can withhold from it a tribute of admiration, or can remain
insensible of the influence for good which that man must by
personal example have shed around him, and which through
his works he still diffuses. And, says Ben Jonson at the
conclusion of his sketch of Bacon's genius, "There is not
one color of the mind and another of the works." Such as
works are as a whole, such on the whole is their author.
Goodness, as well as greatness, is impressed upon the writings
of Bacon. We may be awe-struck in the contemplation of his
magnificent powers of mind, enchanted with his language, and

with the consummate ability with which he treats of all subjects, great or small; but we feel that this is not all. Mere intellect may attract attention and admiration, but it does not win esteem. Running through the whole of his works there is a thread of genuine goodness. It is a thread rather underlying the substance than superficially exhibited, but it is inextricably interwoven. Everywhere from Bacon's works there radiates this goodness, kindness of heart, large-minded toleration, " enthusiasm of humanity," respect for authority, reverence for, and trust in, a great and good God. This it is which " enthralled" his personal friends and " enamoured" his later biographer. This it is which prompts us to exclaim of him as Holofernes did of Virgil:

" Who understandeth thee not, loveth thee not."

CHAPTER IV

FRANCIS BACON: AN OUTLINE OF HIS LIFE AND AIMS.

> " All is not in years to me; somewhat is in hours well spent."
> —*Promus.*

> "Yet hath Sir Proteus, for that's his name,
> Made use and fair advantage of his days;
> His head unmellow'd, but his judgment ripe."
> —*Two Gentlemen of Verona,* ii. 4.

MANY and various opinions have been expressed in modern times concerning Francis Bacon, and the motives and aims supposed to have influenced his course and actions in public capacities. We may safely pass by these phases of his wonderful career, so carefully and devotedly recorded in the calm pages of James Spedding,[1] and will for the present consider the personality and life of Bacon from two different aspects: first, as the poet; secondly, as the most ardent promoter, if not the founder, of a vast secret society, destined to create a complete reformation in learning, science, literature, and religion itself, throughout the whole wide world. In the lively works of Hepworth Dixon, and in scattered episodes in Spedding's *Life of Bacon*, we get occasional peeps behind the scene. But, in the last named work especially, it appears as if we were not meant to do so. The facts that Bacon in his youth " masked and mummed," and led the revels at Gray's Inn; that throughout his life he was appealed to on all great occasions to write witty speeches for others to deliver at the gorgeous " entertainments " which were the fashion of the day (and in which, doubtless, he took a leading part, *in the background*); that he and his brother Anthony, who was living with him in 1594,

---

[1] See "Letters and Life of Bacon," seven vols., 8vo, or the abridgment of them, "Life and Times of Bacon," and especially "*Evenings with a Reviewer,*" 2 vols., 8vo—James Spedding.

actually removed from their lodgings in Gray's Inn to a house in Bishopsgate Street, *in the immediate neighborhood of The Bull Inn, where plays and interludes were acted.* These and many such important factors in his private history are slipped over, or altogether omitted in most accounts of him. They should not be so passed by, for Bacon's theatrical proclivities were no mere boyish or youthful taste; they grew with him and formed a very important part of his " method of discourse," a means by which he could inform those who could not read, instilling through the eyes and ears of the body sound teaching on all sorts of subjects. The stern morality which was often thus inculcated would not for one instant have been listened to, with patience, from the pulpit or the professed teacher, by the class of persons for whose benefit we believe that Francis Bacon wrote his earliest (and unacknowledged) plays. It will be seen that this love and *respect* for the theatre was with him to the end of his life. Nearly fifty metaphors and figures based upon stage-playing are to be found in his grave scientific works, and in the Latin edition of the *Advancement of Learning,* published simultaneously with the collected edition or " Folio " of the *Shakespeare* plays in 1623, he inserts a brave defence of stage-playing and a lament for the degradation of the theatre in his day.

Most persons who peruse these pages are probably acquainted with the outlines of Bacon's life. We therefore merely piece together particulars extracted from the works of his most painstaking and sympathetic biographer, James Spedding, and from the shorter " lives" and biographies of his secretary, Dr. Rawley, Hepworth Dixon, Prof. Fowler, and others.

Francis Bacon was born on the 22d of January, 1561, at York House, in the Strand. His father, Sir Nicholas (counsellor to Queen Elizabeth, and second prop in the kingdom), was a lord of known prudence, sufficiency, moderation, and integrity. His mother, Lady Anne Cooke, a choice lady, was eminent for piety and learning, being exquisitely skilled, for a woman, in the Greek and Latin languages. " These being the parents," says Dr. Rawley, " you may easily imagine what the issue was like to be, having had whatsoever nature or breeding could put in him."

Sir Nicholas is described as " a stout, easy man, full of contrivance, with an original and projective mind." The grounds laid out by him at Gorhambury suggested to his son those ideas of gardening which he himself afterwards put into practice, and which, developed in his essays and other writings,[1] have led to the foundation of an English style of gardening.[2] So with regard to cultivation of another kind. The scheme which Sir Nicholas presented to Henry VIII. for the endowment of a school of law and languages in London, is thought to have been, perhaps, the original germ of the *New Atlantis*, the idea being transferred from statecraft to nature. In politics the Lord Keeper held to the English party; that party which set its face against Rome, and those who represented Rome; against the Jesuits, the Spaniards, and the Queen of Scots. If he felt warm against any one, it was against the latter, whom he detested, not only as a wicked woman, but as a political tool in the hands of France and Spain. By the help of his clear head and resolute tongue, the great change of religion, which had recently taken place, had been accomplished, and it may easily be believed that " Burghley himself was scarcely more honoured by invective from Jesuit pens." But on the bench he had neither an equal nor an enemy. Calm, slow, cautious in his dealings, he was at the same time merry, witty, and overflowing with humour and repartee; qualities which recommended him very highly to the irritable, clever Queen, who loved a jest as well as he, and who seems to have appreciated the value of a faithful minister imbued with so much strong common sense, and with no dangerous qualities. Francis Bacon records a saying concerning his father, which was, doubtless, to the point, or he would not have entered it amongst his apophthegms: " Some men look wiser than they are,—the Lord Keeper is wiser than he looks."

---

1 There seem to be many books of gardening and kindred subjects which will some day be traced to Bacon.

2 Hepworth Dixon's Story of Bacon's Life, p. 17, from which we shall make large extracts, the book being out of print.

So many circumstances and little particulars crop up as these things are looked into, allusions and hints about Sir Nicholas as well as doubts and obscurities concerning his early life and doings, and such particulars all tend toward making us regard with more attention, and to attach more importance to this note of Francis Bacon. The thought suggests itself, Was it, perhaps, this wise, witty, cautious man, " full of contrivance, and with an original, *projective* mind," who first contrived and projected a scheme for the accumulation, transmission, and advancement of learning, which it was left to his two sons, Anthony and Francis, to develop and perfect ?

This is amongst the problems which at present we cannot answer, because so little is known — or perhaps it should be said, so little is *published* — concerning Sir Nicholas and Anthony. Later on we hope to contribute to the general stock all the information about Anthony which we have been able to collect from unprinted MSS., and to show that there can be no doubt of his having been a poet and a considerable author, as well as an active propagandist for the secret society of which he seems always to acknowledge his still more talented and versatile brother, Francis, to have been the head.

For the full and satisfactory elucidation of many difficulties and obscurities which will arise in the course of this study, *it is of imperative importance that the histories and private life of Sir Nicholas and Anthony Bacon shall be submitted to a searching and exhaustive investigation;*[1] for the present we must pass on.

---

[1] The notices of Anthony in ordinary books, such as Spedding, Hepworth Dixon, etc., are quite brief and imperfect. A good summary of all these is to be found in the *Dictionary of National Biography*, edited by Leslie Stephen (Smith, Elder & Co., 1885). See vol. ii., Nicholas Bacon and Anthony Bacon. See also *Memoirs of the Reign of Queen Elizabeth*, vols. i. and ii. (A. Miller, Strand, 1754), and *Historical View of the Negotiations between the Courts of England, France, and Brussels from the year* 1592-1617. (London, 1749.) Both of these by *Thomas Birch*. They are out of print and should be republished. The hard worker will also find plenty of material in the 16 folio vols. of Anthony Bacon's unpublished correspondence — *Tenison MSS.*, Lambeth Palace, and in the British Museum the following: *Harleian MSS.* No. 286, art. 144, 145, 146, 147, 148. *Cotton Lib.*, Calig, E, vii. 205; Nero, B, vi. 290, 291, 293-303, 337, 371, 380, 383-395, 398, 403, 413 b. *Lansdown MSS.* No. 38, 53, 87, 29, 44, 74, 87, 107, 11, 12.

The mother of Anthony and Francis was an important and interesting personage. She was the second wife of Sir Nicholas. The first wife seems to have been a quiet, ordinary woman, of whom there is little or nothing to say excepting that she left three sons and three daughters. Of these half-brothers and sisters, not one appears to have been in any way " brotherly," kind, or useful to Francis, excepting the second son, Nathaniel, who took to the arts, and painted a portrait of his mother standing in a pantry, habited as a cook. It is probable that Nathaniel assisted his younger brother by making some of the designs and pictures which will be explained further on.

Lady Anne Bacon was a woman of higher birth, of loftier character, than her husband. If the three life-like terra cotta busts at Gorhambury and other existing portraits are compared, it will be seen that it is from the mother that the boy derived the chiseled features and the fine development of the brow. From the father came the softer expression, the side-long look, the humourous twinkle in the eye. Lady Anne, though we know her to have been a tender mother and a woman of strong affections, was yet a somewhat stern, masterful and managing head of the house, and so she appears in her portraits. The daughter of Sir Anthony Cooke of Geddy Hall in Essex, scholar and tutor to Edward VI., she inherited the whole of her father's religious creed, and not a little of his accomplishments in Greek. That religion was to fear God and hate the Pope. For a papist she had no tolerance, for this indiscriminating repugnance had been born in her blood and bred in her bone.

The importance of these particulars can hardly be over-estimated when taken in connection with what we know of the development of Francis Bacon's character, and with the aims and aspirations which he set up for himself. There never was a period in his life when judgment seems to have been lacking to him. His earliest and most childish recorded speeches are as wise, witty, and judgmatical in their way as his latest. " His first and childish years," says Dr. Rawley, " were not without some mark of eminency; at which time he was enslaved with that pregnancy and towardness of wit, as they were pre-

sages of that deep and universal apprehension which was manifest in him afterwards."

Having, then, this excellent gift of discernment or "judgment," Francis Bacon was never intolerant, for intolerance is a
sign of want of judgment, of that power or desire to grasp both
sides of a question and to judge between them which was a pre-
eminent faculty and characteristic of Bacon's mind. The tendency to turn every question inside out, hind-side before and
wrong side upwards, is perceptible, not only in his arguments, theories, and beliefs, but it pervades the whole of his
language, and is the cause of that antithetical style which is so
peculiarly characteristic in his writings.

Although he must, from his earliest infancy, have been influenced by the mother whom he esteemed as a " saint of God,"
with a deep interest in the condition of the church, Francis
Bacon never allowed fervour to degenerate into the " over-ween-
ing zeal or extremes " in religion which " do dissolve and
deface the laws of charity and of human society." Lady
Anne perfectly believed that the cause of the Non-Conformists
was the whole cause of Christ.[1] Francis never believed that;
and it seems to be a reasonable explanation of much that took
place between mother and son, that he was forever putting in
practice his own injunctions regarding the necessity for great
tenderness and delicacy in matters of religion, and urging that
unity could only be hoped for in the church when men should
learn that " fundamental points are to be truly discerned and
distinguished from matters not merely of faith, but of opinion,
order, or good intention." On fundamental points, on all that
is " of substance," they were of one accord; but Francis
Bacon's religion was built upon a far wider and broader basis
than that of his pious, Calvinistic mother, or of many of her
relations. For the Greys,[2] the Burleighs, Russells, Hobys, and
Nevilles, in short, the whole kindred of Francis Bacon by the
male and female lines, professed the severest principles of the

---

[1] Spedding, Let. and L. i. 3.

[2] The wife of William Cooke (Lady Anne's brother) was consin to Lady
Jane Grey.

Reformation. Some of them had been exiled (amongst them Lady Anne's father, Sir Anthony Cooke), some even sent to the block in the time of Queen Mary. " In her own fierce repugnance to the Italian creed she trained her sons," says Hepworth Dixon. She may have made them intolerant *to the errors* of the Roman creed, but she certainly did not make them so to the believers themselves; for in after years Francis Bacon's intercourse with and kindness to members of the Roman Catholic church was a great cause of anxiety to his mother, yet his intimacy and correspondence with these friends continued to the end of his life.

Little Francis was ten years old when he attracted the attention of the Queen, and paid her his pretty compliment : " How old are you, my child?" " I am just two years younger than your Majesty's happy reign." We see him in these early days, a man amongst boys; now playing with the daisies and speedwells, and now with the mace and seals; cutting posies with the gardener, or crowing after the pigeons, of which, his mother tells us, he was fond, roast or in a pie. Every tale told of him wins upon the imagination, whether he hunts for the echo in St. James' Park, or eyes the jugglers and detects their tricks, or lisps wise words to the Queen.[1]

" At twelve years of age he was sent to Cambridge and entered with his brother Anthony as fellow-commoner of Trinity College, of which John Whitgift, afterwards Archibishop of Canterbury, was then master. Repeated entries in Whitgift's accounts prove the brothers to have been delicate children, and the state of their health a continual cause of anxiety to their mother, Lady Anne. Many of her letters are extant, and show her, even to the end of her life, feeding them from her cellars and her poultry yard, looking sharp after their pills and ' confections,' sending them game from her own larder, and beer from her own vats, lecturing them soundly on what they should eat and drink, on their physic and blood-lettings, on how far they might ride or walk, when safely take supper, and at what

---

[1] Rawley's Life of Bacon. Hepworth Dixon's *Story of Bacon's Life.*

hour of the morning rise from bed.   From notices, scant but clear,
of the Lord Keeper's household, we may see the two boys growing up together; both gentle and susceptible in genius; as strong
in character as they were frail in health.[1]   One sees Francis by
the light of Hilyard's portrait, as he strolled along the lawn or
reclined under the elms, with his fat round face, his blue-grey
eyes, his fall of brown curls, and his ripe, jesting mouth; in his
face a thought for the bird on the tree, the fragance in the air, the
insect in the stream; a mind susceptible to all impressions."[2]

"Brief and barren as the record of his childhood appears, it
may yet help us," says Spedding, "when studied in the light
which his subsequent history throws back upon it, to understand in what manner, and in what degree, the accidents of his
birth had prepared him for the scene on which he was entering.
When the temperament is quick and sensitive, the desire of
knowledge strong, and the faculties so vigorous, obedient, and
equally developed, that they find almost all things easy, the
mind will commonly fasten upon the first object of interest that
presents itself, with the ardour of a first love."   The same sympathetic writer goes on to describe the learned, eloquent,
religious mother trying to imbue her little son with her own
Puritanic fervour in church matters; the affectionate father, the
Lord Keeper, taking him to see and hear the opening of Parliament, and instilling into him a reverence for the mysteries of
statesmanship, and a deep sense of the dignity, responsibility,
and importance of the statesman's calling.   Everything that he
saw and heard,—the alarms, the hopes, the triumphs of the
time, the magnitude of the interests that depended upon the
Queen's government; the high flow of loyalty which buoyed
her up and urged her forward ; the imposing character of her
council,—must have contributed to excite in the boy's heart a
devotion for her person and cause, and aspirations after the
civil dignities in the midst of which he was bred up.   For the

---

1 *Ib.* From *Whitgift's Accounts*, in Brit. Mag. xxxii. 365.   Heywood's University Transactions, i. 123–156.   Athenæ Cantabrigienses, ii. 314.   Lambeth MSS.
650, fol. 54.

2 Dixon.   Spedding, Letters and Life, 1, 2, 3.

present, however, his field of ambition was in the school-room and library, where, perhaps, from the delicacy of his constitution, but still more from the bent of his genius, he was more at home than in the playground. His career there was victorious; new prospects of boundless extent opening on every side,[1] until at length, just about the age at which an intellect of quick growth begins to be conscious of original power, he was sent to the university, where he hoped to learn all that men knew. *By the time, however, that he had gone through the usual course, he was conscious of a disappointment,* and came out of college at fifteen, by his own desire apparently, and, without waiting to take a degree, in precisely the same opinion as *Montaigne* when he left college, as he says, " having run through my whole course, as they call it, and, in truth, without any advantage that I can honestly brag of."

Francis stayed at Cambridge only for three years, being more than once driven away by outbreaks of the plague; once for so long as eight or nine months. Yet he had made such progress in his studies that he seems to have begged his father to remove him, because he had already found that the academical course which he was pursuing was " barren of the production of fruits for the life of man." Leaving the university before he was sixteen and without taking a degree, he yet carried with him the germs of his plan for reconstituting the whole round of the arts and sciences, a plan from which he never departed, and upon which he was still working at the time of his death.

That this should have been possible, argues an unusually extensive reading, and an acquaintance with branches of learning far beyond the subjects prescribed by the university authorities, and taking together all the facts concerning his great schemes, and the indications which he gives as to the origin of one of them, it is probable that during his sixteenth year, and perhaps earlier, he embarked in the study of the Indian, Arabian,

---

[1] It seems probable that in these early days the ideas and schemes of Sir Nicholas regarding an improved system of education and learning were discoursed of to his little son, and that the germs of his own great plans were thus planted.

Egyptian, and other ancient philosophers and religious writers, who gained such an influence over his imagination, and from whom he seems to have derived many hints for the symbolism employed in the teaching of his secret society.

However this may be, it is certain that Francis Bacon was, in very early childhood, possessed with an extraordinary clear-headedness, and with a maturity of judgment which caused him to form, when he was but a mere boy, those "*fixed and unalterable and universal opinions*" upon which the whole of his after life-work and philosophy were based—opinions as characteristic as they were in advance of his age; theories and ideas which we shall presently find claimed for others, but which, wherever they make themselves heard, echo to our ears the voice of the "Great Master."

During his three years' stay at the university, Francis fell, says Dr. Rawley, "into the dislike of the philosophy of Aristotle, not for the unworthiness of the author, *to whom he would ascribe all high attributes*, but for the unfruitfulness of the way, being a philosophy (his lordship used to say) only strong for disputations and contentions, but barren of the production of works for the benefit of the life of man, in which mind he continued to his dying day."

It seems not a little strange that this "dislike" of Bacon, which has been even made the subject of reproach to him, and which is decidedly treated as an unreasonable prejudice peculiar to himself, should not have been equally observed in the writings of nearly every contemporary author who makes mention of Aristotle. Let this point be noted. To cite passages would fill too much space, but readers are invited to observe for themselves, and to say if it is not true that every distinguished "author" of Bacon's day, and for some years afterwards, even whilst ascribing to Aristotle "all high attributes," decries his system of philosophy, and *for the same reasons which Bacon gives*, namely, that it was "fruitless"—that it consisted more of words than of matter, and that it did not enable followers of Aristotle to rise above the level of Aristotle. Yet this had not hitherto been the general opinion.

7

" It seemed that toward the end of the sixteenth century, men neither knew nor desired to know more than was to be learned from Aristotle; a strange thing at any time; more strange than ever just then when the heavens themselves seemed to be taking up the argument on their behalf, and by suddenly lighting up within the region of 'the unchangeable and incorruptible,' and presently extinguishing a fixed star [1] as bright as Jupiter, to be protesting by signs and wonders against the cardinal doctrine of the Aristotelian philosophy.

" *It was then that a thought struck him, the date of which deserves to be recorded, not for anything extraordinary in the thought itself,* which had perhaps occurred to others before him, *but for its influence upon his after life.* If our study of nature be thus barren, he thought, our method of study must be wrong: might not a better method be found? The suggestion was simple and obvious, and the singularity was in the way he took hold of it. With most men such a thought would have come and gone in a passing regret. . . . *But with him the gift of seeing in prophetic vision what might be and ought to be was united with the practical talent of devising means and handling minute details. He could at once imagine like a poet, and execute like a clerk of the works.* Upon the conviction, This may be done, followed at once the question, *How* may it be done? Upon that question answered, followed the resolution to try to do it." [2]

We earnestly request the reader to observe that *the subject of this paragraph is a little boy twelve or thirteen years old.* The biographer continues:

---

[1] The new star in Cassiopeia which shone with full lustre on the youthful Bacon's freshmanship (and to which he is said to have attached great importance as an augury of his own future) was the same star—or, as some think, comet—which guided the wise men of the East, the Chaldean astronomers and astrologers to the birth-place of our blessed Saviour. This star of Bethlehem has since appeared thrice, at intervals varying slightly in length. According to astronomical calculations, it might have re-entered Cassiopeia in 1887, but its uninterrupted movements will correspond with those previously recorded if it appears again in 1891. We should then say truly that Bacon's star is still in the ascendant.

[2] Let. and Life, i. 4. Again we would remind the reader of the great probability that Sir Nicholas Bacon had implanted this idea in the mind of his brilliant little son.

" Of the degrees by which the suggestion ripened into a project, the project into an undertaking, and the undertaking unfolded itself into distinct proportions and the full grandeur of
its total dimensions, I can say nothing. But that the thought
first occurred to him at Cambridge, therefore before he had completed his fifteenth year, we know upon the best authority — his
own statement to Dr. Rawley. I believe it ought to be regarded
as the most important event of his life; the event which had a
greater influence than any other upon his character and future
course. "

This passage seems, at first sight, rather to contradict the
former, which says that the thought came to Bacon when first
he went to Cambridge. But the discrepancy appears to have
been caused by the difficulty experienced, as well by biographer
as reader, in conceiving that such thoughts, such practical
schemes, could have been the product of a child's mind.

All evidence which we shall have to bring forward goes to
confirm the original statement, that Francis conceived his plan
of reformation soon after going up to the university; that he
matured and organised a system of working it by means of a
secret society, before he was fifteen years old, by which time
he had already written much which he afterwards disdained as
poor stuff, but which was published, and which has all found a
respectable or distinguished place in literature.

It is not difficult to imagine what would have been the effect
upon such a mind as this of grafting on to the teaching received
in a strict Puritan home the study, by turns, of every kind of
ancient and pagan philosophy. And it is clear that Francis Bacon
plunged with delight into these occult branches of learning, his
poetic mind finding a strong attraction in the figurative language
and curious erudition of the old alchemists and mystics. Did
such studies for awhile unsettle his religious ideas, and prepare
him to shake off the bands of a narrow sectarianism? If so,
they certainly never shook his faith in God, or in the Bible as
the expression of " God's will. " Such researches only increased
his anxiety and aspiration after light and truth. He never wrote
without some reference to the Divine Wisdom and Goodness,

some " laud and thanks to God for his marvellous works, with prayers imploring His ayde and blessing for the illumination of our labours, and the turning of them to good and holy uses. "

Bright, witty, and humourous as Francis naturally was, sanguine and hopeful as was his disposition, there is yet a strain of melancholy in most of his writings. " A gravity beyond his years " in youth — in mature age a look " as though he pitied men." And he did pity them; he grieved and was oppressed at the thought that " man, the most excellent and noble, the principal and mighty work of God, wonder of nature, created in God's image, put into paradise to know him and glorify him, and to do his will — that this most noble creature, O pitiful change! is fallen from his first estate, and must eat his meat in sorrow, subject to death and all manner of infirmities, all kinds of calamities which befall him in this life, and peradventure eternal misery in the life to come. "[1]

The more he cogitated, the more he was assured that the cause of all this sin and misery is ignorance. " Ignorance is the curse of God, but knowledge is the wing by which we fly to heaven. "[2]

He reflected that " God created man in His own image, in a reasonable soul, in innocency, in free-will, in sovereignty. That He gave him a law and commandment which was in his power to keep, but he kept it not; but made a total defection from God. . . . That upon the fall of man, death and vanity entered by the justice of God, and the image of God was defaced, and heaven and earth, which were made for man's use, were subdued to corruption by his fall, . . . but that the law of nature was first imprinted in that remnant of light of nature which was left after the fall; . . . that the sufferings and merits of Christ, as they are sufficient to do away the sins of the whole world, so they are only effectual to those who are regenerate by the Holy Ghost, who breatheth where He will, of free grace which quickeneth the spirit of a man.

1 *Anatomy of Melancholy*, i. 174.

2 3 Henry VI. iv. 7.

That the work of the Spirit, though it be not tied to any means in heaven or earth, yet is ordinarily dispensed by the preaching of the word, . . . prayer and reading, by God's benefits, His judgments and the contemplation of His creatures."

Since most of these means are cut off from those who are plunged in dark, gross ignorance, an improved method of study must precede the universal reformation which Bacon contemplated in literature, science, philosophy, and in religion itself. To bring about such a reformation would be the greatest boon which could be conferred upon suffering humanity. By God's help he could and would bring it about.

It would be almost unreasonable to suppose that the boy-philosopher did not communicate the germs of such thoughts and aspirations to the father to whom he was deeply attached, and whose ideas are known to have been in close sympathy with those of his favourite son. Dr. Rawley says, significantly: " Though he was the youngest son in years, *he was not the lowest in his father's affection;* " and, as has been said in a previous chapter, the visions of Francis seem to have been in some degree foreshadowed by or based upon earlier plans of the old Treasurer. At all events, the sagacious father seconded the plans, and perceived the growing genius of his favourite son, and when Francis complained that he was being taught at Cambridge mere words and not matter, Sir Nicholas allowed him to quit the university, and Francis, after lingering a year or more at home, at his own desire, and, most probably, in accordance with a conviction which he afterwards expressed, that " travel is in the younger sort a part of education,"was sent in the train of Sir Amias Paulet, the Queen's Ambassador to France, " to see the wonders of the world abroad."

Hitherto we have scarcely mentioned Anthony Bacon, the elder of the two sons of Sir Nicholas by his second wife, Lady Anne; and, indeed, very little is known to the world in general of this man, who yet, we have reason to believe, was a very remarkable person, and who, although he rarely appeared upon the scene, yet played a very important part behind the curtain, where by and by we will try to peep. Anthony was two years

older than Francis, and the brothers were deeply attached to
each other. They never address or speak of each other but in
words of devoted affection—" My deerest brother," " Antonie
my comforte." As they went together to Cambridge, so probably they left at the same time, but even of this we are not
sure. What next befell Anthony is unknown to his biographers,
and there is a strange obscurity and mystery about the life of
this young man, who, nevertheless, is described by Dr. Rawley as
" a gentleman of as high a wit, though not of such profound
learning, as his brother." That he was a generous, unselfish,
and admiring brother, who thought no sacrifice great which
could be made for the benefit of Francis, and for the forwarding
of his enterprises, we know, and there is abundant proof of the
affection and reverence which he had for his younger and more
gifted brother. The mystery connected with Anthony appears
to be consequent upon his having acted as the propagandist on
the continent of Francis Bacon's secret society and new philosophy. He conducted an enormous correspondence with
people of all kinds who could be useful to the cause for which
the brothers were laboring. He seems to have received and
answered the large proportion of letters connected with the
business part of the society; he collected and forwarded to
Francis all important books and intelligence which could be of
use, and devoted to his service not only his life, but all his
worldly wealth, which we see mysteriously melting away, but
which, no doubt, went, like that of Francis, into the common
fund which was destined, as one of the correspondents expresses
it, to " keep alight this fire " so recently kindled.

Sixteen folio volumes of Anthony Bacon's letters lie, almost
unknown, in the library at Lambeth Palace. These leave no
loophole for doubt as to his real mission and purpose in living
abroad. We hope to return to them by and by, in a chapter
devoted to these letters alone. For the present they are only
mentioned to indicate the source of much of our information
as to Anthony's life and aims.

Neither of the brothers was strong in health. Anthony,
especially, soon became a martyr to gout and other ailments

which were supposed to explain the fact of the comparative retirement in which he lived at home and abroad. Francis seems
chiefly to have suffered from those nervous disorders—tooth-
ache, sleeplessness, and " vapours, " " clouds and melancholy "—
which too often beset the body where the spirit over-crows it.
In later life, looking back, he speaks of having had good health
in his youth; so the " puddering with the potigarie " was probably entailed by the overstrain of such unremitting and exciting
work as he undertook. His natural constitution must have been
singularly good, and his strength unusual, for to the labours of
Hercules he added those of Atlas, cleansing and restoring the
world, and bearing the weight of the whole tremendous work
upon his own shoulders.

But for the present we may look on Francis Bacon as free from
care or anxiety. " We must picture him as in the season of all-
embracing hope, dreaming on things to come, and rehearsing
his life to himself in that imaginary theatre where all things go
right; for such was his case when—hopeful, sensitive, bashful, amiable, wise and well-informed for his age, and glowing
with noble aspirations—he put forth into the world with happy
auspices in his sixteenth year." [1]

What a change of scene, what a revulsion of ideas, what an
upsetting of habits, opinions and prejudices, for a boy to be sent
forth from the quiet college life under the supervision of Whitgift,
and from the still more strict routine of a Puritan home, into the
gaiety, frivolity, dissipation of the life of courts and camps!
True, Sir Amias and Lady Margaret Paulet, in whose suite
Francis was to travel, were kind and good, and, if young in
years, Francis was old in judgment. But all the more, let us
picture to ourselves the effect on that lively imagination, and
keenly observant mind, of the scenes into which he was now
precipitated. For the English Ambassador was going on a mission to the court of Henri III. at Paris, and from thence with the
throng of nobles who attended the King of France and the Queen
Mother. The English embassy, with Francis in its train, went in

---

[1] Spedding, Letters and Life, i. 6.

royal progress down to Blois, Tours and Poictiers, in the midst of alarms, intrigues, and disturbances, intermixed with festivities and license, such as he could never have dreamed of. The French historian of the war, though a witness of and actor in this comedy, turned from it in disgust.[1] "When two courts which rivalled each other in gallantry were brought together the consequence may·be guessed. Every one gave himself up to pleasure; feasts and ballets followed each other, and love became the serious business of life."[2]

At Poictiers, which he reached in 1577, Francis Bacon set up headquarters for three years. Yet we are quite sure, from remarks dropped here and there, that, during these three years, he made various excursions into Spain and Italy, learning to speak, or, at least, to understand, both Spanish and Italian. He also made acquaintance with Michel de Montaigne, then Mayor of Bordeaux, and perhaps he travelled with him, and kept his little record of the travels.[3] For during the time of Francis Bacon's sojourn in France we still hear of him as *studying and writing*. Plunged for the first time into the midst of riotous courtly dissipation, the record of him still is, that he was *observing*, drawing up a paper on the state of Europe — and what else? We think also that he was writing essays on the society which was spread out before him, and which he regarded as a scene in a play. He wrote as the thoughts ran into his pen, with never-failing judgment and perception, with the naiveté of youth, with much enjoyment, but with mistrust of himself, and with profound dissatisfaction, not only with the state of society, but with his own enjoyment. Society, he knew, would neither relish nor be improved by essays which were known to be written by a youth of eighteen or nineteen; he would, therefore, borrow the robe of respected eld, and the essays should come forth with authority, fathered by no less a person than the Mayor of Bordeaux.[4]

---

1 Hepworth Dixon. 2 Sully's Memoirs.

3 The Journal du Voyage de Michel de Montaigne en Italie, par la Suisse et l'Allemagne, 1579 (Old Style), is written in the third person: "*He, M. de Montaigne*, reported," etc.

4 Of course it will be understood that the *first edition* only of the Essays is sup-

These are by no means the only works which were (in our opinion) the products of those light-hearted, exciting days, when with youth, health, genius, keen powers of enjoyment, of observation, and of imagination, with endless energy and industry, and ample means at his disposal,—" Wealth, honour, troops of friends,"—he caught the first glimpses of a dazzling phase of life, and of the " brave new world that hath such people in it." We may judge, from the inscription on a miniature painted by Hilliard in 1578, of the impression made by his conversation upon those who heard it. There is his face, as it appeared in his eighteenth year, and round it may be read the graphic words — the natural ejaculation, we may presume, of the artist's own emotion: *Si tabula daretur digna, animum mallem;* if one could but paint his mind!

He was still at Paris, and wishing to be at home again, when, on February 17, 1579, Francis dreamed that his father's country house, Gorhambury, was plastered over with black mortar. About that time, Sir Nicholas, having accidentally fallen asleep at an open window, during the thaw which followed a great fall of snow, was seized with a sudden and fatal illness of which he died in two days. The question whether in future Francis " might live to study " or must " study to live," was then trembling in the balance. This accident turned the scale against him. Sir Nicholas, having provided for the rest of his family, had laid by a considerable sum of money, which he meant to employ in purchasing an estate for his youngest son. His sudden death prevented the purchase, and left Francis with only a fraction of the fortune intended for him, the remainder being divided amongst his brothers and sisters.

Thenceforward, for several years, we find him making strenuous efforts to avoid the necessity of following the law as a profession, and endeavouring to procure some service under the Queen, more fitted to his tastes and abilities. But the Cecils, now in power, not only refused to help their kinsman (of whom it is said they

posed to have been written at this time. The large and unexplained additions and alterations are of a much later period. and the *enlarged* edition did not appear in England till long after Bacon's death.

were jealous), but, that he might receive no effectual assistance from higher quarters, they spread reports that he was a vain speculator, unfit for real business. Bacon was thus driven, " against the bent of his genius," to the law as his only resource. Meanwhile he lived with his mother at Gorhambury, St. Albans.

Any one who will be at the pains to study the *Shakespeare* plays, in the order in which Dr. Delius has arranged them (and which he considered to be the most correct chronological order), will see that they agree curiously with the leading events of Bacon's external life. So closely indeed do the events coincide with the plots of *the plays, that a complete story of Bacon's true life has been drawn from them. The following notes may be suggestive:

1st Henry VI. The plot is laid in France, and the scenes occur in the very provinces and districts of Maine, Anjou, Orleans, Poictiers, etc., through which Bacon travelled in the wake of the French court.

2nd Henry VI. The battle of St. Albans. The incident recorded on the tomb of Duke Humphrey, *in an epitaph written circa 1621* (when Bacon was living at St. Albans), of the impostor who pretended to have recovered his sight at St. Alban's shrine, is the same as in the play. See 2 Henry VI. ii. 1.

The Taming of the Shrew, The Two Gentlemen of Verona, etc., *Romeo and Juliet*, and *The Merchant of Venice*, all reflecting Francis Bacon's studies as a lawyer, combined with his correspondence with his brother Anthony, then living in Italy. When Francis fell into great poverty and debt, he was forced to get help from the Jews and Lombards, and was actually cast into a sponging-house by a " hard Jew," on account of a bond which was not to fall due for two months. Meanwhile Anthony, returning from abroad, mortgaged his property to pay his brother's debts, taking his own credit and that of his friends, in order to relieve Francis, precisely as the generous and unselfish Antonio is represented to do in *The Merchant of Venice.* This play appeared in the following year, and the hard Jew was immortalised as Shylock. The brothers spent the summer and autumn of 1592 at Twickenham.

The *Midsummer Night's Dream* appears shortly afterwards. In this piece Bacon seems, whilst creating his fairies, to have called to his help his new researches into the history of the winds, and of heat and cold.

The plays and their various editions and *additions* enable us to trace Bacon's progress in science and ethical and metaphysical studies. The politics of the time also make their mark.

Richard II. was a cause of dire offence to the Queen, since it alluded to troubles in Ireland, and Elizabeth considered that it conveyed rebukes to herself, of which Essex made use to stir up sedition. The whole history of this matter is very curious, and intimately connected with Bacon, but it is too long for repetition here.[1]

Hamlet and *Lear* contain graphic descriptions of *melancholia* and raving madness. They appeared after Lady Anne Bacon died, having lost the use of her faculties, and " being," said Bishop Goodman, " little better than frantic in her age." She

> Fell into a sadness, then into a fast,
> Thence to a watch, thence into a weakness,
> Thence to a lightness, and by this declension
> Into the madness wherein,

like Hamlet, she raved, and which her children wailed for.

The particulars of the death of Queen Elizabeth, which Bacon learned from her physician, bear a striking resemblance to passages in *King Lear*.

Macbeth appears to reflect a combination of circumstances connected with Bacon. About 1605–6 an act of Parliament was passed against witches, James implicitly believing in their existence and power, and Bacon, in part, at least, sharing that belief. James, too, had been much offended by the remarks passed upon his book on demonology, and by the contemptuous jokes in which the players had indulged against the Scots. Mixed up with Bacon's legal and scientific inquiries into witch-

---

[1] See Bacon's Apophthegms, Devey, p. 166, and the *Apologia* of Essex.

[2] See *Did Francis Bacon write Shakespeare*, part ii. p. 26, and Bacon's *Apologia* and *Apophthegms.*

craft, we find, in *Macbeth*, much that exhibits his acquaintance
with the *History of the Winds*, of his experiments on *Dense
and Rare*, and his observations on the *Union of Mind and
Body.*

A Winter's Tale is notably full of Bacon's observations on
horticulture, hybridising, grafting, etc., and on the virtues of
plants medicinal, and other matters connected with his notes
on the *Regimen of Health.*

Cymbeline, and *Antony and Cleopatra*, show him studying
vivisection, and the effects of various poisons on the human
body. The effects of mineral and vegetable poisons are also
illustrated in *Hamlet*, and if these plays were written so early
as some commentators suppose, then we may believe that certain portions were interpolated after Bacon's investigations
into the great poisoning cases which he was, later on, called
upon to conduct.

The Tempest describes a wreck on the Bermudas, and Caliban, the man-monster or devil. It was published soon after
the loss of the ship *Admiral*, in which Bacon had embarked
money to aid Southampton, Pembroke, and Montgomery in the
colonisation of Virginia. The ship was wrecked on the Bermudas, the " Isle of Divils." About this time the *History of
the Winds and of the Sailing of Ships* was said to be written.

Timon of Athens, showing the folly of a large-hearted and
over-generous patron in trusting to " time's flies " and " mouth-
friends," who desert him in the time of need, seems to have
been written by Bacon after his fall and retirement, to satirise
his own too sanguine trust in parasites, who lived upon him so
long as he was prosperous, but who, on his reverse of fortune,
deserted, and left him to the kindness of the few true friends
and followers on whom he was absolutely dependent.

Henry VIII. completes the picture. In a letter from Bacon to
the King, in 1622, he quotes (in the original draft) the words
which Wolsey utters in the play of *Henry VIII.*, iii. 2, 454–457,
though Bacon adds: " My conscience says no such thing; for I
know not but in serving you I have served God in one. But it
may be if I had pleased men as I have pleased you, it would

have been better with me." This passage was cut out of the
fair copy of the letter; its original idea appeared next year in
the play of *Henry VIII.*

Ben Jonson describes, in well-known lines, the labour and
artistic skill necessary for the production of mighty verse so
richly spun and woven so fit as *Shakespeare's.* To a profound
study of Nature, which is exalted by, " made proud of his designs," must be added the art which arrays Nature in " lines
so richly spun and woven so fit:"

> " For though the poet's matter *Nature* be,
> His *art* must give the fashion ; and that he
> Who casts to write a living line must sweat
> (Such as thine are) and strike the second heat
> Upon the Muses' anvil; turn the same
> *And himself with it,* that he thinks to frame ,
> Or for the laurel he may gain a scorn ;
> For a good poet's *made* as well as born.
> And such wert thou."

But, as a mere child, he seems to have written, not words
without matter, but *matter without art,* and we can well imagine
him saying to himself in after years :

> " Why did I write ? What sin to me unknown
> Dipt me in ink, my parents', or my own ?
> As yet a child, nor yet a fool to fame,
> I lisped in numbers, and the numbers came."

There is not one, not even the poorest, amongst the *Shakespeare* plays, which could possibly have been *the first* or nearly
the earliest of its author's efforts in that kind. A careless perusal of some of the " mysteries " or play interludes which were
in favour previous to the year 1579 will enable any one to perceive the wide chasm which lies between such pieces and — say
— *Titus Andronicus* and the plays of *Henry VI.* There are
passages in these plays which no tyro in the arts of poetry and of
playwriting could have penned, and for our own part we look,
not backward, but forward, to the crowd of " minor Elizabethan
dramatists" in order to find the crude, juvenile effusions which,

we believe, will prove to have been struck off by Francis Bacon[1] at the *first heat* upon the Muses' anvil. These light and un-labored pieces were probably written, at first, chiefly for his own amusement, or to be played (as they often were) in the Inns of Court, or by the private " servants" of his friends, and in their own houses.

Later on, we know that he took a serious view of the impor-tant influence·for good or for bad which is easily produced by shows and " stage-plays," set before the eyes of the public. As has been said, he always, and from the first, regarded the stage, not as a mere " toy," but as a powerful means of good — as a glass in which the whole world should be reflected — " a mirror held up to nature; to show virtue her own feature, scorn her own image, and the very age and body of the time his form and pressure."

" Men," he said, " had too long ' adored the deceiving and deformed imagery which the unequal mirrors of their own minds had presented to them,' " the " deformities " of ignorance, su-perstition, affectation, and coarseness. They should see these deformities of vice and ignorance reflected so truly, so life-like, that virtue should charm, whilst vice should appear so repulsive that men should shrink from it with loathing.

Many of the plays which we attribute to Francis Bacon and his brother Anthony treat of low life, and contain not a few coarse passages. But the age was coarse and gross, and it must be observed that, even in such passages, vice is never attrac-tive; on the contrary, it is invariably made repelling and con-temptible, sometimes disgusting, and in every case good and the right are triumphant. It is a matter for serious consideration whether the pieces which are exhibited before our lower and middle classes possess any of the merits which are conspicuous in the plays (taken as a whole) of the time of Elizabeth. We see them, we admire or laugh, and we come away, for the most part, without having heard a single phrase worthy of repetition or record. We remember little of the play twenty-four hours

---

[1] Again we add a saving clause in favour of the little known Anthony, also " a concealed poet."

after we have seen it, and we are no whit the wiser, though at
the time we may have been the merrier, and that is not a bad
thing.

Bacon perceived, doubtless by his own youthful experience,
that men are far more readily impressed by what they see than
by what they hear or read. That, moreover, *they must be
amused,* and that the manner and means of their recreation are
matters of no slight importance. For the bow cannot always
be bent, and to make times of leisure truly recreative and
profitable to mind as well as body, was, he thought, a thing
much to be wished, and too long neglected. The lowest and
poorest, as well as the most dissipated or the most cultivated,
love shows and stage plays. He loved them himself. Would it
not be possible to make the drama a complete (though unrecognised) school of instruction in morals, manners, and politics,
and at the same time so highly entertaining and attractive
that men should unconsciously be receiving good and wholesome
doctrines, whilst they sought merely to amuse themselves?

There is no question that such things were to him true recreation and delight. Sports and pastimes have for one object
" to drive away the heavy thoughts of care," and to refresh the
spirits dulled by overwork, and by harping on one string. Idleness, especially enforced idleness, is no rest to such a mind as
Bacon's; and we know that he was always weariest and least
well in " the dead long vacation." So we are sure that he often
exclaimed, like Theseus, in the *Midsummer Night's Dream:*

> "Come, now; what masques, what dances shall we have,
> To wear away this long age of three hours
> Between our after-supper and bedtime?
> Where is our usual manager of mirth?
> What revels are in hand? Is there no play
> To ease the anguish of a torturing hour?
> Say, what abridgment have you for this evening?
> What masque? what music? How shall we beguile
> The lazy time, if not with some delight?"

Like Theseus and his friends, he finds little satisfaction in
the performance of the ancient play which is proposed, and

which he knows by heart, or in the modern one, in which
" there is not one word apt or one word fitted." He mourns
the degradation of the stage—in ancient times so noble, and
even in the hands of the Jesuits wisely used, as a discipline for
the actor, and a means of wide instruction for the spectators.

There is reason to think that Francis, in childhood, showed
great talent for acting, and that he took leading parts in the
Latin plays which were performed at college. At home, such
doings were checked by Lady Anne's Puritan prejudices. The
strong tendency which Anthony and Francis evinced for the
theatre, and for " mumming and masquing " with their companions, was a source of great anxiety and displeasure to this good
lady. She bewailed it as a falling-off from grace, and prayed
yet that it might not be accounted a sin that she should permit
her dear son Francis to amuse himself at home in getting up
such entertainments, with the help of the domestics. All this
renders it improbable that he ever had the opportunity of going
to a public theatre until he went abroad, and perhaps the very
coarseness and stupidity of what he then saw put on the stage
may have disgusted him, acting as an incentive to him to attempt
someting better.

At all events, hardly had he settled down in Gray's Inn, before
the plays began to appear. From this time there are frequent
allusions, in the records of the Gray's Inn Revels, to the assistance which he gave, and which seems, in most cases, to have
consisted in writing, as well as managing, the whole entertainment. If any names are mentioned in connection with such
revels, or with the masques and devices which were performed
at court, these names almost always include that of Francis
Bacon. Sometimes *he is the only person named* in connection
with these festivities.

All this might be taken as a matter of course, so long as
Bacon was but a youth, though even at that time the fact of
his being a playwright, or stage-manager, would seem to be
remarkable, considering the horror with which his mother, and
no doubt many others of his near and dear Puritan relatives,
regarded the performance of stage-plays and masques.

Lady Anne, in a letter written to Anthony, just before the Revels and the first performance of the *Comedy of Errors*, at Gray's Inn, in 1594, exhorts him and Francis that they may "not mum, nor mask, nor sinfully revel. Who were sometime counted first, God grant they wane not daily, and deserve to be named last." [1]

Considering the low estimation in which the degraded stage of that date was held by all respectable people, it is not astonishing that during Bacon's lifetime (if there were no more potent motive than this) his friends should combine to screen his reputation from the terrible accusation of being concerned with such base and despised matters. But it is long since this feeling against the stage has passed away; and, moreover, in some cases, we find Bacon actually instrumental in producing the works of " *Shakespeare,*" not to mention those which have become classical and of much esteem. It is, therefore, not a little surprising to find that particulars and records, which would have been reckoned as of the greatest interest and importance, if they had concerned Shakspere or Ben Jonson, should be hushed up, or passed over, when they are found closely to connect Francis Bacon with theatrical topics. As an illustration of our meaning, it may be mentioned that in the voluminous " Life" of Spedding the index, at the end of each of the five volumes, does not enable the uninitiated reader to trace the fact that Bacon wrote either *devices, masques, interludes, entertainments, or sonnets;* none of these words appear in any index. Moreover, although the device of the *Order of the Helmet,* and the masques of the *Indian Boy,* and the *Conference of Pleasure,* are partly printed and all described in that work, we seek in vain for the pieces under these or any other titles, and they are only to be found by looking under *Gray's Inn revels.* Evidently there has been no great desire to enlighten the world in general as to Bacon's connection with the theatrical world of his day— perhaps it was thought that such a connection was derogatory to his position and reputation as a great philosopher.

---

[1] Lambeth MSS. 650, 222, quoted by Dixon. So here again we see Anthony also mixed up with play-writing.

8

Hepworth Dixon goes into the opposite extreme when he speaks of Lady Anne, in letters written as late as 1592, " loving and counselling her two *careless* boys." Francis was at that date thirty, and Anthony thirty-two years of age. A year later Francis wrote to his uncle, Lord Burleigh: " I wax somewhat ancient. One and thirty years is a good deal of sand in a man's hour-glass. My health, I thank God, I find confirmed; and I do not fear that action shall impair it, because I account my ordinary course of study and meditation to be more painful than most parts of action are." He goes on to say that he always hoped to take some " middle place" in which he could serve her Majesty, not for the love either of honour or business, " for the contemplative planet carrieth me away wholly," but because it was his duty to devote his abilities to his sovereign, and also necessary for him to earn money, because, though he could not excuse himself of sloth or extravagance, " yet my health is not to spend, nor my course to get." Then he makes that remarkable declaration which further explains his perpetual need of money: " I confess *that I have as vast contemplative ends* as I have moderate civil ends; for *I have taken all knowledge to be my province.* This, whether it be curiosity or vainglory, or, if one may take it favorably, *philanthropia,* is so fixed in my mind that it cannot be removed."

That the biographer should have thought fit to use such an expression as " careless boy " in regard to the indefatigable philosopher, " the most prodigious wit," who in childhood had a gravity beyond his years, and who at thirty felt " ancient," speaks volumes as to the impression made on the mind of a sympathetic reader by the various small particulars which shed light on the gay and sprightly side of Francis Bacon's many-sided character.

In the letter to his uncle Bacon goes on to say, " I do easily see that place of any reasonable countenance *doth bring commandment of more wits than a man's own, which is the thing I greatly affect.*" Here is a reason, the only reason, why he desired to gain a good position in the world. With place and wealth would come power to carry out his vast contemplative ends.

Without money or position he could have no such hope, and he adds, " If your lordship will not carry me on, I will not do as Anaxagoras did, who reduced himself with contemplation unto voluntary poverty; but this I will do: I will sell the inheritance that I have, and purchase some lease of quick revenue, or some office of gain that shall be executed by deputy, and so give over all care of service, and become some sorry book-maker, or a true pioneer in that mine of truth which he said lay so deep. This which I have writ unto your Lordship is rather thoughts than words, being set down without art, [1] disguising, or reservation, wherein I have done honour, both to your Lordship's wisdom, in judging that that will best be believed by your Lordship which is truest, and to your Lordship's good nature, in retaining nothing from you."

Bacon wrote this letter from his lodging at Gray's Inn at the beginning of the year 1592. He was now just entering his thirty-second year, and, on the surface, little had appeared of his real life and action. But still waters run deep. He had already accomplished enough to have filled the measure of a dozen ordinary lives, and apart from his own actual writings we have now abundant evidence to show how his vast plans for universal culture and reformation were spreading—more abroad than at home, but everywhere, manifesting themselves in the revival, the " *renaissance* " of literature and science.

The rearing of the new " Solomon's House " was begun. Poor as he was, almost solitary on the heights of thought, but yet with many willing minds struggling to approach and relieve him, he knew with prophetic prescience that his work was growing, imperishable, neither " subject to Time's love nor to Time's hate."

> No, it was builded far from accident;
>   It suffers not in smiling pomp, nor falls
> Under the blow of thralled discontent,
>   Whereto the inviting time our fashion calls:
> It feels not policy, that heretic,
>   Which works on leases of short-numbered hours;
> But all alone stands hugely politic. [2]

---

[1] Spedding, L. L., i. 109. Comp. Hamlet, ii. 2, 95-99, etc. [2] Sonnets cxxiv, cxxv.

To witness this he calls the fools of time. What was it to him that he had " borne the canopy, with his externe the outward honouring"?   Whilst living thus externally, as fortune forced him to do, as mere servant to greatness, a brilliant but reluctant hanger-on at the court, he was meanwhile collecting materials, *digging the foundations, calling in helpers* to " lay great bases for eternity."

CHAPTER V.

PLAYWRIGHT AND POET-PHILOSOPHER.

"Playing, whose end, both at the first and now, was, and is, to hold, as 'twere, the mirror up to nature; to show virtue her own feature, scorn her own image, and the very age and body of the time his form and pressure."

—*Hamlet.*

ABOUT the year 1592 Bacon wrote a device entitled *The Conference of Pleasure.* [1] It was evidently prepared for some festive occasion, but whether or not it was ever performed in the shape in which it is seen in the existing manuscript, is not known.

The paper book which contained this device bore on its outside leaf a list of its original contents, but the stitches which fastened the sheets together have given way, or were intentionally severed, and the central pages are gone—a great loss, when we know that these pages included copies of the plays of *Richard II.* and *Richard III.*, of which it would have been interesting to have seen the manuscript.

The *Conference of Pleasure* represents four friends meeting for intellectual amusement, when each in turn delivers a speech in praise of whatever he holds "most worthy." This explains the not very significant title given to this work in the catalogue which is found upon the fly-leaf of the paper book: "Mr. Fr. Bacon Of Giving Tribute, or that which is due."

The speeches delivered by the four friends are described as *The Praise of the Worthiest Virtue,* or Fortitude, "The Worthiest Affection,"—Love; "The Worthiest Power,"—Knowledge; and the fourth and last, "The Worthiest Person." This is the same that was afterwards printed and published under

[1] This device was edited by Mr. Spedding (1867) from the manuscript, which he found amongst a quantity of paper belonging to the Duke of Northumberland.

the title of " Mr. Bacon in Praise of his Soveraigne." It bears
many points of resemblance to Cranmer's speech in the last
scene of *Henrg VIII.*,[1] and is ostensibly a praise of Queen Elizabeth. Covertly it is a praise of Bacon's sovereign lady, the
Crowned Truth. The editor of the *Conference* observes, as so
many others have done, that there is in the style of this piece a
certain affectation and rhetorical cadence, traceable in Bacon's
other compositions of this kind, and agreeable to the taste of
the time. He does not, however, follow other critics in saying
that this courtly affectation was Bacon's style, or that the
fact of his having written such a piece is sufficient to disprove
him the author of other compositions written more naturally
and easily. On the contrary, he describes this stilted language as
so alien to his individual taste and natural manner, that there
is no single feature by which his own style is more specially distinguished, wherever he speaks in his own person, whether formally or familiarly, whether in the way of narrative, argument,
or oration, than the total absence of it."

The truth is that the style of Francis Bacon was the best
method, whatever that might be, for conveying to men's minds the
knowledge or ideas which he was desirous of imparting. There
should, he says, be "a diversity of methods *according to the
subject or matter which is handled.*" This part of *knowledge of
method* in writing he considers to have been so weakly inquired
into as, in fact, to be deficient. He explains that there must be,
in this "method of tradition," first the invention or idea of that
which is to be imparted; next, judgment upon the thing thought
or imagined, and lastly, delivery, or imparting of the thought or
idea. Then he shows that knowledge is not only for present use,
but also for its own advancement and increase. With regard
especially to present use, he points out that there are times and
seasons for knowledges, as for other things. How to begin, to
insinuate knowledge, and how to refrain from seeming to attempt
to teach? " It is an inquiry of great wisdom, what kinds of wits

[1] Further on we shall have occasion to show how in many of Bacon's poems,
sonnets, etc., where "the Queen" is praised, the allusion is ambiguous, referring
chiefly, though covertly, to Bacon's Sovereign Mistress, Truth.

and natures are most apt and proper for most sciences." He is actually speaking of the use of mathematics in steadying the mind, "if a child be bird-witted and hath not the faculty of attention;" but he leads this argument into another which again brings before us his ideas about the immense importance of the stage. "It is not amiss to observe, also, how small and mean faculties, gotten by education, yet when they fall into great men and great matters, do work great and important effects; whereof we see a notable example in Tacitus, of two stage players, Percennius and Vibulenus, who, by their talent for acting, put the Pannonian armies into extreme tumult and combustion. For, there arising a mutiny amongst them upon the death of Augustus Cæsar, Blæsas, the lieutenant, had committed some of the mutineers, which were suddenly rescued; whereupon Vibulenus got to be heard speak — (*and charged Blæsas, in pathetic terms, with having caused his brother to be murdered*) — with which speech he put the army into an infinite fury and uproar; whereas, truth was, he had no brother, neither was there any such matter; but he played it merely as if he had been on the stage."

This anecdote is partly an illustration of what Bacon has previously been saying, that the duty of rhetoric is "*to apply reason to imagination*, for the better moving of the will." Rhetoric, therefore, may be made an aid to the morality whose end is to persuade the affections and passions to obey reason. He shows that "the vulgar capacities" are not to be taught by the same scientific methods which are useful in the delivery of knowledge "*as a thread* to be spun upon, and which should, if possible, be insinuated" in the same method wherein it was invented. In short, matter, and not words, is the important thing; for words are the images of cogitations, and proper thought will bring proper words. It may in some cases be well to speak like the vulgar and think like the wise. This was an art in which Bacon himself is recorded to have been especially skilful: he could imitate and adopt the language of the person with whom he was conversing and *speak* in any style. If so, could he not equally well *write* in any style which best suited the matter in hand, which would most readily convey his

meaning to educated or uneducated ears, to minds prosaic or
poetical, dull in spirit, and only to be impressed by plain and
homely words, or not impressed at all, except the words were
accompanied by gesture and action as if the speaker were
" upon the stage " ?

And so Bacon was " content to tune the instruments of the
muses," that they should be fit to give out melodies and harmonies of any pitch, and suited to every frame of mind.   In his
acknowledged writings (which seem to be an ingenious map of,
or clue to, his whole body of works) we find, as it were,
samples of many and varied styles of writing which he desires
to see studied and more perfectly used; and although in his
greatest productions he has built up a noble model of language
which the least observant reader must recognise as Baconian,
yet there are amongst his writings some so unlike what might
be expected from his pen, and so very unlike each other, as to
dispel the idea that his many-sided mind required, like ordinary
men, merely a one-sided language and " style " in which to
utter itself.

The manner of speaking or writing which pleases him best
was plain and simple, " a method as wholesome as sweet."
But, just as in the poems and plays which we attribute to him the
styles are so various as to raise doubts, not only of the identity
of the author, but even as to various portions of the same work,
so the style of writing of the *Gesta Grayorum* or the *Conference
of Pleasure* is totally unlike the *New Atlantis* or the *Confession of Faith*.   Neither is there, at first sight, anything which
would cause the casual reader to identify the author of any of
these with the *Wisdom of the Ancients*, or *Life's a Bubble*, or
the *History of the Winds*, or the *Essay of Friendship*, or
many more widely different works or portions of works *known*
to have been written by Bacon.   Because this is known, no one
is so bold or so foolish as to point to the immense differences in
style as proof that one man could not have written all.   One man
did write them; no one can challenge the statement, and consequently no question has arisen about this particular group of
works; yet they differ amongst themselves more than, individ-

ually, they differ with a vast number of works not yet generally acknowledged to be Bacon's. They differ more essentially from each other than do the works of many dramatists and poets of the sixteenth and seventeenth centuries. Their style is sometimes indistinguishable from treatises by various "authors." In short, nothing but a complete comparative anatomy of Bacon's writings at different periods and on different topics would enable any one (without evidence of some other sort) to assert of every work of Bacon's that it was or was not of his composition; so varied is his style.

To return to the paper book. Besides the pieces which are still contained in it, eight more appear to have formed part of the contents of this and another small volume of the same kind, now lost. According to the list on the cover the lost sheets should contain:

1. The conclusion of Leycester's Commonwealth.

2. The speeches of the six councillors to the Prince of Purpoole, at the *Gray's Inn Revels,* 1594. The exterior sheet of the book has in the list, *Orations at Gray's Inn Revels.*

3. Something of Mr. Frauncis Bacon's about the Queen's Mat⁸.

4. Essaies by the same author.

5. Richard II. The editor calls these "*Copies of Shakespeare's Plays.*" The list does not say so.

6. Richard III.

7. *Asmund and Cornelia* (a piece of which nothing is known).

8. A play called *The Isle of Dogs.* The induction and first act of this play are said to have been written by Thomas Nashe, and the rest by "the players." No copy has been found of *The Isle of Dogs;* and after the title in the list appears the abbreviated word *frmnt.*[1]

In a line beneath, "*Thomas Nashe, inferior plaies.*"

It is curious and interesting to observe the pains which are taken to explain away the simplest and most patent documentary evidence which tends to prove Bacon's connection with plays or poetry. The following is an instance: Commenting

[1] This seems to have puzzled the editor, but can it mean more or less than "*fragment*"?

upon the startling but undeniable fact of the two *Shakespeare* plays being found enumerated, with other plays not known, in a list of Bacon's works amongst his papers, the careful editor proceeds to make easy things difficult by explanation and commentary:

" That *Richard II.* and *Richard III.* are meant for the titles of Shakespeare's plays, so named, I infer from the fact—of which the evidence may be seen in the *fac-simile*—that, the list of contents being now complete, the writer (or, more probably, another into whose possession the volume passed) has amused himself with writing down promiscuously the names and phrases that most ran in his head; and that among these the name of *William Shakespeare* was the most prominent, being written eight or nine times over for no other reason that can be discerned. That the name of Mr. *Frauncis Bacon*, which is also repeated several times, should have been used for the same kind of recreation, requires no explanation. . . . In the upper corner . . . may be seen the words *ne vile velis*, the motto of the Nevilles, twice repeated, and there are other traces of the name of Neville. Other exercises of the same kind are merely repetitions of the titles which stand opposite, or ordinary words of compliment, familiar in the beginnings and endings of letters, with here and there a scrap of verse, such as:

" Or,

        Revealing day through every cranie peepes,

      Multis annis jam transactis,
      Nulla fides est in pactis,
      Mel in ore, verba lactis;
      Fell in corde, fraus in factis.

" And most of the rest appear to be merely exercises in writing *th* or *sh;* . . . but the only thing, so far as I can see, which requires any particular notice is the occurrence, in this way, of the name of *William Shakespeare;* and the value of that depends, in a great degree, upon the date of the writing, which, I fear, cannot be determined with any approach to exactness. All I can say is that I find nothing . . . to indicate a date later than the reign of Elizabeth; and if so, it is probably one of the earliest evidences of the growth of Shakspere's *personal* fame as a dramatic author, the beginning of which cannot be dated much earlier than 1598. It was not till 1597 that any of his plays appeared in print; and though the earliest editions of *Richard II., Richard III.*, and *Romeo and Juliet* all bear that date, his name is not on the title-page of any of them. They were set forth as plays which had been 'lately,' or 'publicly,' or 'often with great applause,' acted by the Lord Chamberlain's servants. Their title to favour was their popularity as acting plays at the Globe; and it was not till they came to be read as books that it occurred to people unconnected with the theatre to ask who wrote them. It seems, however, that curiosity was speedily and effectually excited by the publication, for in the very next year a second edition of both the *Richards* appeared, with the name of William Shakespeare on the title page; and the practice was almost invariably followed by all publishers on like occasions afterwards. We may conclude, therefore, that it was about 1597 that play-goers and readers of plays began to talk about him, and that his name would naturally present itself to an idle penman in want of something to use his pen upon. What other inferences will be drawn from its appearance on the cover of this manuscript by those who start with the conviction that Bacon, and not Shakespeare, was the real author of *Richard II.* and *Richard III.*, I cannot say; but to myself the fact which I have mentioned seems quite sufficient to account for the phenomenon." [1]

The phenomenon does not seem to require any explanation. Everything in the list, excepting the plays, is known to be Bacon's. Essays, orations, complimentary speeches for festivals, letters written for, and in the names of, the Earls of Arundel, Sussex, and Essex. Only the plays are called " *copies*, " because in their second editions, when men first began to be curious as to the " concealed poet, " and Hayward, or some other, was to be " racked to produce the author, " the name *Shakespeare* was printed on the hitherto anonymous title-page. The practice was so common at that date as to cause much bewilderment and confusion to the literary historian; and this confusion was, probably, the very effect which that cause was intended to produce.

It is worthy of note that in the writing-case, or portfolio, which belonged to Bacon (and which is in the possession of the Howard family at Arundel) a sheet is found similarly scribbled over with the name William Shakespeare. Considering the amount of argument which has been expended upon the subject of the scribbled names on the fly-leaf of the *Conference of Pleasure*, it would appear too strange for credibility

---

[1] Introduction to the *Conference of Pleasure*, p. xxiv.

that this witness of Bacon's own portfolio should be ignored, were it not that we now have other and such strong proofs of a combination to suppress particulars of this kind.

Besides the name of *Shakespeare*, there are, on the outer leaf of the manuscript book, some other curious jottings which are to our point. The amanuensis, or whosoever he may have been, who beguiled an hour of waiting by trying his pen, scribbles, with the name Shakespeare, some allusions to other plays besides *Richard II.* and *Richard III.*

Love's Labour's Lost satirises " the diseases of style," and " errors and vanities," which Bacon complains were intermixed with the studies of learned men, and which " caused learning itself to be traduced." The utterances of Holofernes, Nathaniel, Biron, and Armado, respectively, illustrate the " vain affections, disputes, and imaginations, the effeminate and fantastical learning," which infected all the teaching and the books of the period.

Making fun of the pedantic talk of Holofernes and his friends, *the pert page Moth* declares that " they have been at a feast of languages and stolen the scraps."

Costard answers: " Oh! they have lived long on the almsbasket of words. I marvel thy master hath not eaten thee for a word; for thou art not so long by the head as *Honorificabilitudinitatibus.*"

This alarming polysyllable was in the mind of the amanuensis, though his memory failed before he got through the thirteen articulations, and he curtails it to " *Honorificabilitudino,*" yet cannot we doubt that this amanuensis had seen in or about the year 1592 the play of *Love's Labour's Lost*, which was not published or acted until 1598.

The scrap of English verse, in like manner, shows the amanuensis to have been acquainted with the poem of *Lucrece*, published for the first time in 1594, or two years after the supposed date of the scribble. Writing from memory, the copyist makes a misquotation. In the poem is the line:

" Revealing day through every cranie *spies.*"

But he writes:

> "Revealing day through every cranie *peepes.*"

A confusion, doubtless, between this line and one which follows, where the word *peeping* is used.

In *Love's Labour's Lost,* v. 2, the whole scene turns upon the ideas involved in the Latin lines which are also written on this communicative fly-leaf:

> *Mel in ore, verba lactis;*
> *Fell in corde, fraus in factis.*

Biron's way of talking is, throughout the scene, compared, for its ultra suavity, to honey and milk:

Biron. White-handed mistress, one sweet word with you.
Princess. Honey and milk and sugar — there are three.

After a quibble or two on Biron's part, the Princess begs that the word which he wishes to have with her may *not* be sweet:

Biron. Thou griev'st my gall.
Princess. Gall? bitter.

Presently, in the same scene, the affectations of another young courtier are satirised, and he is called " Honey-tongued Boyet." Perhaps the scribe knew from whence his employer derived the metaphors of talk, as *sweet, honied, sugared,* and smoother than *milk,* and, antithetically, the *gall of bitter words.* [1]

There are many proofs that Bacon utilised his talents by writing speeches for his friends, to deliver on important occasions, and for public festivities.

---

[1] It is observable that the name *Shakespeare* on the fly-leaf of the *Conference,* though written some dozen times, is invariably spelt as it was *printed* on the title-pages of the plays, and not as he, or any of his family, in any known instance, wrote it during his lifetime. The family of Shakspere, Shakspeyr, Shakspurro, Shakespere, or Shaxpeare never could make up their minds how to spell their names. Perhaps it would be more accurate to say that their friends never could decide for them. There are at least fourteen different spellings, of which *Shaxpeare* is the most frequent, and appears sixty-nine times in the Stratford records. It seems as if the author of the plays must have made some compact with the family, which prevented them from adopting, till long after Shakspere's death, the spelling of the pseudonym. The doctrine of chances, one would think, must have caused one or more to hit upon the printed variety, in some signature or register. See, for excellent information on this matter, " *The Shakespeare Myth,*" p. 170, etc.— Appleton Morgan.

" As Essex aspired to distinction in many ways, so Bacon studied many ways to help him, among the rest by contributing to those fanciful pageants or 'devices,' as they were called, with which it was the fashion of the time to entertain the Queen on festive occasions. On the anniversary of her coronation in 1595, we happen to know positively (though only by the concurrence of two accidents) that certain speeches, unquestionably written by Bacon, were delivered in a device presented by Essex; and I strongly suspect that two of the most interesting among his smaller pieces were drawn up for some similar performance in the year 1592. I mean those which are entitled " Mr. Bacon in Praise of Knowledge, " and " Mr. Bacon's Discourse in Praise of his Sovereign. " [1]

" My reason for suspecting they were composed for some masque, or show, or other fictitious occasion, is partly that the speech in praise of knowledge professes to have been spoken in a *Conference of Pleasure*, and the speech in praise of Elizabeth appears by the opening sentence to have been preceded by three others, one of which *was* in praise of knowledge."

The writer goes on to say that he has little doubt about this device having been written by Bacon for performance on the Queen's day, though, unfortunately, no detailed account remains of the celebration of that day in 1592; we only know that it was " more solemnised than ever, and that *through my Lord of Essex his device.*"[2] The reporter Nicholas Faunt, " being a strict Puritan, and having no taste for devices, " adds no particulars, but an incidental expression in a letter from Heury Gosnold, a young lawyer in Gray's Inn, tells us that Francis was at this time attending the court:—" Mr. Fr. Bacon is, *maulgre the court,* your kind brother and mine especial friend. "

The *Praise of Knowledge*, which sums up many of Bacon's most daring philosophical speculations, as to the revival, spread,

---

1 These were found among the papers submitted to Stephens by Lord Oxford, and printed by Locker in the supplement to his second collection in 1734. The MSS. are still to be seen in the British Museum, fair copies in an old hand with the titles given above, but no further explanation.

2 Nich. Faunt to A. Bacon, Nov. 20, 1592—Lambeth MSS. 648, 176.

and ultimate catholicity of learning, — the happy match which shall be made between the mind of man and the nature of things, and the ultimate " mingling of heaven and earth,"—is printed in Spedding's *Letters and Life of Bacon*,[1] and should be read and considered by all who care to understand what Dr. Rawley describes as certain " grounds and notions within himself," or, as it is elsewhere said, " fixed and *universal* ideas " which came to him in his youth, and abode with him to the end of his life.

This speech is succeeded by the far longer *Discourse in Praise of the Queen* — " an oration which for spirit, eloquence, and substantial worth may bear a comparison with the greatest panegyrical orations of modern times. "[2] The biographer explains that, although this oration seems too long and elaborate to have been used as part of a court entertainment, yet it might have been (and probably was) worked upon and enlarged afterwards, and that the circumstances under which it was delivered caused it to be received as something of much greater importance than a mere court compliment.

Probably no one who has read the life and works of Bacon is so foolish and unsympathetic as to believe that such a man, in exalting the theatre, writing for it, interesting others in its behalf, had no higher aim than to amuse himself and his friends, still less to profit by it, or even to make himself a name as a mere playwright.

Considering merely the position which he held as a man of letters and a philosopher, it is impossible to conceive that for such purposes he would have risked his reputation and prospects — running in the face of public opinion, which was strong against stage-playing, and risking the displeasure of most of the members of his own Puritan family, some of whom would surely hear reports of what he was doing. -

---

1 i. 123–126.

2 See the remarks in Spedding, *Letters and Life*, i. 143, on this piece. The editor shows its fitness for the occasion when it was delivered. Yet we are convinced that it had a second and still more important aim than that which at first sight appears. *There was no need to answer an invective against the Government*, when Bacon ordered the printing and publication of this speech to be done after his death.

In 1594 Anthony Bacon, that "dearest brother," "Antonie my comforte," had lately returned from Italy and had joined Francis in Gray's Inn; but he did not stay there long. Soon afterwards, to the alarm and displeasure of his mother, Lady Anne, he removed from these lodgings to a house in Bishop's Gate Street, close to the Bull Inn. Here there was a theatre at which several of the *Shakespeare* plays were performed, and from this date the plays of *Shakespeare, Ben Jonson* and "twenty more such names and men as these" pour on to the stages of this and other theatres. What share had Anthony in the writing and "producing" of these plays?

The Christmas revels in which the students of Gray's Inn had formerly prided themselves were for some cause intermitted for three of four years. In the winter of 1594 they resolved to redeem the time by producing "something out of the common way." As usual, Francis Bacon is called in to assist in "recovering the lost honour of Gray's Inn." The result was a device, or elaborate burlesque, which turned Gray's Inn into a mimic court for which a Prince of Purpoole and a Master of the Revels were chosen, and the sports were to last for twelve days.

The Prince, with all his state, proceeded to the Great Hall of Gray's Inn on December 20th, and the entertainment was so gorgeous, so skilfully managed, and so hit off the tastes of the times, that the players were encouraged to enlarge their plan, and to raise their style. They resolved, therefore (besides all this court pomp, and their daily sport amongst themselves), to have certain "grand nights," in which something special should be performed for the entertainment of strangers. But the excitement produced on the first grand night, and the throng, which was beyond everything which had been expected, crowded the hall so that the actors were driven from the stage. They had to retire, and when the tumult partly subsided, they were obliged, in default of "those very good inventions and conceits" which had been intended, to content themselves with dancing and revelling, and when that was over, with *A Comedy of Errors, like to Plautus his Menæchmus,* which was played by the players. As this was, according to Dr. Delius, *the first allusion to the Comedy of Errors* — in other words, since this comedy was, for the first time, heard of and acted in Gray's Inn, at the revels of December, 1594 — we may well suppose that this play was the very "invention and conceit" arranged by Francis Bacon for the occasion; and that, whilst the dancing went on, he took the opportunity of getting things set straight which were disordered by the unexpected throng of guests, after which the comedy was "played by the players," according to the original plan. This was on December 28th.

The next night was taken up with a mock-legal inquiry into the causes of these disorders, and after this, (which was a broad parody upon the administration of justice by the Crown in Council), they held a grand consultation for the recovery of their lost honour, which ended in a resolution "that the Prince's Council should be reformed, and some graver conceits should have their places." Again Bacon is to the front, and it is a striking proof of the rapidity with which he was able to devise and accomplish any new thing, that in four or five days he had written and "produced" an entertainment which is described as "one of the most elegant that was ever presented to an audience of statesmen and courtiers." It was performed on Friday, January 3, 1595, and was called *The Order of the Helmet.* This entertainment (which is in many ways suggestive of the Masonic ceremonies) includes nineteen articles, which the knights of the order vowed to keep; they are written in Bacon's playful, *satirical* style, and full from beginning to end of his ideas, theories, doctrines, antitheta, allusions, and metaphors. To these follow seven speeches. The first, by the Prince of Purpoole, gives a sly hit at other princes, who, like Prince Hal, "conclude their own ends out of their own humours," and abuse the wisdom of their counsellors *to set them in the right way to the wrong place.* The prince gives his subjects free leave to set before us " *to what port, as it were, the ship of our government should be bounden.*"

"The first counsellor," then evidently having Bacon's notes

on the subject ready to hand,[1] delivers a speech, " advising the
exercise of war; " the second counsellor extols the study of
philosophy. This counsellor is very well read in *Shakespeare.*
He describes *witches, whose power is in destruction, not in preservation,* [2] and advises the Prince not to be like them or like *some
comet or blazing star* [3] *which should threaten and portend nothing
but death and dearth, combustions and troubles of the world.* He
begs him to be not as a lamp that shineth not to others, and yet
seeth not itself, but as the eye of the world, that both carrieth
and useth light. To this purpose he commends to him the collecting of a perfect library of books, ancient and modern, and of
MSS. in all languages; of a spacious, wonderful garden (botanic
and zoological gardens in one), " built about with rooms to
stable all rare beasts and to cage all rare birds, " and with lakes,
salt and fresh, " for like variety of fishes. And so you may have
in small compass *a model of universal nature made private.*"[4]
Thirdly, he proposes " a goodly huge cabinet, " a museum of all
the rarities and treasures of nature and art, wherein shall be
collected " whatsoever singularity chance and the shuffle of
things hath produced." The fourth " monument" which is to
perpetuate the fame of the Prince is to be " so furnished with
mills, instruments, furnaces, and vessels as may be *a palace fit
for a philosopher's stone.*" Laboratories for experimental
science are here indicated; they are, we see, the same as are
more fully described in the Rosicrucian journey, *New Atlantis,*
and it appears probable that they expressed in the device, as in the
Rosicrucian document, a meaning and aim which tended to unite
the works of Vulcan (art) with those of Minerva (wisdom or
nature).[5]

---

[1] See Spedding —Military arts compatible with learning, iii. 269 ; promoted
by it, iii. 307–314 ; when just, successful, iv. 28, 29 ; warlike disposition the
strength of a nation, v. 81 ; injured by the sedentary arts, v. 84 ; healthful,
x. 85 ; the history of war, proposed, as deficient, iv. 270.

[2] See Macb. i. 3, 18-29 ; iii. 5, 24-34 ; iv. 1, 48-60.

[3] Jul. Cæs. ii. 2, 25-30. All's W. i. 3, 81-85. Macb. ii. 3, 55-60.

[4] " A small model of the barren earth." Richard II. iii. 2.

[5] See Essay of Erichthonius. Spedding, Works, vi. 736.

Then follows the *third counsellor, advising eternizement and fame by buildings and foundations.* This speech is written with the same metaphors and emblems which we find elsewhere in Bacon's acknowledged works and in the documents of the Rosicrucians and Freemasons. Wars, it is agreed, often offer immoderate hopes which issue only in tragedies of calamities and distresses. Philosophies equally disappoint expectation, by turning mystical philosophy into comedies of ridiculous frustration, conceits and curiosities. But the day for a monarch to "*win fame and eternize his name*" is "in the visible memory of himself in the magnificence of goodly and royal buildings and foundations, and the new institution of *orders, ordinances, and societies;* that as your coin be stamped with your own image, so in every part of your state there may be something new, which, by continuance, may make the founder and author remembered."[1] The desire "*to cure mortality by fame*" "caused men to build the Tower of Babel, which, as it was a sin in the immoderate appetite for fame, so it was punished in kind; for the diversities of languages *have imprisoned fame* ever since." He goes on to show that the fame of Alexander, Cæsar, Constantine, and Trajan was thought by themselves to rest not so much upon their conquests as in their buildings. "And surely they had reason; for the fame of great actions is *like to a landflood which hath no certain head or spring;* but the memory and fame of buildings and foundations hath, as it were, *a fountain in a hill which continually refresheth and feedeth the other waters.*"[2]

The fourth counsellor advises *absoluteness of state and treasure.* His speech will be found paraphrased and more gravely and earnestly traced in Bacon's essays of *Empire* and of *The Greatness of Kingdoms,* and in other places which deal with similar subjects.

The fifth counsellor advises the Prince to virtue and a gracious government. If he would "*make golden times*" he must be

---

1 This passage aptly describes the principle upon which Bacon established his orders and societies. See chapters of the Rosicrucians and Freemasons.

2 See Emblems — Hill, Water, etc.

" *a natural parent to the state.*" The former speakers have, says
this counsellor, handled their own propositions too formally.
" My Lords have taught you to refer all things to yourself, your
greatness, memory, and advantage, but whereunto shall yourself
be referred ? If you will be heavenly, you must have influence.
Will you be as a standing pool, that spendeth and choketh his
spring within itself, and hath no streams nor current to bless and
make fruitful whole tracts of countries whereby it cometh? . . .
Assure yourself of an inward peace, that the storms without do
not disturb any of your repairs within; . . . *visit all the parts of*
your state, and let the balm distill everywhere from your sovereign
hands, to the medicining of any part that complaineth; . . . *have*
a care that your intelligence, which is the light of your state, do not
burn dim; . . . *advance men of virtue, not of mercenary minds;*
. . . *purge out multiplicity of laws;* . . . *repeal those that are*
snaring, and press the execution of those that are wholesome and
necessary; . . . *think not that the bridle and spur will make the*
horse go alone without time and custom; . . . *when you have*
confirmed the noble and vital parts of your realm of state, proceed
to take care of the blood, and flesh, and good habit of the body.
Remedy all cankers and causes of consumption."[1] The speaker
ends by saying that, if he wished to commend the beauty of
some excelling lady, he could best do it by showing her picture;
so it is in commending a virtuous government, though he fears
that his " pencil may disgrace it," and therefore leaves the
prince to fill in the picture for himself.

He is succeeded by the sixth and last counsellor, who
" persuades to pastimes and sports." The speeches of his
predecessors were, he thought, " as if a man should come to
some young prince, and, immediately after his coronation, be in
hand with him to make himself a sumptuous and stately tomb,
and, to speak out of my soul, I muse how any of your servants
can endure to think of you as of a prince past; . . . their lessons
were so cumbersome, *as if they would make you a king in a play,*
who, when one would think he standeth in great majesty and

---

[1] Compare Emblems and Metaphors of Bacon.

felicity, he is troubled to say his part. What! nothing but tasks; nothing but working days ? No feasting, no music, no dancing, no triumphs, no comedies, no love, no ladies ? Let other men's lives be as pilgrimages; . . . princes' lives are, as progresses, dedicated only to variety and solace."

(Again an echo of the speeches of Theseus and Philostratus in *A Midsummer Night's Dream,* quoted before.[1])

This lively counsellor entreats his prince to leave the work to other people, and to attend only to that which cannot be done by deputy. *" Use the advantage of your youth; . . . in a word, sweet sovereign, dismiss your five counsellors, and only take counsel of your five senses."*

The prince briefly thanks them all for their good opinions, which being so various, it is difficult to choose between them. " Meantime it should not be amiss to choose the last, and upon more deliberation to determine of the rest; and what time we spend in long consulting, in the end we gain by prompt and speedy executing." Thereupon he takes a partner, and the dance begins. The rest of the night was spent in this pastime, and the nobles and other auditory, says the narrator, were so delighted with their entertainment, that " thereby Gray's Inn did not only recover their lost credit, but got instead so much honour and applause as either the good reports of our friends that were present or we ourselves could desire."

In this same year, 1595, *Lucrece* was published, and dedicated, as the poem of *Venus and Adonis* had been also dedicated in 1593, to Francis Bacon's young friend, Lord Southampton, who is said to have given a large sum of money toward the erection of the " Globe" theatre, which was in this year opened on Bankside with William Shakspere as its manager.[2]

Until Anthony Bacon's return from Italy Francis was very poor, and often in debt, and, although he lived frugally

---

[1] See Mid. N. Dream, v. 1, and Rich. II. iii. 4. L. L. L. iv. 3, 370-380, etc.

[2] This gift was held by Shakspereans to be an evidence of Southampton's friendship for Shakspere. Baconians see in it an evidence of the young Earl's desire to assist in the production of the dramatic works of his friend and associate, Francis Bacon.

and temperately, he was at one time forced to get help from the
Jews. Though Anthony was better off and able to help him,
Francis could hardly contrive to live as a gentleman and at the
same time to publish and carry forward scientific researches as we
find him doing. Anthony was performing the part of secretary
to the Earl of Essex, a work in which his brother shared, Anthony
writing his letters and drafting his despatches to secret agents
in foreign lands; Francis aiding him in getting information, and
in steering his course through the shifting sands of the political
stream. He drew up for Essex that remarkable paper on his
conduct at court, which should have been the rule, and would
certainly have been the salvation, of his life.[1] These services,
occasional on the part of Francis, daily on the part of Anthony,
led them into expenses which they ought to have been repaid.
No salary had been fixed for Francis, but Anthony was to have
received a thousand pounds a year, none of which was ever
paid him.[2] It was probably on account of the large outstanding
debt to the brothers that Essex sued to the Queen for the places
of Solicitor-General or Attorney-General for Francis Bacon. It is
probable that, had it not been for his interference, Bacon would at
this time have been appointed to the former of these offices. But
the injudicious and arrogant behaviour of Essex, which was a
constant subject of remonstrance from Bacon, now again destroyed Bacon's hopes of obtaining a substantial position and
means of livelihood. The Queen would not be driven, nor suspected of bestowing offices at the bidding of her fascinating but
troublesome kinsman. Bacon was again passed over, and retired much hurt, and feeling disgraced in the eyes of the world,
to Twickenham, where, perhaps, he employed himself in writing some of his comedies. For in consequence, perhaps, of this
episode, or in part payment of his large debt to the brothers, Essex
granted Francis a piece of land worth about £1,800, adjoining
the estate of his half-brother, Edward Bacon, at Twickenham.

1 Hepworth Dixon, Story. p. 53. Ath. Cant. ii. 315. Devereux, Lives of
the Earls of Essex, i. 277. Sydney Papers, i. 360.

2 It is very probable in view of the Rosicrucian rules, which we shall consider further on, that the Bacons *would not be paid* for this work.

To this year, when Bacon was in retirement at Twickenham, *The Merchant of Venice*, and *A Midsummer Night's Dream* are attributed. In the first of these " the hard Jew " who persecuted Francis Bacon is immortalised in the person of Shylock, whilst in Antonio   we recognise the generous brother, Anthony Bacon, who sacrificed himself and " taxed his credit " in order to relieve Francis. [1]

A Midsummer Night's Dream is the first piece in which Bacon, whilst creating his fairies from " the vital spirits of nature, " brings his studies of the winds to his help.[2]   This play, as has been said, bears points of strong resemblance to the *Device of an Indian Prince*, which Bacon had written a few months previously, when the stormy passages between the Queen and Essex had passed away, and when the Earl had apparently applied to him for a device which should be performed on the " Queen's Day."

January 27, 1595, is the latest date on any sheet in Bacon's *Promus of Formularies and Elegancies.* Judged by the handwriting, it appears to be the latest sheet, although it is not placed last in the collection of MSS. One entry is suggestive [3] — " Law at Twickenham for ye merry tales."   The merry tales for which Bacon was thus preparing *Law*, are supposed to be those already named, with *The Taming of the Shrew, King John*, two parts of *Henry IV.* and *All's Well that Ends Well*, soon to appear, and full of abstruse points of law, such as afterwards exercised the mind of Lord Campbell.   The play of *Richard III.* is attributed to 1594 by Dr. Delius, but the list of Bacon's MSS. on the outside leaf of the *Conference of Pleasure* seems to show that *Richard II.* and *III.* were sketched together, though apparently the former was not heard of till the year 1596.

Very little is known for some years of the private proceedings of Bacon. He had no public business of importance, and it is

---

[1] Note, Antonio, in *Twelfth Night*, is another impersonation of the same generous and unselfish character.

[2] See Of Vital Spirits of Nature.

[3] *Promus*, 1165. The Promus is a MS. collection of Bacon's private notes.

evident that the published records of his work are not by any
means adequate. With his tremendous energy and powers, the
scanty information concerning him assures us that at this time
he was either travelling or most busy upon his secret and unacknowledged works. In 1596-7 he wrote the *Colours of Good
and Evil,* and the *Meditationes Sacræ,* for which preparations
are found amongst the *Promus* notes; a speech in Parliament
against enclosures, and a general statement that he continued
his scientific studies, are all that is recorded as to his labours at
that time. No doubt, however, that, amongst other matters, he
was preparing the first edition of his essays, which were published in the following year (*with a dedication " to Mr. Anthony
Bacon, his deare brother, you that are next myself"*). Money
troubles still continued, which may be explained in the same
manner as before. All his money, and Anthony's as well, was
going in the expense of publishing, in getting up plays, and in
other enterprises connected with his great schemes.

In a letter of October 15, 1597, written to the Earl of Shrewsbury from Gray's Inn, Francis Bacon requests the loan of a
horse and armour for some public show. In another letter to
Lord Mountjoy, he says that " it is now his manner and rule to
keep state in contemplative matters." Clearly much trouble
was taken to obscure his history and his private proceedings
about this period.

In letters to Sir Tobie Matthew,[1] with dates and other particulars mysteriously obliterated or garbled, Bacon, whilst alluding
by name to several of his acknowledged works, which Sir Tobie
had been reading and criticising, speaks (without naming them)
of his " other works," " works of his recreation." Elsewhere
he refers to other works, but does *not* specify them. They are

---

[1] Sir Tobie Matthew, son of the Bishop of Durham, afterwards Archbishop
of York, was an early friend of Bacon, and one whom he calls his "kind in-
quisitor," since he was in the habit of sending his works for Matthew's perusal
and criticism. A collection of his letters (London, 1660) is extant. These
letters *are without dates.* Tobie Matthew appears to have purposely obliterated
or disguised names and particulars. If the "headings were inserted by himself, he had either forgotten the dates or intended to confuse and conceal
them." (Spedding, *Letters and Life,* iv. 132.)

" deeds without a name," which, in this correspondence, are referred to as the *Alphabet,* a pass-word, perhaps, for his *Tragedies and Comedies,* since, in his private notes, or *Promus,* there is this entry (before 1594):

> " *Iisdem e' literis efficitur tragœdia et comedia.*"
> "Tragedies and comedies are made of one *alphabet.*"

In 1598 the Queen, who had again quarrelled with Essex, was greatly offended by the play of *Richard II.,* which plainly alluded to the troubles in Ireland, with which he was concerned. Not only had this new play drawn crowds of courtiers and citizens to the Globe Theatre, when first it appeared, but it had a long and splendid run, being played not only in the theatre, but in the open street and in the court-yards of inns. The Earl of Essex (who, before his voyage, had been a constant auditor at the Globe) lent the play his countenance; it is even said that he ordered it to be played at his own expense, when Phillips, the manager, declared that the piece had been so long before the public that another performance could not pay. No wonder, then, that the Queen was angry and disturbed by this play, which, she thought, was part of a plot to teach her subjects how to murder kings. " *I am Richard,*" she said; " know you not that ? "

A pamphlet by a young doctor of civil law, John Hayward, published almost simultaneously with the play, increased the Queen's wrath and apprehension. Taking as its basis the story of the play, this pamphlet drew from it morals which were supposed to be seditious. In one place it even affirmed the existence of a title superior to the Queen.[1] This book proved too much for Elizabeth's patience, and, sending the scribe to prison, she summoned Francis Bacon " to draw up articles against him," says the biographer; but, perhaps, also, because she had reason to think that Bacon would know more than others about the matter. Bacon, in his *Apophthegms,* or witty sayings, and again in his *Apologia* concerning Essex, relates this episode.

---

[1] See *Emblems and Metaphors,* Queen. We think that time may alter judgment and interpretation of this pamphlet.

But he, apparently, *intentionally and ingeniously confuses his story*, in the same manner of which examples will be given in the chapter on "*Feigned Histories;*" in the same way, too, as the accounts of the origin of Freemasonry are garbled and mixed up, in order to puzzle the uninitiated reader.

He remembers (he says in the *Apologia*) an answer of his " in a matter which had some affinity with my Lord of Essex's cause, *which, though it grew from me, went after about in others' names.*[1] For her Majesty, being mightily incensed with that book which was dedicated to my Lord (being a story of the first year of King Henry IV.), thinking it a seditious prelude to put into the people's heads boldness and faction, said she had a good opinion there was treason in it, and asked me if I could not find any places in it that might be drawn within case of treason; whereunto I answered, for treason surely found I none, but for felony very many. And when her Majesty hastily asked me wherein? I told her the author had committed very apparent theft, for he had taken most of the sentences of Cornelius Tacitus and translated them into English, and put them into his text."

This we see is of *the play*; but the story continues: "*Another time,* when the Queen would not be persuaded that it was his writing whose name was to it, but that it had some more mischievous author, and said, with great indignation, that she would have him racked to produce his author, I replied, 'Nay, Madame, he is a doctor [*Bacon, therefore, had now turned the argument on to Dr. Hayward's pamphlet*]; never rack his person, rack his stile; let him have pens, ink, and paper, and help of books, and be enjoined to continue the story where it leaves off, and I will undertake, by collecting the stiles, to judge whether he were the author or no.' " It should be observed that Bacon does not propose to " collect " or collate the style of the pamphlet with that of the play, which would be the obvious thing to do if the author of the obnoxious play and the author of the equally obnoxious pamphlet were supposed to be in collusion.

---

[1] Does this enigmatical sentence mean that the play in question was his, although it passed under the name of another?

His object, evidently, is to get the young doctor of law (probably a member of his secret society) out of the difficulties into which he had fallen through his complicity in the publication of a political squib against tyranny, which Bacon was well aware that Dr. Hayward did not write.

Does no one think it strange that Francis Bacon should have told the Queen that the finest passages in *Richard II.* are taken from Cornelius Tacitus and translated into English in that text, and yet that no commentator on *Shakespeare*, no student of Tacitus, should have been at the pains of pointing out these passages? They must be cleverly used, to be so indistinguishable to these learned readers, for they are there.

And is it to be taken as a mere matter of course that Bacon, who as a rule mentions himself so little, should have recorded this scene and his own speech amongst his collection of witty sayings, when that speech (which is not very witty) would have had no point if it had not been true?

And we ask again, Did it not appear strange to Queen Elizabeth that Bacon should show such intimate knowledge of the sources from which some of the chief passages in *Richard II.* were derived — a knowledge beyond any which has been displayed by the most learned and authentic Shakespeare societies which have existed until now?

These episodes about Dr. Hayward's tract and the play of *Richard II.* incline us to a conviction, which is strengthened by other evidence, that Queen Elizabeth had a very shrewd suspicion, if not an absolute knowledge, that Francis Bacon was intimately connected with the revival of the stage in her times. Sometimes it almost seems as if she had a still deeper acquaintance with the aims and objects of his life; that sometimes she disapproved, and was only kept from venting upon him all the vials of her wrath, first by her strong esteem and regard for his father, Sir Nicholas Bacon, and secondly, by her admiration of Francis Bacon himself. It seems not impossible that the Queen's reverence for Sir Nicholas may have been increased by her knowledge of his schemes for the revival of learning, and she may have known, probably did know, that it was the aim of the son to carry out the plans of his father. All this is conjectured, though based upon observation of small particulars. Yet it does not appear that the Queen, although she admired Francis, ever valued him as equal to his father. On the contrary, she often thwarted him, or publicly passed him over in a manner which was very painful to him. Probably, as is so often the case with old people, she could not comprehend that the son, whom she looked on as a boy, would so far outshine the father that the latter should hereafter be chiefly known as " Francis Bacon's father."

On the occasion of the marriage of the Princess Elizabeth with the Count Palatine, February 14, 1612–13, the usual rejoicings took place: triumphs, fire-works, sham fights upon the water, masques, running at the ring, and the rest of it, " concerning which," says Spedding, [1] " it would not have been necessary to say anything were it not that *Bacon took a principal part in the preparation of one of the masques.*" This was the joint masque presented by the gentlemen of Gray's Inn and the Inner Temple, " written by Francis Beaumont," and printed shortly after with the following dedication :

" TO THE WORTHY SIR FRANCIS BACON, HIS MAJESTY'S SOLIC-
ITOR-GENERAL, AND THE GRAVE AND LEARNED BENCH OF
THE ANCIENTLY ALLIED HOUSES OF GRAY'S INN AND THE
INNER TEMPLE, THE INNER TEMPLE AND GRAY'S INN.

" Ye that spared no pain nor travail in the setting forth, ordering, and furnishing of this masque (being the first fruits of
honour in this kind which these two societies have offered to
His Majesty), will not think much now to look back upon the
effects of your own care and work; for that, whereof the success
was then doubtful, is now happily performed, and graciously
accepted; and that which you were then to think of in straits of
time, you may now peruse at leisure. And you, Sir Francis
Bacon, especially, as you did then by your countenance and
loving affections advance it, so let your good word grace it and
defend it, which is able to add value to the greatest and least
matters."

---

1 Life and Letters, iv. 343.

There we perceive that the gentlemen (exclusive of Bacon) who had taken so much pains in the setting forth of this important and almost national tribute of respect to the royal family are thanked for their aid in the " ordering and furnishing " of a masque with which, clearly, they were not as a whole well acquainted. They helped, as modern phrase has it, to " get up " the masque, but of its drift they had so little knowledge that what they could only think of in " straits of time, " perhaps during the performance, they could now enjoy by reading it at leisure. None of these busy helpers, then, had contributed to the writing of the masque, and the wording of the dedication, although it does not say that Bacon was the author, yet seems to indicate as much; for it skilfully brings him to the front, and entirely ignores Beaumont, who, however, doubtless *did* " write " the masque —*fair, with a pen and ink.*

" It is easy to believe, " says the biographer, " that if Bacon took an active part in the preparations of a thing of this kind, in the success of which he felt an interest, he would have a good deal to say about all the arrangements. But as we have no means of knowing what he did say, and thereby learning something as to his taste in this department,[1] it will be well to give a general account of the performance as described by an eye-witness. "

" On Tuesday, " writes Chamberlain, February 18, 1612-13, " it came to Gray's Inn and the Inner Temple's turn to come with their masque, whereof Sir Francis Bacon was the chief contriver; and because the former came on horseback and in open chariots, they made choice to come by water from Winchester Place, in Southwark; which suited well with their device, which was the marriage of the River Thames to the Rhine; and their show by water was very gallant, by reason of infinite store of lights, very curiously set and placed, and many boats and barges with devices

---

1 Why the writer should say this we know not, for two pages farther on he says: " *For what Bacon had to say about such things, see his essay of Masques and Triumphs,* which was very likely suggested by the consideration he had to bestow on this." This essay was never published until one year before Bacon's death, *i. e.,* 1625. It shows us that Bacon's love of the stage and of masquing was as keen in his old age as in his youth. In the posthumous edition of the Essays, published in 1638, *the essay is suppressed.*

of lights and lamps, with three peals of ordnance, one at their taking water, another in the Temple Garden, and the last at their landing; which passage by water cost them better than £300. They were received at the privy stairs, and great expectation there was that they should every way excel their competitors that went before them, both in device, daintiness of apparel, and above all in dancing, wherein they are held excellent, and esteemed for the properer men.

"But by what ill planet it fell out I know not, they came home as they went, without doing anything; the reason whereof I cannot yet learn thoroughly, but only that the hall was so full that it was not possible to avoid[1] it, or make room for them; besides that, most of the ladies were in the galleries to see them land, and could not get in. But the worst of all was that the King was so wearied and sleepy with sitting almost two whole nights before, that he had no edge to it. Whereupon Sir Francis Bacon adventured to entreat of his Majesty that by this difference he would not, as it were, bury them quick;[2] and I hear the King should answer that then they must bury *him* quick, for he could last no longer; but withal gave them very good words, and appointed them to come again on Saturday.

"But the grace of their masque is quite gone, when their apparel hath been already showed, and their devices vented, so that how it will fall out, God knows, for they are much discouraged and out of countenance, and the world says, it comes to pass after the old proverb, the properer man, the worse luck."[3]

Their devices, however, went much beyond the mere exhibition of themselves and their apparel, and there was novelty enough behind the curtain to make a sufficient entertainment by itself, without the water business for overture. Chamberlain writes again on the 25th:

"Our Gray's Inn men and the Inner Templars were nothing discouraged for all the first dodge, but on Saturday last performed their part exceeding well, and with great applause and approbation, both from the King and all the company. The

---

1 "*Clear* it."   2 "*Alive*."   3 Court and Times of James I. i. 227.

next night the King invited the masquers, with their assistants, to the number of forty, to a solemn supper in the new marriage-room, where they were well treated, and much graced with kissing his majesty's hand, and everyone having a particular accoglienza with him." [1]

None of Bacon's biographers or critics have expressed the smallest surprise that, iu days when Shakspere and Ben Jonson were at the height of their fame, it was neither the one nor the other of them, but *the Solicitor-General*, who was employed to "contrive," and ultimately to manage, the first masque which had been "presented" to the King. Under similar circumstances we should expect that Mr. Beerbohm Tree or Mr. Irving would be invited to undertake such a management; it would not have occurred to us to apply for help to Sir Edward Clarke, Q. C., M. P.

In 1613 Francis Bacon was appointed Attorney-General. This happened just before the marriage of the Earl of Somerset with Lady Essex, on December 26th. There were very unpleasant circumstances connected with this marriage, which are now known to historians, but which it is unnecessary here to enter upon. As Spedding says, it is but fair to the world of rank, wealth, fashion, and business, which hastened to congratulate the bride and bridegroom with gifts unprecedented in number and value, to remember that it does not follow that they would have done the same if they had known what we know.[2] It was proposed that during the week of festivities which celebrated this marriage the four Inns of Court (the Middle and Inner Temple, Gray's Inn and Lincoln's Inn) should join in getting up a masque, but they could not manage it, and once more we find Bacon called upon to supply their dramatic deficiencies.

It appears that Bacon considered that he owed Somerset some complimentary offering, because Somerset claimed (though Bacon doubted it) to have used his influence with the King to secure Bacon's promotion. The approaching marriage gave the latter an opportunity for discharging an obligation to a man for whom

---

[1] Ib. 229.

[2] Letters and Life, iv. 392. The following passages are nearly all extracted from this volume of Spedding.

he had no esteem, whom, indeed, he disliked too much to be willing to owe even a seeming and pretended obligation.

The offering was well chosen for this purpose, although, as Spedding allows, it was " so costly (considering how little he owed to Rochester, and how superficial their intercourse had been), and at the same time so peculiar, that it requires explanation." [1] While all the world were making presents—one of plate, another of furniture, a third of horses, a fourth of gold—he chose a masque, for which an accident supplied him with an excellent opportunity. When the united efforts of the four inns of court failed to produce the required entertainment, Bacon offered, on the part of Gray's Inn, to supply the place of it by a masque of their own.

The letter, in Bacon's own hand, which was at first supposed to be addressed to Burghley, but which, upon close examination, Spedding believed to be written to Somerset, acquires a new value and significance from the latter circumstance, giving fresh evidence both as to the tone of Bacon's intercourse with the favourite, and as to the style in which he did this kind of thing. " The fly-leaf being gone, the address is lost, and the docket does not supply it; there is no date." (Just as we should expect when the record has anything to connect Bacon with plays or masques.) " The catalogue assumes that it is addressed to Lord Burghley," and this erroneous assumption adds one more little obstruction to the discovery or recognition of the letter, which is a single leaf, and contains only the following words:

" *It may please your good L.:*

" I am sorry the masque from the four Inns of Court faileth; wherein I conceive there is no other ground of that event but impossibility. Nevertheless, because it falleth out that at this time Gray's Inn is well furnished of gallant young gentlemen, your L. may be pleased to know that, rather than this occasion shall pass without some demonstration of affection from the four Inns of Court, there are a dozen gentlemen that, out of the honour which they bear to your Lordship and my Lord Chamberlain (to whom at their last masque they were so bounden), will be ready to furnish a masque; wishing it were in

---

1 Let. and Life, iv. 392.

their powers to perform it according to their minds. And so for the present I humbly take my leave, resting

"Your L.'s very humbly
"and much bounden
"Fr. Bacon."

The Lord Chamberlain was the Earl of Suffolk, who was the bride's father; so that everything seems to fit. But though Bacon speaks of it as a compliment from Gray's Inn, Gray's Inn was in reality to furnish only the performers and the composers. The care and the charges were to be undertaken by himself, as we learn from a news letter of Chamberlain's, whose information is almost always to be relied upon. Writing on the 23d of December, 1613, he says:

"Sir Francis Bacon prepares a masque to honour this marriage, which will stand him in above £2,000; and though he have been offered some help by the House, and especially by Mr. Solicitor, Sir Henry Yelverton, who would have sent him £500, yet he would not accept it, but offers them the whole charge with the honour. Marry! his obligations are such, as well to his Majesty as to the great Lord, and to the whole house of Howards, as he can admit no partner."

The nature of the obligation considered, there was judgment as well as magnificence in the choice of the retribution. The obligation (whether real or not) being for assistance in obtaining an *office*, to repay it by any present which could be turned into money would have been objectionable, as tending to countenance the great abuse of the times (from which Bacon stands clear) — the sale of offices for money. There was no such objection to a masque. As a compliment, it was splendid, according to the taste and magnificence of the time; costly to the giver, not negotiable to the receiver; valuable as a compliment, but as nothing else. Nor was its value in that kind limited to the parties in whose honour it was given. It conferred great distinction upon Gray's Inn, in a field in which Gray's Inn was ambitious and accustomed to shine.

The piece performed was published shortly after, with a dedication to Bacon, as " the principal, and in effect the only person that doth encourage and warrant the gentlemen to shew their good affection in a time of such magnificence; wherein"

10

(they add) " we conceive, without giving you false atributes, which little need where so many are true, that you have graced in general the societies of the Inns of Court, in continuing them still as third persons with the nobility and court, *in doing the King honour;* and particularly Gray's Inn, *which, as you have formerly brought to flourish, both in the ancienter and younger sort, by countenancing virtue in every quality,* so now you have made a notable demonstration thereof in the lighter and less serious kind, by this, that one Inn of Court by itself, in time of a vacation, and in the space of three weeks, could perform that which hath been performed; which could not have been done but that *every man's exceeding love and respect to you* gave him wings to overtake time, which is the swiftest of things. "

The words which we print in italics seem to show that the true object of this celebrated masque was *to do the King honour;* and, probably, we shall one day find that it was at some expressed desire or regret of his that Francis Bacon was moved to undertake this work, which had proved (as he said in his letters to Rochester) an " impossibility" when attempted by the whole of the four Inns of Court in conjunction.

Observe, too, the unexplained debt which Gray's Inn is said to owe to Bacon for its flourishing condition, and the exceeding love which the members bore to him, and which alone enabled them to carry out his elaborate devices in the short space of three weeks. We would like to ascertain who were J. G., W. D. and T. B., who signed the dedication. Spedding says that, from an allusion to their " graver studies," they appear to have been members of the society. The allusion, coupled with the description of the masque as a show or " demonstration, in *the lighter and less serious kind,"* made *to please the King,* again carries our minds to the opening words of the *Essay of Masques:* " These things are but toys to come amougst such *serious matters; but since princes will have them,"* etc., they should be properly done.

This piece, entitled *The Masque of Flowers,* may be seen at full length in Nichol's Progresses: " A very splendid trifle, and answering very well to the description in Bacon's Essays of

what a masque should be,—with its loud and cheerful music,
abundance of light and colour, graceful motions and forms, and
such things as do naturally take the sense, but having no
personal reference to the occasion beyond being an entertainment given in honour of a marriage, and ending with an offering
of flowers to the bride and bridegroom." [1]

In March, 1617, Bacon was installed as Lord Chancellor upon
the death of Egerton. On May 7th he rode from Gray's Inn to
Westminster Hall to open the courts in state. "All London
turned out to do him honour, and every one who could borrow a
horse and a foot-cloth fell into the train; so that more than two
hundred horsemen rode behind him. Through crowds of citizens
. . . *of players from Bankside,* of the Puritan hearers of Burgess,
of the Roman Catholic friends of Danvers and Armstrong, he
rode, as popular in the streets as he had been in the House of
Commons, down Chancery Lane and the Strand, past Charing
Cross, through the open courts of Whitehall, and by King Street
into Palace yard." [2]

The Bankside players, then, came in a bevy, sufficiently numerous to be conspicuous and registered in history, and all the way
from Southwark, in order to do honour to the newly made Chancellor. "My friends, chew upon this."

The *Essay of Masques and Triumphs* would suffice to show any
unbiased reader that the author was intimately acquainted with
the practical management of a theatre. There is something
particularly graphic in this little essay, which we commend to
the consideration of those who interest themselves in private
theatricals. It should be remembered that Bacon would not
insert amongst his most polished and well filed essays two
pages of *small particulars with which every one was acquainted.*
He is clearly instructing those who do not know so much of the
matter as he does.

True, he takes a high ground, and prefaces his remarks with
the reflection that "these things are but toys to come amongst
such serious considerations; but yet, since princes will have such

---

1 Spedding, Letters and Life, iv. 394-5.   2 Story of Bacon's Life, 317.

things, it is better they should be graced with elegancy than daubed with cost," and he tells us how to ensure this, giving many suggestions which have been adopted until this day. " Acting in song hath an extreme good grace; I say acting, not dancing, for that is a mean and vulgar thing." The things he sets down are such as " take the sense, not petty wonderments," though he considers that change of scene, so it be quietly and without noise, is a thing of beauty. The scenes are to abound with light, but varied and coloured — the masquers when appearing on the scene from above are to " make motions " which will draw the eye strangely and excite desire to see that which it cannot perfectly discern. The songs are to be loud and cheerful, " *not chirpings and pulings*," and the music sharp and well-placed. The colours that show best by candle-light are " white, carnation, and a kind of seawater-green." Short and pithy as this essay is, we wonder that it had never struck Shakspereans how wonderfully well Mrs. Page, in her little device to frighten and confuse Falstaff, carried out the instructions here conveyed. The music placed in the saw-pit; the many rounds of waxen tapers on the heads of the fairies; the rush out of the saw-pit with songs and rattles " to take the sense." The fairies in *green and white, singing a scornful rhyme* as they trip and pinch Falstaff. Although the masque is intended to frighten him, there is in it nothing frightful, for " anything that is hideous, as devils and giants, is unfit." Satires, antics, *sprites and pigmies* Bacon allows; so Mrs. Page introduces " my *little* son and those of the same growth," dressed " like urchins, ouphes and fairies."

Even the " *diffused*" song which they sing seems to be arranged with care and intention, for, says Bacon, " I understand it, that *the song be in quire*, with some *broken* music." But he concludes, " Enough of these toys," and perhaps when the Bankside players came to see him ride in state as Chancellor, there may have been some amongst them who knew that indeed he would no more be able to indulge in meddling with such toys as these.

Public and political business now increased with Bacon so that, without even taking other enterprises into consideration, no one will find it strange that from this time no more is heard of his performing the part of stage-manager or master of the revels on any occasion later than that of the marriage of the King's favourite. Probably, however, want of time had very little to do with the matter, for Bacon seems always to have found time for doing all that it was desirable should be done. It is more likely that he felt the incongruity which would appear between the trivialities of such " toys " and the dignity of his position as Attorney-General and prospective Chancellor. Nevertheless, even in the published records of his later years hints drop out here and there as to his continued devotion to theatrical performances, and his unfading interest in playwrights and all concerning them. He knew that the stage was a great engine for good, and for teaching and moving the masses, who would never read books or hear lectures.

In January, 1617, Bacon " dined at Gray's Inn to give countenance to their Lord and Prince of Purpoole, and to see their revels." [1] At this time, according to a letter from Buckingham to the King, a masque was performed; but we know not what it was. A masque appears also to have been in preparation for Shrove Tuesday, though it could not be performed till Tuesday, owing to the occupation of the banqueting hall by an improved edition of the " Prince's Masque " — a piece of Ben Jonson's, which had been acted on Twelfth Night with little applause. " The poet," says Nathaniel Brent, " is grown dull, that his device is not thought worth the relating, much less the copying out. Divers think fit he should return to his old trade of bricklaying again." [2] Nevertheless, " their fashion and device were well approved " on the second occasion, when the " dull " device must have undergone a good deal of alteration, since Chamberlain adds, " I cannot call it a masque, seeing they were not disguised nor had vizards."

" Ben Jonson had seen something of Bacon off the stage, though we do not know how much," says Spedding, writing of the last years of Bacon's life. Tradition is persistent in repeat-

---

1 Chamberlain to Carleton. 2 To Carleton, February 7, 1617–18.

ing that Ben Jonson was one of Bacon's "able pens," an assistant in his writings, superior to an ordinary amanuensis. Drummond of Hawthornden records that Ben Jonson mentioned having written an "*apology*" for the play of Bartholomew Fair, "*in my Lord St. Aubanie's house,*" in 1604.

Jonson "bursts into song," says one biographer, when politics or events favour Bacon's view, and in 1620 he "celebrates his birthday," says another, "in words breathing nothing but reverence and honour. Since these lines, often alluded to, are little known, it may be worth while to quote them here:

> "Hail, happy genius of this ancient pile !
> How comes it all things so about thee smile ?
> The fire, the wine, the men ! and in the midst
> Thou stand'st as if a mystery thou didst !
>
> Pardon, I read it in thy face, the day
> For whose returns, and many, all these pray ;
> And so do I. This is the sixtieth year
> Since Bacon and thy lord was born, and here ;
> Son to the grave, wise keeper of the seal,
> Fame and foundation of the English weal.
> What then his father was, that since is he,
> Now with a little more to the degree ;
> England's High Chancellor, the destin'd heir
> In his soft cradle to his father's chair:
> Whose even threads the Fates spun round and full
> Out of their choicest and their whitest wool.
> 'Tis a brave cause of joy, let it be known,
> For 'twere a narrow gladness, kept thine own.
> Give me a deep-bowl'd crown, that I may sing,
> In raising him, the wisdom of my King."

However much or little Bacon may have known of Ben Jonson "off the stage," it is certain that Ben Jonson formed a very accurate estimate of Bacon's abilities as a writer and *a poet*. It is impossible so to wrest the ordinary and accepted meaning of words as to insist that Ben Jonson did not mean what he so plainly says (and in connection with the poetic writings of Greece and Rome, as in the eulogy of Shakespeare), namely, that he "*filled up all numbers,*" or wrote poetry in all styles and metres. Enumerating the learned and eloquent men of the early days of Elizabeth, when " Sir Nicholas Bacon was singular and almost alone, he mentions Sir Philip Sydney, Master Richard Hooker, Robert, Earl of Essex, Sir Walter Raleigh, Sir Henry Savile, Sir Edwin Sandys, and Sir Thomas Egerton, " a grave and great orator, and best when he was provoked. But his learned and able, though unfortunate successor, is *he who hath filled up all numbers, and performed that in our tongue which may be compared or preferred to insolent Greece and haughty Rome.*"

It will be observed that *Shakespeare* and the whole of the Elizabethan poets and dramatists, excepting Sir Philip Sydney, are here omitted, and that Jonson considers that with Bacon's death the main prop of learning, wit, eloquence, and poetry had been taken away.

" In short, within his view, and about his time, were all the wits born that could honour a language or help study. Now things daily fall, wits go backward; so that he may be named and stand as the mark or ἀκμή of our language."

Jonson is not here speaking of Bacon's scientific works. He comes to them in a subsequent paragraph, wherein he again shows his intimate knowledge of Bacon's powers, aims, and character. " The *Novum Organum,*" he says, is a book " which, though by the most superficial of men, who cannot get beyond the title of nominals, it is not penetrated nor understood, it *really openeth all defects of learning whatsoever,* and is a book,

Qui longem noto scriptori proroget œvum."[1]

In connection with Bacon's acquaintance with actors and his interest in the theatre, we must add a few words about one distinguished member of the profession. Edward Allen, or Alleyn, was the founder of Dulwich College, a munificent endowment which has been the subject of much wonder and of a considerable amount of unrewarded inquiry. How Alleyn became possessed of the means to enter upon and carry through so large and costly an enterprise has not yet been satisfactorily explained to the public at large, but the facts are clear that in

---

[1] Horat. de Art. Poetica.

1606 he began to acquire land at Dulwich, and the most important of the valuable estates which now collectively form the endowment of the college; that in 1613 he contracted with a certain John Benson for the erection of a school-house and twelve alms-houses, and that in the course of the years of 1616 and 1617 the first members of his foundation were admitted to the college. Alleyn now endeavoured to obtain from the King a patent for the permanent establishment of his college by its endowment by the King of lands to the value of £800. Bacon opposed this, not because he objected to the charity, in which he was interested, but because he considered that the crown property would suffer if the King once began the system of " amortizing his tenures " for charitable purposes. Moreover, alms-houses, he thought, were not unmixed blessings, whereas endowments for educational purposes were much needed. The King had lately rejected the applications of Sir Henry Savile and Sir Edward Sandys for grants of money for such purposes; why, then, should he give such a large sum to Alleyn ?

Bacon's good judgment in preferring educational institutions to alms-houses has been vindicated by the action of the Charity Commission. By an act of Parliament passed in 1857 the almsmen of the " hospital " were all pensioned off, and the foundation completely reconstructed, simply as a collegiate institution, with upper and lower schools.

Since, even in this matter, it has been attempted to put Bacon in the wrong, by representing that " the impediments which Alleyn experienced proceeded from the Lord Chancellor," and by the implication that these impediments were needlessly vexatious. Here is the letter which Bacon wrote on this occasion to the Marquis of Buckingham. It has been truly described as characteristic in point and quaintness:

" MY VERY GOOD LORD :

" I thank your lordship for your last loving letter. I now write to give the King an account of a patent I have stayed at the seal. It is of licence to give in mortmain eight hundred pound land, though it be of tenure in chief, to Allen, that was the player, for an hospital.

" I like well that Allen playeth the last act of his life so well; but if his Majesty give way thus to amortize his tenures, his courts of wards shall decay, which I had well hoped should improve.

" But that which moveth me chiefly is, that his Majesty did now lately absolutely deny Sir Henry Savile for £200, and Sir Edwin Sandys for £100 to the perpetuating of two lectures, the one in Oxford, the other in Cambridge, foundations of singular honour to his Majesty (the best of learned kings), and of which there is a great want; whereas hospitals abound, and beggars abound never a whit the less.

" If his Majesty do like to pass the book at all; yet if he would be pleased to abridge the £800 to £500, and then give way to the other two books for the university, it were a princely work. And I make an humble suit to the King, and desire your lordship to join in it, that it mought be so. God ever preserve and prosper you.

" Your lordship's most obliged friend
" and faithful servant,
" FR. VERULAM, Canc.
" YORK HOUSE, this 18th of August, 1616."

Whether or no the money for the lectures at the university was granted by the King, deponents say not, but on June 21st, 1619, Bacon affixed the great seal of England to letters patent from James I. giving license to Edward Alleyn " to found and establish a college in Dulwich, to endure and remain forever, and to be called *The College of God's Gift* in Dulwich, in the County of Surrey."

On September 13th of the same year the college was completed, " and so, in the quaint words of Fuller "[1] — words which strangely echo those in Bacon's letter to the Duke of Buckingham —" *he who out-acted others in his life, outdid himself before his death.*"

Amongst the distinguished guests at the opening of the college Bacon and his friends are conspicuous. Alleyn gives a list of them, beginning with " The Lord Chancellor (Bacon), the Lord of Arondell, Lord Ciecill (Cecil), Sir John Howland, High Shreve, and Inigo Jones, the King's Surveyor."

Perhaps the latest, as it is the greatest tribute openly paid by

---

[1] Old and New London, vi. 298.

Bacon to the value of the theatre as a means of popular education, is the passage which he *omitted* from the *Advancement of Learning* in its early form, but *inserted* in the *De Augmentis* in 1623, when that work, the crowning work of his scientific and philosophical labours, appeared simultaneously with the first collected edition of the *Shakespeare* plays. The passage was not intended to be read by the "profane vulgar," who might have scorned the Chancellor for praising the much-despised stage. It was, therefore, reserved for the Latin, and thus rendered, for the time, accessible only to the learned — for the most part Bacon's friends:

"Dramatic poesy, which has the theatre for its world, would be of excellent use if well directed. For the stage is capable of no small influence, both of discipline and of corruption. Now, of corruptions in this kind we have enough; but the discipline has, in our times, been plainly neglected. And though in modern states play-acting is esteemed but as a toy, except when it is too satirical and biting, yet among the ancients it was used as a means of educating men's minds to virtue. Nay, it has been regarded by learned men and great philosophers as a kind of musician's bow, by which men's minds may be played upon. And certainly it is most true, and one of the greatest secrets of nature, that the minds of men are more open to impressions and affections when many are gathered together, than when they are alone." [1]

The brief records which are published of Bacon's last days show him, still in sickness and poverty, possessing the same sweet, gentle, patient, and generous spirit which had been with him in the brilliant and exciting days of prosperity; even in his misfortune and ruin making himself happy with his looks and his experiments, trying to leave his work in such a condition that others could readily take up and complete that which life was too short and fortune too adverse for him to accomplish before his death.

His will is brief, but touching in its thought for everybody connected with him, and for the sanguine spirit which it displays.[2] "My name and memory I leave to men's charitable speeches,

---

[1] De Aug. ii. 13.

[2] The following is from Hepworth Dixon's *Story*, p. 479.

and to foreign nations, and to the next ages." He desired to be laid near the mother he so dearly loved and so closely resembled, in St Michael's Church, near Gorhambury. Sir John Constable, his brother-in-law, was to have the chief care of his books.[1] Bequests were made to the poor of all the parishes in which he had chiefly resided. An ample income, beyond the terms of her marriage settlement, was secured to his wife; though, for reasons only darkly hinted in his will, a subsequent clause or codicil revoked these bequests, and left the Viscountess to her legal rights. Legacies were left to his friends and servants; to the Marquis d'Efflat "my book of orisons, curiously rhymed;" to the Earl of Dorset "my ring with the crushed diamond, which the King gave me when Prince;" to Lord Cavendish "my casting bottle of gold."

Where are these relics? Surely the recipients must have valued such gifts, and handed them down to their posterity as curiosities, if not as precious treasures. The *book of orisons*, especially, we should expect to find carefully preserved. Can no one produce this most interesting prayer-book?

The lease of Bacon's rooms in Gray's Inn, valued at three hundred pounds, was to be sold, and the money given to poor scholars. The residue of his estate, he believed, would be sufficient to found two lectureships on natural history and the physical sciences at the universities. "It was a beautiful, beneficent dream," but not to be realized, for the property and personalty left by Bacon hardly sufficed to pay his debts; yet in the last clause, which has just been quoted, we see a repetition of the earnest expression of his opinion as to the "great want" of foundations for the perpetuating of lectures, which he mentioned in his letter to Buckingham. As usual, he endeavours, poor as he now is, to supply the necessary funds, which the King had "denied." Probably, had the grant been denied to Alleyn, Bacon intended himself to raise the money for the completion of Dulwich College and its alms-houses.

The winter of 1625-6 was the most dismal he had known;

---

[1] Another copy of his will consigns the charge of his "cabinet and presses full of papers" to three trustees, Constable, Selden, and Herbert.

the cold intense, the city blighted with plague, the war abroad disastrous. Bacon remained at Gorhambury, "hard at work on his *Sylva Sylvarum*." But that work is merely a newly-arranged collection of old notes, and its construction would not have been nearly sufficient occupation for such a mind. It seems probable that Bacon was now engaged in putting together, arranging, or polishing the works which he was about to leave behind, to be brought out in due season by the faithful friends to whom he entrusted them, and to whom he must, at this time, have given instructions as to their future disposition and publication.

A Parliament was called at Westminster, for February, to which he received the usual summons, for he had been restored to his legal rights, and reinstated amongst his peers. But he was too ill to obey the writ. He rode once to Gray's Inn, but it was in April, and the severity of the winter had not yet passed. He caught the cold of which he died. Taking the air one day. with his physician, Dr. Witherbourne, towards Highgate, the snow lying deep, it occurred to Bacon to inquire if flesh might not be preserved in snow[1] as well as in salt. Pulling up at a small cottage near the foot of Highgate Hill, he bought a hen from an old woman, plucked and drew it; gathered up snow in his hands, and stuffed it into the fowl. Smitten with a sudden chill, but doubting the nature of his attack, Bacon drove to the house of his friend Lord Arundel, close by, where Witherbourne had him put into the bed from whence he rose no more.

It is hardly possible to keep patient on reading that the sheets between which the invalid was laid "were damp, as no one had slept in them for a year," and, although the servants warmed the bed with a pan of coals, the damp inflamed his cold.

From the first a gentle fever set in; he lingered just a week; and then, on the 9th of April, 1626, expired of congestion of the lungs.[2]

---

[1] This idea was the original thought which has since given rise to the various systems of preserving and transporting frozen meat from distant countries.

[2] H. Dixon, from *Court and Times of Charles*, i. 74; *Lord's Journal*, iii. 492; *Aubrey*, ii. 227.

He was buried, as directed, near his mother, in the parish church of St. Michael, near St. Albans. This picturesque and lonely little church became a place of pilgrimage, and will, we believe, become so once more. The obligations of the world are, as his biographer says, of a kind not to be overlooked. There is no department in literature or science or philanthropy, no organization for the promulgation of religious knowledge, which does not owe something to Francis Bacon.

To him the patriot, the statesman, the law reformer, the scientific jurist, the historian, are also indebted, and, apart from all debatable works, the collector of anecdote, the lover of good wit, of humourous wisdom, and of noble writing, must all find that he has laid them under obligations far greater than they may be aware of. It is hard, indeed, to say who amongst us is not the easier in circumstances, the brighter in intellect, the purer in morals, the worthier in conduct, through the teachings and the labours of Francis Bacon. The principles of his philosophy are of universal application, and they will endure as long as the world itself.

To this conclusion must those come who contemplate his life and works from the standpoint which we have been occupying. But not all will care to take the same view. Let us, therefore, shift our position and take a more particular observation of some circumstances connected with Bacon which seem to be mysterious, or at least not thoroughly explained.

CHAPTER VI.

DEFICIENCIES OF LEARNING IN THE TIMES OF ELIZABETH AND JAMES I.

"Defect is a reptile that basely crawls upon the earth."—*Bacon.*

"What a piece of work is man! how noble in reason! how infinite in faculty! . . . Yet man delights not me. . . What should such fellows as I do, crawling between heaven and earth?"—*Hamlet.*

BEFORE trying to follow Bacon in his inquiries as to the deficiencies of learning, let us reflect upon the herculean nature of the work which he was proposing to himself. He might satirise his own vast speculations; he may even have been perfectly well aware that his enthusiastic visions could never be realised, but a universal reformation was his aim, and who will say that he failed to achieve it?

Those " good old times " in which Bacon lived were anything but good; they were coarse, ignorant, violent, " dark and dangerous." The church, Bacon said, " which should be the chief band of religion, was turned to superstition, or made the matter of quarrelling and execrable actions; of murdering princes, butchery of people, and subversion of states and governments. The land full of oppression, taxation, privileges broken, factions desperate, poverty great, knowledge at a standstill; learning barren, discredited by the errors, contentions, conceit, and fantastical pedantry of so-called learned men. The literary spirit of the ancients dead. At the universities and schools words were taught, but not matter. He even questions whether it would not be well to abolish the scholastic system altogether, and to set up a new form of teaching. The list of sciences taught, and which he finds to be full of follies and errors, or totally deficient, forbids any wonder at his verdict, that, whereas present methods were rotten and useless to advance learning, the old fabric should be rased to the ground, and a new Solomon's House erected.

But is it not a little surprising that, even if Bacon could thus speak in his early days of the ignorance, the folly, the futility of the learning of his time, the dullness, apathy, or ignorant bigotry of his contemporaries, the degradation of the stage, the decay of the wisdom of the ancients, the barrenness of the modern muse, yet that we should find him reiterating, with even more forcible expressions, these same opinions at the very end of his life? In his crowning work, the *De Augmentis*, published in 1623, he is as earnest in his strictures on the prevailing learning (or the want of it) as he was in the days of his youth. Was he a detractor, or a boastful, self-satisfied man, who could see no good in any works but his own? Or was he a rash and inconsiderate speaker, uttering words which do not bear the test of time, or which were confuted and rejected by his contemporaries? We turn to the short life of Bacon by his secretary, Dr. Rawley, a man who does not waste words, and whose statements have become classical as they are unassailably accurate:

" He was no dashing[1] man, as some men are, *but ever a countenancer and fosterer of another man's parts. Neither was he one that would appropriate the speech wholly to himself, or delight to outvie others. He contemned no man's observations, but would light his torch at every man's candle. His opinions were for the most part binding, and not contradicted by any, which may well be imputed either to the well-weighing of his sentences by the scales of truth and reason, or else to the reverence and estimation in which he was held. I have often observed, and so have other men of great account, that if he had occasion to repeat another man's words after him, he had an use and faculty to dress them in better vestments and apparel than they had before, so that the author should find his own speech much amended, and yet the substance of it still retained, as if it had been natural to him to use good forms, as Ovid spake of his faculty of versifying:*

---

[1] Rawley means, not a man who used his wit to put others out of countenance. See Costard in Love's Labour's Lost, v. 2: " An honest man, look you, and soon dashed." Spedding, Works, ii. 12.

'*Et quod tentabam scribere, versus erat.*'" [1]

Bacon's most malicious enemies have not attempted to contradict or disprove these statements of one of his most intimate friends and faithful " servants." Why, then, does Bacon entirely ignore the unparalleled outburst of learning, the prodigious strides made in every department of science, the spirit of inquiry and of longing after truth, the galaxy of wits and poets, the " giant minds " with whom, so we are told, the age was teeming? We might read Bacon's acknowledged works from cover to cover without suspecting that such persons as Hooker or Ben Jonson, Burton, Spenser, or Shakspere, ever existed. Comprehensive as are his works, summing up the deficiencies of knowledge in all its departments, we find no allusion to that marvellous phenomenon—patent apparently to all eyes but those of Bacon himself—of the sudden and simultaneous revival of learning which began to take place immediately after he left Cambridge at the age of fifteen

The great impediments of knowledge, and the points which, in Bacon's judgment, rendered his times so unfavourable for its advance, were, in the first place, the scattering or " diversion " of clever men, the want of " a collection of wits of several parts or nations," and of any system by which wits could contribute to help one another, and mutually to correct errors and " customary conceits."

This deficiency was the cause of another impediment to knowledge, the lack, namely, of any means for keeping " a succession of wits of several times, whereby one might refine the other." There was no system by which newly acquired knowledge could be handed down, for the manner of the traditions of learned men " was utterly unfit for the amplification of knowledge."

The result of such impediments in and before Bacon's time was, he said, such as to lead men to conclude, either that knowledge is but a task for one man's life (and then vain was the complaint that life is short and art is long); or else that the knowledge that now is, is but a shrub and not that tree which is

---

[1] "He lisped in numbers, for the numbers came." (*Pope's Epistle to Dr. Arbuthnot.*)

never dangerous but where it is to the purpose of knowing good and evil in order that man may choose the evil. A desire which rises into a desire rather to follow one's own will than to obey, contains, he says, a manifest " defection " or imperfection.

He is also of opinion that " the pretended succession of wits," such as it is, has been ill-placed, and that too much absolute reliance was put upon the philosophy of one or two men to the exclusion of others. Also that the system of handling philosophy by parts, and not as a whole, was very injurious, and a great impediment to knowledge. He deprecates " the slipping-off particular sciences from the root and stock of universal knowledge," quoting the opinion of Cicero, that eloquence is not merely " a shop of good words and elegancies,[1] but a treasury and receipt of all knowledges; " and the example of Socrates, who, instead of teaching " an universal *sapience* and knowledge, both of words and matter, divorced them, and withdrew philosophy, leaving rhetoric to itself, which thereby became a barren and unnoble science."

Bacon argues that a specialist in any branch of science, " whether he be an oculist in physic, or perfect in some one tittle of the law, may prove ready and subtile, but not deep or sufficient, even in the one special subject which is his province ; *because* it is a matter of common discourse of *the chain of sciences, how they are linked together*," inasmuch as the Grecians, who had terms at will, have fitted it of a name of *circle learning.*

Although Bacon speaks of this chain of sciences as *a matter of common discourse*, it seems to have been so only in the circle of his own friends. To forge such links and to weld such a chain was, it would seem, one part of his method, and the conventional design which represents this linking together of universal knowledge, both earthly and heavenly, is to be seen on a vast number of the title-pages and ornamental designs of the books which emanated from Bacon's great society for the advancement of learning. As a rule these chains will be found in combination with a figure of Pan, or universal nature, with the head of Truth,

---

[1] Compare Bacon's own Promus of Formularies and Elegancies.

11

or universal philosophy or religion, and with the peculiar wooden
scroll or frame-work which we interpret as figuring " the universal frame of the world."

Since then the end and scope of knowledge had been so generally mistaken that men were not even well-advised as to what
it was that they sought, but wandered up and down in the way,
making no advance, but setting themselves at last " in the right
way to the wrong place," Bacon takes in hand the business of
demonstrating " what is the true end, scope, or office of knowledge, and to make, as it were, a calendar or inventory of the
wealth, furniture, or means of man, according to his present
estate, as far as it is known." By this means, he adds, " I may,
at the best, give some awaking note, both of the wants in man's
present condition, and the nature of the supplies to be wished;
though, for mine own part, neither do I much build upon my
present *anticipations*, neither do I think ourselves yet learned or
wise enough to wish reasonably; for, as it asks some knowledge
to demand a question not impertinent, so it, asketh some sense
to make a wish not absurd."

The Interpretation of Nature, from which these passages are
taken, includes only a fragment of the " inventory," which is to
be found in the form of a separate " catalogue " of one hundred
and thirty histories which are required for the equipment of
philosophy. It is also in the *De Augmentis*, which is in truth an
Exposition of the Deficiencies which Bacon noted in every conceived branch of science and literature, and of the practical
means which he proposed to adopt for the supply of these tremendous gaps in the chain of universal knowledge.

The " Catalogue of Histories " was published at the end of the
Novum Organum in 1620, but it appears to have been written
much earlier; for a few lines at the end show that at the time
when he penned this list he was looking forward to the accomplishment of all that is included in it. It seems improbable that
he would, so late in life, have published this catalogue, had it
been merely the airy fabric of a vision. On the other hand,
there are works extant which were first published anonymously
during his life-time, and which answer admirably to the titles of

many of these " particular histories," which, we observe, are not necessarily to be *original* works, but " collections " or " contributions to the equipment of philosophy." In other words, they were to be the furniture and household stuff of the new Solomon's House.

It will be profitable to spend a few minutes in noting with Bacon some of the departments of knowledge which he found to be either totally uncultivated, or so weakly handled as to be unproductive. In so doing we must not overlook the fact that, in every case where he notes such deficiencies, he makes, as he says, some effort toward supplying them.

Unless we take some pains to follow Bacon's meaning and line of argument, it is impossible to realize what is meant by his statement that truth was barren of fruits fit for the use of man. Modern teaching and traditions as to the marvellous revival of learning in the time of Elizabeth have blinded us to the fact that knowledge was at the very lowest ebb. The first attempt made by William Grocyn, in the end of the fifteenth century, to introduce the study of Greek into the University of Oxford, was regarded as an alarming innovation, and roused strong opposition. His distinguished pupil John Colet, afterwards Dean of St. Paul's, and founder of St. Paul's School, was exposed to the persecution of the clergy through his promotion of a spirit of inquiry and freedom of thought and speech. We read that in Paris, about the same time,[1] " The Juris Consult, Conrad Heresbach, affirms that he heard a monk announce from the pulpit, 'A new language, called Greek, has been found, against which strict precautions are requisite, as it propagates all kinds of heresie. A number of persons have already procured a work in that tongue called the *New Testament* — a book full of briars and vipers. As to Hebrew, all those who learn it turn Jews at once.' "

These dense prejudices were about to be dissipated by the creation, by Francis I., of the Royal College. Its professors were to be nominated by the King, regardless of university

---

[1] Francis I. and His Times. C. Coignet. Translated by F. Twemlow Bentley. London, 1888.

degrees, and the college was to be the refuge of free-thinkers of all countries. Such an innovation was reprobated by the pedants of the old school, and a tempest of wrath and indignation greeted the enterprise. Béda, syndic of the theological faculty, who later on headed a religious persecution, was a leader in this contest, and in this curious struggle we trace the germ of the conflict between Faith and Science, between Church and State, a conflict which Bacon spent his life in trying to appease and terminate.

Béda pretended that religion would be lost if Greek and Hebrew were taught by others than theologians. Were not all Bibles brought from that heretical nest, Germany, or from the Jews? The royal professors replied: We are not theologians, but grammarians and scholars. If you understand Greek and Hebrew, attend our classes and denounce our heresies; but if you do not understand these languages, why interfere with us?

Parliament was puzzled what to do. Theology and Hebrew were dead letters to it. King Francis was in fits of laughter at its evident embarrassment. Finally it decided to wash its hands of the affair, and to leave the disputants to settle it amongst themselves. Francis now completed the discomfiture of his adversaries by nominating as royal printer of Hebrew and Latin classics Robert Estienne, the distinguished editor and typographer. Theologians detested Estienne, because his translations of Holy Writ corrected their falsifications and misrepresentations, and exposed their ignorance and insincerity. His first translation of the Hebrew Bible appeared in 1532. It was denounced as sacrilegious, and its author as meriting the stake. During the King's absence from Paris, Estienne's house was ransacked, and he was forced to fly. But on the King's return Estienne was reinstated. Search was made throughout Europe and Asia for the old manuscripts, and these Estienne reproduced, the King superintending, with great interest, the beauty and perfection of type, destined, as these books were, to enrich his magnificent library at Fontainebleau.

Amongst the distinguished men who, in these early days, were connected with the Royal College of Francis I. are the names of men whose works were afterwards studied and quoted by Bacon and his own school, and whose successors seem to have become some of the most able and earnest workers on behalf of his far more liberal and far-reaching secret society. It is easy to see that Bacon, during his residence in the French court, must almost certainly have been drawn into the society of many members of this Royal College, whose duty it was to bring before the notice of the King " all men of the greatest learning, whether French or foreigners."

But, in spite of this Royal College, learning had not made much advance, even in France. Although Bacon must have witnessed the working of the college when he was in Paris, yet he says nothing in its praise. The *method* was as faulty as ever, although speech, and consequently thought, had become freer. Bacon's chief complaint against the " schoolmen," and against the ancient philosophies, was not so much regarding their matter as their method. The matter had become mere words, and the continual repetition of the same words made even " truth itself tired of iteration." He rightly complained that the writers of his time only looked out for facts in support of preconceived theories, or else, where authority and prejudice did not lead the way, constructed their theories on a hasty and unmethodical examination of a few facts collected at random.[1] In either case they neglected to test or verify their generalizations, whilst they wasted time and study in drawing out, by logical arguments, long trains of elaborate conclusions, which, for aught they knew, might start from erroneous theories.

The whole of Bacon's teaching, then, goes to enforce upon his disciples the necessity of examining and proving every statement, trusting to no " authority," however great, whose assertions or axioms cannot stand the test of microscopic inspection, or which are not seen to be " drawn from the very centre of the sciences."

" How long," he asks, " shall we let a few received authors stand up like Hercules' Columns, beyond which there shall be no

---

[1] See an excellent and very clear exposition of this in "*Francis Bacon*," by Prof. Fowler.

sailing or discovery in science?" He proceeds to indicate the various parts of his method by which learning was to be collected, rectified, and finally stored up in the "*receptacles*" which he would have provided in "places of learning, in books, and in the persons of the learned." In other words, he would provide schools, colleges, and libraries; he would facilitate printing, the publication of good books, and the institution of lectures, with paid professors of all arts and sciences. We look around, and are overwhelmed with admiration of all that has been accomplished upon Bacon's method. But he did not live to see it. Doubtless his life was one long series of disappointments, lightened only by his joyous, hopeful spirit, and by the absolute conviction which possessed him that he had truth on his side, and that "Time, that great arbitrator, would decide" in his favour.

"For myself," he says, "I may truly say that, both in this present work, and in those I intend to publish hereafter, *I often advisedly and deliberately throw aside the dignity of my name and wit (if such thing be) in my endeavour to advance human interests; and being one that should properly, perhaps, be an architect in philosophy and the sciences, I turn common labourer, hodman, anything that is wanted; taking upon myself the burden and execution of many things* which must needs be done, and which others, through an inborn pride, shrink from and decline."[1]

Dr. Rawley records Bacon's gentle regret that he that should be an architect in this erecting and building of the new philosophy "should be forced to be a workman and a labourer, to dig the clay and make the brick, and, like the Israelites, to gather the stubble and straw over all the fields, to burn the bricks withal. But he knoweth that, except he do it, nothing will be done: men are so set to despise the means of their own good. And as for the baseness of many of the experiments, as long as they be God's works, they are honourable enough; true axioms must be drawn from plain experience, and not from

---

[1] *De Aug.* vii. 1.

doubtful, and his course is, to make wonders plain, and not plain things wonders."

So, in the thousand paragraphs of the Natural History, or *Sylva Sylvarum*, we find each paragraph recording, not mere speculations, or repetitions of theories or conclusions supposed to have been established by former philosophers, but reports of *experiments* (sometimes very strange and original) made always with a definite object, and generally accompanied by some remarks explaining the causes of the phenomena observed. Bacon is never ashamed to admit his own ignorance of causes, and nothing which tends to their recovery is, in his eyes, insignificant or unimportant.

" It is," he says, " esteemed a kind of dishonour to learning, to descend into inquiries about common and familiar things, except they be such as are considered secrets, or very rare." Plato, he says, ridiculed this " supercilious arrogancy;" and " the truth is that the best information is not always derived from the greatest examples, but it often comes to pass that mean and small things discover great, better than great can discover the small, as that secret of nature, the turning of iron touched with the loadstone to the earth, was found out in needles, and not in bars of iron."

The collector of facts he compares to the ant heaping up its store for future use. He does not despise the ant, but commends its intelligence, as superior to that of the grasshopper, which, like the mere talker, keeps up a chirping noise, but does no work. The notes which he collects in such a store as the *Sylva Sylvarum* (although, as we firmly believe, ambiguous in meaning, and in their more important bearings symbolical or parabolic) give a good idea of the want of observation and general ignorance in Bacon's times on matters with which children in the poorest schools are now made familiar. Whatever double purpose this work on Natural History may have had, these simple notes were offered to the public as interesting and instructive information, and as such were received by the learned in the seventeenth century.

For instance, we read that alkali or potash is used in making glass; that airs may be wholesome or unwholesome; that some flowers are sweeter than others; that some, but not all, can be distilled into perfumes; that some have the scent in the leaf, as sweetbriar, [1] others in the flower, as violets and roses; that most odours smell best crushed or broken; that excess in nourishment is hurtful — if a child be extremely fat it seldom grows very tall; all mouldiness is a beginning of decay or putrefaction; heat dries and shrivels things, damp rots; some parts of vegetables and plants are more nourishing than others; yolks of eggs are more nourishing than the whites; soup made of bones and sinews would probably be very nourishing; bubbles are in the form of a sphere,[2] air within and a little skin of water without. No beast has azure, carnation or green hair;[3] mustard provoketh sneezing, and a sharp thing to the eyes, tears. Sleep nourishes — after-dinner sleep is good for old people. Boiling gives a bubbling sound; mincing meat makes it easier for old teeth; Indian maize when boiled is good to eat; flax and white of eggs are good for wounds.

Now, although it is true that here is hardly one particular which is not turned to excellent account in the Shakespeare plays, and in many minor works of Bacon's time, it is impossible to ignore the fact that Bacon makes notes of these *as things not generally known;* that the book in which he registered them was not published until after his death, and then, as we are especially told, with the notes revised, or not arranged in the order in which they were written.

Amongst the commonplaces which we have enumerated, there are other statements incorrect as they are picturesque and poetical. Probably Bacon did not believe them himself; they are often introduced with some such modification as " It may be that," or " It is said that." Thus we are told that gums and rock crystals are the exudations of stones; that air can be turned into water, water into oil; that the celestial bodies are

---

1 "The leaf of eglantine out-sweetened not thy breath." Cymb. iv. 2.

2 See *Emblems* of a Bubble, in reference to the world.

3 This is alluded to in *Troilus and Cressida*, i. 2, where Pandarus says that they are laughing at the white hair on Troilus' chin, and Cressida answers: "An't had been a *green hair*, I should have laughed too."

most of them true fire or flames; that flame and air do not mingle except for an instant, or in the vital spirits of vegetables
and living creatures. Everywhere the Paracelsian and very
poetical idea of the vital spirits of nature is perceptible, and the
whole of these notions are resolved into poetry in *Shakespeare*
and elsewhere. It is not too much to say that there is in
the plays hardly an allusion to any subject connected with science or natural history which is not traceable to some note in
these commonplace books, the apparently dry records of disjointed facts or experiments.

Not only arts and arguments, but demonstrations and proofs
according to analogies, he also " notes as deficient." And here
is a point in which his observations are distinctly in touch with
the Rosicrucian doctrines, or, to put it more accurately, a point
in which the Rosicrucians are seen to have followed Baconian
doctrines. For they made it a rule to accept nothing as *scientific truth* which did not admit of such proof and demonstration
by experiment or analogy.

As an example of the deficiency in this quarter, Bacon gives
the form and nature of light.[1] That no due investigation should
have been made of light, he considers " an astonishing piece of
negligence." Let inquiry be made of it, and, meanwhile, let it
be set down as *deficient*. So of heat and cold, of flame, of dense
things and rare, of the nature of sulphur, mercury, salt, and
metals, the nature of air, of its conversion into water, and of
water into oil; almost everything, in fact, which we now call
natural science, he either marks among the deficients, or as
being handled in a manner of which he " prefers to make no
judgment."

Since doubts are better than false conclusions, Bacon sets
down a calendar of doubts or problems in nature as wanting,
and probably few students of works of the class here indicated
will find much difficulty in identifying the works written to
supply these needs.

---

[1] Here, we think, is the customary double allusion, light being, in his symbolic language, synonymous with pure truth.

In short, Bacon shows that the sciences, whether of natural philosophy, physics, or chemistry, were in a parlous state, full of barren doctrines, empty theories, and bootless inquisitions; that if ever they were to be revived and made to bring forth fruits for the food of man, they must be " proyned " about the roots, nourished and watered, lopped of an infinite number of excrescences and useless branches, and grafted anew.

So with all the allied sciences of husbandry, horticulture, distillation, fermentation, germination, putrefaction, etc., we have but to consider the " experiments, " proposed or explained, in the *Sylva Sylvarum* (for the special use, as we believe, of Bacon's learned brotherhood or " Illuminati "), to realise the fact that the world (*even the learned world*) was indeed very ignorant, and that these scientific studies were part of the great " birth of time, " the *Renaissance*, the seeds and weak beginnings which time should bring to ripeness. Many of these observations are repeated in the *Anatomy of Melancholy*, which seems to be another " collection, " this time the sweepings of Bacon's commonplace books on subjects medical and metaphysical; a detailed examination of the mutual relations between mind and body, which are briefly treated of in the *Advancement of Learning*, and other places.

The *History of Winds* supplies particulars for all the poetic allusions to meteorological or nautical matters which are met with in the plays, poems, and emblem books of the time. Here it will be seen how weirdly and exquisitely these studies of meteorological facts are interwoven with metaphysical subtleties, such as are met with in *Macbeth* and *The Tempest*. Meteorology and the " sane astrology " which Bacon finds to be a desideratum, mix themselves up with the science of medicine —in his time " forsaken by philosophy, " " a weak thing, not much better than an empirical art, " " a science more practised than laboured, more laboured than advanced; the labours spent on it being rather in a circle than in progression. "

As for the *art of prolonging life*, he " sets it down as deficient, " and writes a book (apparently with a double meaning) on the subject. *The History of Life and Death* is bound up with the

Rosicrucian *New Atlantis* and the *Natural History*, which we believe correspond with the *Librum Naturæ* of the fraternity, and the simple remedies and recipes which Bacon prescribes and publishes stand as records of the elementary state of knowledge in his time. Metaphysics lead to the consideration of the doctrine of dreams—" a thing which has been laboriously handled and *full of follies.*" It is connected with the " doctrine of the sensible soul, which is a fit subject of inquiries, even as regards its substance, but such inquiries appear to me *deficient.*" [1]

The knowledge of human nature, of men's wants, thoughts, characters, is also *entirely neglected* yet. " The nature and state of man is a subject which deserves to be emancipated and made a knowledge of itself." In the *Sylva Sylvarum* he devotes many paragraphs to preparations for advancing this much-neglected art, noting even the small gestures and tokens by which the body of man reflects and betrays the mind. These notes furnish a compendium of hints not only for the metaphysician, but also for the artist, the orator, and the actor; there is hardly one which is not sure to be used with effect in the Shakespeare plays.

Let us sum up briefly the deficiencies in knowledge which, so far, we have learnt from Bacon to observe in the works of his predecessors, but which were being rapidly supplied during his life and in the succeeding generation:

Natural Science,[2] or Physics and Chemistry, with experiments and demonstrations — deficient.

Natural History,[3] excepting a few books of subtleties, varieties, catalogues, etc. — deficient.

Horticulture and Husbandry,[4] totally or partially deficient.

Meteorology [5] in all its branches — deficient.

---

1 *De Aug.* iv. Spedding, iv. 372–379.

2 See Advancement of Learning and De Augmentis; Nov. Organum; New Atlantis; Sylva Sylvarum.

3 Sylva Sylvarum; New Atlantis; Parasceve.

4 Sylva Sylvarum; Ess. Of Gardens; Plantations.

5 Nov. Org.; Hist. of Winds; Ebb and Flow of the Sea, etc.

Astronomy, [1] weak, with good foundations, but by no means sound.

Astrology,[2] not to be despised, but not practised so as to be useful or *sane.*

Medicine,[3] Pathology and the Art of Prolonging Life—deficient.

Metaphysics,[4] or the Doctrine of the Human Soul, and of the influence of mind on body—deficient.

Physiognomy and Gestures,[5] study of them—deficient.

In order to minister to the extreme poverty of science in all these departments, Bacon, as has been said, drew up a catalogue of 130 "Histories" which he found wanting, and which he strove, by his own exertions, and with help from friends, to furnish, or at least to sketch out.

Those who nourish the belief that, in the sixteenth century, the ordinary scribe or author could pick from casual reading, by intercourse in general society, or by his penny-worth of observation, such a knowledge of scientific facts as is exhibited (though in a simple form) in the best plays of the time, will do well to consider this catalogue, and to reflect that the particulars in it are, for the most part, discussed as *new and fruitful branches of information, or food for speculation,* in the works of Bacon. To this consideration it would be well to add a study of the works of a similar description *current before Bacon began to publish,* and to see how much of the " popular science " which we connect with Bacon was known, say, in the year 1575, beyond the walls of the monastery or the cell of the philosopher. Then see how far such knowledge reappears in any pre-Baconian poetry.

Bacon's method, says Spedding, in his dialogue with Ellis, " presupposed a *History* (or dictionary as you call it) of universal nature, as *a storehouse of facts to work on.*" [6] In these words

---

1 Thema Cœli.

2 De Aug.; Sylva Sylvarum.

3 Hist. Life and Death, etc.; Ess. Regimen of Health, Recipes, etc.

4 Doctrine of the Human Soul; De Aug., etc., etc.

5 De Aug.; Sylv. Sylv.

6 Spedding, Works, Preface to Parasceve.

the speaker uses the term expressing the idea of *Promus et Condus* — the idea of a store from which things new and old should be drawn, of a store of rough material from which perfect pieces should be produced. Such a store he was himself engaged in making.

To Spedding's inquiry his interlocutor replies : " Bacon wanted a collection large enough to give him the command of all the avenues to the secrets of nature." It almost seems as if Mr. Ellis were quoting from the *Promus* itself, where many hints seem to be given of Bacon's proposals for working his secret society, and where we find these entries: " Avennes — Secrett de Dieu; Secrett de Dieu." Are not these *secrets of God* correspondent to the *secrets of nature* to which Bacon would open avenues? Are they not the " things " known to the soothsayer who confesses, when taxed with his unusual knowledge:

> "In nature's infinite book of secresy
> A little I can read." [1]

And we cannot fail to observe that the study of such things was attended with some perils to the student whose object was to keep them as much as possible out of sight and screened from hostile observation. The catalogue, instead of being incorporated, as one would naturally expect, with the treatise itself, is detached from it, and sometimes omitted from the publication. Some of the entries, moreover, are incomprehensible, excepting on the assumption that they, again, moralise two meanings in one word—of which more anon.

But, we hear it said, " Grant that science, in modern acceptation of the term, was a new thing in Bacon's time, and that he held nearly every department in it to be deficient; what of that? Grant that there was then no such thing as popular teaching on these subjects, and that all branches of science have made tremendous strides during the past century. The same arguments cannot apply to the literature of the sixteenth and seventeenth centuries. Have we not all been taught that those were the times when Spenser and Shakespeare grew to their full

---

1 Ant. and Cleo. i. 2

powers, Spenser representing England with its religious sense of duty combative; Shakespeare, enabled by that English earnestness to speak through the highest poetry the highest truth? That the depths were stirred, and the spirit of the time drew from the souls of men the sweetest music, ennobling and elevating rough soldiers, mechanics, and country louts into poets of the highest degree?"

But in truth Bacon condemned the literary part of the knowledge of his own time before he touched upon the scientific part, although, for convenience, the order is here reversed. The second book of the *Advancement* treats of " the Divisions of the Sciences." There " all human learning " is divided into *History, Poesy*, and *Philosophy*, with reference to the three intellectual faculties, *Memory, Imagination, Reason*, and we are shown that the same holds good in theology or divinity.

History he again divides into natural and civil (which last includes ecclesiastical and literary history), and natural history is subdivided into histories of generations and arts, and into natural history, narrative and inductive. So we see that the science comes *last* in Bacon's contemplations and method, although, in the chair of sciences, it connects itself with the first part of human learning—history. But here at once he discovers a deficiency. " The history of learning—without which the history of the world seems to me as the statue of Polyphemus without the eye, that very feature being left out which marks the spirit and life of the person — *I set down as wanting.*" As usual he gives a summary of the requisites for this work, and the best method of compiling such a history from the principal works written in each century from the earliest ages, " that by tasting them here and there, and observing their argument, style, and method, the literary spirit of each age may be charmed, as it were, from the dead."

Such a history would, he considers, greatly assist the skill of learned men. " It would exhibit the movements and perturbations which take place no less in intellectual than in civil matters. In short, it would be a step toward the true study of human nature," which was his aim.

Civil history, though pre-eminent amongst modern writings, he finds to be "beset on all sides by faults," and that there is nothing rarer than a true civil history, which he subdivides into Memorials, Commentaries, Perfect History, and Antiquities. "For memorials are the rough drafts of history, and antiquities are history defaced, or remnants of history, which, like the spars of a shipwreck, have recovered somewhat from the deluge of time."

No defects need be noticed in the annals, chronologies, registers, and collections of antiquities, which he classes with "imperfect histories." They are of their very nature imperfect, but they are not to be condemned like epitomes, "things which have fretted and corroded the bodies of most excellent histories, and wrought them into unprofitable dregs." There are many collections, annals, chronologies, chronicles, commentaries, registers, etc., which began to appear in Bacon's time, in accordance with his instructions and suggestions, if not with direct help from him.

"Just and perfect history is of three kinds, according to the object which it propoundeth or pretendeth to present; for it presenteth either a time or a person or an action. The first of these we call *Chronicles*, the second *Lives*, and the third *Narratives*. Though the first be the most complete, and hath most glory, yet the second excelleth it in use, and the third in truth. For history of times representeth the greatness of actions, and the public faces and behaviour of persons; it passeth over in silence the smaller events and actions of men and matters. But such being the workmanship of God, that He doth hang the greatest weight upon the smallest wires,[1] it comes to pass that such histories do rather set forth the pomp of business than the true and inward resorts (or springs) thereof. Insomuch that you may find a truer picture of human life in some satires than in such histories." But well-written "lives and histories are likely to be more purely true, because their argument is within the knowledge and observation of the writer.[2] All three kinds of history are,

---

[1] "Thus hast thou hang'd our life on brittle pins." Translation of Psl. xc. "The whole frame stands upon pins." 2d Henry IV. iii. 2.

[2] Advt. ii. 1.

nevertheless, " so full of many and great deficiencies," that he says: " Even to mention them would take too much time." He would himself have undertaken the business in good earnest if James had given him any encouragement. But in this, as in many other things, he failed to rouse the dull King, whom he vainly tried to make as wise as he thought himself. The fragment of the " History of Great Britain " hints at Bacon's efforts in this direction, and there are several large books which will probably some day be acknowledged as part of the " collections" made by Bacon, or under his direction, to this end.[1]

For lives, he thinks it most strange that they have been so neglected, and counts them among the deficients.

Narrations and relations are also to be wished, since a good collection of small particulars would be as a nursery-ground, raising seedlings to plant when time will serve a fair and stately garden.[2]

Other parts of learning, as appendices to history, as orations, letters, brief speeches or sayings and letters, he considers an important branch of history. " Letters are according to the variety of occasions, advertisements, advices, directions, propositions, petitions, commendatory, expostulatory, satisfactory, of compliment, of pleasure, of discourse, and all other passages of action. And such as are written from wise men are, of all the words of man, in my judgment, the best, for they are more natural than orations and public speeches, and more advised than conferences or present speeches. So, again, letters of affairs, from such as manage them or are privy to them, are, of all others, the best instructions for history and, to a diligent reader, the best histories in themselves." [3]

Bacon's own letters are, of themselves, a good illustration of his doctrine; but there are other collections of letters, such as Sir Tobie Matthew's correspondence, with names and dates can-

---

[1] See "The Chronicles of the Kings of England from the Time of the Romans Government to the Death of King James." By *Sir Samuel Baker.* On the frontispiece of the third edition is a vignette of Verulam.

[2] *De Aug.* ii. 7. See, also, "The Collection of the History of England." *Samuel Daniel,* 3d edn. 1636.

[3] Advt. ii. 1.

celled, and the collection by Howell, entitled *Horæ Elianæ*, which seem as if they had been written with a further purpose than that of mere correspondence between friend and friend. The vast chasm, in point of diction, between these and the letters written by ordinary persons of good breeding and education in Bacon's time, may be well gauged by a compar'son with them of the sixteen folio volumes of Anthony Bacon's correspondence at the library belonging to Lambeth Palace, or the letters in the Cottonian and Hatton Finch collections at the British Museum.

Next, Bacon commends the collecting of apophthegms or witty sayings. "The loss of that book of Cæsar's" is, he thinks, a misfortune, since no subsequent collection has been happy in the choice. His own collection, with the supplementary anecdotes, which are sometimes ranked as "spurious," still remain to us; the former, we think, possessing a double value, inasmuch as it seems probable that, in one edition at least, it forms a kind of cipher or key to the meaning of other works.

As to the heathen antiquities of the world, "it is in vain to note them as deficient," for, although they undoubtedly are so, consisting mostly of fables and fragments, "the deficiency cannot be holpen; for antiquity is like fame — *caput inter nubile condit* — her head is muffled from our sight."[1] He does not allude to his own *Wisdom of the Ancients*, or to other kindred works, which, although they seem to have been published later, yet bear traces of having been the more diffuse and cruder studies which were the early products of Bacon's youthful studies.[2]

He draws attention to the history which Cornelius Tacitus made, coupling this with annals and journals, which again he finds to be in his own day deficient.

We observe that no hint is dropped about Camden's Annals. The omission is the more significant, seeing that in that work we have before us Bacon's own notes and additions.

Now he passes on to "Memorials, commentaries, and registers, which set down a bare continuance and tissue of actions

---

[1] Advt. lii. 1.

[2] See particularly Mystagogus Poeticus, or the Muses' Interpreter, 2nd edn., much enlarged by Alexander Ross, 1648.

12

and events, without the causes and pretexts, and other passages of action; for this is the true nature of a commentary, though Cæsar, in modesty mixed with greatness, chose to apply the name of commentary to the best history extant."[1] There are some "Observations on Cæsar's Commentaries"[2] which are deserving of notice in connection with this subject, although they bear on the title-page the name of *Clement Edmundes*, yet that very title-page is adorned with a portrait which strikingly resembles portraits of Francis Bacon. Here he is as a lad of about sixteen years old, and the internal evidence of the work renders it highly probable that this was merely one of his many juvenile productions. Several other works of a similar nature, with some geographical manuals, such as "Microcosmus, or a Little Picture of a Great World," and large works, such as the "Discovery of Guiana" and "A History of the World" (in which history, politics, and personal adventure are largely intermixed with geography), began to make their appearance about this time, and assisted in completing Bacon's great plan for the dissemination of universal knowledge. He affirms, "to the honour of his times and in a virtuous emulation with antiquity, that this great Building of the World never had through lights made in it till the age of us and our fathers. For, although they had knowledge of the antipodes, yet that might be by demonstration and not by fact, and if by travel, it requireth the voyage but of half the globe. But to circle the earth, as the heavenly bodies do, was not done nor attempted till these later times, and therefore these times may justly bear in their word not only *plus ultra* in precedence of the ancient *non ultra*, and *imitabile fulmen* in precedence of the ancient *non imitabile fulmen*, etc., but, likewise, *imitabile cœlum*, in respect of the many memorable voyages, after the manner of heaven, about the globe of the earth."

He never loses sight of the great object which he has at heart, of bringing lights into the darkness in which the world is lying; never for an instant forgets his darling hope that the advance-

---

[1] De Aug. ii. 6.

[2] Published, Lowndes, 1609.

ment of geographical knowledge may be made a means of
"mingling heaven and earth." When considering the deficiencies not only of knowledge, but of language in which to express
knowledge, it will not be amiss to draw attention to the words
of Hallam concerning the works of Sir Walter Raleigh,[1] especially
"The History of the World." The reader should reflect whether
it is more probable that the adventurous soldier and busy man
of the world should have been capable of writing such a book as
the one in question (filled as it is with Baconian beauties of diction and sentiment), or that Bacon, visiting his interesting friend
in the Tower, should have induced him to beguile the tedious
day and drive away the heavy thoughts of care by writing or
compiling, with his help, the work to which Sir Walter contributed the experience of his own travels, but for which Bacon
himself furnished the plan, the erudition, and the diction.

"We should," says Hallam, "expect from the prison-hours
of a soldier, a courtier, a busy intriguer in state affairs, a poet,
and a man of genius, something well worth our notice; but
hardly a prolix history of the ancient world, hardly disquisitions
on the site of Paradise and the travels of Cain. The Greek
and Roman story is told more fully and exactly than by any
earlier English author, and with a plain eloquence which has
given this book a classical reputation in our language. Raleigh
has intermingled political reflections and illustrated his history
by episodes from modern times, which perhaps are now the most
interesting passages. It descends only to the second Macedonian
war. There is little now obsolete in the words of Raleigh, nor
to any great degree in his turn of phrase; . . . he is less pedantic
than most of his contemporaries, seldom low, never affected."

Not science only, or natural history, or the history of the
world and of individuals, but arts and inventions of all kinds
were, in Bacon's opinion, equally "at a standstill." "As to
philosophy, *men worship idols, false appearances, shadows, not*

---

[1] It is not unworthy of inquiry, Was Raleigh (whose name is variously spelt)
any relation of the Dr. Rawley who was Bacon's chaplain and confidential secretary?

substance; [1] they satisfy their minds with the deepest fallacies.
The methods and frameworks which I have hitherto seen, there
is none of any worth, all of them carry in their titles the face
of a school and not of a world, having vulgar and pedantical
divisions, not such as pierce the heart of things."

Then, for the art of memory, " the inquiry seems hitherto to
have been pursued weakly and languidly enough; . . . it is a
barren thing, as now applied for human uses. *The feats of
memory now taught, I do esteem no more than I do the tricks and
antics of clowns and rope-dancers' matters,* [2] perhaps of strange-
ness, but not of worth."

Passing from natural and physical science to philology, or, as
Bacon calls it, " philosophic grammar," we again find it " set
down as wanting." " Grammar," he says, " is the harbinger of
other sciences—an office not indeed very noble, but very
necessary, especially as sciences, in our age, are principally
drawn from the learned languages, and are not learned in our
mother's tongue. . . . Grammar, likewise, is of two sorts—the
one being literary, the other philosophical." The first of these
is used chiefly in the study of foreign tongues, especially in the
dead languages, but " the other ministers to philosophy." This
reminds him that Cæsar wrote some books on " analogy," and
a doubt occurs whether they treated of this kind of philosophical
grammar. Suspecting, however, that they did not contain anything subtle or lofty, he takes the hint as to another deficiency,
and thinks " of a kind of grammar which should diligently
inquire, not the analogy of words with one another, but the
analogy between words and things, or reason, not going so far
as that interpretation which belongs to logic. Certainly words
are the footsteps of reason, and the footsteps tell something
about the body. . . . The noblest kind of grammar, as I think,
would be this: If some one well seen in a number of tongues,

---

1 Compare: "He takes *false shadows* for *true substances.*" (*Tit. And.* iii. 2.)
"Your falsehood shall become you well *to worship shadows and adore false
shapes.*" (*Tw. G. Ver.* iv. 1, 123–131.) *Mer. Wiv.* ii. 2, 215. *Mer. Ven.* iii. 2,
126–130; and comp. l. 73–80. *Richard II.* ii. 2, 14. 1 *Henry VI.* ii. 3, 62, 63.

2 This line seems to throw light upon Petrucio's powers of vituperative
rhetoric—"He'll rail in his *rope tricks.*" (*Tam. Sh.* i. 2.)

learned as well as common, would handle the various properties of languages, showing in what points each excelled, in what it failed. For so, not only may languages be enriched by mutual exchanges, but the several beauties of each may be combined, as in the Venus of Apelles, into a most beautiful image and excellent model of speech itself, for the right expression of the meanings of the mind."

As in everything else which Bacon noted as unattempted or unachieved, we find him endeavoring to supply the deficiencies in language which were universal in his day. He does not hint that Ben Jonson, Shakespeare, and others had been for years pouring Latin words into our language, trying experiments in words which had never been tried before, coining, testing, and rejecting, in the same manner, precisely, in which Bacon himself was coining, testing, rejecting, or making current, the new words which he entered in his *Promus*. That he was coining, *intentionally*, we know from his habit of supplementing his new word with its nearest synonym, and also from the frequent recurrence of such expressions as: " So I call it," " As it were," " As I term it," etc.

Bacon suggests[1] the making of " a store " of forms of speech, prefaces, conclusions, digressions, transitions, excusations, and a number of the kind, as likewise deficient. He subjoins specimens of these. " Such parts of speech answer to the vestibules, back-doors, ante-chambers, withdrawing-chambers, passages, etc., of a house, and may serve, indiscriminately, for all subjects. For as, in buildings, it is a great matter, both for pleasure and use, that the fronts, doors, windows, approaches, passages, and the like, be conveniently arranged, so, also, in a speech, such accessories and passages, if handsomely and skilfully placed, add a great deal, being both of ornament and effect to the entire structure." Surely he is here thinking of the construction of his Solomon's House. He then gives a few instances from Demosthenes and Cicero, having " nothing of his own to add to this part." Nothing, he means, which he chose to publish at that time, as a store of the kind. That he had it,

---

[1] De Aug. vi. 3, 492.

and had used it in all his works for thirty or forty years, and
with marvellous effect, we now know well from the internal
evidence of those works. In the *Promus* is a consecutive list
of one hundred and twenty-six short expressions of single
words, and farther on eighty more, which are all to be found in
the early *Shakespeare* plays, and more rarely elsewhere. Some of
these, such as " O my L. S." (the " O Lord, Sir, " of *Love's Labour's
Lost* and *All's Well*), are dropped in later plays. But by far
the larger number, as " Believe me," " What else ? " " Is it
possible ? " " For the rest," " You put me in mind," " Nothing
less, " " Say that, " etc., are met with throughout all the works
which will hereafter be claimed as Bacon's. Most of these
expressions are now such familiar and household terms that it
seems strange to imagine that three hundred years ago they
were not in everybody's mouth. What would be thought if it
were found that any great orator of our own time had written
down, intermixed with literary notes, which were carefully
preserved, such notes as these : " Will you see ? " " You take it
right, " " All this while, " " As is, " " I object, " " I demand, "
" Well, " " More or less, " " *Prima facie*, " " If that be so, " " Is
it because ? " " What else ? " " And how now ? " " Best of all, "
" I was thinking, " " Say, then, " " You put me in mind, " " Good
morning, " " Good night " ?

Yet these are amongst the private notes " for store of forms
and elegancies of speech. " They are of the kind which Bacon,
in his learned works, describes as *deficient;* which, even in his
last great work, the *De Augmentis*, he still pronounces to be
deficient and much needed for the building-up of a noble model
of language. Can we doubt that in such collections as this we
see Bacon in labourer's clothes, digging the clay and gathering
the stubble from all over the desolate fields of learning, to burn
the bricks wherewith he would rebuild the temple of wisdom?

Careful study and examination of these questions will surely
prove that to Francis Bacon we owe, not only the grand speculative philosophy and the experimental science which are associated with his name, and a vast number of works unacknowledged
by him, though published during the sixteenth and seventeenth

centuries, but also the very language in which those books are written, the " noble model of language " which has never been surpassed, and which constitutes the finest part of the finest writing of the present day.

Now, to return to our hasty sketch of deficiencies in grammar and philology, we find, as might be expected, that, inasmuch as words and graceful forms of speech were lacking, and the very machinery or organs of discourse imperfect, so " the proper rational method of discourse, [1] or rhetoric, for the transmission of knowledge, has been so handled as to defeat its object. " Logicians, by their artificial methods, have " so forced the kernels and grains of the sciences to leap out, that they are left with nothing in their grasp but the dry and barren husks. "

Changing the metaphor, Bacon declares that he finds the road to knowledge abandoned and stopped up, and, setting himself to the task of clearing the way, he quotes Solomon as to the use of eloquence, and again enforces the necessity of making *collections*. This time they are to be collections of " illustrations " which shall consider the opposite sides of every question, and show that there is a good as well as a bad side to every proposition. " It is the business of rhetoric to make pictures of virtue and goodness that they may be seen. And a store of sophisms, or the colours of good and evil, should be made, so that when men's natural inclinations mutiny, reason may, upon such a revolt of imagination, hold her own, and in the end prevail. " These " points and stings of things " are by no means to be neglected ; yet they, like the rest, are deficient.

Bacon wishes it to be plainly understood that the object of all this " provision of discourse" is to enable men readily to make use of their acquired knowledge. The system of noting, tabulation, and indexing which he enjoined, practised, and developed into a perfect system in his secret society is, he says, rather an exercise of patience, a matter of diligence, than of erudition. " Aristotle derided the sophists who practised it, saying that they did as if a shoemaker should not teach how to make a shoe, but should only exhibit a number of shoes of all fashions

---

[1] "An honest method, as wholesome as sweet." (*Ham.* ii. 2.)

and sizes. Far otherwise said our Saviour, speaking of divine knowledge: Every scribe *that is instructed* in the Kingdom of Heaven is like a householder that bringeth forth old and new store." His own notes were to him the store or *Promus* from which he drew. They correspond to the last collection, which he specially recommends, namely, " a store of *commonplaces*, in which all kinds of questions and studies, prepared beforehand, are argued on either side, and not only so, but the case exaggerated both ways with the utmost force of wit, and urged unfairly, and, as it were, beyond the truth." For the sake of brevity and convenience, these commonplaces should be contracted into concise sentences, " to be like reels of thread, easily unwound when they are wanted." These he calls the "antitheses of things," and, having a great many by him, he gives, " by way of example," *forty-seven* antitheta, which, "although perhaps of no great value, yet as I long ago prepared them, I was loth to let the fruit of my youthful industry perish — the rather (if they be carefully examined) they are *seeds only*, and not flowers."

These antitheta, which pervade the whole of Bacon's works, and which indeed tend to the formation of the most remarkable points in his style, may equally well be seen in the Shakespeare plays and poetry, whose "highly antithetical style" is the subject of comment by nearly every critic of the varied resources of his expressive diction.

From the discussion of words, phrases, life, and rhetoric (all of which he finds to be fundamentally defective), Bacon passes on to sound, measure, and accent; explaining, as to novices in the art, the most elementary principles of elocution, rhythm, and prosody. " The sound belonging to sweetnesses and harshnesses, the hiatus caused by vowels coming together," the difference in the use of diphthongs in Greek and Latin, and some peculiarities in various languages — of these things he has soon " had more than enough," and he gladly turns to his congenial subject, poesy.

Now on this score, at least, one might expect that he could congratulate his countrymen. But all that he is able to say is that " Poesy has produced a vast body of art, considered, *not to the matter of it, but to the form of words.*" All words, no matter, nothing from the heart![1] Is this all that can be said for the poetry of an age which produced the *Faerie Queene, The Shepherd's Calendar*, the Shakespeare plays, poems and sonnets, the works of Ben Jonson, Marlowe, Middleton, Chapman, Webster, the hymns and spiritual songs of Herbert, Quarles, Withers, Cowley, Crashaw, and a host of " minor poets "? Are we to believe that Bacon included these in his vast body of *art* considered, not in regard to the matter, but to the words of it?

Poetry to be lovely must have matter as well as art. It should be the spontaneous overflow of a full mind, stored to the brim with " true history," with a knowledge of nature, and especially of human nature; for " by Poesy," says Bacon, " *I mean here nothing else than feigned history.*"[2] *Shakespeare* formed the same estimate of true poetry:

Audrey. I do not know what *poetical* is; . . . is it a true thing?

Touchstone. No, truly, for *the truest poetry is the most feigning*, and what they swear in poetry may be said, as lovers, *they do feign.* . . . If thou wert a poet, I might have some hope thou didst feign?[3]

Bacon reminds us more than once of *all that poets feign*[4] in their histories, but he fails not to show that "*all invention*" or imaginative power "*is but memory,*" and that " a man is only *what he knows.*" In vain would weaker wits endeavour to persuade us that " reading and writing come by nature," or that a man can write well about matters concerning which he can never have had the opportunity of duly informing himself. Poesy, indeed, being " free and licensed, may at pleasure make unlawful matches and divorces of things," but the poet must be acquainted with those things before he can either match or divorce them.

---

[1] Compare: "Who will *for a tricksy word defy the matter.*" (*Merchant of Venice*, iii. 5) "*More rich in matter than in words.*" (*Romeo and Juliet*, ii. 6.) "Words, words, mere words, nothing from the heart." (*Troilus and Cressida*, v. 3.) "*More matter with less art.*" (*Hamlet*, ii. 2.) "This nothing's more than matter." (*Ibid.* iv. 5.) "When priests are more in words than matter." (*Lear*, iii. 2 and iv. 6.)

[2] *De Augmentis.*   [3] *As You Like It*, iii. 5.

[4] 3 *Henry VI.* i. 2. *Merchant of Venice*, v. 1, etc.

The first study of the poet should be history, " which is *properly* concerned with individuals,[1] and whose impressions are the first and most ancient guests of the human mind, and are as *the primary material of knowledge.*"   This is no passing thought of Bacon's, but a firm conviction, of which he set forth a visible illustration on the title-page of the *Advancement of Learning*. Here we see two pyramids, that on the right based upon Divinity, and rising into the study of human nature; that on the left based on Philosophy, and issuing in History and Poetry.   Bacon describes the process of poetic evolution :

" The images of individuals are received into the sense, and fixed in the memory. They pass into the memory whole, just as they present themselves.   Then the mind recalls and reviews them, and, which is its proper office, compounds or divides the parts of which they consist.   For individuals have something in common with each other, and again something different, and the composition of one characteristic with another is either according to the pleasure of the mind or according to the nature of things as it exists in fact.   If it be according to the pleasure of the mind of the composer, and that the various characteristics of one person are mixed or compounded with those of another, then the work is a work of imagination; which, not being bound by any law or necessity of nature, may join things which are never found together in nature, and separate things which in nature are never found apart."

Now, truly, Bacon realised the " tricks of strong imagination,"

" Shaping fantasies that apprehend
More than cool reason ever comprehends,"

bodying forth the forms of things unknown, whilst the poet's pen

" Turns them to shapes and gives to airy nothing
A local habitation and a name." [2]

The antithetical view of the question is best seen in *Antony and Cleopatra*, where Cleopatra, recalling the memory of Antony, " whole as it presents itself," is yet struck by the inadequacy of her efforts to combine so many noble features in one image:

---

[1] " The *proper* study of mankind is man."

[2] See M. N. D. v. 1, 1–28.

> " Nature wants stuff
> To vie strange forms with fancy, yet *to imagine*
> *An Antony* wore nature's peace 'gainst fancy,
> Condemning shadows quite. 1

" If, on the other hand, these same parts or characteristics of individuals are compounded or divided, as they really show themselves in nature, this is the business and duty of *Reason.* From these three fountains of Memory, Imagination, and Reason flow three emanations of History, Poesy, and Philosophy, and there cannot be more or other than these; they even include Theology. For whether information enters or is conveyed into the mind by revelation or by sense, the human spirit is one and the same, and it is but as if different liquors were poured through different funnels into one and the same vessel."

He goes on to show that Poesy is to be taken in two senses, in regard to words or matter. " In the first sense it is but a kind of speech, verse being only a kind of style and having nothing to do with the matter or subject; for true history may be written in verse, and feigned history or fiction may be written in prose."2 Bacon adds, in the *De Augmentis*, that in the " *style and form of words, that is to say, metre and verse, the art we have is a very small thing*, though the examples are large and innumerable."

" The art which grammarians call Prosody should not be confined to teaching the kinds and measures of verse, but precepts should be added as to the kinds of verse which best suit each matter or subject." He shows how the ancients used hexameters, elegiacs, iambic and lyric verse, with this view. Modern imitation fell short, because, with too great zeal for antiquity, the writers tried to train the modern languages into ancient measures, incompatible with the structure of the languages, and no less offensive to the ear. " But for poesy, whether in stories or metre, it is like a luxuriant plant that cometh of the lust of the earth and without any formal seed. Wherefore it spreads everywhere, and is scattered far and wide, so that it would be vain to take thought about the defects of it." Yet he levels a parting shaft at these defects, observing that, although accents in *words* have been carefully attended to, the accentuation of sentences has not been observed at all.

---

1 Ant. and Cl. v. 2.　　　　2 Intellectual Globe.

Narrative Poesy is a mere imitation of History, such as might pass for real, only that it commonly exaggerates things beyond probability.

Dramatic Poesy is History made visible, for it represents actions as if they were present, whereas History represents them as past.

Parabolic Poesy is typical history, by which ideas that are objects of the intellect are represented in forms that are objects of the sense.

As for *Narrative or Heroical Poesy*, " the foundation of it is truly noble, and has a special relation to the dignity of human nature. For as the sensible world is inferior in dignity to the rational soul, poesy seems to bestow upon human nature those things which history denies to it, and to satisfy the mind *with the shadows of things when the substance* cannot be obtained."

So, in his *Device of Philautia*, the soldier is made to say: " The *shadows of games are but counterfeits and shadows*, when *in a lively tragedy* a man's enemies are sacrificed before his eyes," etc.

Theseus has the same thought that poetry is the *shadow of things*. He does not despise the shadow when the substance cannot be obtained, although Hippolyta pronounces the rural play to be the silliest stuff that e'er she heard. He replies: " *The best in this kind are but shadows*, and the worst are no worse, *if imagination* mend them."[1]

Puck, too, in his apology for himself and his fellow-players, calls them *shadows*.

" And the reason why poesy is so agreeable to the spirit of man is that he has a craving for a more perfect order and more beautiful variety than can be found in nature since the fall. Therefore, since the acts and events of real history are not grand enough to satisfy the human mind, poesy is at hand to feign acts more heroical; since the issues of actions in real life are far from agreeing with the merits of virtue and vice, poesy corrects history, exhibiting events and fortunes as according to merit and the law of Providence. Since true history wearies the mind with common events, poetry refreshes it by reciting things unexpected and various. So that this poesy conduces not only to

[1] M. N. D. v. 2.

delight, but to magnanimity and morality. Whence it may
fairly be thought to partake somewhat of *a divine nature*, because *it raises the mind aloft*, accommodating the shows of
things to the desires of the mind, not (like reason and history)
buckling and bowing down the mind to the nature of things."[1]

" By these charms and that agreeable congruity which it has
with man's nature, accompanied also with music, to gain more
sweet access, poesy has so won its way as to have been held in
honour even in the rudest ages and among barbarous people,
when other kinds of learning were utterly excluded."[2]

Can it be doubted that he intended so to use it in his own age,
still so rude, though so self-satisfied? In a previous chapter
he has described Minerva as " forsaken," and he proposes " to
make a hymn to the muses, because it is long since their rites
were duly celebrated."[3] Years before this he said the same in
the *Device of Philautia*, which was performed before the Queen
A hermit is introduced, who, in his speech, exhorts the squire
to persuade his master to offer his services to the muses. " It is
long since they received any into their court. They give alms
continually at their gate, that many come to live upon, but few
have they ever admitted into their palace." Elsewhere he
speaks of " the *poverty* of experiences and knowledge,"[4] " the
poverty and scantiness" of the subjects which till now have
occupied the minds of men."[5]

And so in the *Midsummer Night's Dream* (v. 1) we find:

> " The thrice-three muses mourning for the death
> Of Learning, late deceas'd in beggary."

And the Princess in *Love's Labour's Lost* (v. 2), exclaims,
when the King and his masque and musicians depart:

> " Are these the breed of wits so wondered at?
> Well-liking wits they have; gross, gross; fat, fat.
> *O poverty in wit, kingly-poor* flout!"

And Biron says the study of

> " *Slow arts* entirely keep the brain;
> And, therefore, finding *barren* practisers,
> Scarce show a harvest of their heavy toil."

---

[1] De Aug. ii. 13.

[2] De Aug. ii. 13. "Aye, much is the force of heaven-bred poesy."—Tw 'G
Ver. iii. 2. [3] Advt. L. i. [4] Int. Nat. 10. [5] Nov. Org. i. 85.

In the *Anatomy of Melancholy*, the author (Bacon, as we believe) says that " poetry and beggary are Gemini, twin-born brats, inseparable companions.

> "And to this day is every scholar poor:
> Gross gold from them runs headlong to the boor."

And now we come to dramatic poesy, a section which Bacon seems carefully to have omitted in the *English* edition of the *Advancement of Learning.* That edition would, during his own lifetime, be chiefly read by his own countrymen, and might draw attention to his connection with the drama and stage plays, arts which, as we have seen, he held to be of the highest value and importance, although in his time corrupt, degraded, plainly neglected, and esteemed but as toys.

" Dramatic poesy, which has the theatre for its world, would be of excellent use *if well directed.* For the stage is capable of no small influence, both of discipline and of corruption. Now, of corruptions in this kind we have had enough; but the discipline has, in our times, been plainly neglected. And though *in modern states play-acting is esteemed but as a toy*, except when it is too satirical and biting, yet among the ancients it was used as a means of educating men's minds to virtue. Nay, it has been regarded by learned men and great philosophers as a kind of musician's bow, by which men's minds may be played upon. And certainly it is most true, and one of the great secrets of nature, that the minds of men are more open to impressions and affections when many are gathered together, than when they are alone." [1]

He returns to the subject later on, in connection with rhetoric and other arts of transmitting knowledge:

" It will not be amiss," he says, " to observe that even mean faculties, when they fall into great men or great matters, work great and important effects. Of this I will bring forward an example worthy to be remembered, the more so because the Jesuits appear not to despise this kind of discipline, therein judging, as I think, well. It is a thing indeed, if practised professionally, of low repute; but if it be made a part of discipline it is of excellent use. I mean stage playing — an art which strengthens the memory, regulates the tone and effect of the

---

[1] De Aug. ii. 13.

voice and pronunciation, teaches a decent carriage of the countenance and gesture, gives not a little assurance, and accustoms
young men to bear being looked at."

He then gives an example from Tacitus (not from *Hamlet*) of
a player who

> " in a fiction, in a dream of passion,
> Could force his soul so to his whole conceit
> That, from her working, all his visage wann'd .
> *Tears in his eyes,* distraction in 's aspect,
> A broken voice, and his whole function suiting
> To his conceit,

and who so moved and excited his fellow-soldiers with a fictitious
account of the murder of his brother that, had it not shortly
afterward appeared that nothing of the sort had happened, or,
as Hamlet says, that it was " *all for nothing* " — " nay, that he
never had a brother, would hardly have kept their hands off the
prefect; but the fact was, that he played the whole thing as if it
had been a piece on the stage." [1]

Highly as Bacon extols Poetry in all its branches, but especially
in the narrative and dramatic forms, he yet gives to Parabolic
Poetry a still more distinguished place, and this would certainly
strike us as strange if it were not that this parabolic method is
found to be so intimately connected with the whole question
of secret societies, their symbols, ciphers, and hieroglyphics.

In the *De Augmentis* we cannot fail to see that he is everywhere leading up to a secret description of his own system of
conveying covert or hidden information and of moralising two
meanings in one word.

" Parabolic Poesy is of a higher character than the others,
and appears to be something sacred and venerable, especially
as religion itself commonly uses its aid as a means of communication between divinity and humanity. *But this, too, is corrupted*
by the levity and idleness of wits in dealing with allegory. It
is of double use, and serves for contrary purposes, for it serves
for an infoldment, and it likewise serves for illustration. In the
latter case the object is a method of teaching, in the former an

---

[1] De Aug. vi. 9.

artifice for concealment." He goes on to show how, in days
when men's minds were not prepared for the reception of new
ideas, they were made more capable of receiving them by means
of examples; and hence the ancient times are full of parables,
riddles, and similitudes.

That this was Bacon's strong and well considered opinion
appears from its frequent repetition in his works. The admirable
preface to *The Wisdom of the Ancients* enters into this subject
with considerable detail, and is peculiarly interesting on account
of the indisputable evidence which it affords that *these things
were new* in Bacon's day; that it was he who revived the use of
trope and metaphor; who taught men, in days when this
knowledge of the ancients had been all but extinguished, to
light up or illustrate, "not only antiquity, but the things
themselves."

Again, repeating that there are two contrary ends to be
answered by the use of parable, which may serve as well to
wrap up and envelop secret teaching, as openly to instruct, he
points out that, even if we drop the concealed use, and consider
the ancient fables only as stories intended for amusement.

" *Still the other use must remain, and can never be given up.*
And every man of any learning must allow that this method of
instructing is grave, sober, or exceedingly useful, and sometimes
necessary in the sciences, as it opens an easy and familiar passage to the human understanding in all new discoveries that are
abstruse and out of the road of vulgar opinions. Hence, in the
first ages, when such inventions and conclusions of the human
reason as are now trite and common were new and little known,
all things[1] *abounded with fables, parables, similes, comparisons,
and allusions*, which were not intended to conceal, but to inform
and teach, whilst the minds of men continued rude and unpractised in matters of subtlety and speculation, or even impatient,
and in a manner uncapable of receiving such things as did not
directly fall under and strike the senses. For, as hieroglyphics
were in use before writing, so were parables in use before
arguments. And even to this day, if any man would let new

---

[1] "If you look in the maps of the 'orld, you shall find in the comparisons
between Macedon and Monmouth, that the situations, look you, is both alike. . . .
For there's figures in all things. . . . I speak but in *the figures and comparisons*
of it." — *Henry V.* iv. 8.

light in upon the human understanding, and conquer prejudice, without raising contests, animosities, opposition, or disturbance, he must still go on in the same path, and have recourse to the like method of allegory, metaphor, and allusion.

"Now, whether any mystic meaning be concealed beneath the fables of the ancient poets is a matter of some doubt. For my own part I must confess that I am inclined to think that a mystery is involved in no small number of them. . . . I take them to be a kind of breath from the traditions of more ancient nations, which fell into the pipes of the Greeks. But since that which has hitherto been done in the interpretation of these parables, being the work of skilful men, not learned beyond commonplaces, does not by any means satisfy me, I think fit to set down philosophy according to the ancient parables among the *desiderata.*"

He then selects, as examples of his own interpretation of the ancient myths, Pan interpreted of the Universe and Natural Philosophy; Perseus, of War and Political Philosophy; Dionysus, of Desire and Moral Philosophy.

Who can read the scientific works of Bacon, or try really to understand his philosophy, without perceiving that, whatever he may have discovered, revived, instilled, or openly taught, his main object was to teach men to teach themselves? His "method" everywhere tends to this point. To get at general principles, to find out first causes, and to invent the art of inventing arts, and of handing down as well as of advancing the knowledge acquired — these were his aims. He is fully conscious that life is short and art is long, and therefore does not attempt to perfect any one department of science. He gives *the keys* and expects others to decipher the problems by means of those keys. He had very small respect for mere accumulations of detached facts, but he knew that generalisations could only be properly based upon such accumulations, classified and reduced to order, and that axioms to be true must be "drawn from the very centre of the sciences." That he organised and supervised the making of such stores of facts and scraps of knowledge as fill the ponderous volumes of the encyclopedists of the ·sixteenth century, we do not for an instant doubt. Modern science, in its pride or conceit, has too often been inclined to disown its vast debts to

Bacon, because, forsooth, having worked with the whole mass of his accumulated knowledge to begin upon, whereas he began upon nothing, they now find short cuts to the invention of sciences for which he laboured when science was an empty name, and the art of invention unknown excepting by Bacon himself. That his works are ostensibly and intentionally left unfinished, and that the book-lore of his time was to his mind thoroughly unsatisfactory, and the store of knowledge acquired inadequate for the *invention* and advancement of arts and sciences, is made very plain in the " *Filum Labyrinthi sive Formula Inquisitionis*," in which he relates *to his sons*[1] (the Rosicrucian Fraternity, of which he was the father) the thoughts which passed through his mind on this subject:

" Francis Bacon thought in this manner. The knowledge whereof the world is now possessed, especially that of nature, extendeth not to magnitude and certainty of works. . . . When men did set before themselves the variety and perfection of works produced by mechanical arts, they are apt rather to admire the provisions of man than to apprehend his wants, not considering that the original intentions and conclusions of nature, which are the life of all that variety, are not many nor deeply fetched, and that the rest is but the subtle and ruled motion of the instrument and hand, and that the shop therein is not unlike the library, which in such number of books containeth, for the far greater part, nothing but iterations, varied sometimes in form, but not new in substance. So he saw plainly that opinion of store was a cause of want, and that both books and doctrines appear many and are few. He thought, also, *that knowledge is uttered to men in a form as if everything were finished*, for it is reduced into arts and methods, which in their divisions do seem to include all that may be. And how weakly soever the parts are filled, yet they carry the shew and reason total, and thereby the writings of some received authors go for the very art; whereas antiquity used to deliver the knowledge which the mind of man had gathered in observations, aphorisms, or short and dispersed sentences, or *small tractates of some parts that they had diligently meditated and laboured*, which did invite men to ponder that which was invented, and to add and supply further."

---

1 In the left-hand corner of the MS., in the British Museum (Harl. MSS. 6797, fo. 139), there is written in Bacon's hand· *Ad Filios.*

A vast number of such " small tractates " as Bacon here mentions will be found amongst the works which sprang up in his
time and immediately after his death. They seem to be the
result, for the most part, of diligent pondering upon the works
which Bacon himself had " invented;" they reproduce his sayings, paraphrasing, diluting, abridging, or delivering them in
short and dispersed aphorisms, according to the method which
he advocates as one means for the advancement of learning.
The method is still extant, and Bacon continues, like evergreen
history, to repeat himself. Often when unexpectedly we come
upon his own words and apparently original thoughts, familiarly
used as household words, or calmly appropriated by subsequent
writers, we think how true it is that one man labours and others
enter into his labours.

Once more, a brief summary of the *deficiencies* which Bacon
found in the literature and arts of discourse of his own times:

1. A history of learning (anything in fact corresponding to
Prof. H. Morley's *Tables of English Literature*).

2. Civil history, biographies, commentaries, antiquities,
chronicles, perfect histories.

3. Appendices to history, orations, letters, apophthegms or
brief sayings, etc.

4. Registers, journals, memorials, etc.

5. Helps to the art of memory.

6. Philosophic grammar — (*a.*) Words new-coined. (*b.*)
Words from foreign sources. (*c.*) A true grammar of language.

7. A store or provision for discourse, forms of speech, elegancies, prefaces, conclusions, digressions, etc.

8. A method of discourse and for the transmission of
knowledge.

9. " Collections," dictionaries, encyclopediæ, books of reference.

10. Store of sophisms.

11. Store of antitheta, or arguments on all sides; commonplaces.

12. Treatises on elocution and prosody, on sound, measure,
and accent in poetry.

13. Dramatic poesy and the art of stage-playing.

14. Parabolic poetry; the use of symbols, emblems, hiero-glyphics, metaphors; the power of using analogies, etc.; fables, parables, allegories.

Not one word does Bacon say about the prodigious increase in the richness of language which had taken place during his own life. As he wrote in the prime of his manhood, so he writes in the complete edition of the *Advancement of Learning*, published simultaneously with the Shakespeare plays in 1623. Ending where he began, and disregarding the mass of splendid literature which filled up all numbers and surpassed the finest efforts of Greece and Rome, he calmly sets down philosophic grammar and the art of using beautiful language as " wanting."

CHAPTER VII.

THE ROSICRUCIANS: THEIR RULES, AIMS, AND METHOD OF WORKING.

" Woorke when God woorkes." — *Promus.*

" To see how God in all His creatures works!"— *2d Henry VI.*

" Ripening would seem to be the proper work of the sun, . . . which operates by gentle action through long spaces of time, whereas the operations of fire, urged on by the impatience of man, are made to hasten their work." — *Novum Organum.*

BRIEF and incomplete as are the previous chapters, it is hoped that they may serve their purpose of unsettling the minds of those who suppose that the history, character, aims, and work of Bacon are thoroughly understood, and that all is known that is ever likely to be known concerning him.

The discrepancies of opinion, the tremendous gaps in parts of the story, the unexpected facts which persistent research and collation of passages have continued to unearth, the vast amount of matter of every description which (unless philology be an empty word and the study of it froth and vanity) must, in future years, be ascribed to Bacon, are such as to force the explorer to pause, and seriously to ask himself, Are these things possible? Could any one man, however gigantic his powers, however long his literary life, have produced all the works which we are forced by evidence, internal and, sometimes, also, external, to believe Bacon's — his in conception, in substance, in diction, even though often apparently paraphrased, interpolated, or altered by other hands?

The mind of the inquirer turns readily toward the history of the great secret societies which were formed during the Middle Ages, and which became, in troublous times of church or state,

such tremendous engines for good and evil. A consequent study
of these secret societies, their true origin, their aims, and, so far
as they can be traced, their leaders, agents, and organs, renders
it evident that, although, single-handed, such self-imposed
labours as Bacon proposed and undertook would be manifestly
impracticable, yet, with the aid of such an organisation as that
of the Rosicrucian Fraternity, the thing could be done, for this
society, whether in its principles, its objects, its proceedings, or
in the very obscurity and mystery which surrounds it, is, of all
others, the one best calculated to promote Bacon's aims, its very
constitution seeming to be the result of his own scheme and
method.

So much interest has lately been roused on the subject of the
Rosicrucians, that we shall curtail our own observations as much
as possible, trusting that readers will procure the books which,
in these later days, have made the study of this formerly
obscure and difficult subject so pleasant and easy. [1]

Is it still needful to say that the Rosicrucians were certainly
not, as has been thought, atheists or infidels, alchemists, or
sorcerers? So far as we could find, when investigating this subject some years ago (and as seems to be fully confirmed by the
recent researches of others), there is no real ground for believing that the society was an ancient one, or that it existed before
1575, or that it issued any publication in its own name before
1580.   All the legends concerning the supposititious monk
Christian Rosenkreuz, and the still more shadowy stories which
pretend that the Rosy Cross Brethren traced their origin to
remote antiquity, and to the Indians or Egyptians, melt into thin
air, and, like the baseless fabric of a vision, dissolve away, when
we approach them with spectacles on nose and pen in hand.

" A halo of poetic splendour surrounds the order of the Rosicrucians; the magic lights of fancy play round their graceful
day-dreams, while the mystery in which they shrouded themselves lends additional attraction to their history.   But their
brilliancy was that of a meteor. It just flashed across the

<hr>

[1] See especially *The Real History of the Rosicrucians*, A. E. Waite, 1887.
Redway (Kegan, Paul & Co.).   *Bacon and the Rosicrucians*, 1889, and *Francis
Bacon, etc.*, 1890; both by W. F. C. Wigston (*Kegan, Paul, Trubner & Co.*).

realms of imagination and intellect, and vanished forever; not, however, without leaving behind some permanent and lovely traces of its hasty passage. . . . Poetry and romance are deeply indebted to the Rosicrucians for many a fascinating creation. The literature of every European country contains hundreds of pleasing fictions whose machinery has been borrowed from their system of philosophy, *though that itself has passed away.*"[1]

As will be seen, there is strong reason to doubt whether the words which we have rendered in italics are correct. The philosophy, the work of the Rosy Cross Brethren, *has never passed away;* it is, we feel sure, still green and growing, and possessing all the earth.

It is only just to readers to whom this subject is new, to say that there is still a wide divergence of opinion concerning the origin and true aims of the secret society of the Rosicrucians. Bailey gives the following account:

" Their chief was a German gentleman, educated in a monastery, where, having learned the languages, he travelled to the Holy Land, *anno* 1378; and, being at Damascus, and falling sick, he had heard the conversation of some Arabs and other Oriental philosophers, by whom he is supposed to have been initiated into this mysterious art.   At his return into Germany he formed a society, and communicated to them the secrets he had brought with him out of the East, and died in 1484.

" They were a sect or cabal of hermetical philosophers, who bound themselves by a solemn secret, which they swore inviolably to observe, and obliged themselves, at their admission into the order, to a strict observance of certain established rules.

" They pretended to know all sciences, and especially medicine, of which they published themselves the restorers; they also pretended to be masters of abundance of important secrets, and, among others, that of the philosopher's stone; all which, they affirmed, they had received by tradition from the ancient Ægyptians, Chaldeans, the Magi, and Gymnosophists.

" They pretended to protract the period of human life by means of certain nostrums, and even to restore youth.   They pretended to know all things.   They are also called the Invisible Brothers, because they have made no appearance, but have kept themselves *incog.* for several years."

As will be seen, we cannot agree with the opinions of Bailey and

---

[1] Heckethorn, Secret Societies of all Ages and Countries.

others, who have claimed for the society a very great antiquity, finding no evidence whatever that the hermetical philosophers last described, the supposed alchemists and sorcerers, were ever heard of until the end of the sixteenth century. That a secret religious society did exist for mutual protection amongst the Christians of the early church and all through the darkest ages until the stormy times of persecution at the Reformation and Counter-reformation, there can be no doubt. Probably the rude and imperfect organisation of the early *religious* society was taken as a basis on which to rear the complete and highly finished edifice as we find it in the time of James I. But, in honest truth, all statements regarding Rosicrucians as a society of men of letters existing before the year 1575 must be regarded as highly doubtful, and the stories of the Rosicrucians themselves, as fictions, or parabolical " feigned histories," devised in order to puzzle and astonish the uninitiated hearer.

In the *Royal Masonic Cyclopædia* there is an article on the Rosicrucians which seems in no way to run counter to these opinions. The article begins with the statement that in times long ago there existed men of various races, religions, and climes, who bound themselves by solemn obligations of mutual succor, of impenetrable secresy, and of humility, to labour for the preservation of human life by the exercise of the healing art. But no date is assigned for the first appearance of this society in any form, or under any name. And the title *Rosicrucian* was, we know, never given or adopted until after the publication of the *Chymical Marriage of Christian Rosencreutz*, in 1616. The writer in the cyclopædia seems to acknowledge that the truth about the origin of the Rosicrucian Fraternity *is known*, though known only to a few, and we have strong reasons for believing that, in Germany at least, a certain select number of the learned members of the " Catholic" (not the *Papal*) Church are fully aware of how, when, and where this society was formed, which, after awhile, assumed the name of Rosicrucian, but which the initiates in Germany call by its true name—" Baconian." It is very difficult, in all Masonic writings, for the uninitiated to sift

¹ Bailey's Dictionary—*Rosicrucians.*

the true from the false; or, rather, *fact* from *disguised history*, prosaic statements from figurative language, genuine information from garbled statements framed expressly to mislead. Yet, in spite of these things, which must never be lost sight of, the article in question gives such a good summary of some of the chief facts and theories about the Rosy Cross brethren, that, for the benefit of those who cannot easily procure the cyclopædia, we transcribe some portions:

" Men of the most opposite worldly creeds, of diverse habits, and even of apparently remote ideas, have ever joined together, consciously or unconsciously, to glorify the good, and *despise, although with pity, the evil that might be reconciled to the good.* But in the centuries of unrest which accompanied the evolution of any kind of civilisation, either ancient or modern, how was this laudable principle to be maintained? [1] This was done by a body of the learned, existing in all ages under peculiar restrictions, and at one time known as the Rosicrucian Fraternity. The Fraternity of the Rosy Cross, unlike the lower orders of Freemasons, seldom had gatherings together. The brethren were isolated from each other, although aware of their mutual existence, and corresponding by secret and mysterious writings, and books, after the introduction of printing. They courted solitude and obscurity, and sought, in the contemplation of the divine qualities of the Creator, that beatitude which the rude outside world despised or feared. In this manner, however, they also became the discoverers and conservators of important physical secrets, which, by slow degrees, they gradually communicated to the world, with which, in another sense, they had so little to do. It is not, at the same time, to be supposed that these occult philosophers either despised the pleasures or discouraged the pursuits of their active contemporaries; but, as we ever find some innermost sanctuary in each noble and sacred fane, so they retired to constitute a body apart, and more peculiarly devoted to those mystical studies for which the great mass of mankind were unfitted by taste or character. Mildness and beneficence marked such courteous intercourse as their studious habits permitted them to have with their fellowmen; and in times of danger, in centuries of great physical suffering, they emerged from their retreats with the benevolent object of vanquishing and alleviating the calamities of mankind. In a rude period of turmoil, of battle, and of political change,

---

[1] This, it is seen, was the very question which Francis Bacon, at the age of fifteen, proposed to himself. See Spedding's Life, i. 3; and *ante*, chap. iv.

they placidly pursued their way, the custodians of human learning, and thus acquired the respect, and even the reverence, of their less cultivated contemporaries. . . . The very fact of their limited number led to their further elevation in the public esteem, and there grew up around them somewhat of 'the divinity that doth hedge a king.' . . .

" It is easy at the present day to see that which is held up before every one in the broad light of a tolerant century; but it was not so in the days of the Rosicrucians and other fraternities. There was a dread, amongst the masses of society in bygone days, of the unseen — a dread, as recent events and phenomena show very clearly, not yet overcome in its entirety. Hence, students of nature and mind were forced into an obscurity not altogether unwelcome or irksome, but in this obscurity they paved the way for a vast revolution ir mental science. . . . The patient labours of Trittenheim produced the modern system of diplomatic cipher-writing. Even the apparently aimless wanderings of the monks and friars were associated with practical life, and the numerous missals and books of prayer, carried from camp to camp, conveyed, to the initiated, secret messages and intelligence dangerous to be communicated in other ways. The sphere of human intelligence was thus enlarged, and the freedom of mankind from a pitiless priesthood, or perhaps, rather, a system of tyranny under which that priesthood equally suffered, was ensured.

" It was a fact not even disputed by Roman Catholic writers of the most Papal ideas, that the evils of society, ecclesiastical and lay, were materially increased by the growing worldliness of each successive pontiff. Hence we may see why the origin of Rosicrucianism was veiled by symbols, and even its founder, Andreä, was not the only philosophical romancer — Plato, Apuleius, Heliodorus, Lucian, and others had preceded him in this path.

" It is worthy of remark that one particular century, and that in which the Rosicrucians first showed themselves, is distinguished in history as the era in which most of these efforts at throwing off the trammels of the past occurred. Hence the opposition of the losing party, and their virulence against anything mysterious or unknown. They freely organised pseudo-Rosicrucian and Masonic societies in return, and these societies were instructed to irregularly entrap the weaker brethren of the True and Invisible Order, and then triumphantly betray anything they might be so inconsiderate as to communicate to the superiors of these transitory and unmeaning associations.

" Modern times have eagerly accepted, in the full light of

science, the precious inheritance of knowledge bequeathed by the Rosicruciaus, and *that body has disappeared from the visible knowledge of mankind, and re-entered that invisible fraternity of which mention was made in the opening of this article. . . . It is not desirable, in a work of this kind, to make disclosures of an indiscreet nature. The Brethren of the Rosy Cross will never, and should not, at peril and under alarm, give up their secrets.* This ancient body *has apparently disappeared from the field of human activity, but its labours are being carried on with alacrity, and with a sure delight in an ultimate success.*" [1]

Although, during our search for information, experience has made us increasingly cautious about believing anything which we read in printed books concerning the Rosicrucians or the Freemasons, still it seems almost impossible to discredit the statements which have just been quoted; at least it will be granted that the writer is intending to tell the truth. He seems also to speak with knowledge, if not with authority, and such a passage as has been last quoted must, we think, shake the opinion of those who would maintain that the Rosicrucians, if ever they really existed and worked for any good purpose, have certainly disappeared, and that there is no such secret organisation at the present time. The facts of the case, so far as we have been able to trace them, are entirely in accordance with the assertion that the non-existence of the Rosicrucian Society is only apparent; true, they work quietly and unrecognised, but their labours are unremitting, and the beneficial results patent in our very midst.

A great light has been shed upon our subject by the publication in 1887 of Mr. Waite's remarkable little book, which has, for the first time, laid before the public several tracts and manuscripts whose existence, if known to previous investigators, had certainly been ignored, including different copies and accounts of the " *Universal Reformation of the Whole Wide World* " (the title of one of the chief Rosicrucian documents), as well as original editions of the " *Chymical Marriage of Christian Rosy*

---

[1] From the Royal Masonic Cyclopædia, edited by Kenneth R. H. Mackenzie, IX °, pub. Bro. John Hogg, 1877.

Cross," which are not in the Library Catalogue. [1] It is true, as
Mr. Waite says, that he is thus enabled to offer for the first time
in the literature of the subject *the Rosicrucians represented by
themselves.* [2]

This invaluable book should be read in connection with another
important volume which has since been published, and which
follows the subject into recesses whither it is impossible now to
attempt to penetrate. [3] Mr. Wigston enters boldly and learnedly
upon the connection perceivable between Bacon's philosophy
and Rosicrucianism, and the whole book goes to prove, on very
substantial grounds, that Bacon was probably the founder and
certainly the mainstay of the society.

For those who have not the time or opportunity for much
reading, it may be well again, briefly, to summarize the aims of
the Rosicrucians, as shown by their professed publications, and
the rules and system of work by which they hoped to secure
those aims. [4] We gather from the evidence collected that the
objects of the fraternity were threefold :

1. To purify religion and to stimulate reform in the church.

2. To promote and advance learning and science.

3. To mitigate the miseries of humanity, and to restore man to
the original state of purity and happiness from which, by sin, he
has fallen.

On comparing the utterances of the supposed authors of the
Rosicrucian manifestoes with Bacon's reiterated statements as
to his own views and aspirations, we find them to be identical in
thought and sentiment, sometimes identical in expression. It
is only necessary to refer to the eloquent and beautiful chapter
with which Spedding opens his *Letters and Life of Bacon*, and

---

[1] Note how often this is found to be the case where particulars throwing
fresh light on Bacon or on matters connected with him are found in old books
or libraries.

[2] See The Real History of the Rosicrucians, by A. S. Waite, London, Redway, 1887.

[3] Bacon, Shakespeare, and the Rosicrucians, by W. F. C. Wigston, London,
Redway, 1889.

[4] The following is chiefly extracted from an article in the Bacon Journal,
January, 1889 (Redway).

from which some portions have been already quoted, in order to perceive how striking is the general resemblance in aim, how early the aspirations of Bacon formed themselves into a project, and with what rapidity the project became a great fact.

" Assuming, then," concludes the biographer, " that a deep interest in these three causes—the cause of reformed religion, of his native country, and of the human race through all their generations — was thus early implanted in that vigorous and virgin soil, we must leave it to struggle up as it may, according to the accidents of time and weather. . . . Of Bacon's life I am persuaded that no man will ever form a correct idea, unless he bear in mind that from very early youth his heart was divided by these three objects, distinct, but not discordant."

Bacon, as we have seen, was *not fifteen years old* when he conceived the thought of founding a new system for the advancement of knowledge, and for the benefit of humanity. The Rosicrucian manifestoes inform us that *the founder of the society,* and the writer of one of the most important documents, *The Chymical Marriage,* was *a boy of fifteen.*

Mr. Waite observes, naturally enough, that the knowledge evinced by the writer of the paper in question, of the practices and purposes of alchemy, must be impossible to the most precocious boy. But in mind Francis Bacon never was a boy. Some men, he said, were always boys, their minds never grew with their bodies, but he reflected, evidently thinking of himself in relation to others, that " *All is not in yeares, somewhat also is in houres well spent.*"[1]   Never had he been " idle truant, omitting the sweet benefit of time," but rather had, like Proteus, " *for that's his name,*"

> " Made use and fair advantage of his days,
> His years but young, but his experience old;
> His head unmellowed, but his judgment ripe!"[2]

Wonderful as it is, improbable as it would appear, did we not know it to be the case, the fact remains, that at the age of fif-

---

[1] Promus.

[2] Two Gentlemen of Verona, ii. 4.

teen Francis Bacon had run through the whole round of the arts and sciences at Cambridge, had outstripped his tutors, and had left Cambridge in disappointment and disgust, finding nothing more to learn there. He did not wait to pass a degree, but, practically, it was acknowledged that he had more than deserved it, for the degree of Master of Arts was conferred upon him some time afterward.

How he spent the next year is not recorded by his biographer, but another R. C. document, the *Fama Fraternitatis*, throws a side-light upon the matter. In this paper, full as all these Rosicrucian manifestoes are of Bacon's ideas and peculiarities of expression, we read that " the high and noble spirit of one of the fraternity was stirred up to enter into the scheme for a general reformation, and to travel away to the wise men of Arabia." This we interpret to mean that, at this time, the young philosopher was entering his studies of Rhazis, Avenzoar, Averroes, Avicenna, and other Arabic physicians and " Hermetic" writers, from whom we find him quoting in his acknowledged, as well as in his unacknowledged, writings.

At this time, the *Fama* informs us, this young member *was sixteen years old*, and *for one year he had pursued his course alone.*

What is this likely to mean but that, having left college, he was pursuing his advanced studies by himself? It seems almost a certainty that at this period he was endeavouring, as so many other ardent minds have done, to get at a knowledge of the first causes of things. How could he better attempt to achieve this than by going back to the most ancient philosophies in order to trace the history of learning and thought from the earliest recorded period to his own times?

We shall presently have occasion to show the immense influence which the study of the occult philosophies of India, Persia, Arabia, and Egypt had upon the mind and writings of Francis Bacon, and how he drew from them the most elementary and universal symbols and emblems which are the foundations of Freemason language and hieroglyphics. But there is another particular which especially links Bacon with the whole system of Rosicrucianism, and this is that very matter of making *collections* or *dictionaries* which we spoke of in the last chapter. Now, this was not only one of the ostensible objects of the fraternity, but also the ostensible object of Francis Bacon. He claims the idea as his own, and declares that neither Aristotle nor Theophrastus, Dioscorides or Pliny, and much less any of the modern writers, have hitherto proposed such a thing to themselves. Spedding says Bacon would have found that such a dictionary or index of nature as he contemplated in the *Novum Organum* must be nearly as voluminous as nature herself, and he gives the impression that such a dictionary was not attempted by Bacon. Here, as will be seen, we differ from this admirable biographer, and believe that Bacon did organise, and himself commence, such a system of note-taking, alphabetising, collating, "transporting," etc., as by the help of "his twenty young gentlemen," his able pens, devoted friends in every corner of the civilised world, and especially from the Illuminati, Rosy Cross brethren, and skilled Freemasons, to produce, within a few years, that truly cyclopedian mass of books of reference, which later writers have merely digested or added to.

Bacon claims as his own the method by which this great deficiency is to be supplied.

Behold, then, the author of the *Fama Fraternitatis* making a precisely similar claim :

"After this manner began the Fraternity of the Rosie Cross — first by four persons only, and by them was made *the Magical Lannage and Writing with a large Dictionary.*"

May not the sentence just quoted help somewhat to account for the extraordinary likeness, not only in ideas, but in words, of books, scientific and historical, which appeared before the publication of the great collections? Is it possible that copies or transcripts may have been made from Bacon's great manuscript dictionaries by those who would, with his ever-ready help, proceed to "make" or "produce" a book? Were such budding authors (Rosicrucians) allowed to come under his roof to write their books, and use his library and his brains?—questions at present unanswerable, but to be answered. Visions of Ben

Jonson writing his " Apology for Bartholomew Fair at the house
of my Lord St. Albans;" of Bacon visiting Raleigh in prison;
of the young Hobbes pacing the alleys at Gorhambury with the
Sage of Verulam — these and many other suggestive images
rise and dissolve before the eyes of one who has tried to live in
imagination the life of Francis Bacon, and to realize the way in
which his faithful followers endeavoured to fulfil his wishes.

Dictionary is a dry, prosaic word to modern ears; the very
idea of having to use one damps enthusiasm, and drops us
" when several yards above the earth" into the study or the
class-room. But

> " It so falls out
> That what we have, we prize not to the worth
> Whiles we enjoy it; but being lack'd and lost,
> Why, then, we rack the value." [1]

Now think, if we had no dictionaries, how we should *lack*
them, and having made even one poor little note-book on any
subject which closely concerns us, how we prize it, and *rack its
value!* So did Bacon. The making of dictionaries was to him
a sacred duty, one of the first and most needful steps toward
the accomplishment of his great ends.

" I want this primary history to be compiled *with a religious
care, as if every particular were stated on oath; seeing that is the
book of God's works,* and (so far as the majesty of the heavenly
may be compared with the humbleness of earthly things) *a kind
of second Scripture.* "

He sees that such a vast and difficult work is only to be accomplished by means of co-operation, and by co-operation on a
methodical plan. These convictions are most clearly seen in
Bacon's most Rosicrucian works, the *New Atlantis, Parasceve,
Natural and Experimental History,* and other " fragmentary"
pieces. " If," he says, " all the wits of all ages, which hitherto
have been, or hereafter shall be, were clubbed together; if all
mankind had given, or should hereafter give, their minds wholly
to philosophy, and if the whole world were, or should be, composed of nothing but academies, colleges, and schools of learned

---

1 M. Ado, iv. 1.

men; yet, without such a natural and experimental history as we shall now prescribe, we deny that there could be, or can be, any progress in philosophy and other sciences worthy of mankind."

The author of *Fama* reflects in precisely the same fashion, writing the thought of the *sacred nature* of such a work, and the thought that it is *a kind of second Scripture*, with that other most important reflection as to the necessity for *unity*, and a combination of wits, if real progress is to be made and a book of nature or a perfect method of all arts be achieved.

" Seeing the only wise and merciful God in these latter days hath poured so richly His mercy and goodness to mankind, whereby we do attain more and more to the knowledge of His Son Jesus Christ, and of nature, . . . He hath also made manifest unto us many wonderful and never-heretofore-seen works and creatures of nature; . . so that finally man might thereby understand his own nobleness and worth, and why he is called *Microcosmus*, and how far his knowledge extendeth in nature.

" Although the rude world herewith will be but little pleased, but rather smile and scoff thereat; also the pride and covetousness of the learned is so great, *it will not suffer them to agree together; but were they united, they might, out of all those things which in this our age God doth so richly bestow upon us, collect* Librum Naturæ, *or a perfect method of all arts.*" [1]

" The College of the Six Days," which Bacon described, is, we know, the College of the Rosicrucians, who accept the *New Atlantis*, in its old form, as a Rosicrucian document, and allow it to be circulated under a changed title.

The hopelessness and impossibility of attempting to perform single-handed all that his enthusiasm for humanity prompted, and that his prophetic soul foresaw for distant ages, often oppressed his mind, and as often he summoned his energies, his philosophy, and his faith in God, to comfort and encourage him to the work. This is all very distinctly traceable in the *Promus* notes, which are so frequently quoted in the Shakespeare plays. Amongst the early entries, in the sprawling Anglo-Saxon handwriting of his youth, he records his intention to use " Ingenuous honesty, and yet with opposition and strength. Good means

---

1 *Fama Fraternitatis* — Real History of the Rosicrucians; A. S. Waite.
14

against badd, hornes to crosses ." [1] " The ungodly," he next
reflects, " walk around on every side." " I was silent from
good words, and my grief was renewed," but " I believed and
therefore have I spoken ; " and he is resolute in trying to do what
he feels to be his duty, for " The memory of the just lives with
praise, but the name of the wicked shall rot." Here we find
him registering his resolves to do good to others, *regardless of
private advantage or profit.* This, it will be seen, is one of the
cardinal rules of the Rosy Cross Brethren. They were " *to cure
the sick gratis,*" to seek for no pecuniary profit or reward for the
works which they produced for the benefit of others. " Buy the
truth," say Bacon's notes, " and sell it not." " He who hast-
eth to be rich shall not be innocent," but " Give not that which
is holy unto dogs." He foresaw, or had already experienced in
his own short life, the manner in which the " dogs " or cynics of
public opinion and of common ignorance would quarrel over
and tear to pieces every scrap of new knowledge which he presented to them. " The devil," he says farther on, " hath cast
a bone to set strife." But this should not hinder him. " We
ought to obey God rather than man," " and the fire shall try
every man's work, of what sort it is ; " " for we can do nothing
against the truth, but much for the truth." And then he seems
to prepare his mind *to suffer* on account of the efforts which he
was making on mankind's behalf. He remembers that our
Blessed Lord Himself suffered in the same way, and writes a
memorandum from this verse: " Many good works have I showed
you of my Father ; for which of those works do ye stone me? "
Whatever might be the judgment upon him and his works, he
would rest in the assurance of St. Paul: " I have fought a good
fight, I have finished my course, I have kept the faith." We
hardly think that he stopped here in the quotation. Although
he does not write down the other half of the passage, his ardent
soul treasured, and his works reflect in a thousand different ways
the inspiring and triumphant hope of recognition in that future
life to which he was always looking: " Henceforward there is

---

[1] See in the chapter on Paper Marks the Symbols of Horns and Crosses, to
which, perhaps, the entry alludes.

laid up for me a crown of righteousness, which the Lord, the righteous Judge, shall give me at that day, and not to me only, but to all that love His appearing."[1]

But meanwhile, how to do all that he felt and knew to be necessary, and yet which could only be done by himself, we see him again in the notes reflecting that victory can be gained by means of *numbers;* that " things united are more powerful or better than things not united; " that " two eyes are better than one; " " So many heades so many wits; " " Friends have all things in common; " " Many things taken together are helpful, which taken singly are of no use; " " One must take men as they are, and times as they are; " but, on the whole, he seems to think that most men are serviceable for something, that every properly instructed tongue may be made to bear witness, and that it must be one part of his work to draw together so great a cloud of witnesses as may perform the part of a chorus, endorsing, echoing, or capping the doctrines of the new philosophy as they were uttered, and giving a support, as of public opinion, both at home and abroad.

We now know that many of Bacon's works were transmitted " beyond the seas," to France, Spain, Italy, Germany, and Holland, where they were translated and surreptitiously published, usually under other names than his own. There are, when we come to collect them, many indications in the *Promus* of a secret to be kept, and of a system planned for the keeping of it.

" *The glory of God,*" we read, is " *to conceal a thing* "—and there are many " *secrets of God.*" " *Woorke as God woorkes* "—quietly, persistently, secretly—unheeded, except by those who read in His infinite book of secresy. " *Plutoe's helmet*" is said to have produced " invisibility." " *The gods have woollen feet* "—i. e., *steal on us unawares.* " *Triceps Mercurius, great runying,*" alludes, perhaps, to the little anonymous book of cipher called " *Mercury, the Secret and Swift Messenger,*" which reproduces so accurately (and without acknowledging him) Bacon's biliteral cipher, and many other particulars told precisely after his manner, that we believe it to be the brief summary by himself

[1] 2 Tim. iv. 7, 8.

of some much larger works.   But he also notes that " a Mercury cannot be made of every word," that is, a dull fellow will never be made a clever one; nevertheless " a true servant may be made of an unlikely piece of wood,"[1] and he had a faculty for attaching people to him and for bringing out all that was best and most serviceable in their natures.

The next note says that " *Princes have a cypher.*"   Was he thinking that he, the prince of writers, would use one for his royal purposes?   A few lines earlier is this entry:

> " Iisdem e' literis efficitur tragœdia et comedia"
> (Tragedies and comedies are made of one *alphabet*),

which we now know refers to the cipher narrative for which the pass-word was the *alphabet*, and which is found running through the Shakespeare tragedies and comedies. [2]

Such entries as these, suggestive of some mystery, are interesting when taken in connection with other evidence derivable from Bacon's manuscript books, where the jottings have been more methodised or reduced from other notes.   In the *Commentaries* or *Transportata*, which can be seen in MS. at the British Museum, we find him maturing his plans for depreciating " the philosophy of the Grecians, with some better respect to ye Ægiptians, Persians, and Chaldees, and the utmost antiquity, and the mysteries of the poets."   " To consyder what opynions are fitt to nourish *Tanquam Ansæ*, so as to graft the new upon the old, *ut religiones solent*," of the " ordinary cours of incompe-

---

1 See letter to Lord Pickering, 1594.

2 " I have sent you some copies of the *Advancement*, which you desired; and a little work of my recreation, which you desired not.   My *Instauration* I reserve for our conference—it sleeps not.   *Those works of the alphabet* are, in my opinion, of less use to you where you are now, than at Paris, and, therefore, I conceived that you had sent me a kind of tacit countermand of your former request.   But in regard that some friends of yours have still insisted here, I send them to you; and for my part I value your own reading more than your publishing them to others.   Thus, in extreme haste, I have scribbled to you I know not what. "—(*Letter from Bacon to Sir Tobie Matthew*, 1603.)

" What these *works of the alphabet* may have been, I cannot guess; unless they related to Bacon's cipher," etc. — (*Spedding's comment on the above words*, i. 659.)

See also the *Advancement of Learning*, ii.; Spedding, iii. 399, where Bacon quotes Aristotle to show that words are the images of cogitations, and *letters* are the images of words.

tency of reason for natural philosophy and invention of woorks."
" Also of means to procure 'histories' of all things natural and
mechanical, lists of errors, observations, axioms, &c." Then
follow entries from which we abridge:

" Layeing for a place to command wytts and pennes, Westminster, Eton, Wynchester; spec(ially) Trinity Coll., Cam.; St.
John's, Cam.; Mandlin Coll., Oxford.

" Qu. Of young schollars in ye universities. *It must be the
post nati.* Giving pensions to four, to compile the two histories,
ut supra. Foundac: Of a college for inventors, Library, Ingi-
nary.

" Qu. Of the order and discipline, the rules and præscripts of
their studyes and inquyries, allowances for travailing, intelligence, and correspondence with ye universities abroad.

" Qu. Of the maner and præscripts touching secresy, traditions, and publication."

Here we have a complete sketch of the elaborate design which
was to be worked out; and we wonder — yes, we wonder, with
an astouishment which increases as we approach the matter —
how these remarkable jottings, so pregnant with suggestion,
speaking to us in every line of a vast and deeply-laid scheme,
should have been so lightly (or can it be *so purposely*) passed
over in every life or biography of Bacon. Here he was laying
his plans to " command wits and pens " in all the great public
schools, and especially in the principal colleges of the universities. He was endeavouring to secure the services of the cleverest
scholars to assist him in working out a scheme of his own. They
were especially to be *young scholars*, who should have imbibed,
or who were capable of imbibing, the advanced ideas produced by
the " new birth of time, " which he had himself inaugurated. To
work out new ideas, one must have fresh and supple material; and
minds belonging to bodies which have existed for nearly half a
century are rarely either supple or easily receptive of new ideas.
Bacon, therefore, did not choose, for the main staff and fibre of
his great reforming society, men of his own age (he was now
forty-seven); he wisely sought out the brightest and freshest of
the sons of the morning, the cream of youthful talent, wherever it was to be discovered.

Would it not be a pursuit as exciting as profitable to hunt

out and track the footsteps of those choice young wits and pens
of the new school, of the *Temporis Partus Masculus,* and *Partis
Secundo Delineatio,* of which Bacon thought and wrote so much,
and to see what various aids these " young schollars " were able
to afford for his great work? One line of work is clearly indicated: they were, *under his own instructions,* to collect materials
for compiling " histories" on natural philosophy and on inventions in the mechanical arts—as we should now say, the applied
sciences. One work is specified, as to its contents and nature.
It is to be a " history of marvailes" with " all the popular
errors detected." Such a book was published shortly after
Bacon's death by a young Oxford man, of whom we shall by-
and-by have occasion to speak. Another history is of " Mech-
anique;" it is to be compiled with care and diligence, and a
school of science is to be established for the special study of the
art of invention. " A college, furnished with all necessary
scientific apparatus, workshops and materials for experiments."
Not only so, but Bacon proposes *to give pensions* to four of his
young men, in order that they might freely devote themselves
to scientific or philosophic research. Some were also to have
" *allowances for travelling,*" which proves that their field of
research and for the gleaning of materials was not to be confined
only to their own country, but " inquiries and correspondence with
ye universities abroad" were to form an important element in
the scheme.

The works which were the product of this wise and liberal
scheme of Bacon's will not be difficult of identification. They
belong to the class of which the author said that they did not
pretend to originality, but that they were flowers culled from
every man's garden and tied together by a thread of his own.

It is clear that the wits and pens of the " young schollars"
(who, we learn from the Rosicrucian documents, were to be
sixty-three in number) were chartered and secured under the
seal of secresy. The last of the manifestoes in Mr. Waite's
book contains this passage, in which few who have read much
of Bacon will fail to recognise his sentiments, his intentions—
nay, his very words:

" *I was twenty when this book was finished;* but methinks I have outlived myself; I begin to be weary of the sun.[1] . . . I have shaken hands with delight, and know all is vanity, and I think no man can live well once but he that could live twice. For my part I would not live over my hours past, or begin again the minutes of my days;[2] not because I have lived well, but for fear that I should live them worse. At my death I mean to make a total adieu of the world, not caring for the burthen of a tombstone and epitaph, but in the universal Register of God I fix my contemplations on Heaven. I writ the Rosicrucian *Infallible Axiomata* in four books, and study, not for my own sake only, but for theirs that study not for themselves. In the law I began to be a perfect clerk; I writ the *Idea of the Law*, etc., for the benefit of my friends, and practice in King's Bench.[3] I envy no man that knows more than myself, but pity them that know less. . . . Now, in the midst of all my endeavours there is but one thought that dejects me, *that my acquired parts must perish with myself, nor can be legacied* amongst my dearly beloved and honoured friends."

This is the very sentiment which caused Bacon to contrive some method of handing down, by means of those very friends, the *Lamp of Tradition*, which he could not legacy, but which, wherever forthcoming and by whomsoever rubbed, brings up on the spot the spirit of the Lamp, Francis Bacon himself.

Let us glance for a few minutes at " the order and discipline, the rules and prescripts," which were instituted for the use of the Rosicrucian Fraternity, or may we not safely say, for the use of Bacon's " young schollars " and friends? The original rules were fifty-two in number, but only the leading features of them can be noted, numbers being placed against them for the sake of brevity in reference:

1. The society was to consist of sixty-three members, of various grades of initiation, apprentices, brethren, and an " imperator."

2. These were all sworn to secresy for a period of one hundred years.

---

1 " I 'gin to be *aweary of the sun.*"—*Macb.* v. 5. " Cassius is aweary of the world."—*Jul. Cæs.* iv. 3.

2 Compare Bacon's posthumous or second Essay *Of Death*.

3 See Bacon's Tracts of the Law, Spedding, Works, vii.

3. They were to have secret names, but to pass in public by their own names.

4. To wear the dress of the country in which they resided.

5. *To profess ignorance*, if interrogated, on all subjects connected with the society, except the Art of Healing.

6. To cure the sick gratis (sickness and healing seem to have been terms used, metaphorically, for ignorance, and instruction or knowledge).

7. In all ways and places to oppose the aggressions and unmask the impositions of the Romish church — the Papacy.

8. To aid in the dissemination of truth and knowledge throughout all countries.

9. Writings, if carried about, were to be written in *ambiguous language*, or in " secret writing." (Query, in cipher ?)

10. Rosicrucian works were, as a rule, *not* to be published under the real name of their author. Pseudonyms, mottoes, or initials (*not the author's own*) were to be adopted.

11. These feigned names and signatures were to be frequently changed. The "imperator" to change his name not less frequently than once in ten years.

12. The places of publication for the " secret writings " to be also periodically changed.

13. Each member was to have at least one " apprentice " to succeed him and to take over his work. (By which means the secret writings could be passed down from one hand to another until the time was ripe for their disclosure.)

14. The Brethren must suffer any punishment, even to death itself, sooner than disclose the secrets specially confided to them.

15. They must apply themselves to making friends with the powerful and the learned of all countries.

16. They must strive to become rich, not for the sake of money itself, for they must spend it broadcast for the good of others, but for the sake of the advantages afforded by wealth and position for pushing forward the beneficent objects of the society.[1]

---

1 The working of this rule is observable throughout the whole of Bacon's life and writings. It accounts for the diametrically opposite accusations which have been levelled against him and which his enemies have delighted to magnify, of *meanness and lavishness.* " Riches," he says, " are for spending, and spending

17. They were to promote the building of "fair houses" for the advancement of learning, and for the relief of sickness, distress, age, or poverty.

18. When a Rosicrucian died he was to be quietly and unostentatiously buried. His grave was either to be left without a tombstone, or, if his friends chose to erect a monument in his honour, *the inscription upon it was to be ambiguous.*

It is needless to show what an engine such a society would be, driven by such a motive power as Bacon, one original mind, endowed in almost equally balanced proportions with every intellectual faculty; equally capable of the quick perception of ideas, as of their prompt acquisition and application to useful purposes. With all this, Bacon possessed the still rarer faculty of being able to communicate his ideas, to impress them upon the dull, dead minds of the many, as well as upon the more receptive apprehensions of the few. Where opposition to direct teaching or advance in any kind of knowledge existed, there his versatile genius, the "nimbleness of mind," of which he was conscious, enabled him to devise methods "to let new light in upon the understanding, and conquer prejudice without raising contests, animosities, opposition or disturbance,"[1] to speak truth with a laughing face.[2]

We are disposed to shrink from the facts which stare us in the face, and to say: Is it possible that one man can have dared and accomplished so much? Is it possible that any one brain could have been capable enough, any life long enough, to enable one man to have not only planned, but carried through, the

---

for honour and good actions. . . . I cannot call riches better than the baggage of virtue; the Roman word is better, 'impedimenta,' for as the baggage is to an army, so is riches to virtue; it cannot be spared nor left behind, but it hindereth the march. . . . *Of great riches there is no real use except it be in the distribution; the rest is but conceit.*" "*Money is like muck, not good except it be spread.*" In the same spirit, and with the same metaphor, *Coriolanus* is said to have regarded riches. "Our spoils he kicked at, and looked upon things precious as they were *the common muck o' the world.*"—Cor. ii. 3. Compare Essays *Of Expense* and *Of Riches* with the speeches of the fallen Wolsey, *Henry VIII.* iii. 2, 106, etc., and with *Timon of Athens*, i. 2, 90, etc., ii. 1, etc.

1 Pref. to Wisdom of the Ancients.

2 Promus, 10;1.

amount of works of infinitely varied kinds in which we find
Bacon engaged? *Is it possible* that he could have found time
to read, cogitate, write, and publish this enormous quantity of
valuable. works, each pre-eminent in its own way; to have filled
some of them with elaborate ciphers, and to have made many of
them means of conveying information secret as well as ostensible? With all this can we conceive him also experimenting to
the extent which we know he did in every branch of natural
philosophy, breaking a gap into every fresh matter, noting deficiencies in old studies, and setting to work to supply them; in
each case *originating* and inaugurating new ideas—a very different affair from merely imitating, or following where another
has gone before?

In truth, a hasty judgment would pronounce these things to
be impossible and contrary to common sense. But this merely
means unparalleled in the speaker's experience. No other man
has ever been known to perform such work as we claim for
Francis Bacon.

But Bacon was no ordinary man. He was an intellectual
giant, born into a world which seemed to him to be chiefly peo-
pled with pigmies; the spiritual and intellectual life of the
world stunted, deformed, diseased, and sick unto death through
ignorance and the sins which ignorance nourishes and strengthens. With his herculean powers and eagle-sighted faculties of
imagination, keen to perceive, subtle to devise, prompt to act,
skilful in practical details, what might he not do with four
" pensioned" able pens continually at his " command," and
sixty-three of the choicest scholars of the universities to assist
in the more mechanical parts of the work; to transcribe, collate,
and reduce into orderly form the " collections," historical, scientific, ethical, or phraseological, which, during his life, were to
stand for him and for them in the place of modern books of
reference, and which, after his death, were to be published as
" histories," " dictionaries, " " collections," etc., under the names
of those who were the ostensible editors or " producers" of
works which they would have been incapable of originating?

Whilst these men were thus writing under his eye, or accord-

ing to his " prescripts, " Bacon himself, in the quiet of his library
or tower, sometimes in his " full poor cell" in Gray's Inn, was
cogitating, note-taking, dreaming, experimenting, composing,
or " inventing."

> " Out of 's self-drawing web he gives us note;
> The force of his own merit makes his way:
> A gift that Heaven gives for him." [1]

The credibility of such assumptions is increased when we
endeavour to realise how things would stand with ourselves if,
from our earliest childhood, everything that we had lisped had
been noticeable; if our earliest writings had been worthy of
preservation; if every letter, every word we wrote had been
religiously stored, revised, and by and by published. " I add,
but I never alter; " that seems to have been part of Bacon's
method, and thus edition after edition, each time improved
and augmented, was produced, the same material being utilised
in various ways over and over again.

Bacon was never idle. Recreation with him was not idleness,
but merely a change of occupation. He never plodded upon
books, but read, taking notes, or perhaps marking extracts for
others to write out. Thus he wasted no moment of time, nor
allowed one drop of his freshly distilled knowledge to evaporate
or be lost, but carefully treasured and stored it up in " vases "
or note-books, where he could at any moment draw it out
afresh.

There is good reason for thinking that he largely encouraged
the use of stenography or shorthand writing; that his friends
sat round him as the disciples of the ancient philosophers sat
round their masters, listening to his words, and often writing
down his utterances, or his entire discourses. The facility with
which he expressed himself, the grace and sweetness of his
language, and the marvellous fulness of his conversation were
perpetual themes of admiration and wonder. " His meals,"
says Dr. Rawley, " were refections of the ear as well as of the
stomach, like the *Noctes Atticæ*, or *Convivia Deipus-Sophistarum*,
wherein a man might be refreshed in his mind and understand-

---

[1] Henry VIII. i. 1.

ing, no less than in his body. And I have known some, of no mean parts, *that have professed to make use of their note-books* when they have risen from table."[1]

Both the matter and the manner of *John Selden's " Table Talk "* assure us that this and several other similar books are merely transcripts of such hasty notes of words which dropped from Bacon's lips, reproduced as accurately as possible, and treasured up for the benefit of posterity by his loving friends.

To look a little into the rules of the Rosicross brethren, Bacon's " Sons of Science," and of whom we believe him to have been the " Imperator " or supreme head :

Rules 1, 13 and 15 help us to grasp the possibility of Bacon's having produced the enormous quantity of books which will surely, in the future ages, be claimed for him, and which can be proved, by all that has hitherto passed as conclusive evidence with regard to other works, to be the work of one author.

Rules 2, 10, 11, 12 and 14 suffice to answer the oft-repeated query: Why did not Bacon acknowledge his own works? or why did not his friends vindicate his claim to them? He, as well as his friends, had sworn solemnly to keep the secrets of the society for a period of one hundred years.

Rules 3, 10 and 11 enable us to reconcile many difficulties as to the authorship of certain works. For instance, in the anthology entitled " England's Helicon," there are poems which have, at different times, borne two, three or even four different signatures. If the Rosicrucian publications were not, as a rule, to bear the name of the author, and if the feigned names of the brethren were to be frequently changed, confusion and mystification as to the true author would inevitably be produced. It would be impossible to draw any irrefutable conclusions as to the date and sometimes as to the aim of the works in question, and this, doubtless, was precisely what the secret society desired.

---

[1] It seems possible that traditions of such delightful meals as Dr. Rawley here records, and in which Bacon delighted " to *draw a man on, and allure him to speak upon such a subject as wherein he was peculiarly skilful*," may have taken place at the " Mermaid," where the chief wits of the day are said to have enjoyed their " wit combats."

Rules 8 and 13, especially when taken together with the preceding, throw great light on the publication of such works as " Montaigne's Essays " in France, *of its supposed translation, in 1603, from French into pure Baconian English, by the Italian Florio, tutor to the English royal family,* and of the large addi-- tions and alterations, such as none but the author could have presumed to make, in the later edition published by Cotton in 1685–6.

Rule 8 seems also to explain the fact of many of Bacon's most intimate friends having passed so much of their time abroad, in days when to travel was a distinction, but not an every-day occurrence, and when, indeed, it required the royal sanction to leave the country.   So Anthony Bacon lived for many years in Italy and the south of France, very little being absolutely known about his proceedings.   Mr. Doyly, Bacon's first recorded correspondent, was at Paris when he received a mysterious letter explaining something in an ambiguous manner.   Bacon's answer is equally misty: " he studiously avoids particulars, and means to be intelligible only to the person he is addressing."[1]

This Mr. Doyly had travelled with Anthony Bacon, and after residing in Paris, went to Flanders, where " he was of long time dependent on Mr. Norris. "   What his business was is unknown; he returned to England in 1583.   The letter from Mr. Doyly to Francis Bacon shows great intimacy: it begins, " To my verye deare friend, Mr. Doylie."

Then there was Anthony Bacon's very intimate friend Nicholas Faunt, at one time Walsingham's secretary, a gentleman attached to the Puritan party.   From 1580 to 1582 we find him traveling, with no ostensible object, through France and Germany, spending seven months between Geneva and the north of Italy, back to Paris, and home to London in 1582.   He is described as an " able intelligencer," and is just such a man as we should expect to find Bacon making good use of.

The young Earl of Rutland receives in 1595 a licence to pass over the seas, and (although they pass for awhile as the writing of Essex) it is Bacon who writes for him those " Letters of

[1] Spedding, Letters and Life, ii. 9.

Advice " which were published anonymously nearly fifty years
. later.

Then we find another of his most intimate friends, Tobie Matthew, abroad, wandering, and sometimes, perhaps, rather mysteriously occupied. Although, to Bacon's deep regret, he joined the
Roman branch of the Church, the correspondence and intimacy
between the two never ceases, and we think that it will transpire
that Sir Tobie, having become a priest in the Jesuit college at
Douai, continued to serve Bacon in many ways by aiding in the
translation and dissemination of his works, and especially in the
production of the Douai Bible. The proceedings and writings
of other travellers and writers, or supposed authors, of Bacon's
time, should be examined and reviewed in this connection. They
are too numerous to speak of here, but we would remind the
reader of his life-long friends, the Sidneys, Herberts, Nevilles,
Howards, Careys, Sandys, Cottons, of Lord Arundel, Sir Thos.
Bodley, Camden, and the Shirleys; of John Selden, his trusted
friend and one of his executors; Sir Henry Wotton, his cousin;
of Sir Walter Raleigh, whom, during his imprisonment, he is
known to have visited in the Tower, whilst he was engaged in
writing *The History of the World;* of Ben Jonson, who, according to Drummond of Hawthornden, wrote from under Bacon's
roof; of Sir Kenelm Digby, Montaigne, Florio, Davies, and other
foreigners, as well as Englishmen, whose names and works are
found to be so curiously interwoven with the lives and writings
of Anthony and Francis Bacon.

By and by we shall have to return to the subject of Bacon's
friends and collaborators, and to the light which is let in upon
their agency through the large collection of Anthony Bacon's
correspondence, preserved in the library at Lambeth Palace.
To return to the Rosicrucian ordinances:

Rule 5 shows that the *incognito* maintained by the brethren
was to extend, not merely to their names and authorships, but
also to their knowledge and mental acquirements. The very
fact of their belonging to a secret society was to be concealed;
they were to pass through the world as ordinary members of
society, wearing the dress of the country in which they lived,

and doing nothing to draw upon them the special notice of others. *They were even to conceal any special or superior. knowledge which they might have acquired,* [1] *actually professing ignorance when interrogated,* the only science of which they were allowed to show any knowledge being "the science of healing." Perhaps this is to be taken partly in its literal sense, and the rule may have been made with the benevolent intention of encouraging the study of medicine and surgery, which Bacon found to be terribly deficient; also, this permission would enable the experts in these subjects to come to the rescue on emergency, and to help to alleviate the bodily sufferings of their fellow-creatures. Still, a comparison of the Rosicrucian works obliges us to see that it was to remedy the deformities of the age, to heal the sores and cankers of miserable souls, to minister to the mind diseased, that the Rosy Cross brethren were really labouring; and this fifth rule gives a good hint as to the reason why Bacon did not "*profess to be a poet,*" why "Burton" should not *profess to be a theologian,* or Montaigne "*profess to be a philosopher.*"

The thought arises: What could be the object of this rule? Even if it were desirable, for the safety of the author of dangerous or advanced publications, that his name should be concealed, what reason could there be for obliging the man himself to feign ignorance of subjects which he had specially studied, and this, too, in days when the revival of learning was a subject of discussion and pride, and when to be supposed learned was a feather in a man's cap?

There seems to be only one really satisfactory explanation of this and other rules, namely, that *the so-called authors were not the true authors of the books which passed under their names;* that at the best they were translators, revisors, or editors, often mere transcribers and media for publication. Under these circumstances it would not only have been false, had they claimed the authorship of works which they did not write, but it would have been fatal and foolish in the extreme had they gone about *professing* to talk of matters which they did not understand.

[1] We wonder if this rule is still in force. Experience persuades us that it is.

·Rosicrucians were *to heal the sick, gratis.* This seems to mean that their work was, throughout, to be a labour of love. Not for the sake of profit or of fame did they labour, but simply for the love of God, and of man created in God's image. Truly we believe that for this end the brothers Anthony and Francis lived poor for many years, flinging into the common fund, for publishing, etc., every penny which they could spare, after defraying the most necessary expenses for themselves, and to keep up appearances. We equally believe that their work has never died out, but has been taken up in the same spirit by numberless individuals and societies—now in full activity, and recently mightily on the increase.

Rule 17 would account for the extraordinary impetus given in Bacon's time to the building and endowing of libraries, schools, colleges, hospitals, almshouses, theatres, etc. The names of many such " fair houses, " munificently endowed, will rise to the minds of all who are well acquainted with London and the two great universities. Let the reader inquire into the history of Gresham College, Sion College, and the splendid library attached to it; Dulwich College, with its school, almshouses, and library, originally intended to benefit poor actors; the Bancroft Hospital and many other similar establishments; the library and other buildings at Trinity College, Cambridge; the additions to the Bodleian Library, Oxford, the library at Lambeth Palace, and the great printing-houses established at both universities — he will find that he can never get away from Bacon and his friends. Either we find Bacon suggesting the need or encouraging the performers, or inspecting and approving the work, but himself, as a rule, unrecognised in public documents; so with the societies. His portrait alone hangs in the great library of the Royal Society. His friends are all closely associated with the founding of the Arundel Society, the Society of Antiquaries, the Camden Society, the Ray Society, and, we think, with the Colleges of Surgeons and Physicians; but, as usual, although the names appear, in connection with these and other institutions, of his intimate friends, Bacon, the great instigator and promoter of them all, remains in the background. It is sufficient to read of such institutions that their origin is " veiled " or " obscure " for us to feel tolerably well assured that behind the veil is Francis Bacon.

In Rosicrucian books not included amongst the short pieces in MS. published by Mr. Waite, it is shown that one great work of the society was the publication and dissemination of Bibles. There are, says Bacon, two books of God, *the Book of the Bible, expressing His will*, and the *Book of Nature, setting forth His works*. Neither can be fully understood or interpreted without the other, and men should be made equally acquainted with either. The revised Bibles of 1594, 1611, and 1613 bear witness to his personal efforts in this direction. The commentary published at Geneva, by " John Diodati," *the Messenger Given by God* (or the *Messenger of God's Gift*, which Bacon says was the gift of reason with speech), should be examined in connection with this part of the subject. It will surely transpire that Francis Bacon played no minor part in promoting the knowledge of God's first book, and that his faithful followers have nobly fulfilled their vows and duty of carrying on his great work.

For the *Second Book of God*, it is easier at once to make plain the enormous services which he rendered. *He founded the Royal Society.* In these words we sum up the fact that he planned and set going the vast machinery which has produced such wonderful results upon science, and upon almost every department of human knowledge.

The history of the origin of the Royal Society, which, according to its chief chroniclers, is, like so many other matters connected with Bacon, " *veiled in obscurity*," appears to be this: A few choice spirits met first in Bacon's private room, then at various places in Oxford and Cambridge, until the friends formed themselves into a small philosophical society, under Dr. Wilkins, in Wadham College. Meetings were sometimes held in taverns. When too large for these, they adjourned to the parlour of Gresham College. Lord Arundel " offered the Royal Society an asylum in his own palace when the most fierce and merciless of the elements subverted her first abodes," all of which is printed with many italics and very large type in the

1 5

dedication " to the illustrious Henry Howard, Earl of Norfolk,"
at the beginning of a curious little book " *written in French*
by Roland Freart, Sieur de Cambraye,*" and " *rendered English* "
by John Evelyn, Fellow of the Royal Society. [1]

Evelyn obtained a charter for the society from Charles II.,
and named it The Royal Society. The rare literary accumulations of the noble family of the Howards were contributed to the
library. [2]

The rules which forbid the publication of *names* would, of
course, prohibit the Rosicrucians from writing their names in
books which were likely to reveal the course of their studies, or
their connection with a certain clique of persons; and so, in effect, we find. They must adopt feigned initials, or mottoes, in
order to identify themselves amongst their initiated friends
alone. This again explains the disfigurement which so often distresses the purchaser of good old books of a certain class, and
which is caused by the cutting out of large pieces of the title-
pages, or frontispieces, or fly-leaves, or the cancelling, by scrib-
bling with pen and ink, sometimes six or eight names on the
page. It is the exception and not the rule, in books professedly
Rosicrucian, and previous to the eighteenth century, to find in
them the name of any owner, although they may, apparently,
have passed through many hands.

The same circumstance explains the mystery as to the disap-
pearance of Bacon's library — *which is a mystery,* although the
world has been content to take it very apathetically. Bacon's
library must have been something quite remarkable for his day.
Like Prospero, we know that his books were dearer to him far
than state or public life, which was always a toil and burden to
his nature.

---

[1] This little work is entitled *An Idea of Painting.* We commend the consideration of it to Baconian readers, believing that Evelyn merely " rendered
English" that which had first appeared in France, by publishing the original
English of Bacon, written when he was a young man living and travelling in
the south of France, and perhaps in Italy.

[2] See Disraeli's Curiosities of Literature.

> " Being so reputed
> In dignity, and for the liberal arts,
> Without a parallel ; those being all my study, . . .
> I to my state grew stranger, being transported
> And rapt in secret studies."

Prospero, in his fall and banishment, is represented as most highly commending the kindness of the noble Gonzalo, who

> " Of his gentleness,
> Knowing I loved my books, he furnished me
> *From my own library* with volumes that
> I prize above my dukedom."

Without trespassing on the domain of the novelist, we may fairly believe that Bacon's feelings were the same, even if he did not actually experience a similar episode in the days of his cruel ruination and banishment from the home of his youth.

Where is Bacon's library? Undoubtedly the books exist and are traceable. We should expect them to be recognisable by marginal notes; yet these notes, whether in pencil or in ink, may have been effaced. If annotated, Bacon and his friends would not wish his books to attract public attention. Yet not only their intrinsic worth, but their priceless value as belonging to their beloved master, would have made the friends and followers of Bacon more than commonly anxious to ensure the safety of these books. Bacon himself, we feel sure, would have taken steps to this end. Yet it is observable that in neither of his wills (elaborate and detailed in particulars though they be) does he mention his library. Copies of all his writings, " fair bound," were to be placed in the King's library, and in the university libraries at Cambridge and Oxford, in Trinity College, Cambridge, and " Bennet College, where my father was bred," and in the libraries of Lambeth and Eton.

The MSS. in his " *cabinets, boxes, and presses* "—(think of the quantity of papers suggested by these words)—were to be taken possession of by three trustees, Constable, Selden, and Herbert, and to be by them perused and by degrees published. But of *books* there is not a word, and observation has led the present writer to the conclusion that during his life Bacon assigned his books to certain of his friends for life, or for use, and that eventually these books were to find their way into the great libraries where they now repose, and where future research will oblige them to yield up their secret, and to say what hand first turned their pages, whose eyes first mined into them to extract the precious ore so long buried beneath the dust of oblivion? Where, in what books, do we find this gold of knowledge, seven times tried in the crucible of poetic philosophy, cast into living lines, and hammered upon the muses' anvil into the " well-tuned and true-filed lines " which are not of an age but for all time?

We earnestly exhort young and able scholars, whose lives lie before them, to follow up this subject. Think of the new worlds of knowledge that remain to be explored and conquered. Who can tell the contents of the library at Eton, in which Bacon took such a lively interest? Who has ever thoroughly examined the hoards of manuscripts of Bacon's time at Lambeth Palace, at the Record Office, at Dulwich, or at the British Museum? Baconians, reading with modern search-lights rather than by the dim rays shed from even the best lamp of the last century, cannot fail in future to perceive many things which escaped the notice of previous observers, however diligent.

The Selden and Pembroke collections of books at the Bodleian Library, the Cotton Library at the British Museum, the libraries of the Royal Society, the Antiquaries, and others directly connected with Bacon, the theological library at Sion College, Gresham College, the collection of Bacon's works in the University Library, Cambridge, and at Trinity College, should be examined, and every collection, public or private, which was commenced or much enlarged between 1580 and 1680, should be most thoroughly ransacked with a special eye to records, direct and indirect, of the working of Bacon and his friends, and with a view *to tracing his books*. It is probable that the latter will seldom or never be found to bear his name or signature. Rather we should expect, in accordance with Rosicrucian rules, that no *name*, but only a motto, an enigmatic inscription, or the initials of the title by which he passed amongst the brethren, would be found in these books. Yet it may reasonably be anticipated that some at least are " noted in the margin," or that some will be found with traces of marks which were guides to the transcriber or amanuensis, as to the portions which were to be copied for future use in Bacon's collections or book of " commonplaces."

One word more, before quitting these rules of the Rosicrucians. The eighteenth rule shows that on the death of a brother nothing should be done which should reveal his connection with the fraternity. His tomb was to be either without epitaph or the inscription must be ambiguous. It is remarkable how many of the tombs of Bacon's friends and of the distinguished names of his time come under one or the other of these descriptions. Some of these will be noticed in their proper place. Meanwhile, let us remark that there seems to be only one satisfactory way of accounting for this apparently unnecessary rule. The explanation is of the same kind as that given with regard to rule 5, which prohibits the members of the society from *professing* a knowledge which they did not possess.

For suppose that the friends of deceased Rosicrucians had inscribed upon their tombs epitaphs claiming for them the authorship of works which had passed current as their writings, but which they did not really originate. The monuments would, in many cases, have been found guilty doing positive dishonour, not only to the sacred place in which they were erected, but even to the dead, whose memory they were to preserve, for they would actually declare and perpetuate untruths, or at the best half-truths, certain in the end to be discovered.

It is rare to find any epitaph by way of eulogium over the grave of any person who seems to have collaborated with Bacon, or to have been accredited with the authorship of any work which is suspiciously Baconian. Rarer still do we find on such tombs any hint that the so-called poet or philosopher ever *wrote* anything. In the few cases where this is asserted or suggested, there are reasons for believing, or actual proof, that the inscription, perhaps the monument itself, was put up by descendants or admirers some years after the death of the individual to whom the memorial was erected.

CHAPTER VIII.

THE VITAL SPIRITS OF NATURE.

"In Nature's infinite book of secresy, a little I can read."
—*Antony and Cleopatra.*

BACON seems to have been strongly influenced and stimulated by the study of the works of the celebrated theosophist, physician, and chemist, Paracelsus, whom he often cites (not always with approval), and from whose doctrine of the " Vital Spirits of Nature " it is clear that he must have derived the original germ of those lovely ideas of all-pervading life which reappear throughout his writings, and preëminently in the *Midsummer Night's Dream, Macbeth,* and *The Tempest.*

When the comet or new star suddenly shone forth in 1572, in the constellation of Cassiopeia, it was marked as a portent or harbinger of success for the boy Francis, who in that year went up for the first time to Cambridge, and who even at that early age was manifesting signs of future greatness.

Now it is worthy of note that this same portent was observed by Paracelsus as heralding the advent of " the artist Elias, " by whose means a revelation was to be made which would be of the highest importance to the human race; and, again, this prophecy of Paracelsus was accepted by the Rosicrucians as true, and as finding its fulfilment in the fact that in the year 1572 the wonderful boy did make his appearance, and became the founder of their society.

" Paracelsus, in the eighth chapter of his *Treatise on Metals,* gives utterance to the following prognostication : ' *God will permit a discovery of the highest importance to be made ; it must be hidden till the advent of the artist Elias.*'

" In the first chapter of the same work he says: ' *And it is true, there is nothing concealed which shall not be discovered; for*

*which cause a marvelous being shall come after me, who as yet
lives not, and who shall reveal many things.'*

"These passages[1] have been claimed as referring to the
founder of the Rosicrucian order; and as prophecies of this
character are usually the outcome of a general desire rather
than of an individual inspiration, they are interesting evidence
that then, as now, many thoughtful people were looking for
another saviour of society. At the beginning of the seventeenth century 'a great and general reformation,' says Buhle,—
'a reformation more radical and more directed to the moral
improvement of mankind than that accomplished by Luther —
was believed to be impending over the human race, as a necessary forerunner to the day of judgment.' The comet of 1572
was declared by Paracelsus to be '*the sign and harbinger of the
coming revolution,*' and it will readily be believed that his
innumerable disciples would welcome a secret society whose vast
claims were founded on the philosophy of the Master whom
they also venerated as a supreme factor in the approaching
reformation.   Paracelsus, however, had recorded a still more
precise prediction, namely, that '*soon after the decease of the
Emperor Rudolph, there would be found three treasures that had
never been revealed before that time.*'"

The author then claims that these are the three great Rosicrucian documents which were issued at the time appointed,
and which he has recently published for the first time in English,
under the titles of "The Universal Reformation of the Whole
Wide World," "*Fama Fraternitatis;* or, a Discovery of the Fraternity of the Most Laudable Order of the Rosy Cross," and
"The Confession of the Rosicrucian Fraternity, addressed to
the Learned of Europe."

It is easy to picture to ourselves the effect of these prognosti-
cations of Paracelsus, joined to the fact that the wonderful star
did appear at the very time when the youthful philosopher was
himself sent forth to shine as a prodigy and portent — it is easy
to imagine the impression produced upon a highly-strung, sensitive boy by such a combination of circumstances, to which,
doubtless, his admiring friends and tutors were not slow in
drawing his attention.   Years afterward we find him making

---

[1] The Real History of the Rosicrucians, A. E. Waite, pp. 34–5.   Published by
Redway.

" experiments," " touching emission of immateriate virtues from
the minds and spirits of men, either by affections, or by imaginations, or by other impressions." He speaks of the force of
imagination, and of the means to exalt it, and endeavours to
solve this problem: *Whether a man constantly and strongly
believing that such a thing shall be, it doth help anything to the
effecting of the thing itself.* He decides that it is certain that
such effects result; but that *the help is, for one man to work by
means of another, in whom he may create belief, and not by himself,* and we think it by no means improbable that in childhood
his own imagination was thus wrought upon and kindled into
enthusiasm concerning the work to which he was called, and
which he regarded as sacred.

Bacon does not, in his scientific works, often *quote* Paracelsus;
in some points he entirely differs from him, disapproving of his
doctrines, and of their effects upon popular belief. He protests
against the excessive freedom in the interpretation of Scripture,
which either explains " the divinely-inspired Scriptures as
human writings," or else " which presupposes such perfection in
Scripture that all philosophy likewise should be derived from
its sources, as if all other philosophy were something profane
and heathen. This distemper has principally grown up in the
school of Paracelsus and some others, but the beginnings thereof
came from the rabbis and Cabalists." [1] He shows the error of
Paracelsus and his school, who, " seeking a place for its three
principles even in the temple of Juno, that is, the air, established
three winds, and for the east found no place." [2] He reproves
the intemperate extremes of these " disciples of pretended natural magic," who exalted " fascination," or " the power and apprehension of the imagination, to be much one with the power
of miracle-working faith." [3] He laughs at the " prodigious
follies" of those who aim at making Paracelsus' pigmies. [4]
" Vast and bottomless follies which ascribe to imagination exalted the power of wonder-working faith, [5] fancies as wild as

---

[1] De Aug. ix.　[2] Hist. of Winds.　[3] De Aug. iv. (It is curious to see how
fashions and delusions return. Note the present "faith-healing" fancies.)　[4] Nat.
Hist. i. 99, and Hist. Dense and Rare.　[5] Nat. Hist. i. 1.

that by which Paracelsus was to have it that nutrition is caused only by separation, and that in bread and meat lie eye, nose, brain, liver, and in the moisture of the ground root, leaf, and flower." [1] Neither does he share the " idle notion of Paracelsus that there are parts and correspondences between man's body and all the species of stars, plants, and minerals; misapplying the emblem of man as a microcosm or epitome of the world in support of this fancy of theirs." [2]

Bacon differed on many points from Paracelsus, and, as we see, did not wish to be supposed a disciple of his; yet he studied very closely all that he had to say, and quoted him by name as if to lead others to the consideration of his works, from which he drew so much, although, perhaps, not of the kind, or after the fashion, which the alchemist philosopher might have desired and expected. The notion which is prominent in the writings of Paracelsus concerning the " Vital Spirits of Nature" fell in perfectly with Bacon's own ideas, and this poetical and beautiful fancy pervades his writings to such a degree as to be inseparable from them. The method in which he handles the subject is also so peculiar as to form another touchstone by which the authorship of certain works may be tested, since the thought of any two men, forming the same fanciful theories, and deriving from them the same subtle thoughts and conclusions, is too improbable to be seriously entertained.

In the preface to the *History of Life and Death*, the editor says:

" The idea on which Bacon's idea of longevity is founded, namely, that the principle of life resides in a subtle fluid or spirit, which permeates the tangible parts of the organisation of plants and animals, seems to be coeval with the first origin of speculative physiology. Bacon was one of those by whom this idea was extended from organised to inorganised bodies. In all substances, according to him, resides a portion of spirit which manifests itself only in its operations, being altogether intangible and without weight. This doctrine appeared to be to him of most certain truth, but he has nowhere stated the grounds of his conviction, nor even indicated the kind of evidence by which

---

1 Nov. Org. i. 48.   2 De Aug. iv. 2.

the existence of the *spiritus* is to be established. In living bodies he conceived that two kinds of spirits exist: a crude or mortuary spirit, such as is present in other substances, and the animal or vital spirit, to which the phenomena of life are to be referred. To keep this vital spirit, the wine of life, from oozing away ought to be the aim of the physician who attempts to increase the number of our few and evil days." [1]

The writer is here treating chiefly of the body, but wherever Bacon speaks of inorganic matter, or of organised forms of plants, etc., he uses language which expresses that they are more or less living and sentient, having vital spirits which act somewhat as in the bodies of living creatures. Doubtless his poetical nature led him always into metaphoric language; his "nimbleness to perceive analogies," his sense of beauty and of the wonderful harmony in which the world was created tended to make him speak and write thus; but a deeper feeling still moved him continually to connect the "crude," "gross," and "earthy" with the "rare," "airy and flamy" of the sensitive soul. He was forever mentally endeavouring to bring about a union or marriage between things natural and things spiritual, to "mingle earth with heaven." "I am labouring with all my might to make the mind of man a match for the nature of things." [2]

It is, therefore, to be expected, as a single outcome of his cogitations and philosophy, that we shall read of "Motion which *invites* an excited body;" "Materials which *refuse* to be heated; "*Master spirits* which, in any body, *curb, tame, subdue, and regulate* other parts," etc. "Bodies which delight in motion and *enjoy* their own nature," and which, in spontaneous rotation, "*follow* themselves, and *court*, so to speak, *their own embraces.*" Other "bodies *abhor* motion, and remain at rest." Others "move by the shortest path, to *consort* with bodies of their own nature." "By this appetite for motion all bodies of considerable density *abhor* motion; indeed, the *desire* of not moving is the only *appetite* they have; and though, in countless ways, they be *enticed and challenged* to motion, they yet, *as far as they*

---

[1] Prof. *Hist. Vitæ et Mortis*, by Robert Leslie Ellis. Spedding, Bacon's Works, ii. p. 91.

[2] De Aug. v. 2.

can, maintain their proper nature; and if compelled to move, they, nevertheless, *seem always intent* on recovering their state of rest, and moving no more. While thus engaged, indeed, *they show themselves active, and struggle for it with agility and swiftness* enough, as *weary and impatient of all delay. . . .* Of the motions I have set forth, *some are invincible, some are stronger than others, fettering, curbing, arranging them; some carry further than others; some outstrip others in speed; some cherish, strengthen, enlarge, and accelerate others.*" [1]

How lifelike all this is! Surely, it might be supposed that we were reading of two-legged or four-legged creatures instead of particles of matter. In the same vein the philosopher-poet tells of opiates and kindred medicaments, which *put the spirits utterly to flight by their malignant and hostile nature.* [2] How, if taken internally, their fumes, ascending to the head, *disperse in all directions the spirits contained in the ventricles of the brain,* and these spirits, thus withdrawing themselves, and unable to escape into any other part, are . . . sometimes *utterly choked and extinguished.* Rosewater, on the other hand, "*cherishes*" the spirits.

We read, too, of *Continuance* as the *steward or almoner of Nature;* [3] of Heat and Cold as the *hands* by which she works. Cold as an *enemy* to growth, and bad air an *enemy* to health; of the west wind *friendly* to plants, and of *strife and friendship in nature.* Bodies, at the touch of a body that is *friendly,* . . .

---

1 Nov. Org. i. 47. Compare with the preceding sentences "*Passion invites* me." *Twelfth Night,* ii. 2. "A *spirit* too delicate . . . *refusing* [the foul witch's] grand hests." *Temp.* i. 2. "All hail, *great master.*" *Ib.* "Her *more potent ministers. Ib.* "My *potent master.*" *Ib.* iv. 1. "*Curb* this cruel devil of his *will.*" Mer. Ven. iv. 1, and Ham. iii. 4. "*Tame* the savage spirit of wild war." *John,* v. 2. "The *delighted spirit* to bathe in fiery floods." *Meas. for Meas.* iii. 1. "More *spirit* chased than *enjoyed.*" *Mer. Ven.* ii. 6. "The air smells *wooingly here.*" *Macb.* i. 6. "Nature doth *abhor* to make his bed," etc. *Cymb.* iv. 4. "Night's swift dragons cut clouds full fast . . . damned *spirits,* all . . . all gone, and must for aye *consort* with black-browed night." *Midsummer Night's Dream,* iii. 2., etc.

2 See Nov. Org. ii. 48, 50. *Hist. Winds, Qualities,* 27. Hist. Heavy and Light, Cog. Naturæ, vi., etc.

3 "The gifts of Nature." *Twelfth Night,* i. 3; *Ham.* i. 5, etc. "Frugal nature." iv. i. "*Our foster nurse of nature is repose.*" "Poison and treason are the *hands* of sin." *Pericles,* i. 1. "Care's an *enemy* to life." *Twelfth Night,* i. 2. "Nature is thy *friend.*" *Merry Wives,* iii. 3.

open themselves; but, at the touch of an *unfriendly body, they shrink up.*" [1]

In the *Anatomy of Melancholy* (which, as has been said, seems to be the sweepings of Bacon's note-books on all subjects connected with the *Doctrine of the Union of Mind and Body*) all these ideas are reproduced and expanded.

The chapter containing the passages of the *Digression of Spirits* is particularly interesting and instructive, forming, as it does, a connecting link between the science and the poetry of the plays. Who that reads such sentences as the following, which catch the eye as it travels hastily down those pages, but must be reminded of the scenes and lines in the *Tempest, Macbeth, Lear,* and the *Midsummer Night's Dream,* and other plays, which are familiar in our mouths as household words?

" Fiery spirits [2] are such as commonly work by blazing-stars, fire-drakes, [3] or *ignis fatui* ; [4] which lead men oft *in flumina aut præcipitia,* saith Bodine, *lib.* 2, *Theat. Naturæ, fol. 221;* . . . likewise they counterfeit suns and moons, [5] stars oftentimes, and *sit on ship-masts,* . . . or which never appear, saith Cardan, but they signify some mischief or other to come unto men, though some again will have them to pretend good and victory; . . . and they do likely come after a sea-storm. . . .

" *Aerial spirits,* or devils, are such as keep quarter most part in the air, *cause many tempests, thunder and lightnings, tear oaks, fire steeples, houses, strike men* [6] *and beasts, make it rain stones,* [7] . . . *counterfeit armies in the air, strange noises,*

---

1 " A south wind *friendly.*" Winter's Tale, v. i. " *Friendly* drop" (of poison). *Romeo and Juliet,* v. 3. " A huge infectious troop of pale distemperatures and *foes* to life."— *M. M.* v. 1.

2 Comp. 3 Hen. VI. ii. 1, 21–38, and with " That *fire-drake* did I hit. . . . The *devil* was amongst them."—*Henry VIII.* v. 3.

3 *Fierce, fiery* warriors fight upon the clouds. The heavens blaze forth the death of princes.—*Jul. Cæs.* ii. 2.

4 *The will o' the wisp.* Lob. "Thou Lob of Spirits " of Puck.—M. N. D. ii. 1. See Puck's behaviour, *ib.* iii. 1. " Sometimes a horse I'll be ; . . sometime *a fire.*" See also the Fool of the *Walking Fire* and Flibbertigibbet, *Lear,* iii. 2, and Ariel's tricks upon Stephano and his fellows in *The Tempest,* iv. i.

5 Comp. 3 Hen. VI. ii. 1, 25–31.

6 Compare Prospero's account of his own performances in his speech to the elves (Temp. v. 1), and Macb. iv. 1, 44–61.

7 "The gods throw stones of sulphur."—*Cymb.* v. 5. " Are there no stones in heaven ?"—*Oth.* v. 2. " Let the sky rain potatoes."—*Mer. Wiv.* v. 5.

swords,[1] etc. . . . They cause whirlwinds on a sudden, and tempestuous storms, which, though our meteorologists generally refer to natural causes, yet I am of Bodine's mind (Theat. Nat. i. 2), *they are more often caused by those aerial devils,[2] for Tempestatibus se ingerunt,* saith Rich. Argentine, *as when a desperate man makes away with himself,* which by hanging or drowning they frequently do.[3] . . . These can corrupt the air and cause plagues, sickness, storms, shipwrecks, fires, inundations." Such devils or aërial spirits can " sell winds to mariners[4] and cause tempests; they consort with witches and *serve magicians.*[5] . . . Cardan's father had one of them (as he is not ashamed to relate), an aërial devil, bound to him for twenty-eight years."

Many other instances are given of men who employed such familiar spirits; Paracelsus being supposed to have one confined to his sword pommel, others who wore them in rings.

" Water-devils are those naiads or water-nymphs conversant with waters and rivers.[6] The water (as Paracelsus thinks) is their chaos, wherein they live; some call them fairies, and say that Habundia is their queen; *these cause inundations, many times shipwrecks,* and deceive men divers ways, as succuba, or otherwise, appearing most part (saith Tritemius) in women's shape.[7] Paracelsus hath several stories of them that have lived and been married to mortal men, and so continued for certain years with them; and after, upon some dislike, have forsaken them.[8] Such a one as Ægaria, . . . Diana, Ceres, etc. Olaus Magnus hath a narration of a King of Sweden, that, having lost his company one day, as he was hunting, met with these water-nymphs, or fairies, and was feasted by them; and Hector Boethius tells of Macbeth and Banquo, two Scottish lords, that,

---

[1] See of the portents before the murder of Cæsar. "*The noise of battle hurtled in the air.*"—*Jul. Cæs.* ii. 2.

[2] "Away! *the foul fiend* follows me! . . . Who gives anything to poor Tom? whom the *foul fiend* hath led through fire and through flame, through ford and whirlpool, over bog and quagmire. . . . *Bless thee from whirlwinds, star-blasting,* and taking."—*Lear,* iii. 4.

[3] See how the murder of Macbeth is accompanied and foreshadowed by tempests (*Macb.* i. 1). This has been well accentuated in Mr. Irving's reproduction of the play.

[4] Note the witches and the mariners (Macb. i. 3), and especially the *giving of a wind.*   [5] Ariel and Prospero.

[6] Prospero summons them, through Ariel, the most perfect impersonation of a Paracelsian nymph.—*Tempest,* v. 1.

[7] Ib. i. 2. Macb. i. 3.

[8] Such is Undine in the lovely story of La Motte-Fouque.

as they were wandering in the woods, had their fortunes told them by three strange women.

" Terrestrial devils are those Lares, Genii, Fauns, Satyrs, Wood-Nymphs, Foliots, Fairies, ¹ Robin Good-fellows, ² etc., which, as they are most conversant with men, so they do them most harm. Some think it was they alone that kept the heathen people in awe of old, and had so many idols and temples erected to them. Of this range was Dagon among the Philistines, Bel among the Babylonians, Astarte among the Sidonians, Baal among the Samaritans, Isis and Osiris among the Egyptians, etc. Some put our fairies into this rank, which have been in former times adored with much superstition, with *sweeping their houses*, and *setting of a pail of clear water, good victuals, and the like*, and then they should not be *pinched*,³ but find money in their shoes, ⁴ and be fortunate in their enterprises. ⁵ These are they that *dance on heaths and greens*,⁶ as Lavater thinks with Tritenꞏnius, and, as Olaus Magnus adds, leaving that *green circle*⁷ which we commonly find in plain fields, which others hold to proceed from a meteor falling, or some *accidental rankness of the ground*, so nature sports herself. . . . Paracelsus reckons up many places in Germany where they do usually walk in little coats, some two feet long. A bigger kind of them is called with us *hobgoblins* and *Robin Goodfellows*, that would, in those superstitious times, *grind corn for a mess of milk, cut wood, or do any manner of drudgery work*. . . . Cardan holds, ⁸ they will make strange noises in the night, howl sometimes pitifully, and then laugh again, cause great flame and sudden lights, fling stones, rattle

---

1 See *M. N. D.* ii. 1. The fairies of Shakespeare are always Bacon's vital spirits of nature, and this seems to be now recognized. The sprites and fairies in Mr. Benson's recent representation of the *Midsummer Night's Dream* were properly attired as flowers, insects, bullrushes, river weeds, etc., and not, as formerly, in ballet skirts and satin shoes. In *Macbeth* Mr. Irving not only departs from the old idea of witches as hags in red cloaks and poke bonnets, but the witches are distinctly arrayed to imitate the winds, and a scene in dumb show is interpolated where these wind-witches filled the sails which are to carry Macduff to England.

2 *M. N. D.* ii. 1.

3 "Let the supposed fairies pinch him." *Mer. Wiv.* iv. 4 "*Pinch* the maids blue; . . . *pinch* them, arms and legs and backs; . . . still pinch him, fairies, pinch him to your time." *Ib.* v. 5, and *Temp.* i. 2, 328, and iv. 1, 233.

4 "It was told me I should be rich by the fairies." *W. T.* iii. 3.

5 "Fairies and gods prosper it with thee." *Lear.* iv. 6.

6 "Dance our ringlets to the whistling winds." *M. N. D.* ii. 2.

7 "Yon demi-puppets, that by moonshine do the *sour-green ringlets make, whereof the sheep bites*."—*Temp.* v. 1.

8 See of Ariel, who makes music in the air. Twanging instruments, voices humming, or howling and thunder.

chains, shave men, open doors and shut them, *fling down plat-ters, stools, chests,* [1] sometimes appear *in likeness of hares, crows, black dogs,* [2] etc., of which read Pit. Thyræus the Jesuit, in his tract, *de locis infestis,* i. 4, who will have them to be devils, or the souls of damned men that seek revenge, or else souls out of purgatory that seek ease. . . . These spirits often foretell men's deaths by several signs, as knockings, groanings, [3] etc. Near Rupes Nova, in Finland, in the Kingdom of Sweden, there is a lake in which, before the Governor of the Castle dies, a spec-trum, in the habit of Arion with his harp, appears and makes excellent music. . . . Many families in Europe are so put in mind of their last by such predictions, and many men are fore-warned, (if we may believe Paracelsus), by familiar spirits in di-vers shapes, as *cocks, crows, owls, which often hover about sick men's chambers,* . . . for that (as Bernardinus de Bustis thinketh) God permits the devil to appear in the form of crows, and such-like creatures, to scare such as live wickedly here on earth."

Farther on, when discoursing of idleness as a cause of melan-choly, the Anatomist describes the men who allow themselves to become a prey to vain and fantastical contemplation, as unable " to go about their necessary business, or to stave off and extri-cate themselves," but as " ever musing, melancholising, and carried along *as he that is led round about a heath with Puck in the night,* they run earnestly on in this labyrinth of anxious and solicitous meditation."

Such notes and studies as these appear most conspicuously in the *Shakespeare* and other plays of Bacon. It is hard to believe that he could have created the fairy world of the *Midsummer Night's Dream* without some such preparation as is recorded in the scientific notes. Let us give a few minutes' consideration to this play, with the view of showing how dry facts, business-like notes, and commonplace observation were distilled into

---

1 See how this is illustrated in *M. N. D.* ii. 1. Puck takes the form of a stool.
2 "*In likeness of* a filly foal." *M. N. D.* ii. 1.
  "Sometime a horse I'll be, sometimes a hound,
  A hog, a headless bear, sometime a fire;
  And neigh, and bark, and grunt, and roar, and burn,
  Like horse, hound, hog, bear, and fire, at every turn."
  M. N. D. iii. 1.

3 Compare the sounds, etc., before the deaths of Duncan, Macbeth, and Julius Cæsar.

4 "It was the owl that shrieked, that fearful bellman." *Macb.* ii 3.

poetry in that wonderful mind of which John Beaumont said tnat it was able " to lend a charm to the greatest as well as to the meanest of matters." [1]

To begin with Puck's well-known speech. Oberon desires him to fetch a certain herb and to return " ere Leviathan can swim a league." Puck answers:

> " I'll put a girdle round about the earth
> In forty minutes."

Bacon, in studying the winds, made many inquiries as to the parts of the globe in which the winds chiefly occur, and where they blow with the greatest swiftness. He finds this to be the case at the tropics. " In Peru, and divers parts of the West Indies, though under the line, the heats are not so intolerable as they are in Barbary and the skirts of the torrid zone. The causes are, first, *the great breezes which the motion of the air in great circles, such as are under the girdle of the earth, produceth.*" Puck, then, is the ministering wind, Oberon's familiar or aërial spirit, who will, at his bidding, sweep round *the girdle of the earth,* where, according to Bacon's observations, winds travel with the greatest speed.

Puck is " one of the free winds which range over a wide space." We know this, because he calls himself [2] " a merry wanderer of the night," and the *free winds,* Bacon tells us, " last, generally, for twenty-four hours;" it is the " smaller and lighter winds " which " generally rise in the morning and fall at sunset." [3]

The first scene in which the fairies enter suggests the *airiness* of the elves, the " rare " and wind-like nature which Bacon says resembles fame, " for the winds penetrate and bluster *everywhere.*" The fairies here seem to be " the free winds blowing from every quarter," and the first speaker " an attendant wind," whose duty it is " to collect clouds," and which are, according to the " History," of a *moist* nature.

---

[1] The following is reprinted from an article published in *Shakespeariana,* April, 1884.

[2] M. N. D. ii. 1.

[3] History of Winds. Spedding, Works, v. 143.

Puck. How now, spirit, whither wander you?
Fai. Over hill, over dale,
    Thorough bush, thorough brier,
  Over park, over pale,
    Thorough flood, thorough fire.
I do wander everywhere,
Swifter than the moon's sphere;
And I serve the fairy queen,
To dew her orbs upon the green.
The cowslips tall her pensioners be:
In their gold coats spots you see;
Those be rubies, fairy favours,
In those freckles live their savours:
I must go seek some dewdrops here,
And hang a pearl in every cowslip's ear.

There is something infinitely pleasurable in tracing in the speeches of the fairies which follow all the details, as to their nature, avocations, and abode, of the spirits of fire, air, earth, and water, which are here so exquisitely presented to us—

> The fairies who meet in groves and green —
> By fountain clear or spangled starlight sheen.

And although the more popular idea of fairies, because (so we think) it was first so presented in this play, is the idea of "*wood nymphs*," "terrestrial spirits," we still find the fairies of the hill and dale, of forest and mead, mixed up and consorting with lighter winds and breezes which spring up beside rivers and running water. Titania upbraids Oberon because

> Never, since the middle summer's spring,
> Met we on hill, in dale, forest or mead,
> By paved fountain or by rushy brook,
> Or on the beached margent of the sea,
> To dance our ringlets to the whistling wind,
> But with thy brawls thou hast disturb'd our sport.

In a speech of nearly forty lines, she continues to pour out a string of Baconian observations on the "contagious" effects of fogs, sucked up from the sea by the revengeful winds; of the "rotting" produced by warm, damp winds (which, Bacon adds, are usually from the south or southwest); of the rheumatic disorders and changes of season and consequent "distempera-

16

tures" resulting from inundations, which have "drowned" the
fields and filled the nine men's morris with the unwholesome
"mud" which Bacon's soul abhorred.   The influence of the
moon is also noted here, as in the scientific notes:

> "The moon, the governess of floods,
> Pale in her anger, washes all the air."

And the effect which she produces, of raising the tides and so
of causing inundations and destruction of vegetation, is as clearly
marked as in the notes on the *Ebb and Flow of the Sea*, or in the
Sylva Sylvarum.

"The periodical winds," says Bacon, "*do not blow at night,
but get up the third hour after* sunrise.   All free winds, likewise,
blow oftener and more violently in the morning and evening
than at noon and night."   So, *when midnight approaches*, Oberon
and his train retire, "following darkness like a dream," but
with commands to "meet me all *by break of day.*"

In the last scene of this charmingly spiritual piece, Puck
again declares himself the true child of Bacon's imagination.
In describing the frolics of the fairies (perhaps the "frivolous
winds," which he describes as "*performing dances*, of which it
would be pleasing to know the order"), Puck speaks of sprites
who are let forth to "glide about":

> ". . . fairies that do run
> By the triple Hecate's team,
> From the presence of the sun."

For, Bacon says, "*the winds cease at noon.*"   Of himself,
Puck says:

> "I am sent *with broom* before,
> *To sweep* the dust behind the door."

For as we again read in the *History of Winds*: "To the
earth, which is the seat and habitation of men, *the winds serve
for brooms, sweeping and cleansing* both it and the air itself."

The poet, then, according to these observations, derived his
lovely conceptions of the fairies, in the first instance, from his

careful but suggestive notes on the zephyrs and breezes, of whom he makes Puck chief or swiftest. To many other airy nothings he gives neither a local habitation nor a name. Yet we feel sure that they are the vital spirits of nature — " water-nymphs conversant with waters and rivers," such as Oberon has employed to " cause inundations " — or they are terrestrial spirits, like the Hobgoblins and Robin Goodfellows of the *Anatomy*, and who do the same domestic drudgery, and play the same pranks that are there described in similar detail, bringing, in spite of their fun and mischief, good luck to the houses which they frequent.

> *Fai.* Either I mistake your shape and making quite,
> Or else you are that shrewd and knavish sprite
> Call'd Robin Goodfellow: are not you he
> That frights the maidens of the villagery;
> Skim milk, and sometimes labour in the quern
> And bootless make the breathless housewife churn;
> And sometimes make the drink to bear no barm;
> Mislead night-wanderers, laughing at their harm?
> Those that Hobgoblin call you and sweet Puck,
> You do their work, and they shall have good luck:
> Are not you he?
>
>   *Puck.*   Thou speak'st aright;
> I am that merry wanderer of the night.
> I jest to Oberon and make him smile
> When I a fat and bean-fed horse beguile,
> Neighing in likeness of a filly foal;
> And sometime lurk I in a gossip's bowl,
> In very likeness of a roasted crab,
> And when she drinks, against her lips I bob,
> And on her wither'd dewlap pour the ale.
> The wisest aunt, telling the saddest tale,
> Sometime for three-foot stool mistaketh me;
> Then slip I from her, then down topples she,
> And "tailor" cries, and falls into a cough;
> And then the whole quire hold their hips and laugh,
> And waxen in their mirth, and neeze and swear,
> A merrier hour was never wasted there.[1]

" Sir Fulke Greville . . . would say merrily of himself: that he was like Robin Goodfellow, for when the maids spilt the milk-

---

[1] Midsummer Night's Dream.

pans, or kept any racket, they would lay it on Robin; so, what tales the ladies about the Queen told her, or other bad offices they had, they would put it upon him."[1]

There are four fairies besides Puck, who, somewhat less ethereal than the rest, specially connect themselves with the studies of the natural philosopher, and appear to be the very coinage of his brain. In recalling the flowers which perfume the air most delightfully in gardens, when crushed or trodden upon, Bacon begins with "bean flowers," but checks himself by saying that *they are not for gardens, because they are field flowers.*" Elsewhere he says that "the daintiest smells of flowers are those plants whose leaves smell not, as *the bean flower.*" He suggests "the setting of whole alleys of burnet, wild thyme, and mint, to have pleasure when you walk and tread," and in another place he says that "odours are very good to comfort the heart," and the smell of leaves falling and *of bean blossoms* supplies a good coolness to the spirits. Thus, whilst commending the sweetness of

"A bank whereon the wild thyme grows,"

bean flowers are, in his estimation, sweeter still, and in the fairy "Peaseblossom" of the play we seem to recognise the "bean flower," sweetest of perfumes amongst field flowers, and whose mission is to supply a "cooling" and "comforting" odour to the bank whereon the Fairy Queen will repose. "Mustardseed" is a brisk ministering spirit of the fairy court, for "mustard," says Bacon, has in it "*a quick spirit, ready to get up and spread.*"

"Where's Monsieur Mustardseed ?
Ready . . . What's your will ?"

Peaseblossom and Cobweb are also ready, but only the fiery and quick-spirited Mustardseed is *ready to get up and act.*

Then Moth—be not appalled, delicate reader—Moth seems to be the winged product of Bacon's experiments touching living creatures bred of putrefaction. "For putrefaction is the work of the spirits of bodies, which ever are unquiet to get

---

1 Bacon's Apophthegms, 235; Spedding, Works, vii. 158.

forth and congregate with the air" (the wind fairies), "and to enjoy the sunbeams." Titania is the sunbeam, the vivifying and all-cheering spirit of living things. Her name proclaims her nature. We are told "moths and butterflies quicken with heat, and revive easily, even when they seem dead, being brought near the sun." What, then, can be more fitting than that the soft, ephemeral white "Moth" should be found hovering or flitting about where Titania, the Sunbeam, is?

Cobweb, or Gossamer, is another almost immaterial creature, "bred *by dew and sun* all over the ground. . . . Cobwebs are most seen where caterpillars abound, which breedeth *(sic)* by dew and leaves. "They are a sign of dryness, . . . and come when the dry east winds have most blown." The ideas which spring from these details, and which are woven into the "Dream," are as subtile as the Gossamer itself, and almost as difficult to handle without destroying their beauty. By means of the clues offered by the simple names of the attendants upon Titania, we may, if we will, follow, panting, the nimble bounds of the poet's fancy, to bend and twirl and light in unexpected places, while he leads us a dance through the sciences — that "labyrinth," whose paths are "so subtle, intricate, and crossing each other, that they are only to be understood and traced by the clue of experience." *

We conjure up, perhaps faintly, the dream which he was dreaming of universal nature — the Oberon of the play [1] — of the nature upon which the zephyrs and soft winds wait, hasting to assist the operations of the Sunbeam, the life-giver. When the east winds have dried the banks, Cobweb overspreads them with his delicate covering to receive the Fairy Queen, and as she sleeps, her "spirits cooled," and her "heart comforted" by the perfumes which Peaseblossom scatters, Moth fans her with his noiseless wings, and Mustardseed stands ready to spring up to obey her hest or know what is her will.

---

[1] Compare Oberon with Pan as described in the essay by Bacon and in the *De Augmentis.* The universal nature of things, which has its origin from confused matter; the hairiness of his body representing *the rays of things;* his control over the nature and fates of things — as Oberon, in the play, is seen to regulate the general course of events.

Those fairies were the children of an idle brain — considering whose brain it was. Troubles which were but as a summer cloud, in comparison to the storms which broke over his later life, had lately passed away when that rare vision was dreamed. The pert and nimble spirit of mirth was again wide-awake. Francis Bacon's pretty device, *The Masque of the Indian Boy*, had lately been performed before the Queen ; his mind was full of thoughts such as pervade that little, courtly piece, when, in the glades and river-scenes of Twickenham, the poet, as we believe, on some hot summer's night, wrote his fairy story.

Things had changed when he set his pen to write *Macbeth*. "There's nothing either good or ill but thinking makes it so." The world and its joys had grown dark to Francis Bacon, and the very elements, the powers of nature, turned wild and gloomy in the distracted globe of his great mind.

The winds are no longer "frivolous," "dancing," "piping," and whistling to each other," "gamboling with golden locks," "playing with the sedges." They are now the powerful and portentous ministers of fate as well as of nature; their realm is full of hurly-burly, fog and filthy air; their nature, *still spiritual*, is no longer fairy-like, but witch-like and demoniacal. The beneficent merry spirits have been transformed into the evil geniuses and hell-hags, whose mission is to confound unity, to lead men on to their destruction, to tumble all nature together, even till destruction sickens.

The witches of *Macbeth* have about them some points which distinguish them from all other beings of the kind with whom literature acquaints us. They seem to have been created in the poet's brain by a subtle blending or fusion of his lawyer's experience in trials for witchcraft — of " witches, inhabitants of earth " — with his scientific and metaphysical investigations and conceits as to the properties and " versions " of air, breath, and water ; of the " transmissions of spiritual species ; " of " the operations of sympathy in things which have been contiguous." Bacon's witches, inhabitants rather of the air and clouds than of the earth, partake (by sympathy with the elements to which they are " contiguous ") of the virtues and characteristics of

air, vapours, and exhalations. It was a recognised characteristic of witches, that they ride through the air generally on
broomsticks, and vanish, but the more poetical idea of their
conversion, at pleasure, into the elements to which they are
made kindred, is, we believe, only to be found in *Macbeth.*

In the few descriptive words of Macbeth and Banquo[1] the
scientific doctrine of the convertibility of air, vapour, and water
is clearly seen, and with it the poetical and very Baconian
doctrine of the mutual influence of body and spirit. It is *by
sympathy* that the witches can turn themselves into either form.
Spirits they are, airy, or " pneumatic bodies, which partake
both of an oily and watery substance, and which, being converted
into a pneumatic substance, constitute a body composed, as it
were, of air and flame, and combining the mysterious properties
of both. Now, these bodies," continues Bacon, " *are of the
nature of breaths.*"

The witches vanish, and Banquo exclaims:

> " *The earth has bubbles* as the water hath,
> And *these are of them.* Whither are they vanished?"

Macbeth replies:

> " *Into the air: and what seemed corporal, melted
> As breath, into the wind.* "

So, too, he describes to Lady Macbeth how, when he tried to
question the witches:

> " *They made themselves air, into which they vanished.*"

There is in this line something singularly weird, supernatural,
and poetic, drawn. as it surely is, and as Bacon tells us that all
great sayings are drawn, from the very centre of the sciences.

The witches, in the first act, appear to be incarnations of air,
in violent agitation or motion; strong winds, accompanied by
thunder and lightning, such as Bacon describes. In the third
scene two witches, spirits of air, offer to help Hecate by the
gift of a wind. They are more generous than the aërial spirits
mentioned in the *Anatomy,* who " *sell* winds," and Hecate

---

[1] Macbeth, i. 3, 79–82.

acknowledges their merit. "*Thou art kind*," she says, for she is busy raising tempest after the manner described by Bacon,[1] and an extra wind or so is not unacceptable.

In the same scene the weird sisters describe themselves as:

"Posters of the sea and land,"

just as, in the *History of Winds*, Bacon speaks of "clouds that *drive fast*," "winds *traders* in vapours," "winds that are *itinerant*."

It may be remembered that the aërial spirits were specially described in the *Anatomy* as causing tempests in which they *tear oaks, fire steeples*, cause *sickness, shipwrecks*, and *inundations*. A similar description is given in the *History of Winds and of the Management of Ships*. "Winds are like great waves of the air. . . . They may *blow down trees;* . . . they may likewise *overturn edifices;* but the more solid structures they cannot destroy, unless accompanied by earthquakes. Sometimes they hurl down avalanches from the mountains so as almost to bury the plains beneath them; sometimes they cause great inundations of water."

See how all these points are reproduced by Macbeth when he conjures the witches :

> *Macb.* I conjure you, by that which you profess,
> Howe'er you come to know it, answer me :
> Though you untie the winds and let them fight
> Against the churches; though the yesty waves
> Confound and swallow navigation up ;
> Though bladed corn be lodged and trees blown down ;
> Though castles topple on their warders' heads ;
> Though palaces and pyramids do slope
> Their heads to their foundations; though the treasure
> Of nature's germens tumble altogether,
> Even till destruction sicken; answer me
> To what I ask you.[2]

The meetings of the witches in every case derive their picturesqueness and colour from Bacon's notes "on the meetings of the winds together, which, if the winds be strong, produce vio-

---

[1] See Hist. of Winds, Sylva Sylvarum, and the passage from the *Anatomy*, quoted *ante*.

[2] *Macb.* iv. i.

lent whirlwinds," and it is interesting to find that the hint for
" *the sound of battle in the air,*" and which is introduced as a
portent in *Julius Cæsar* —

" The noise of battle hurtled in the air" 1

(and which, by the way, is also included in the notes of the
Anatomist — " Counterfeit armies *in the air, strange noises,
swords,* etc.) — was originally taken from the poet Virgil, from
whom, indeed, the idea of the meeting of the four witches, as
of " *the rushing together of the four winds,*" may have been
taken.

" Virgil . . . was by no means ignorant of Natural Philosophy."
" At once the winds rush forth, the east, and south, and southwest laden with storms." 2

And again:

" I have seen *all the battles of the winds* meet together in the air." 3

In the *Tempest* much of the fun and sprightliness of the *Midsummer Night's Dream* peeps out again, and the "'gross matter "
of prosaic scientific notes is again vapourized into ideas as light
as the airs of the enchanted isle of which the poet-philosopher
wrote.

" Inquire," says the *History,* " into the nature of the winds,
whether some are not *free ?* . . . What do *mountains* contribute
to them ? "

Prospero says to Ariel: " Thou shalt be *free as mountain
winds.*"

" The poets," continues the *History,* " have feigned that the
Kingdom of Sol was situated in subterranean dens and caverns,
where the winds are imprisoned, and whence *they were occasionally let loose. . . . The air will submit to some compression. . . .*
At Aber Barry there is a rocky cliff filled with holes, to which
if a man apply his ear, he will hear *sounds and murmurs.*" In
Potosi are *vents* for hot blasts."

---

1 *Jul. Cæs.* ii. 2. 2 Æneid, i. 85, quoted in *Hist. of Winds.* 3 Georgics, i. 318,
and compare *Macbeth,* ii. 3, 55, 60.

Prospero reminds Ariel of his miserable condition as *an imprisoned bird* under the control of the witch Sycorax, and of how he had to *submit to painful compression*, " *venting* his groans " for a dozen years. He threatens further punishment if Ariel continues to murmur :

> And, for thou wast a spirit too delicate
> To act her earthy and abhorr'd commands,
> Refusing her grand hests, she did confine thee,
> By help of her more potent ministers
> And in her most unmitigable rage,
> Into a cloven pine; within which rift
> Imprison'd thou didst painfully remain
> A dozen years; within which space she died
> And left thee there; where thou didst vent thy groans
> As fast as mill-wheels strike.
>
> .   .   .   .
>
>   Thou best know'st
> What torment I did find thee in; thy groans
> Did make wolves howl and penetrate the breasts
> Of ever angry bears : it was a torment
> To lay upon the damn'd, which Sycorax
> Could not again undo : it was mine art,
> When I arrived and heard thee, that made gape
> The pine and let thee out.
>   *Ari.*   I thank thee, master.
>   *Pr.* If thou more murmur'st, I will rend an oak
> And peg thee in his knotty entrails till
> Thou hast howl'd away twelve winters.[1]

Sooner than undergo any further compression Ariel asks pardon, and promises to do his spiriting gently. Prospero then commands him to make a " version " of himself from air into water (a converse process to that performed by the witches).

" Go, make thyself a nymph of the sea."

" No wonder," Bacon reflects, " that the nature of the winds is ranked amongst the things mysterious and concealed, when the power and nature of the air which the winds *attend and serve* is entirely unknown. . . . Inquire into the nature of the

---

1 *Tempest,* i. 2.

attendant winds, their community, etc." This mysterious and concealed characteristic of the winds is hinted when Ariel *disguises* himself, and appears as a harpy. " I and *my fellows,* " he says, " are ministers of fate," incapable of injury, " invulnerable."

The winds have " *a power of conveying spiritual species, that is, sounds, radiations, and the like;* " these Bacon would have inquired into. The excited imagination and uneasy conscience of Alonzo make him nervously impressionable, and able to recognise these spiritual sounds:

> *Alon.*　　Oh, it is monstrous, monstrous!
> Methought the billows spoke and told me of it;
> The winds did sing it to me, and the thunder,
> That deep and dreadful organ-pipe, pronounced
> The name of Prosper: it did bass my trespass.[1]

A passage which, in gloomier and more tragic language, is echoed in *Macbeth:*

> And pity, like a naked new-born babe,
> Striding the blast, or heaven's cherubim, horsed
> Upon the sightless couriers of the air,
> Shall blow the horrid deed in every eye,
> That tears shall drown the wind. [2]

The notes on the tremendous force of the winds are once more distilled into verse in the *Tempest,* where, also, the gentler winds are described " *driving on the tides and currents, sometimes propelling, and sometimes flying from one another, as if in sport.* " These winds, weak masters though they be, assist, Bacon says, in promoting an " agitation " and " collision " amongst the violent winds, and " *drive them along in mad fury.* " In other words, the tempest, raised by the attendant and ministering winds, is combined with an earthquake, over which the winds have no control, but which the magician has caused by his art.

---

1 *Tempest,* iii. 3.

2 *Macbeth,* i. 7.　　The last line seems to refer to Bacon's observation that " *showers generally allay the winds, especially if they be stormy.* "

See the lovely creation from these elements:

> *Pros.* Ye elves of hills, brooks, standing lakes and groves,
> And ye that on the sands with printless foot
> Do chase the ebbing Neptune and do fly him
> When he comes back; you demi-puppets that
> By moonshine do the green-sour ringlets make,
> Whereof the ewe not bites, and you whose pastime
> Is to make midnight mushrooms, that rejoice
> To hear the solemn curfew; by whose aid,
> Weak masters though ye be, I have bedimm'd
> The noontide sun, call'd forth the mutinous winds,
> And 'twixt the green sea and the azured vault
> Set roaring war: to the dread rattling thunder
> Have I given fire and rifted Jove's stout oak
> With his own bolt; the strong-based promontory
> Have I made shake, and by the spurs pluck'd up
> The pine and cedar: graves at my command
> Have waked their sleepers, oped, and let 'em forth
> By my so potent art.

These lines give us hints of Bacon's curious " Experiments
Touching the Rudiments of Plants, of Excrescences," etc.
" Moss," he says, " cometh of moisture," and is made of the
sap of the tree " which is not so frank as to rise all the boughs,
but *tireth by the way and putteth out moss.*" [1] A quaint idea!
full of that Paracelsian notion of the spirits or souls of things,
and very Baconian, too.   Bacon thought that the winds had
something to do with such growths, for trees are said to bear
most moss that " stand bleak and upon the winds."   Next to
moss he speaks of *mushrooms*, which he associates with moss,
as being " likewise an imperfect plant."   Mushrooms have two
strange properties. " the one is, they yield so delicious a meat "
(therefore they are deserving of the fairies' trouble in growing
them); " the other, that *they come up so hastily, and yet they are
unsown* " (and how could that be except they were sown by the
fairies?).   Like moss, " they come of moisture, and are *windy,
but the windiness is not sharp and griping;*" they are, therefore,
unlike " the green-sour ringlets " which the fairies make in the

---

1 Nat. Hist. vi. 540.

moonlight (where, Bacon says, *nothing will ripen*), and which even the sheep will not eat, though sheep love mushrooms.

The wind-fairies " *rejoice to hear the solemn curfew.*" This tells us that these are the south winds, " *for the south wind is the attendant of the night; it rises in the night, and blows stronger.*" [1]

The south and west winds, too, are " warm and moist, favourable to plants, flowers, and all vegetation ; " hence the mushrooms spring up quickly under their influence.

But the north winds are " more potent ministers ; " with them occur " thunder, lightning, and tornadoes, accompanied with cold and hail." [2]   They are " *unfriendly,*" and even destructive to vegetable life, and either " *bind the flower on the opening of it,* or *shake it off.*" [3]

> "The tyrannous breathing of the north
> Shakes all our buds from growing." [4]

" Storms, " continues our observant naturalist, " when *attended with clouds and fog, are very dangerous at sea.*" Prospero, therefore, to make his tempest the more terrible, " *bedims the noontide sun,*" before calling forth the winds and the thunder. [5]

" The anniversary north winds " come " *from the frozen sea, and the region about the Arctic Circle,* where *the ice and snow are not melted till the summer is far advanced.*" Prospero taunts Ariel :

> " Thou think'st it much to tread the ooze
> Of the salt deep,
> *To run upon the sharp wind of the north
> When it is bak'd with frost.*"

The last lines seem to be suggested by the Latin entry in the *Promus* (No. 1367):   " *Frigus adurit.*"

The idea is repeated in *Hamlet:*

> " Frost itself as actively doth *burn.*" [6]

---

1 Hist. Winds, 1, 2, 10, 12, etc., qualities and powers.

2 Comp. *Macb.* i. 1, 2.   *Ham.* v. 2, 97.

3 Ib. 21, 24.   4 *Cymb.* i. 4.

5 Compare. *Macb.* i. 1, of the witches' storms.

6 *Hamlet,* iii. 4.

The philosophic poet does not forget to allude to the effects of " *warm* winds and *moist* airs in inducing putrefaction, " and in " increasing pestilential diseases and catarrhs. " Caliban's worst imprecation (which, by the way, personifies even dew in true Paracelsian style) is this:

> " As *wicked* dew as e'er my mother brush'd
> With raven's feather from unwholesome fen
> Drop on you both! *A southwest blow on ye*
> *And blister you all o'er.*"

Prospero is equal to the occasion, and answers him in kind:

> "For this, be sure, thou shalt have cramps,
> Side stitches that shall pen thy breath up.
> . . . I'll rack thee with old cramps,
> Fill all thy bones with aches. " [1]

Bacon's cogitations on winds, contagion, putrefaction, and the doctrines of the human body, of the biform figure of nature, and of the sensitive soul, are inextricably interwoven in the Shakespeare plays of the later period. . It is not the intention of this book to enter deeply into anything; the aim is to excite interest, even *opposition*, if that will promote study, and at least to encourage our younger readers to believe that all is not yet known on any of these subjects, and that vast fields of delightful and profitable research lie open for them to explore, delve into, and cultivate. But in order to do this, it is quite certain that the tool absolutely indispensable is a knowledge of Bacon's works — not only of those little pithy essays which embody all that the ordinary reader conceives as Bacon's writings, exclusive of " exploded science, " and law tracts and speeches, too dull to be tackled. Let those who are of this mind take those very works and read them with the belief that they are the keys to all the great literature of the sixteenth and seventeenth centuries; the touchstones by which the authorship of other works may be tried; sketches for finished pictures or condensed editions of more casual and discursive works of Bacon's early

---

[1] *Tempest*, i. 2, and compare where Thersites curses Patroclus (*Troilus and Cressida*, v. 1), and where Marcius curses the Romans (*Coriol.* i. 4, 30, etc.).

days. Let them think that even with regard to the Shake-speare plays only these little-read scientific works of Bacon are invaluable, explaining or elucidating, as they so often do, the meaning or original idea of obscure passages, and often enabling the commentator to trace the thought to some author of antiquity, or to some observation drawn from " nature's infinite book of secresy," in which, says the poet, "a little I can read."

The last scene in *The Tempest* shows us the philosopher returning from the " recreative " writing, which relieved the overflowing of a full brain, to the graver labours and contemplations which drew Bacon to the retirement of his " full poor cell." Play-time was over, and " these things are but toys."

> " Our revels now are ended. These our actors,
> As I foretold you, were all spirits and
> Are melted into air, into thin air :
> And, like the baseless fabric of this vision,
> The cloud-capp'd towers, the gorgeous palaces,
> The solemn temples, the great globe itself,
> Yea, all which it inherit, shall dissolve
> And, like this insubstantial pageant faded,
> Leave not a rack behind. We are such stuff
> As dreams are made on, and our little life
> Is rounded with a sleep. Sir, I am vex'd;
> Bear with my weakness ; my old brain is troubled;
> Be not disturb'd with my infirmity:
> If you be pleased, retire into my cell
> And there repose: a turn or two I'll walk,
> To still my beating mind."

CHAPTER IX.

MASONRY.

> "If I mistake
> In those foundations which I build upon,
> The centre is not strong enough to bear
> A schoolboy's top."
> — *Winter's Tale.*

ACCORDING to many books on Freemasonry, the "*Rosicrucians had no connection with the Masonic fraternity.*" In the face of collective evidence to the contrary, it is very difficult for non-Masonic people to credit the statement; it would rather seem as if the desire of Masonic writers to draw a hard and fast line between the two societies were confirmatory of hints dropped in certain books concerning schisms which, during the last two centuries, have occurred amongst the brethren or brotherhoods. Originally one and the same, alike in aims, alike in symbolic language, with similar traditions tracing back to similar origins, some, at least, of the members supposed to have constituted the Rosicrucian society actually were, we find, members of the Freemason lodge. The only conspicuous differences which appear to have existed three hundred years ago were: (1) That the Rosicrucians were distinctly Christian and church people, and that the magnificent literature brought out under their auspices was all either religious or written with an elevating tendency, invariably loyal, patriotic, and unselfish. (2) That the society was unostentatious and retiring to such an extent as to gain the name of the Invisible Brotherhood. It laboured silently and secretly for the good of men, but not to be seen of men. It went not to church with brass bands and banners; neither did it assume magniloquent titles or garments and decorations of obsolete or grotesque quaintness.

The Rosicrucians were and are a powerful, but unobtrusive, Christian literary society. The Freemasons are, we believe, the lower orders of the same; deists, but not necessarily Christians; moral, but not necessarily religious; bent on benefiting the human race by all means humanitarian and chiefly devoting themselves to the development of the practical side of life; to architecture, printing, medicine, surgery, etc.; to the arts and crafts, the habitations, the recreations of the million. It is easy to see that, in the first instance, such societies might have worked as part of one system. Whether or not they continue in any degree so to work, we cannot positively say; but it seems to the mere looker-on as if, *once one*, the society divided, subdivided, and in its lower branches underwent such changes as to be not only divergent, but, at the present day, different in character and aim. We speak, hoping to be contradicted, and give, as an instance, that the Freemasonry of Germany seems to differ very much from that of the most respectable lodges of England, being in some cases not only *not Christian*, but not even deistic; on the contrary, persons professedly atheists are enrolled amongst its members, and this miserable degradation of the brotherhood has, we are told, unhappily extended to England and America. Need it be said that to atheism and irreligion is too frequently added the so-called socialism, which has, in these later days, done so much to stir up discontent where content reigned, destroying order and respect for authority, and setting men by the ears who should be joined for mutual aid.

Of course, this is the bad and dark side of the question; there is a very bright side, too, and researches (we cannot say *inquiries*, for they are fruitless) encourage us to hope that there are signs, either of the " drawing together " of opposite parties, for which Bacon so earnestly strove, or else that the much-suppressed Rosicrucians, the gallant little band who held together through all the stormy times of the Puritans, the civil wars, the Restoration, and the many subsequent troubles, are now rapidly multiplying in number, increasing in power, and everywhere extending their beneficent operations. " By their fruits ye shall know them. "

But all this is, after all, mere conjecture; it is only submitted as such in order that others may pin down these statements, proving or disproving them. Having no means of doing so, we fall back, for the present, upon our old plan of quoting " the best authorities," and when, as is frequently the case, these doctors disagree, readers will, perhaps, cross-examine them, and decide between them.

Dr. Mackey is positive that the Rosicrucians have no connection with the Masons. He is indignant that any one should doubt this. " Notwithstanding *this fact*," says the Doctor (but bringing no proof of the fact), " Barnel, the most malignant of our revilers, with a characteristic spirit of misrepresentation, attempted to identify the two institutions. This is an error into which others might unwittingly fall, from confounding the *Prince of Rose Croix*, a Masonic degree somewhat similar in name, but entirely different in character." Here, again, it is not explained how the writer has become so intimately acquainted with the characteristics of the Rosicrucians, seeing that he is not himself an initiate of that brotherhood. He proceeds in the same strain of assertion, without proof: " *The Rosicrucians do not derive their name, like Rose Croix Masons, from the rose and cross, for they have nothing to do with the rose*, but with the Latin *ros*, dew, and crux, the cross, as a hieroglyphic of light. . . . A Rosicrucian philosopher is one who, by the assistance of dew (previously explained as the most powerful solvent of gold) seeks for light, or the philosopher's stone." [1]

This author is evidently possessed with the notion that there is something rather discreditable in Rosicrucianism, for he concludes with an apology for having introduced the subject, which only a fear of the error into which Masons might unwittingly fall would, apparently, have induced him to touch upon.

Another work of the same kind has a long article on Rosicrucianism, in which all the old traditions and errors are repeated: that the Rosy Cross brethren were alchemists; that their origin was of great antiquity, etc.; adding, also, other errors, namely,

---

[1] Lexicon of Freemasonry, A. G. Mackey, D. D. (Griffin & Co., Exeter St., Strand), 7th edition, 1883.

that " the fraternity seldom had meetings together," and that
" its corporate character was by no means marked." The
writer, who evidently takes a much more correct view of the
aims of the society than his predecessor, yet adds this statement: " The modern society of Rosicrucians is constituted upon
a widely different basis than that of the parent society. While
the adepts of former times were contented with the knowledge of
their mutual obligations, and observed them as a matter of course
and custom, the eighteenth century Rosicrucians forced the
world to think that, for a time, they were not only the procursors
of Masonry, but, *in essentia,* that body itself. This has led to many
misconceptions. *With Freemasonry the occult fraternity has only
this much to do, i. e., that some of the Rosicrucians were also Freemasons;* and this idea was strengthened by the fact that a portion of the *curriculum* of a Rosicrucian consisted in theosophy;
these bodies had, however, no other substantial connective ties.
In fact, Freemasons have never actually laid claim to the possession of alchymical secrets. Starting from a definite legend —
that of the building of Solomon's temple — they have merely
moralised on life, death, and the resurrection." But this, we
know, is the same definite legend from which the Rosicrucians
started, and they moralised after the same fashion, and in the
same strictly Baconian manner, metaphorically and by analogy;
or, as our author here formidably puts it, " correspondentially
with the increase and decrease and the palingenesia of nature."
He pays a proper tribute to the superiority of the Rosicrucians
over the Freemasons when he says that, as the science of mathematics contains the rude germs of things, and the science of
words comprehends the application of these forms and intellectual purification, so " the Rosicrucian doctrine specifically
pointed out the uses and inter-relations between the qualities
and substances in nature, although their enlarged ideas admitted of a moral survey. *The Freemasons, while they have deserved the esteem of mankind for charity and works of love, have
never accomplished, and, by their inherent sphere of operation,
never can accomplish, what these isolated students effected.*"

But, although the extent and precise nature of the connection between the two societies may not be accurately definable; though, indeed, it may be unknown, excepting to a select few, in the very highest degree of initiation, yet, the ceremonies and symbols of this degree of Prince Rouge Croix approach more nearly to those of the Rosy Cross Brotherhood than they do even to other degrees of their own Masonic lodges. For the *Rose Croix* alone, of all the degrees in Masonry, is said by "the best authorities" to be "eminently a *Christian* degree," and hence unattainable by an immense number of Masons. We observe, moreover, that the "monk" mentioned by the Masonic writer whom we are about to cite is none other than our old friend Johann Valentin Andreas, the formerly accredited author of the "*Chemical Marriage of Christian Rosenkreuz*," which we now find to have been written by Francis Bacon at the age of fifteen.

It will also be observed in the following extracts that *Ragon* attributes to Andreas the same motive for inaugurating the secret society as that which chiefly influenced Bacon, the grief, namely, which he felt at the loss of truth through vain disputes and pedantic pride. *Clavel*, as we shall see, adds another thread to strengthen the evidence which we have collected to show that, whilst on the one hand the Rosicrucians were bound in every way to oppose the bigotry and superstition of the Church of Rome, and the anti-Christian pretences of the pope to infallibility, yet it was not the *Church* of Rome, or its chief head or pope, against which the Rosy Cross brothers were militant; it was against *the errors, the bigotry and superstition* which that church indulged in; against the *ignorance and darkness* in which the mass of its members were intentionally kept by its priesthood. The highly cultivated and sometimes heavenly-minded members of the Society of Jesus must doubtless have often had reason to share the distress attributed to the monk Andreas, and we think that it will probably be found that the Rosy Cross brethren did, in fact, obtain great, though secret, help from the more liberal amongst the Jesuit communities.

Ragon, in his treatise entitled *Orthodoxie Maçonnique*, attributes the origin of the Eighteenth Degree, or the "Sovereign

Prince of Rose-Croix Heredom," to a pious monk named John
Valentine Andreas, who flourished in the early part of the seventeenth century, and who wrote, amongst other works, two treatises, one entitled *Judicorum de Fraternitate R. C.*, the other
Noces Chimiques de Rozen Crutz. Ragon says that Andreas,
grieved at seeing the principles of Christianity forgotten in idle
and vain disputes, and that science was made subservient to
the pride of man, instead of contributing to his happiness,
passed his days in devising what he supposed to be the most
appropriate means of restoring each to its legitimate moral and
benevolent tendency. Clavel absurdly affirms that the degree
was founded by the Jesuits, for the purpose of counteracting
the insidious attacks of free-thinkers upon the Romish faith,
but he offers no evidence in support of his assertion; in fact,
the Jesuits were the great enemies of Masonry, and, so far from
supporting it, wrote treatises against the order. Many of the
Rosicrucians were amongst the reformers of the age, and hence
the hostility of the Romish Church. The almost universal recognition of this degree in all countries would favour the theory
of its being of long standing.

Hurd, in his *Treatise on Religions*, speaks of the Brethren of
the Rose, or *Ne Plus Ultra.* " They were to declare openly that
the Pope was Antichrist, and that the time would come when
they should pull down his triple crown. . . . They claimed a
right of naming their successors, and bequeathing to them all
their privileges; to keep the devil in subjection; and that their
fraternity could not be destroyed, because God always opposed
an impenetrable cloud to screen them from their enemies."

Rosetti, in his work on the Antipapal Spirit of Italy, asserts
similar statements with regard to this and other societies connected with Freemasonry. *" The ceremonies of the degree of the
Rose-Croix are of the most imposing and impressive character,
and it is eminently a Christian degree.* Its ritual is remarkable
for elegance of diction, while the symbolic teaching is not only
pleasing, but consistent with the Christian faith, figuratively
expressing the passage of man through the valley of the shadow
of death, accompanied and sustained by the Masonic virtues —

faith, hope, and charity — and his final reception into the abode of light, life, and immortality." [1]

In the Rose-Croix transparency which is used during the ceremonies there is a cross of Calvary raised on three steps. On the cross is hung a crown of thorns with one large rose in the centre; two smaller crosses are on either side, with skulls and cross-bones.

These symbols would alone be almost sufficient to satisfy our readers of the Christian character of that degree; but the jewel worn by the initiate is even more distinct in its announcement. This jewel includes all the most important symbols of the degree. It is a golden compass, extended on an arc to twenty-two and a half degrees, or the sixteenth part of a circle; the head of the compass is surmounted by a crown with seven emerald points. The compass encloses a cross of Calvary formed of rubies or garnets, having in its centre a full-blown rose, whose stem twines round the lower limb of the cross. At the foot of the cross is a pelican, wounding her breast to feed her young, which are in a nest beneath.

On the reverse is an eagle instead of the pelican, and on the arc of the circle is engraved in cipher the pass-word of the degree. [2]

Taking all things together, evidence favours the following conclusions with regard to the Rosicrucians and the Freemasons:

1. That the aims of the Freemasons are (in a lower degree) much the same as those of the Rosicrucians.

2. That the Masons begin by meeting on a common platform of humanity, and that they propose to raise their initiates step by step to a somewhat higher level.

3. That their highest level is a kind of theosophy or deism, or at least that no more than this is *required*, excepting in the

---

[1] From the Freemason's Manual, J. How, K. T. 30°, pp. 272-3, 3rd edn. revised and illustrated. J. Hogg, London, 1881.

[2] How's Manual. For the meaning of the symbols above mentioned, see *ante*, Emblems and Symbols.

Rose Croix degree.[1] Here the Rosicrucians, therefore, seem to part from them, and to continue to mount. Whereas with the Freemasons Christ and his church are practically ignored, with the Rosicrucians Christianity is the life and soul of all that they have done, and are doing. Whereas the words " Christ, " " Church, " " Religion, " are almost banished from Freemason books, the mighty literature of the sixteenth and seventeenth centuries, and all that is good, great, and enduring in the present age, will probably be traced to the agency of this uni · versal church literary society.

4. There seems to be no evidence that Freemasonry, in the present acceptation of the term, or as a mutual benefit society, existed before the middle of the sixteenth century. Church architects and builders, who had secrets of their own, and to whom, probably, we owe the magnificent structures which continue to be models to our own time, were a trade guild and a church guild too. Their secrets were of the nature of the printer's secrets of the present day, not only for mutual use and protection, but also enclosing certain information to their craft, and, perhaps, to a select few, beyond that enchanted circle. But in no way can we say that these old builders filled the places of the ubiquitous, many-headed Freemasons. Moreover, if we mix them up with the Knights of St. John of Jerusalem, we still find ourselves linked with " the Holy Catholic Church " of our forefathers, to which the Rosicrucians were inseparably bound, but from which the Freemason writers seem most anxious to separate themselves.

Hepworth Dixon[2] tells us that the scheme which Sir Nicholas Bacon presented to Henry VIII. for the endowment of a school of law, policy, and languages, in London, was, perhaps, the

---

1 In connection with the Rose Croix degree, it may be observed, says the same authority, that the initials of the Latin inscription placed on the cross, I. N. R. I., representing *Jesus Nazarenus, Rex Judæorum*, were used by the Rosicrucians as the initials of their Hermetic Secrets — *Igne Natura Renovatur Integra* — " By fire, Nature is perfectly renewed." They also adopted them to express the names of their three elementary principles, Salt, Sulphur, and Mercury, by making the initials of the sentence, *Igne Nitrum Roris Invenitur.*

2 *Story of Bacon's Life,* p. 17.

original germ of the *New Atlantis;* the idea being transferred from statecraft to nature. It is, therefore, possible that Francis Bacon, whose admiration and reverence for his father is very perceptible, may have considered that the foundation-stone of his Solomon's House was laid by Sir Nicholas. Nowhere can we find irrefutable statements or proofs that this society had any earlier history. The professed records of its antiquity seem, like the similar records of the Rosicrucians, to be fictitious, mere shams, which cannot pass current amongst initiated readers; playing upon words, intended to convey to some members a knowledge or reminder of their true origin, whilst veiling it from the profane vulgar.

The object of this concealment was probably the same as with the greater mysteries of the Rosicrucians, and two-fold. It enabled the society to work more freely, and unsuspected of dangerous or reforming aims. It also bestowed upon the fraternity a fictitious dignity and importance, by the glamour shed over its ceremonies of a supposed "antiquity," which, as Bacon shows, men are prone to adore; for in history, as in other matters, we often see " 'tis distance lends enchantment to the view." Moreover, Freemasonry frequently lay under the charge of irreligion, not always without cause. Yet the goodness of the institution should not be rashly maligned because of the wickedness or weakness of some of its members, and its " authorities " come forward to defend it from this charge.

" *Masonry is not an irreligious institution*, but it assumes no special dogmatic form; it demands at the hands of its candidates a sincere and honest belief in a Creative Being, ever attentive to the honourable aspirations of those who seek Him in spirit and in truth, and it rejects with scorn those who would degrade the Contriver into a part of the contrivances, and thus would set bounds to the limitless Author of all Being." [1]

The estimation in which the Masons hold themselves is so amusing to non-Masons, and their traditions concerning themselves so quaint, that we cannot refrain from quoting a few passages:

---

[1] Royal Masonic Cyclopædia.

" Freemasonry is undoubtedly the oldest society in the world, and it is not a political, but a religious society, strange as such an assertion must be to the uninitiated. Before letters were invented, the only means of teaching divine truths, and handing down divine traditions, was by symbols and signs. In that way, before the deluge, the people of the old world had the whole history of the creation, the fall of our first parents, etc., handed down to them by tradition in the primitive lodges, the serpent being a common symbol employed for the purpose then, as it has been since. After the deluge, the ark became one of the commonest symbols, and the history of that event was thereby taught to the initiated. *A lodge must have been in full working order on the plains of Shinar during the lifetime of Noah:* for, when the dispersion took place, lodges of a similar nature were established in every part of the world, though, probably, not for many years after the settlement of the emigrants in their new countries. . . . They all, however, used the same symbols, and it has generally been admitted by scholars that they had one common origin. *That common origin was Freemasonry.* . . . According to the traditions of our venerable society, *Enoch was a very eminent Mason,* and preserved the true name of God, which the Jews subsequently lost. The descendants of Abraham write it Jao; in the mysteries it was Om, but most commonly expressed in a triliteral form, Aum, as we learn from Wilkins' notes on Bhagvat Veta. Both in the genuine and spurious lodges the doctrine of a trinity in unity was taught.

" The Mysteries, *or spurious Masonic rites,* were introduced into India by Brahma; into Egypt by Thoth; into China and Japan by Buddha; into Persia by Zeradusht, *i. e.,* Zoroaster; into Greece by Melampus, according to Herodotus, ii. 4, or by Cadmus, according to Epiphanius; into Boetia by Prometheus; into Samothrace by Dardanus; into Crete by Minos; into Athens by Erectheus; into Thrace by Orpheus; into Italy by Pelasgis; into Gaul and Britain by Gomer; into Scandinavia by Odin; into Mexico by Vitziphtzli (Purch. viii. 10); and into Peru by Manco Capac." [1]

There is no date to the little tract at the British Museum from which these extracts are made, but it seems to be of recent production, and continues throughout in the same strain, assuming that *because* ancient symbols are introduced into Masonic lan-

---

[1] Freemasonry: An Address. Bro. J. Milner, M. A., F. R. G. S. Lond.: Simpkin, Marshall & Co.

guage and ceremonies, *therefore* Masonry is of extremest antiquity.

This same line of argument is adopted in many books which
seem to be of Freemason extraction, and in some of the
modern anti-Christian works on Buddhism and "Theosophy."
These go farther still, maintaining not only the superior antiquity, but the superior beauty and value of the religions of *India
and Arabia*, which, well suited as they doubtless were to the
rude or ignorant minds which they were to impress, can only be
regarded by Christians as gropings before daylight, or as the
altars erected by ignorant but well-meaning worshippers of the
unknown God.

In the ancient mysteries, all sorts of uncomfortable methods
were resorted to in order to test the nerves and constancy of the
initiate. He was made suddenly to see great lights which were
as suddenly eclipsed, leaving him plunged in total darkness.
Terrible sounds and sights were in succession forced upon him.
Thunder and lightning, visions of hideous monsters and horri-
ble objects were designed to fill him with awe and consternation.
Finally he was restored to daylight, and to a delightful calm in
a lovely garden, where music and dancing revived his spirits,
and, perhaps, charmed him the more by reason of all the horrors
to which he had been subjected. It seems to have been held as
a crime, punishable only by death, for a man to reveal what he
had seen in these mysteries, which for ages were kept secret.
But, as with the somewhat similar ordeals which are said to be
imposed upon Masonic initiates, the secrets which now seem to
us foolish, and almost cruel, have leaked out by some means or
another. In the present day such things appear to be anachronisms, and profane rather than impressive. Nevertheless, they
would, doubtless, have an effect on weak nerves, and may possibly aid in deterring the lower orders of initiates from revealing
these secrets, or others of greater importance.

In all cases *initiation* represents death, and a *renaissance* or
renovation, a new birth, not a *resurrection from the dead*. " In
the British mysteries, the noviciate passed the River of Death in
the boat of Garanhir, the Charon of antiquity (the boat typified

the corporal body); and before he could be admitted to this
privilege, it was requisite that he should be mystically buried,
as well as mystically dead, which is implied in the ancient Greek
formulary, 'I was covered in the bed,' the body being a sort of
grave or bed of the spirit." [1]   With the Freemasons, this symbolic death and burial is or was initiated by the ceremony of
putting the noviolate into a coffin and covering him with a pall.
We have heard, but cannot answer for the fact, of a young man
who fainted under this " nerve test." It is hard to conceive
that such things should be done in civilised countries at the
present hour, and if it be true that they are yet practiced, it
must be that vows taken by the initiates bind them to continue
a system which, at its first invention, had some use in conveying
certain instruction to very rude minds, incapable of otherwise
receiving it.

The earliest Rosicrucian documents do not enforce the special
doctrines of any church. The later documents are, however,
professedly Christian. We know that Bacon " was religious;
. . . well able to render a reason of the hope which was in him; "
that he conformed to the ordinances of the Christian religion; [2]
that he died in the communion of the Church of England; and
the thought suggests itself that, during the period of his life
when he was " running through the whole round " of the
ancient philosophies (a terrible and unsettling process to young,
excitable minds)—at that time, when his ardent soul was
striving after definite truth, and trying to free itself from the
clouds of error, bigotry, and superstition which obscured it—he
may have found himself, like Malvolio, " more puzzled than the
Egyptians in their fog." Besides this, the quarrels and divission
on religious questions sorely disturbed him.   He could not
believe in the religion of men who hated each other, who would
" dash the first table against the second, and who would so act
as Christians as to make us forget that they are men." Such

---

1 *The Book of God*, vol. ii. p. 125, quoting from Davies' *Mythology of the
Druids*, p. 392.

2 Life of Bacon, by his Chaplain and Secretary, p. 14.   See *ante*, Bacon's
character.

divisions, he says, " were evils *unknown to the heathen;*" yet he
lived in the very midst of such divisions. He was eleven years
old at the time of the Massacre of St. Bartholomew, when 60,000
Huguenots or Protestants were butchered by the order of
Charles IX. and his mother, the victims including Admiral de
Coligny, one of the most virtuous men that France possessed,
and the mainstay of the Protestant cause. · He was a child
when the tyranny and barbarity of the Inquisition was in full
force, and for thirty-one years of his life he was witness to the
scenes of intolerable cruelty and iniquity which were perpetrated
under the name of religion by the Spanish Tiberius, Philip II.,
not only in his own country and amongst the unhappy Moors,
but, almost worse, in Flanders or the Netherlands, where the
miserable Protestants, at first patient under the extravagant
oppression to which they were subjected, at last rebelled, and,
at the sight of the tribunals of the Inquisition erected in their
principal cities, forgot their own weakness, and, impelled by
rage and fury, pulled down churches, subverted altars, and
obliged the clergy to fly. The atrocities which followed, the
execrable cruelties which were committed, and the detestation of
the papists which was inspired in the formerly peaceable
Flemings, are matters of history. No one will read Motley's
graphic narrative of the events of this time, and marvel that a
thoughtful man, witnessing such scenes, should be led to doubt
if religion, if Christianity, in whose name such deeds of darkness
were performed, could be a true thing ?

In the *Essay of Unity*, Bacon speaks of " Lucretius, the poet,
who, when he beheld the act of Agamemnon, that could endure
the sacrificing of his own daughter, exclaimed: 'Could religion
prompt to deeds so dreadful?'   What would he have said if he
had known of the massacre in France, or the powder treason in
England? He would have been seven times more epicure and
atheist than he was."

But Bacon seems to have said to himself: " Since men thus
quarrel over their religious opinions, I will seek for some ground
upon which all mankind may meet in common consent and harmony. All men who have any claim to intelligence and goodness

acknowledge the existence of a God, an all-wise, all-powerful Being, to whom we must render an account of ourselves. Let us, then, leave quarrelling and controversies, and meet as men and brethren on this wide platform of belief in a God, and desire to benefit each other." Some such sentiment seems certainly to have been in the mind of the founder of Masonry, and, perhaps, the method adopted in rude times for enlisting the sympathies of the majority of ignorant but intelligent persons of various nationalities and creeds was the best that could be devised. There is no doubt that to the great society of the Freemasons we owe a vast debt of gratitude, for the many humanitarian works which they have inaugurated; for the many " fair houses," for purposes of charity and education, which they have reared; for many good lessons in morality and self-control which they have systematically endeavoured to teach. And yet, although the society was founded expressly to uphold order, and respect for authority, as well as to promote learning and works of charity; though its members were to consist of " *men who are not only true patriots and loyal subjects, but the patrons of science and the friends of all mankind,*" there is reason to believe that Bacon found the rules of the society, and the doctrines of pure Deism, insufficient to ensure either patriotism or loyalty; insufficient to ensure the attainment of the highest truth, or of the greatest good to the greatest number.

It is clear that he himself could not endure to remain in this low ground, and he mounted, as we have seen, into the clearest and sublimest heights to which the human intelligence or the human spirit is permitted to penetrate. Not so all his followers, if the scanty gleanings which we have been able to make in this field are of any value. There is reason to think that more than once the harmony of the Masonic brethren has been broken; selfishness, ambition, and other ills which frail humanity is heir to, and which will not be checked by any code of human laws, by morality, however philosophical; by philanthropy, however well meaning, seem to have crept in, creating quarrels and ruptures, and, doubtless, in every case, fresh divergence from the original scheme.

If we read aright some ambiguous narratives in books which are nothing if not mystical, and which bear marks of being of Masonic origin, there have been, not only quarrels, but faithless members in the society, who, instead of "handing down the lamp" which had been consigned to their charge — instead of merely preserving or publishing, in due season, some work, *not their own, have clung to it, claimed it, and endeavoured to profit by it*. Is that true, which such hints in books, endorsed by verbal information, incline us to believe, namely, that the Masons are no longer *all* "true patriots and loyal subjects," and that, *in some countries, at least,* "mutual toleration in matters of speculative opinion and belief" is no longer one of the "valuable characteristics of the craft"? These, joining to their disrespect for religion the kindred disrespect for any authority except their own, are applying themselves to degrade, if possible to demolish, all forms of church worship, defacing the Beauty of Holiness, reducing Christianity to Humanitarianism, and landing their followers in a cold agnosticism, or a worse spirit of antagonism to Christianity.

The causes of atheism are, Bacon says, "divisions in religion, scandal of priests, custom of profane scoffing in holy matters, which doth little by little deface the reverence of religion; and, lastly, learned times with peace and prosperity; for troubles and adversities do more bow men's minds to religion. They that deny a God, destroy man's nobility; for certainly man is of kin to the beasts by his body; and if he be not of kin to God by his spirit he is a base and ignoble creature. It destroys, likewise, magnanimity and the raising of human nature, . . . and as atheism is in all respects hateful, so in this, that it depriveth human nature of the means to exalt itself above human frailty."[1] Bacon's axiom, "Thought is free," expressed something very different from irreverent license of thought; neither did he advocate the idea that "the raising of human nature" was to be achieved by disregard of the Powers that be. The majority of right-minded and loyal Masons are, doubtless, of his opinion, and

---

[1] Essay Of Atheism.

it is suggested that the large and increasing number of the members of the Rose-Croix degree may be a tacit protest against the irreligious tendencies of some of the other lodges. [1] It is possible that Bacon perceived the beginnings of such deviations as have been indicated, and that his foresight as to the ultimate issue caused him to make the Rosy Cross the highest and most secret degree, the members forming a community of the ablest and most earnest and influential *Christians* in the Masonic ranks.

Since the statements and opinions of Masonic writers differ, it is, of course, impossible for a non-Mason to obtain information so accurate as to be incapable of contradiction or refutation. These remarks, therefore, are merely intended to form a basis for further inquiries and researches. *No one book must be taken as an absolute authority;* for if anything is made plain to the uninitiated student of Masonic literature, it is that comparatively few Masons know much about the true origin and aims of their own society. Books ostensibly published for the purpose of giving information consist, for the most part, of names of persons and lodges, of places and orders, with very scanty notices on any subject which will not be found discussed in ordinary cyclopædias. The Masonic books are palpably constructed so as to disclose nothing of any value; some contradict others, and doubtless they are only intended to be thoroughly useful to those who have other and verbal information imparted to them.

Under these circumstances, the most helpful plan which can be adopted seems to be to ignore recent utterances, and to give transcripts from a book whose ninth edition was published nearly a hundred years ago, and which is still continually referred to in the chief Masonic manuals. The subject is " The Idea of Masonry," [2] its tenets, objects, and practical works, the place

---

[1] In 1881 there were eighty-five Rose Croix chapters on the roll, and the members numbered nearly 4,000.

[2] " *Illustrations of Masonry,*" by Wm. Preston, Past Master of the Lodge of Antiquity, 9th edn., *with considerable additions.* London: Wilkie, 57 Paternoster Row, 1796. In the volume before us (carefully preserved as it has been) abundant " *marks*" of six or seven different kinds assure us that the publishers and printers — yes, and the readers themselves — have wished to draw especial attention to it as a work of importance to their society.

where and the person by whom it was first introduced into
England. The reader will judge for himself as to how much or
how little of the historical part he will credit; but he may observe that this author tells us nothing of Masonic lodges before
the deluge, or on the plains of Shinar.

The *Illustrations* are in six "books," of which the first displays the excellence of Masonry, and deals with reflections on
the symmetry and proportion perceptible in the works of nature,
and on the harmony and affection amongst other species of
things.

"Whoever attentively observes the objects which surround
him, will find abundant reason to admire the works of nature,
and to adore the Being who directs such wonderful operations.
He will be convinced that infinite wisdom could alone design,
and infinite power finish, such amazing works. . . . Besides the
symmetry, good order, and proportion which appear in all the
works of creation, something farther attracts the reflecting mind
and draws its attention nearer to the Divinity—the universal
harmony and affection among the d ifferent species of beings of
every rank and denomination. *These are the cements of the
rational world*, and by these alone it subsists. When they cease
nature must be dissolved, and *man, the image of his Maker*, and
the chief of His works, be overwhelmed in the general chaos."

As to the origin of Masonry, we are told that we may trace its
foundations from the beginning of the world. "Ever since symmetry began and harmony displayed her charms, our order has
a being." It almost seems as if the idea of the extreme antiquity of the order was encouraged by the frequent use of quibbles
on the word *order*. Bacon's aim was to reduce knowledge and all
else to a method, or order, for "order is heaven's first law."
In the dark and rude ages of the world knowledge was withheld from our forefathers incapable of receiving it. [1] Masonry
then diffused its influence, science was gradually unveiled, arts
arose, civilization took place, and the progress of knowledge
and philosophy gradually dispelled the gloom of ignorance [2] and
barbarism.

---

1 Compare with Preston's *Illustrations of Masonry*, section iii, Bacon's concluding paragraphs in his preface to the *Wisdom of the Ancients*.

2 "*There is no darkness but ignorance.*" (*Twelfth Night*, iv. 2.)

Next we read of the advantages of secresy, and of a system of secret signs carefully preserved among the fraternity. A universal language is thus formed, and contributes to the union, in an indissoluble bond of affection and mutual interest, of men of the most opposite tenets, of the most distant countries, and of the most contrary opinions. The Chinese, the wild Arab, the American savage, will embrace a brother Briton, and will find a stronger obligation than even the common tie of humanity to induce him to kind and friendly offices.

" As all religions teach morality, if a brother is found to act the part of a truly moral man his private speculative opinions are left to God and himself."

" *Masonry,*" we are told, is a term which expresses a double meaning, the *work,* that is, and the abstract ideas of which that work is the symbol or type. Masonry passes under two denominations, operative and speculative.

" By the former we allude to a proper application of the useful rules of architecture, whence a structure derives figure, strength, and beauty, and whence result a due proportion and a just correspondence in all its parts. By the latter we learn to subdue the passions, *act upon the square,* keep a tongue of good report, maintain secresy, and practice charity.

" Speculative Masonry is so far interwoven with religion as to lay us under the strongest obligations to pay that rational homage to the Deity which at once constitutes our duty and our happiness. It leads the contemplative to review with reverence and admiration the glorious works of creation, and inspires them with the most lofty ideas of the perfections of the divine Creator.

" Operative Masonry furnishes us, indeed, with dwellings and sheltering edifices, and demonstrates how much can be done for the benefit of man by science and industry. Yet the lapse of time and the ruthless hand of ignorance, and the *devastations of war, have laid waste and destroyed many valuable monuments of antiquity* on which the utmost exertions of human genius have been employed. Even the Temple of Solomon, so spacious and magnificent, and constructed by so many celebrated artists, escaped not the unsparing ravages of barbaric force."

We are arrested by the very Baconian and Shakespearian

sentiments, and the combination of words in which they are expressed.

> " Not marble, nor the gilded monuments
> Of princes, shall outlive this powerful rhyme ;
>
> .   .   .   .   .   .
> When *wasteful war shall statues overturn,*
> *And broils root out the work of masonry,*
> Nor Mars his sword, nor war's quick fire shall burn
> The living record of your memory.[1]

" The monuments of wit survive the monuments of power," etc.[2]

" We see, then, how far the monuments of wit and learning are more durable than the monuments of power or of the hands. For have not the verses of Homer continued twenty-five hundred years or more, without the loss of a syllable or letter; during which time infinite palaces, *temples, castles, cities, have been decayed and demolished.* . . . But the images of men's wits and knowledges remain in books, exempted from the wrong of time, and capable of perpetual renovation."[3]

Throughout the Masonic books the reader is led to suppose that *the survival and transmission of Freemasonry* is the matter of extremest importance. Read, however, by the light of Bacon, we perceive that the whole object is to get possession of the rude and ignorant, and, by working upon their innate vanity — or shall we say their self-respect? — to draw them on to works of mutual benefit, and to raise them by gentle stages up the steps of knowledge and morality under the impression that their superiority consists chiefly in the possession of some great and mysterious secret. The lower orders are indeed the stepping-stones for the cleverer and more helpful higher initiates. The subscriptions of the vast number of members are of immense value in promoting many useful works, which, without some such organisation, would never have been attempted ; and doubtless the members of every degree share in the pleasure and pride

---

1 Sonnet lv.   Compare sonnets lxxxi, lxiv, lxv, cvii.

2 Device of Philantia, Hermit's Sp.

3 Advt. of L. i.

which Freemasons evidently take in the numerous charitable works which they have inaugurated and liberally supported. Yet it is much to be doubted if the lower orders of Masons either guess at their own origin, or perceive that the true aim of the society is to raise the level of patriotism and morality until the former may fulfil Heaven's first law of universal order and harmonious obedience to earthly authority, and the latter shall lift man above the flats of mere worldly wisdom and morality to the sublime heights of divinity or religion, to heights, indeed, to which probably many Freemasons do not aspire, but are content to live in the valley.

" The attentive ear," says the Masonic Manual, " receives the soul from the instructive tongue, and the sacred mysteries are safely lodged in the repository of faithful breasts. Tools and implements the most expressive! [*sic*] are selected by the fraternity, to imprint on the memory serious truths; and thus the excellent tenets of the institution are transmitted unimpaired, under circumstances precarious and adverse, through a succession of ages."

The fraternity is said to consist of three classes, each with distinct privileges. Honour and probity are recommendations to the first class. Diligence, assiduity, and application are qualifications for the second class, in which is given an accurate elucidation of science, both in theory and practice. The third class is restricted to a selected few, whom truth and fidelity have distinguished, whom years and experience have improved, and whom merit and abilities have entitled to preferment. We should expect this class to be initiated into some of the mysteries of the printing-house, and of the collating-room, and the ciphers, for, in the next section, the author enters into a discussion of the objections raised to the secrets of Masonry, which, he says, are not mere trivialities, but " the keys to our treasure." He exhorts his readers not to regard the mysteries or the ceremonials of the order as nominal and frivolous. Those who hurry through the degrees or stages, without considering the steps which they pursue, or without possessing a single qualification for the duties which they undertake, are doing a positive injury to the society which they profess to aid, and deriving no benefit themselves; for " the substance is lost in the shadow."

Then comes an explanation of some of the causes why Masons have, from time to time, brought upon themselves discredit and censure. The very " variety of members of which the society of Masons is composed, and *the small number who are really conversant with the tenets of the institution,*" render it almost certain that some will transgress, and prove faithless to their calling. When mild endeavours to reform such persons are fruitless, they are expelled the lodge, as unfit members of the society. But no wise man will condemn a whole community on account of the errors of a few individuals. " Friendship and social delights cannot be the object of reproach, nor can that wisdom which hoary time has sanctified be subject to ridicule. *Whoever attempts to censure what he does not comprehend, degrades himself; and the generous heart will always be led to pity the mistakes of such ignorant presumption.*" In the " charge, at the initiation into the first degree," the initiate is enjoined never to suffer his zeal for the institution, however laudable, to lead him into argument with those who may ridicule it; " but rather extend your pity toward all *who, through ignorance, contemn what they never had an opportunity to comprehend.*" [1]

Charity is next extolled as the chief of every social virtue, and the distinguishing characteristic of the order, and of the Deity himself. [2]

" The bounds of the greatest nation, or the most extensive empire, cannot circumscribe it. It is a Godlike disposition, . . since a mutual chain of dependence subsists throughout the animal creation. The whole human species are, therefore, proper objects of charity."

Further : all kinds of men may, in their different spheres, prove useful; but the officers of a lodge in Freemasonry ought to be principally restricted to those " *whose early years have been dedicated to literary pursuits, or whose circumstances and situation in*

---

1 " *Disparage not the faith thou dost not know.*" (Midsummer Night's Dream)

2 See *Merchant of Venice,* iv. 1, 193-7.

life render them independent." They should also be men of superior prudence and good address, with a tranquil, well-cultivated mind and retentive memory. But *" he who wishes to teach, must be content to learn."* A self-sufficient, conceited person, however able, can, therefore, never be a good Mason. " Arrogance and presumption appear not on the one hand, or diffidence and inability on the other, but all unite in the same plan."

The second book of Masonry gives an illustration of the ceremonies connected with the opening and closing of a lodge, in which account we seem to see a reflection of Bacon's cogitations on the means of ensuring help from worthy and capable men, who should prepare to guard the entrances and approaches to the Temple of Wisdom. In the first sentence note the use of his *Promus* entry, " Avenues." [1]

" Our care is first directed to *the external avenues* of the lodge, and the proper officers, whose province it is to discharge that duty, execute the trust with fidelity." [2]

By certain mystic forms these officers intimate that it is safe for the ceremonies to proceed, or they detect impostors and unfit persons who must be excluded. The ceremonies are religious, and intended not only to remind the master and brethren of their many duties, but also to inculcate a reverential awe of the Deity, that " the eye may be fixed on that object from whose radiant beams light only can be derived."

At the closing of the lodge, " each brother faithfully locks up the treasure which he has acquired in his own repository, and, pleased with his own reward, retires to enjoy and disseminate among the private circle of his friends the fruits of his labour and industry in the lodge." This paragraph seems to imply that the brethren adopted Bacon's advice regarding the taking of notes, and that they habitually stored up their newly gained treasures of learning in order to add to the common fund, and

---

1 Promus, 1432; and comp. Montaigne Ess. " To Learn to Die"—Ed. Hazlitt, p. 76.

2 Preston, p. 33.

to distribute them at a later period for the benefit of the world in general.

We observe amongst other peculiarities in Rosicrucian books the large number of *fly-leaves* at one or both ends. These, however, in the old volumes, have been in most instances cut out. Only one explanation of this singular circumstance seems satisfactory, namely, that the brethren, by Bacon's original instructions, took notes of all that they heard or read, and that these fly-leaves, or note-books, were thus made the " repositories of treasure stored up," so that nothing should be lost, but that ultimately all newly acquired learning should flow into the common treasury.

" No brother is supplanted, or put out of his work, if he be capable of filling it. All meekly receive their rewards . . . and never desert the master till the work is finished. . . . In a lodge Masons meet as members of the same family, and representatives, for the time being, of all the brethren throughout the world. All prejudices, therefore, on account of religion, country, or private opinion, are removed."

In the charge delivered at the closing of the lodge, the Masons are instructed to be " very cautious in your words and carriage, *that the most penetrating stranger may not discover or find out what is not proper to be intimated,* and, *if necessary, you are to waive a discourse,*[1] and manage it prudently, for the honour of the fraternity. . . . If a stranger apply . . . beware of giving him any secret hints of knowledge." The charge ends with renewed exhortations to " brotherly love, the foundation and cap-stone, the cement and glory of this ancient fraternity."

In the first Masonic " lecture," " virtue is painted *in the most beautiful colours,*" and the duties of morality are strictly enforced. In it the Masons are prepared for " a regular *advancement in knowledge and philosophy,* and these are *imprinted on the memory by lively and sensible images,* the lecture being suited to all capacities, and necessary to be known by every person who would wish to rank as a Mason."

---

[1] This injunction is excellently complied with, and is, no doubt, a chief obstruction to non-Masons in the attainment of information.

Unhappily for the uninitiated, the author can annex to this remark no explanation consistent with the rules of Masonry, but refers " *the more inquisitive to our regular assemblies for further instruction.*" So, " out goes the candle, and we are left darkling;" yet we need not despair, but may believe that by a due study of Bacon's *Colours of Good and Evil* (and other works based upon it), his *Advancement of Learning*, and his emblematic and metaphoric language, we may furnish ourselves with all the useful knowledge which the Masonic initiates will gain by their lecture on the colours of virtue, the advancement of philosophy, and the images by which the novices are instructed.

Just as the Rosicrucians in *The New Atlantis*, and elsewhere, are commanded to dispense their medicines *gratis*, so Masons are called upon solemnly to declare themselves uninfluenced by *mercenary motives*, but prompted by a desire for knowledge, and a sincere wish of being serviceable to their fellow-creatures.

They pledge themselves to study the Bible, to consider it as the unerring standard of truth and justice, and to regulate their lives according to its divine precepts. The three great moral duties to be observed are: (1) To God, by reverence and submission to His Will; (2) To your neighbour, by " acting on the square," and by unselfishness in dealing with him; (3) " To yourself, by avoiding irregularity and intemperance, *which might impair your faculties* and debase the dignity of your profession."

This section concludes with another exhortation to secresy and caution in recommending new initiates. Next we come to a page of observations on the origin and advantages of *hieroglyphical instruction*, a subject which, in view of Bacon's instructions on this very subject, and the evidently close relation which his remarks bear to the illustrations and ornaments of the books published during his life, and (with various modifications) from that time till now, possesses for the inquirer a strong attraction and interest.

Since nothing can be more noble than the pursuit of virtue, nor any motive more alluring than the practice of justice, " what instruction," we are asked, " *can be more beneficial than an accurate elucidation of those symbols which tend to embellish and adorn the mind? Everything that strikes the eye more immediately engages the attention, and imprints on the memory serious and solemn truths. Hence, Masons have universally adopted the plan of inculcating the tenets of their order by typical figures and allegorical emblems, to prevent their mysteries from descending to the familiar reach of inattentive and unprepared novices, from whom they might not receive due veneration.* It is well known that the usages and customs of the Masons have ever corresponded with those of the ancient Egyptians, to which they bear a near affinity. These philosophers, unwilling to expose their mysteries to vulgar eyes, concealed their particular tenets and principles of polity under hieroglyphical figures, and expressed their notions of government by signs and symbols, which they communicated to their Magi alone, who were bound by oath not to reveal them. Pythagoras seems to have established his system on a similar plan, and many orders of a more recent date have copied the example. Every character, figure, and emblem, depicted in a lodge, has a moral tendency, and tends to inculcate the practice of virtue."

Here, as will be seen by and by, when we come to emblems and hieroglyphic pictures, Freemasons are again adopting Bacon's ideas and doctrines, and using his words, though their charm is lost by dilution and paraphrase. No addition or alteration seems to improve either his phraseology or his ideas; usually the copyists limp after him in " what imitation they can borrow;" but even where they most craftily prick in, or transfer to their own work his beauties of language and quaint conceits, it is still easy to distinguish the original from the imitation, the pearls from the beads, and at least one-third of *Preston's Illustrations* is, we believe, taken directly from Bacon, perhaps originally dictated by him.

The charge at initiation into the second degree again enforces the study of the liberal arts, " especially of geometry, the basis of our art; geometry and Masonry, originally synonymous terms, *being of a divine and moral nature*, which, while it proves the wonderful properties of nature, *demonstrates the more important truths of morality."* It will readily be perceived that here is a double meaning; for *geometry does not really teach morality,* and no one can believe that the terms geometry and Masonry were ever truly synonymous. The next instructions, concerning the five orders of architecture, further confirm the notion that the teaching is symbolic, and that it requires *verbal* elucidation. The information on architecture is of the most elementary character, and converts itself, at the end of the second page, into " an analysis of the human faculties," where we are taught to consider the five senses as the gifts of nature, " the channels by which knowledge is conveyed."

In the treatment of the senses of hearing, seeing, and feeling,[1] the analogies between the bodily organs and the spiritual faculties are ever present to the writer. It is " the *ear,* the gate of the understanding; the *eye,* the gate of the affections;"[2] the *touch* of nature which makes the whole world kin, which we perceive shadowed in the architectural instructions of Masonry.

When these topics are proposed in Masonic assemblies, the brethren " are not confined to any peculiar mode of explanation," which probably means that the eye may be interpreted the eye of the mind, as well as of the body; that the ear, in the same way, may be intellectual or physical; that the Masonic signs may be palpable to the eye by symbols, gestures, or marks in printing, engraving, and sculptures, or sensible (as they have been found) to the touch, in the pages or edges of books; that the contents of the books themselves may be *tasted, chewed, and swallowed,* or their secrets *smelt out* by discerning initiates. For, though " the senses are the gifts of nature, reason, properly employed, confirms the documents of nature, which are always true and wholesome; she distinguishes the good from the bad; rejects the last, and adheres to the first. Hearing is the sense by which we can best communicate to each other our thoughts and intentions, our purposes and desires, while our reason is capable of exerting its utmost power and energy. (The descrip-

---

1 See " Metaphors." Also of the book-marks, in which not only the sight, but the touch, is appealed to.

2 Promus, 1137, where are many Shakespeare references.

tion of this sense seems to point to the *verbal* teaching of the Masons.) But the " sight is the noblest of all the senses, the organ is the masterpiece of Nature's work," and the large amount of symbols and metaphors which connect themselves with this sense show the important place which it occupies in Masonic symbolism. Then, by feeling, we distinguish the different qualities of bodies (or, it might be added, of *spirits*). They are hot or cold, hard or soft, rough or smooth, and have other qualities which are seen to be connected " *by some original principle of human nature* which far transcends our inquiry." " Hast thou," says Prospero to Ariel — " hast thou, *though a spirit*, some touch, some feeling of their afflictions?" [1] *Shakespeare* makes great use of the metaphor, " The inly *touch* of love." [2] " A sweet *touch*, a quick venue of wit." [3] " The most bitter *touch* of sorrow. " [4] " *Touched* with noble anger," [5] with pity, etc. No one can doubt that Shakespeare, like Enoch, was a good Mason.

Surely, too, *the eye of the perceptive intellect, the ready ear for truth* (in other words, the Will, which, Bacon says, rules thought, free as it is), and *the tender sympathy which is in touch with all created nature*, are the three senses of hearing, seeing, and feeling, which are deemed particularly essential amongst Masons.

Then of smelling, " that sense by which we distinguish odours," we recall " Ovidius Naso smelling out the odoriferous flowers of fancy; " [6] the Fool's exposition of " why one's nose stands i' the middle on 's face, to keep one's eyes of either side 's nose; that *what a man cannot smell out he may spy into,*" [7] with many other similar figures; of *smelling out villainy*, [8] at which " Heaven stops the nose; " [9] of the air and *smell* of the court; of calumny; of sin, offence and corruption; of mortality and Heaven's breath. [10] Ariel's graphic description of the effect produced

---

1 Temp. v. 1. 2 Tw. Gen. Ver. ii. 7. 3 L. L. L. v. 1.
4 All's Well, i. 1. 5 Lear, i. 5. 6 L. L. L. iv. 2.
7 Lear, i. 5. 8 Othello, v. 2. 9 Ib. iv. 2.

10 There are about fifty passages in Shakespeare alone which illustrate this one idea.

upon the varlets Trinculo, Stephano, and Caliban, by his music, shows the tendency throughout Bacon's works to associate many or opposite ideas in such a manner as to make them blend into one harmonious thought. Here all the five senses do their part and are shown to be mutually connected. The men were *drinking*, and striking out, striving to *touch* something. Ariel beats his tabor, and their senses are so confused that they try to *see* or to *smell* his music, following it to the detriment of their shins, the sense of *hearing* beguiling the sense of *touch*, until they are plunged into the midst of *foul-smelling* mud. We feel throughout that the author is illustrating his doctrine of the Biform Figure of Nature, showing how a man who takes no pains to cultivate the intellectual and spiritual side of his nature reduces himself to the level of the brutes, to which by his body he is kin.

> *Ari.* I told you, sir, they were red-hot with *drinking;*
> So full of valour that *they smote* the air
> For breathing in their faces; *beat the ground*
> For kissing of their feet; yet always *bending*
> *Towards their project.* Then I beat my tabor;
> At which, like unback'd colts, *they prick'd their ears,*
> *Advanced their eyelids, lifted up their noses*
> *As they smelt music:* so I charm'd their ears
> That calf-like they my lowing follow'd through
> Tooth'd briars, sharp furzes, pricking goss and thorns,
> Which entered their frail shins: at last I left them
> I' the filthy-mantled pool beyond your cell,
> There dancing up to the chins, that *the foul lake*
> *O'erstunk their feet.*[1]

Lastly, with regard to the organ of taste, " which enables us to make a proper distinction in the choice of our food: this sense guards the entrance of the alimentary canal, as that of smell guards the entrance of the canal for respiration. Smelling and tasting are inseparably connected, and it is by the unnatural kind of life men commonly lead in society that these senses are rendered less fit to perform their natural offices. . . . The senses are the channels of communication to the mind, and *when the*

---

[1] Tempest, iv. 1.

mind is diseased every sense loses its virtue." In the noblest arts the mind of man is the subject upon which we operate, and wise men agree that there is but one way to the knowledge of Nature's works, the way of observation and experiment. " Memory, imagination, taste, reasoning, moral perception, and all the active powers of the soul . . . constitute a proper subject for the investigation of Masons, and are mysteries known only to nature and to nature's god, to whom all are indebted for every blessing they enjoy." In other words, " the proper study of mankind is man," and humanity must be led to *inquire,* and " to look from nature up to nature's God." Yet it is difficult to see how this dissertation has any true connection with the adjoining passages on architecture, or with those which immediately follow, on " geometry, the first and noblest of the sciences," *the same* as symmetry, and " order, Heaven's first law," unless we take the view that all this is the symbolic language. In this section God is called, in Baconian language, *the Divine Artist, the Great Artificer of the Universe, the Architect of Nature.* The universe itself is God's vast *machine, framed by himself,* and through which, by geometry, " *we may curiously trace Nature, through her various windings, to her most concealed recesses.*"

In the really poetical and very Baconian description here given of the beauty and order displayed in the various parts of animate and inanimate creation, the writer delights to prove " the existence of a first cause. . . . Every blade of grass that covers the field, every flower that blows, every insect which wings its way into unbounded space, . . . the variegated carpet of the terrestrial creation, every plant that grows, every flower that displays its beauties or breathes its sweets, affords instruction and delight. When we extend our views to the animal creation, and contemplate the varied clothing of every species, . . . the hues traced by the divine pencil in the plumage of the feathered tribe, how exalted is our conception of the heavenly work. . . . The apt disposition of one part to another is a perpetual study to the geometrician. . . . Even when he descends into the bowels of the earth he finds . . . that every gem and pebble proclaims the handiwork of an Almighty Creator."

In the sixth section of the second degree, previous utterances, suggestions, and lessons are repeated, still in diluted Baconian terms. Evaporating a little superfluous phraseology, we again come upon familiar exhortations to temperance, fortitude, prudence, and justice. Temperance, which *governs* the passions. Fortitude, which he who possesses is seldom *shaken, and never overthrown by the storms that surround him.* Prudence, *the chief jewel of the human frame.* Justice, the *bound* of right, the *cement* of civil society, *which, in a great measure, constitutes real goodness,* and which should be the *perpetual* study of the good Mason. Virtue, *true nobility.* Wisdom, *the channel* through which virtue is directed and conveyed. *The mind, the noblest subject of our studies.* Observation and experiment, the one way to the knowledge of nature's works.

Masonry, we are repeatedly told, is a progressive science, including *almost* every branch of polite learning. The omission implied consists, apparently, in all matters connected with Christianity and the church of Christ; in fact, if, as we think, Bacon framed these rules, we see that this must be so. For, after a dissertation (still in Baconian language paraphrased), upon "geometry, the noblest of the sciences;" . . . upon the "numberless worlds framed by the same Divine Artist, which roll through the vast expanse, conducted by the unerring laws of nature," and of the "progress made in architecture, particularly in the reign of Solomon," these instructions finish up with a short explanation of the liberal arts, which are computed by the Masons to be seven in number.[1]

These arts are grammar, rhetoric, logic, arithmetic, geometry, music, astronomy (which includes the doctrine of the spheres), geography, navigation, and the arts dependent on them. "Thus end the different sections of the second lecture," . . . which, besides a complete theory of philosophy and physics, contains a

---

[1] *Seven,* that mystical number, which, as we have elsewhere said, is so closely associated with Masonic symbols and traditions.

regular system of science, demonstrated on the clearest principles, and established on the firmest foundations.

Truly this must be a wonderful lecture, and it seems quite a pity that the majority of mankind should be excluded from this short cut to the seven liberal arts and sciences. Perhaps, however, it only *points the way*, as Bacon did, to so many studies which ultimately lead to knowledge fitting its possessor for admission to the last and highest degree of initiation. For the third and last lecture consists of twelve sections, composed of " a variety of particulars, *which render it impossible to give an abstract without violating the laws of the order. . . .* Every circumstance that respects government and system, *ancient lore and deep research, curious invention and ingenious,* is accurately traced, while the mode of proceeding, on public as well as on private occasions, is explained. Among the brethren of this degree *the land-marks of the order are preserved;* and from them is derived that fund of information which expert and ingenious craftsmen only can afford, whose judgment has been matured by years and experience."

" To a complete knowledge of this lecture few attain ; . . . *from this class the rulers of the craft are selected;* and it is only from those who are capable of giving instruction that we can properly expect to receive it."

It is, then, this highest class of Masons that we should confidently expect to find in possession of all the histories of the building and endowing of the great libraries, colleges, schools, hospitals, etc., of which we have elsewhere spoken. We should expect them not only to be able to give account of the origin and builders of these and other structures — gateways, fountains, etc., to ancient houses; tombs and monumental tablets and sculptures; of wood-carvings, of pulpits, choir stalls, etc. Iron-work also, in churches, gateways, and old signs; designs in stained windows and ceilings. But we should expect from them a clear and indubitable explanation of the *meaning* of the peculiar designs and figures which we have observed, not only in buildings, but in books.

A very brief account of the building of the Temple of

Solomon, and of the dedication of that edifice, follows. "We can," says the author, "afford little assistance to the industrious Mason in this section, as *it can only be acquired by oral communication.*" A remark which again plainly shows us that the temple to be built is not a mere structure of brick or stone. Two pages móre bring us to an explanation of "the seven liberal arts," of which five at least seem to have nothing to do with architecture — grammar, rhetoric, logic, arithmetic, geometry, music, and astronomy — and as these, together with "the doctrine of the spheres," are all to be included in one lecture, we may rest satisfied that this lecture is not so profound as its title might lead us to suppose.

Here we should be inclined to break off this review of Masonry, because, having extracted as much as we can of the pith and meaning and aim of these Masonic mysteries, it seems undesirable to spend time and space upon particulars which apparently have for their object to puzzle and confuse the uninitiated reader; though to the initiated they may, perhaps, convey some information or reminder. We continue, nevertheless, chiefly for the sake of illustrating a theory set forward in another place, with regard to *feigned or disguised histories, records and biographies, and changed names.*

In Book III. a short paper is printed which professes to contain " *Certayne questions, with answers to the same, concerning the mystery of* Maçonrye, *writtene by the hande of Kynge* Heurye, *the sixthe of the name, and faithfullye copyed by me* Johan LEYLAND, antiquarius, *by the commande of his Highnesse.*" Whether or not this document is what it pretends to be, is not to the present purpose; our object is to draw attention to the strange *footnotes* which accompany the questions, and which occupy much more letter-press than the document itself. None of these notes appear to be both genuine and necessary; some contain the elaborate quibbles or puns which were said to be so irresistible to Bacon, but which, also, we think, formed a part of the secret and ambiguous language of his society; others speak of the *invention of arts* which Bacon suggested or commenced; all include touches of his style; one mentions his name. For instance, foot-note 6 turns upon a supposed confusion between *Venetia* and *Phœnicia: "perhaps similitude of sound might deceive the clerk who first took down the examination."* Then to the question, " Howe commede ytt yn Engelonde? " we are informed that Masonry was brought by " Peter Gower, a Grecian," who, after travelling through Egypt and Syria, and every country where " the *Venetians* " had planted Masonry, " framed a grate lodge at 'Groton.' " The foot-notes again correct this passage at much length :

" Peter Gower must be another mistake of the writer. I was puzzled at first to guess who Peter Gower should be, the name being perfectly English; or how a Greek could come by such a name. But as soon as I thought of Pythagoras, I could scarce forbear smiling to find that philosopher had undergone a metempsychosis he never dreamt of. We need only consider the French pronunciation of his name, *Pythagore*, that is, *Petagore*, to conceive how easily such a mistake may be made by an unlearned clerk."

The true object of this note seems to be to draw attention to the connection between Pythagoras and the wisdom and religious mysteries of the Egyptians. " That he was initiated into several different orders of priests, *who in those days kept all their learning secret from the vulgar*," is a hint which seems to point to a similar system in Masonry, and the subsequent remarks about Pythagoras having discovered the Forty-seventh Book of Euclid, and that he " made every geometrical theorem a secret, and admitted only such to the knowledge of them as had first undergone a five years' silence," seems to contain a further hint concerning the nature of certain highly scientific systems of cipher-writing which we have elsewhere found mentioned in connection with the name of Pythagoras.

With regard to " the grate lodge" which Pythagoras is said to have founded at *Groton*, another *foot-note* corrects the error after this fashion : " *Groton is the name of a place in England.* The place here meant is Crotona," etc. From the many Masons made by Pythagoras " yn processe of tyme, the arte passed yn Engelonde."

In answer to the question, "Whatte artes haveth the Maçonnes techedde mankynde?" we are told that they taught agriculture, architecture, astronomy, numbers, music, poesy, chemistry, government, and "*relygyonne*" *(religion)*. To this a foot-note appends the remark, "What appears most odd is, that *they reckon religion among the arts,*" and this appears to give another hint of the double-meanings, and symbolism, and, perhaps, of the cipher-system introduced, then as now, into religious books, pictures, designs, and edifices.

But the next note is even more suggestive. In reply to an inquiry as to what the Masons conceal, we learn that "*they concelethe the arte of ffyndynge newe artes.*" Here our commentator becomes more than usually communicative:

"The art of finding arts must certainly be a most useful art. *My Lord Bacon's Novum Organum is an attempt toward somewhat of the same kind.* But I much doubt that, if ever the Masons had it, they have now lost it, *since so few new arts have been lately invented and so many are wanted.* The idea I have formed of such an art is, that it must be something proper to be employed in all the sciences generally, *as algebra is in numbers,* by the help of which new rules of arithmetic are and may be found."

The Masons, also, are said *to conceal the art of keeping secrets,* though what kind of an art this may be the commentator professes not to know. They also conceal "*the art of changes*" *(but he knows not what it means)* and "the facultye of Abrac." Here he is utterly in the dark. Lastly, Masons conceal their "universal language." The foot-note to this statement might be supposed to be a mere transcription, either of some rough notes or of verbal instructions given by Bacon himself:

"An universal language has been much desired by the learned of many ages. It is a thing rather to be wished than hoped for. . . . If it be true, I guess it must be something like the language of the pantomines amongst the ancient Romans, who were said to be able, by signs only, to express and deliver any oration intelligibly to all men and languages."

Bacon makes many references to the silent language conveyed
19

by pictures or sculptures, but the passage just quoted may contain a hint of the instruction which may be given by dumb
shows, or stage plays, for it continues as Bacon does where, in
in the *De Augmentis,* he upholds the benefits derivable from a
wise use of the theater. Yet in all that regards these *arts of
concealment,* there are, to the mind of the present writer, strong
hints of a system not so much of *secret studies* as of *secret methods of
communication,* whether by means of cipher-writing, hieroglyphic
designs, pantomimic gestures, or double-meaning language.
This can only be tested by a comparison of many books in which
veiled information of the same kind is to be found. May some
industrious reader follow up the subject, which seems to become
easier as we plod on.

The fourth and last book in this strange little volume professes to give " The History of Masonry in England." Whether
or not any one was ever found to believe the statements made in
the opening chapters of this " History" we know not, but
hitherto we have not found them repeated, excepting in Masonic
dictionaries and manuals. We are to believe that " Masonry"
flourished in England before the time of the Druids; that lodges
and conventions were regularly held throughout the period
of Roman rule until Masonry was reduced to a low ebb
through continual wars. At length *the Emperor Carausius,*
having shaken off the Roman yoke, contrived the most effectual
means to render his person and government acceptable to the
people by assuming the character of a Mason. . . . He raised
the Masons to the first rank as his favourites and *appointed Albanus, his steward,* the principal superintendent of their assemblies. Later on, " he granted them a charter and *commanded
Albanus to preside over them* as Grand Master. Some particulars
of a man so truly exemplary among Masons will certainly merit
attention. *Albanus was born at Verulam, now St. Albans, in
Hertfordshire, of a noble family."* Some account of the proto-
martyr, St. Alban, is then introduced; it ends by saying that St.
Alban built a splendid palace for the Emperor at Verulam, and
that to reward his diligence " the Emperor made him *steward of
his household and chief ruler of the realm. . . . We are assured*

*that this knight was a celebrated architect and a real encourager
of able workmen;* it cannot, therefore, be supposed that Freemasonry would be neglected under so eminent a patron."

This remarkable and authentic history further enlightens us as
to St. Alban's munificence and liberality in paying his servants.
" Whereas before that time, in all the land, a Mason had but a
penny a day and his meat, St. Alban mended it, " for " he gave them
two shillings a day, and threepence to their cheer. . . . He also got
them a charter from the King. "[1]   An additional note adds that
" *a MS. written in the time of James II. contains an account of
this circumstance, and increases the weekly pay to* 3s. 6d. and 3d.
a day for the bearers of burdens. " These payments were liberal
for the seventeenth century. For the days of St. Alban, mar-
tyred A. D. 303, the allowance strikes us as remarkable for
labouring masons and hod-men. Perhaps we may find three
shillings and sixpence per week was the pay for scribes, amanuenses, etc., and threepence a day for messengers.

The editor of the *Royal Masonic Cyclopædia* is so considerate
as to grant his readers the full use of their faculties in this
investigation. To be sure, he complicates it as much as possible
by cross-references, but it seems to be the rule rather than the
exception to hinder students from attaining any information of
value without the exercise of some perseverance and considerable loss of time. Thus, we wish to ascertain the origin of Freemasonry. Finding nothing to the point under " Freemason,"
we try " Origin of Freemasonry," and are more happy.   This
article summarizes the theories promulgated on the subject:
" 1. Masonry derived from the patriarchs.   2. From the mysteries of the pagans.   3. From the construction of Solomon's
Temple.   4. From the Crusades.   5. From the Knights Templars.
6. From the Roman Collegia of Artificers.   7. From the operative masons of the middle ages.   8. From the Rosicrucians of
the sixteenth century.[2]   9. From Oliver Cromwell.   10. From
Prince Charles Stuart, for political purposes.   11. From Sir

---

1 Why has *the Emperor* become suddenly only *the King?*

1 Observe that the Rosicrucians are here traced by the Freemasons no farther back than Bacon's time.

Christopher Wren, at the building of St. Paul's. 12. From Dr.
Desaguliers and his friends, in 1717."

"*It is hardly necessary,*" adds this accommodating instructor,
"*to express any opinion on the point : the Fraternity has the
advantage* of being able to choose for itself, and, as Masonry is
now worked, any decision on the point is as impossible as the
value of that decision would be futile." This is disconraging.
Nevertheless, we cannot fail to observe that, amongst the twelve
distinct theories as to the origin of the Freemasons, the legend
of *St. Alban is omitted.* The writer refers us to a previous
article on the " Antiquity of Freemasonry." The words with
which this article greets us are doubtless intended to deter us
from investigation :

"On this subject *much has been written to little purpose, and it
is not proposed to further discuss them here.* That mystical
societies flourished long before the dawn of history, is not to be
denied, but *that such societies essentially resembled Freemasonry,*
it is more than futile to opine."

Then the writer goes off into a discussion of hieroglyphics
and Egyptian symbolism, and speaks of Hiram, Osiris, and
Adonis, and of Numa Pompilius, king of Rome. He is not much
interested in his own remarks, and evidently does not expect
any one else to be so. " It is idle to speculate upon such a topic
as the antiquity of these secret associations, and it is far wiser
to accept the development, as being *in essentia* all that we
know upon the subject."

Alas ! not every one has so much wisdom as to find bliss in
ignorance. We next try " Alban, St.— See Saint Alban."

"*Saint Alban.*— The proto-martyr of England, born at
Verulam or Saint Alban's, in Herefordshire. He is the reputed
legendary introducer of Freemasonry into England, but without
much vidence."

So the writer takes no heed of all the accurate historic information about the Emperor Carausius which the " Past Master
of the Lodge of Antiquity " was so particular in chronicling !
We are now referred to a sixth article on " Grand Masters of
Freemasonry," which opens by again cautioning the reader

against putting any trust in the information which is about to be imparted to him.

"Grand Masters of England before the Revival of Masonry in 1717. *This list has been collated from several authorities. It is, however, not given as fact, but as tradition.*"

Here the "tradition" of St. Alban, which in *Preston's Illustrations* is presented as true history, is repeated. The first Grand Master is said to have been—

"A. D. 287. *Saint Alban,* a Roman Knight, when Carausius was Emperor of Britain."

Say that the origin of Freemasonry was traditional, yet what need is there to invent an Emperor Carausius?[1]

After a sketch of the History of Masonry in England, under St. Augustine, King Alfred, and the Knights Templars, we are gradually made to perceive how, from very early times, the great family of the Pembrokes and the Montagues were connected with (or *said to be connected with*) Masonry. Roger de Montgomery, Earl of Shrewsbury, is said to have employed the fraternity in building the Tower of London. Gilbert de Clare, Marquis of Pembroke, presided over the lodges in the reign of Stephen, when the Chapel, afterwards the House of Commons, at Westminster, was built by the Masons. On the accession of Edward I., 1272, the care of the Masons was entrusted to the Archbishop of York, the Earl of Gloucester, and "Ralph, Lord of Mount Hermer, the progenitor of the family of the Montagues," who finished the building of Westminster Abbey. Even when we come down to the history of Inigo Jones, as a Mason and architect of the palace at Whitehall, and of many other magnificent structures in the time of James I., we are reminded that it was to *William Herbert, Earl of Pembroke,* that Inigo Jones owed his education; that by his instrumentality Inigo Jones was introduced to the notice of the King, "nomi-

---

[1] We can only suppose that Carausius was either a pseudonym for James I., whose "steward and chief ruler of the realm" Bacon really was; or that two facts are mixed, and that a record of something connected with Prince, afterwards King Charles (Carolus) may be here hinted. Those who follow up these devices for imparting knowledge will not find either of these suggestions to be impossible, or exceptionally strange.

nated *Grand Master of England,* and deputised by his sovereign
to preside over the lodges." Again, we read that William Herbert, Earl of Pembroke, became warden to Grand Master Jones,
and that when the architect resigned, in 1618, the Earl of Pembroke succeeded him, and presided over the fraternity until
1630. Others of Bacon's friends accepted office for short
periods— Henry Danvers, Earl of Derby; Thomas Howard,
Earl of Arundel, and Francis Russel, Earl of Bedford.   Then,
in 1636, Inigo Jones returned to his office of Grand Master,
which he retained till his death, in 1646. He designed Wilton
House, the seat of the Earls of Pembroke, where there was a
private theatre, and where *Measure for Measure* was first performed by Shakespeare's company, in order, it is said, to
propitiate the King at a time when Sir Walter Raleigh was about
to be tried for his life at Winchester, and when James I. and
his suite were staying at Wilton.

In the early accounts of Freemasonry, it really appears that
the actual building of " fair houses," or magnificent edifices
for public utility, or for religious purposes, was the sole
or chief object and mission of the Masons.   Even at these
early dates, however, the friends of Bacon's family were
apparently always mixed up with the affairs of the society.
Long after Bacon's death, the records of Masonry are seen
recording the same connection.   On the 27th December, 1663,
a general assembly was held, at which Henry Jermyn, *Earl
of St. Albans,* was elected Grand Master, who appointed Sir
John Denham his deputy, and Mr. (afterwards Sir) Chisto-
pher Wren and John Webb his wardens."

We pause, in order to draw especial attention to a foot-note
appended to the name of Christopher Wren:

" He was the only son of Dr. Christopher Wren, Dean of Wind-
sor, and was born in 1632. His genius for arts and sciences
appeared early. *At the age of thirteen he invented a new astronomical instrument, by the name of Pan-Organum, and wrote a
Treatise on Rivers.*"

It is, perhaps, needless to say no such " astronomical instru-

ment " is known at the Royal Society; neither is it mentioned
in any other account of Sir Christopher Wren which we have
met with, although the fact that he was, in 1680, chosen President of that society, might naturally suggest some instances of
his connection with mathematical science and mechanical inventions. Observe, that here is another precocious boy who
" invents " or designs a plan for a universal method, a *Novum
Organum.* Will any one produce Sir Christopher Wren's *Treatise on Rivers,* or any proof of his having written such a work?

In no life or biography of Sir Christopher Wren do we find
any of the statements which this work on Freemasonry inserts
concerning him, and which (as usual in these cases) *are rele-
gated to a foot-note.* His biographer continues:

" His other numerous juvenile productions in mathematics
prove him to be a scholar of the highest eminence. He assisted
Dr. Scarborough in astronomical preparations, and experiments
upon the muscles of the human body; whence are dated the first
introduction of geometrical and mechanical speculations in
anatomy. He wrote discoveries on the longitude; on the variations of the magnetical needle; *de re nautica veterum;* how to
find the velocity of a ship in sailing; of the improvements of
galleys, and how to restore wrecks. Besides these, he treated on
the convenient way of using artillery on ship-board; how to
build on deep water; how to build a mole into the sea, *without
Puzzolan dust* or cisterns, and of the improvement of river navigation in joining of rivers. *In short, the works of this excellent
genius appear to be rather the united efforts of a whole century
than the production of one man.*"

Here, it will be observed, the writer is saying of Sir Christopher
Wren the same, in other words, that Dr. Sprat said of Bacon, that
" *though he might not allow him to be equal to a thousand men, he
was at least equal to twenty.*"

And, looking back at the catalogue of Wren's performances,
not only are we disposed to look askance upon statements which
come to us in such questionable shape, and which have such a
curious affinity with particulars of researches which we do know
to have employed the nimble brain and the equally nimble pen
of Bacon; but further (since it is pleasant to understand what

we read) will any one inform us as to *Puzzolan dust*, and what can any kind of dust have to do with the building of a mole, or with cisterns? Is it possible that in *Puzzolan dust* we meet with one of those egregious puns, those quibbles or jests which, according to Ben Jonson, *Bacon never could pass by?* Was this the *dust* which is to be cast in the eyes of the mind to " *puzzle* the understanding," or to " puzzle the will" of man? We read in Rosicrucian works of " *dusty impressions*," [1] of brains which " trot through dust and dirt," [2] and the quibble is as well suited to convey its meaning as many others which we find in these and similar books. Perhaps when Ben Jonson said that Bacon never could pass by a jest, he said it *with a purpose*, to draw attention to these endless ambiguities of speech, the trivial puns which conveyed such weighty meanings.

The names of distinguished Masons are well worthy of note. They afford much insight into the connection between certain famous old firms in printing and kindred trades and those of to-day. It will be seen how many names well known in literature, art, and science are Masons, as it were, *hereditary*, and handing down the lamp of tradition, each in his own line. We have noticed some interesting tombs in connection with this subject, and younger readers are advised (having filled their minds with the symbols of these societies) to keep their eyes open when visiting old churches and church-yards.

To return to the point whence we started in this chapter, we find it almost impossible to believe that the Rosicrucians and the Freemasons were separate and totally disconnected fraternities, all evidence showing them as, originally, one and the same, the Rosicrucians forming the pinnacle to the lower orders of Masons, and although a mass of suggestive evidence has come before us, by means of the Rosicrucian books and documents, the more solid historical facts have all been reached by an examination of the old works which are professedly Masonic.

It is more than probable that at some period within a hundred years from the death of Bacon the " little knowledge" of many

---

[1] Bruno's Heroic Euthusiasts, part II. p. 176, edited by L. Williams, published by Quaritch. [2] Quarles' Emblems, i. 11.

of his followers became indeed " a dangerous thing;" that the " puffed," " swelling" and " windy" pride which he reprobated took the place of the patient, humble, self-effacing spirit of his first fraternity, and that the " Free Thought" for which he laboured " from curbed license pluck'd the muzzle of restraint." Instead of exercising a gentle and benign practice of tolerance in matters of religious ceremonial or of opinion, the Masons, in many cases, seem to have lost sight of the *universality* or *catholicity* of true faith, their religious principles degenerating into mere abuse and vituperation of the Romish church, whereas their duty was but to resist and expose its errors and imposture, and the initiation of Roman Catholics *(not Papists)* was permitted by the laws of the brotherhood. This violent and intemperate behaviour of the Freemasons seems to have produced a rupture, and Freemasonry became not the handmaid, but the enemy and opponent of Christianity, and the result affords a melancholy illustration of the saying of Bacon concerning atheism and its causes:

" The causes of atheism are divisions in religion, if they be many, for one main division addeth zeal to both sides, but many divisions introduce atheism."

Scandal of priests, and a custom of profane scoffing in holy matters are also causes which he notes for that atheism which to him is especially " hateful in that it depriveth human nature of the means to exalt itself above human frailty." He quotes the speech of Cicero to the conscript fathers, in which he says that they may admire themselves as much as they please, yet, neither by numbers, nor by bodily strength, nor by arts and cunning, nor by the inborn good sense of their nation, did they vanquish their many powerful antagonists; " *but through our devotion and religious feeling, and this the sole, true wisdom,— they having perceived that all things are regulated and governed by the providence of the immortal gods,— have we subdued all races and nations.*" [1]

---

[1] Essay Of Atheism.

CHAPTER X.

PAPER-MARKS USED UNTIL THE TIME OF SIR NICHOLAS BACON.

AMONGST the helps to the understanding in the *Interpretation of Nature*, Bacon " puts in the tenth place instances of power, or the fasces, which, also, I call *instances of the wit or hands of man*. These are the noblest and most consummate works in each art, exhibiting the ultimate perfection of it." Such works should, he says, " be noted and enumerated, especially *such as are the most complete and perfect ; because, starting from them, we shall find an easier and nearer passage to new works hitherto unattempted.* . . . What we have to do is simply this, to seek out and thoroughly inspect all mechanical arts, and all liberal, too, as far as they deal with works, and make therefrom a collection or particular history of the great and masterly and most perfect works in every one of them, together with the mode of their production and operation. And yet, I do not tie down the diligence that should be used in such a collection, to those works only which are esteemed the masterpieces and *mysteries of an art*, and which excite wonder. For Wonder is the child of Rarity ; [1] and if a thing be rare, though in kind it be no way extraordinary, yet it is wondered at. . . . For instance, a singular instance of art is paper, a thing exceedingly common."

He proceeds to describe the nature and qualities of paper, " as a tenacious substance, that may be cut or torn," and that, in its resemblance to the skin of an animal, and to the leaf of a vegetable, imitates Nature's workmanship; and he winds up as he began, by pronouncing paper to be " *altogether singular.*"

Then, as it would at first seem, going off at a tangent from

---

[1] *Miranda :* "O brave new world that hath such creatures in it!"

his subject, he says: " Again, as instances of the wit and hand of man, we must not altogether condemn *juggling and conjuring tricks.* For some of them, though, in use, trivial and ludicrous, yet, *in regard to the information they give, may be of much value.* " [1]

The chain of ideas in this passage — *helps to the understanding; many particulars united;* by the *wit and hands of man;* — these helps illustrated by the *masterpieces and mysteries of the art of paper-making;* and these arts, again, connected with *juggling and tricks,* suggested to the present writer the idea of examining the paper on which those books are printed, and which had already been specially noted on account of their " Baconian " matter and style; books which also contain the numberless unaccountable typographical peculiarities which seem to have some relation to a system of cipher, to be discussed in another part of this work.

A few hours of study were sufficient to prove that the very same " method of tradition," or system of secret communication, which is perceptible in the hieroglyphic pictures and wood-cuts, hereafter to be described, prevails, though in a simpler and rougher form, throughout the so-called " water-marks" or paper-marks of the Baconian books, pamphlets and manuscripts.

It was also found that the use and aim of these paper-marks, and their *interpretation,* are to be most easily reached by means of the metaphorical and parabolical language devised and taught by Bacon himself, and which continues to be used, whether consciously or unconsciously, not only by his acknowledged followers, but by the whole civilised world. These symbols were introduced with a purpose higher than that of mere decoration; they were, in the first instance, used not only as a means of mutual recognition, but also for covertly instilling or asserting truths and doctrines, in days when bigotry, ignorance, and persecution prevented the free ventilation of opinions and beliefs. But the secret language of the Renaissance philosophers requires a full volume for its elucidation, so, for the present, we must be con-

1 Nov. Org. xxxi.

tent to limit inquiry to its simplest manifestations, in the *paper-marks* of their printed books or manuscripts.

If one thing more than another can assure the inquirer into these subjects that here he has to do with the workings of a secret society, it is the difficulty which is encountered in all attempts to extract accurate information, or to obtain really useful books concerning paper-making, printing, and kindred crafts. In ordinary books, ostensibly instructive on such matters, the particulars, however detailed and accurate up to a certain point, invariably become hazy or mutually contradictory, or stop short altogether, at the period when works on the subject should teem with information as to the origin of many of our English translations of the Bible, and of the sudden outburst of literature and science in the sixteenth century. This is notably the case with one large and very important work, Sotheby's *Principia Typographica*, [1] which, for no apparent cause, breaks off at the end of the fifteenth century, and to which there is no true sequel.

There are, likewise, at the British Museum [2] eight folio volumes of blank sheets of water-marked paper. But these papers are all of foreign manufacture, [3] chiefly Dutch and German, and the latest date on any sheet is about the same as that at which the illustrations stop in Sotheby's *Principia*.

---

[1] Brit. Mus. Press-mark 2050 G. *Principia Typographica.* The wood-blocks or xylographic delineations of Scripture History, issued in Holland, Flanders, and Germany during the fifteenth century, exemplified and considered in connection with the origin of printing; to which is added an attempt to elucidate the character of the paper-marks of the period. Sam'l Leigh Sotheby. Printed by Walter McDowell, and sold by all antiquarian booksellers and printers. 1858. (Paper-Marks. See vol. iii.)

[2] Since there seems to be no catalogue accessible to the general reader, by which these volumes are traceable, we note the press-mark at the British Museum "Large Room," 318 C.

[3] Two loose sheets are slipped between the pages in two volumes. One is classified as Pitcher, the other as Vase. They are specimens of the one-handled and two-handled pots of which we have so much to say. These are English, and we believe of later date than any of the specimens bound up in the collection. Their presence is again suggestive. They hint at the existence of an English collection *somewhere*. Another particular points to the same conclusion. In "*Paper and Paper-making*," by Richard Herring, of which the third edition was printed in 1863 (Longmans), there are, on page 105, five illustrations of paper-marks. They are all specimens of the patterns used *circa* 1588

If it be worth while to collect, classify, and catalogue, in handsomely bound volumes, the water-marked papers of foreign countries before the middle of the sixteenth century, one would think that it would be of at least equal interest and importance to preserve a similar collection, such as could easily be made from the papers manufactured in England *circa* 1588, the date of the erection of the first great paper mill. If such matters are interesting or important in other respects, it would be natural to suppose that literary experts would find pleasure and instruction in connecting the paper with the matter printed upon it, and that a collection of paper used by the printers of all the greatest works published in the reigns of Elizabeth and James, whether that paper was home-made or imported, would have been formed by the careful observers who were so keen to preserve the older foreign papers, which concern us much less.

But such a collection, we have been repeatedly assured, does not exist at the British Museum, or indeed at any public library or museum to which authorities on such subjects can — or may — direct us. [1]

During this pursuit of knowledge under difficulties we have constantly been told that the subject is one of deep interest. "Instructive," "wide," "complicated," "vast" are the terms by turns applied to it by those to whom we have applied for help, so that sometimes we have been oppressed and discouraged as was perhaps occasionally intended) by the apparent hopelessness of following up the quest, or of fathoming these mysterious difficulties, which seemed to have no bottom.

But then came comfort. The mysteries, such as they are, are evidently traditional, of no real use to living individuals; no one can be personally interested in keeping them up, and where

---

and later, and they are numbered 1418, 1446, 1447, 1449, 1450. These numbers evidently refer to a collection such as we have anxiously sought, but which we have been repeatedly assured is *not known to exist.* That it does exist, we have not the slightest doubt; but where is it, and why is it withheld?

[1] Recently we have been told that the Trustees of the Bodleian Library at Oxford have secured a private collection of the kind, concerning which, however, no information is forthcoming to the present writer.

such mystifications are kept up the thing concealed is pretty sure to be something simple and easy to master when once it is reached. And there must be means of reaching it, because how can it be known that these subjects of inquiry are either instructive or worthy of pursuit unless some one has studied and pursued them, and discovered whither they tend?

Further effort, stimulated by reflections of this kind, have not been altogether unrewarded, and, although much remains to be cleared up, we trust that, regardless of scratches, we may have broken such a gap into the matter as to secure an easier passage for successors.

In *A Chronology of Paper and Paper-making*, [1] there is the following entry:

"1716—John Bagford, *the most extraordinary connoisseur of paper ever known*, died in England. His skill was so great that it is said that he could, at first sight, tell the place where, and the time when, any paper was made, though at never so many years' distance. *He prepared materials for a History of Paper-Making*, which are now in the British Museum, numbered 5891 to 5988." [2]

One hundred and eight volumes by this extraordinary connoisseur of paper! The hint did not remain unheeded, and it was

---

1 Joel Munsell, 4th edition, 1870; 5th edition, 1878.

2 These form, in fact, part of the Harleian collection. For some reason the Bagford portion has recently been divided. The bulk of it now reposes in charge of the librarians of the rare old printed books, "Large Room," British Museum. The MS. portions are in the MS. department, where, until lately, the whole collection were bound together. Most of the folios are scrap-books, containing thousands of book plates and wood cuts, large and small. Of these we shall have to speak by and by. Some were moved from the collection by order of the chief librarian in 1814 and in 1828. These extracts, "transferred to the portfolios of the Print Room," are not to be found. There is said to be no record of them. Similarly, the evidences of John Bagford's extraordinary knowledge of paper are absent from these collections. Some folios are made up of paper bearing six or eight different water-marks, and there are MS. notes of printers, which may lead to further knowledge. But the whole collection gives the impression that it has been manipulated for purposes of concealment, rather than to assist students, and the authorities at the British Museum in no way encourage the idea that information on paper-marks is procurable from this source.

to be hoped that at last some true and reliable information would be forthcoming. But, so far as any fresh knowledge concerning paper and paper-marks is concerned, an examination of many of these curious scrap-books and note-books has proved disappointing. Yet we glean further evidence as to the pains and care which in past years have been bestowed upon the laying of plans, and the carrying of them out in small details, for the purpose of preventing these subjects from becoming public property; for the books bear silent witness that one of two things has occurred: Either the portions relating to paper and paper-marks, their use and interpretation, have been at some time carefully eliminated (and probably stored elsewhere), or else they never were in this collection. In the latter case, Joel Munsell, Hearne, and others, must have derived their information about John Bagford and his extraordinary and almost unique knowledge of paper, *i. e.*, *of paper-marks*, from some other sources which they do not disclose, but which must be discoverable. For the present, we rest in the persuasion that all these " secrets " are in the possession of a certain Freemason circle, or perhaps, more correctly speaking, of the paper-makers' and printers' " Rings," and since it is not possible that these can a tale unfold of the secrets of the printing-house which have come to them traditionally, and under stringent vows, we must be content, as before, to grope and grub after scraps of information which, poor and despicable as they may seem in their disjointed state, afford, when pieced together, a valuable contribution toward the " furniture " of knowledge.

Ordinary works, whether of general information, or particular instruction on matters connected with paper-making, uniformly convey the impression that " water-marks " are either mere ornaments in the paper, or else *trade-marks of the paper-manufacturer.* One writer defines them as " ornamental figures in wire or thin brass, sewn upon the wires of the mould, which, like those wires, leave an impression, by rendering the paper, where it lies on them, almost translucent." [1]

---

[1] *Objects in Art Manufacture.* Edited by Charles Tomlinson. No. 1. Paper. Harrison, 1884.

Another writer, whose book has gone through several editions, and who is cited as an authority, distinctly claims for these water-marks that they are trade signs analogous to those of a public-house, a tea store or a pawnbroker.

" The curious, and in some cases absurd terms, which now puzzle us so much, in describing the different sorts and sizes of paper, may frequently be explained by reference to the paper-marks which have been adopted at different periods. In ancient times, when comparatively few people could read, pictures of every kind were much in use where writing would now be employed. Every shop, for instance, had its sign, as well as every public-house ; and those signs were not then, as they often are now, only painted upon a board, but were invariably actual models of the thing which the sign expressed — as we still occasionally see some such sign as a bee-hive, a tea-cannister, or a doll, and the like.

" For the same reason printers employed some device, which they put upon the title-pages and at the end of their books, and paper-makers also introduced marks by way of distinguishing the paper of their manufacture from that of others — which marks, becoming common, naturally gave their names to different sorts of paper. " [1]

These conclusions are, really, in no way satisfactory. They are in direct opposition to facts which present themselves in the process of collecting these water-marks — facts such as these :

1. That the same designs are often varied *in the same book*, some volumes containing as many as eight, twelve, or twenty-five variations of one pattern. (See Plates, *Ben Jonson*, *Selden*, etc.)

2. That similar designs appear in books of widely different periods *printed and published by various firms*, whilst, *so far as we have found*, they appear in the MS. letters of only one limited period.

3. That three kinds of water-marks (and so, according to Herring, *paper from three different firms*) are often found in one small book.

---

[1] "*Paper and Paper-making*," p. 103, by Richard Herring, 3d edition, 1863. See also Dr. Ure's "*Mines and Manufactures*"—*Paper-making.*

4. That these water-marks, infinitely varied as they are, often contain certain initial letters which seem to connect them with private persons, authors, or members of a secret society.

5. That, even in the present day, two or three firms use the same designs in their paper-mark.

These points, which it is our purpose to illustrate, assure us that it is an error to suppose either the most ancient or the most modern paper-marks to be mere trade-signs. True, that there are now some such which have been used, since the revival, as a fashion, of the hand-made or rough-edged paper. But these are quite easily distinguishable, and those who follow us in this investigation will have no hesitation in deciding to which class each paper belongs. On the other hand, Mr. Sotheby arrives, from his own point of departure, at the same conclusion reached by the present writer.

" I venture," he says, " to assert that until, or after, the close of the fifteenth century, there were no marks on paper which may be said to apply individually to the maker of the paper." With Jansen, he agrees that "the study of water-marks is calculated to afford pretty accurate information as to the country where, and the probable period when, a book without date or place was printed. . . . Until toward the close of the fifteenth century there occur *no marks in paper used for the making of books*, from which we are led to infer that they were intended for the motto or device of the maker. That paper-marks were, *or rather became general, and not confined to particular manufactories*, is in fact inferrible from the fact that we are able to trace similar marks in use from the commencement to the end of the fifteenth century." In some instances the varieties of the same mark are, as Mr. Sotheby says, so abundant that, "instead of the eight plates engraved by Jansen, it would require more than fifty plates of similar size to give the tracings of all the varieties of even two marks; the letter P, and the ' Bull's Head.' ... Hence it is that the frequent remark, ' with little variations,' is so generally found in the writings of all those, even from the earliest period to the present time, who have

20

touched upon this subject, *unaccompanied, however, by any attempt to account for or explain them.*"

Here we are reminded of the dictum of the Freemason Cyclopædia: "*A very minute difference* may make the emblem or symbol differ widely in its meaning," and of Bacon's similar hint as to the necessity for noting small distinctions in order to comprehend great things:

"*Qui in parvis non distinguit, in magnis labitur.*"

This he connects with the following note:

"*Everything is subtile till it be conceived.*" [1]

It is reasonable to attempt this explanation of the "little variations" that the symbol, whatever it may be — a bull's head, unicorn, *fleur-de-lis*, vine, or what not — illustrates some single, fundamental doctrine or *idea*. But the "little variations" may, as Jansen and Mr. Sotheby agree, afford pretty accurate information as to the country where, and the period when, the book was written or "produced." They may even indicate the paper-maker or the printer, or that the persons connected with the writing of the book were members of a certain secret society.

"The marks that are found on the paper used for the printing of the block-books assigned to the Netherlands are," continues Mr. Sotheby, "for the most part confined to the unicorn, the anchor, the bull's head, the letter P, the letter Y, [2] and, as we shall endeavour to show, the arms of the dynasties of the Duke of Burgundy, and their alliances; initials of particular persons, and arms of the popes and bishops. It must not, however, for

---

[1] *Promus*, 186, 187.

[2] In *Principia Typographica* (vol. iii., *Paper-marks*), we read that plain P stood for the initial of Philip, Duke of Burgundy, surmounted in some cases by the single *fleur-de-lis*, arms proper of Burgundy, and that in certain copies Y is added for Isabella — thus, as the author considers, proving the date. Students will, we think, find cause for doubting this explanation of the P and Y so frequent in very old books, and so long used. In Hebrew the sacred name of God is associated with the letter P — *Phoded*, or *Redeemer*. As is well known, this same form, with a cross drawn through the stem, was the sign adopted by the first Christian emperor of Rome, Constantine the Great. The Roman church still uses this symbol, so frequently seen stamped upon our books of Common Prayer. The Y is of far greater antiquity as a symbol, and was held by Pythagoras to signify the different paths of virtue and vice. Hence, says the *Royal Masonic Cyclopædia*, it was termed "*Litera Pythagoræ.*"

a moment be supposed that no marks similar to those we assign to the Netherlands occur in books printed in Germany; but, taking it as a general rule, the paper there used for printing was, no doubt, confined to the manufactories of the country."

These remarks do not touch the matter of English books and paper-marks; nor do they explain the appearance, simultaneously, or at different periods, of the same marks in different countries, and sometimes with the names of different paper-makers.

If the paper used for printing books was usually made in the country where the books were printed (and this seems to be the most natural and reasonable arrangement), then we must inquire at what English mill was the paper manufactured which was to be the means of transmitting to a world then plunged in darkness and ignorance the myriad-minded and many-sided literature of the sixteenth and seventeenth centuries?

As in everything else connected with printing, the inquirer is at once met with difficulties and rebuffs. Authors contradict each other. Experts in the trade plead ignorance, or decline to give information, and once more we are obliged to perceive how jealously everything connected with these matters is guarded and screened from public notice by the Freemasons. The following is extracted from the little book by R. Herring, which we have already quoted:

" With reference to any particular *time* or *place* at which this inestimable invention was first adopted in England, all researches into existing records contribute little to our assistance. [1] *The first paper-mill erected here is commonly attributed to Sir John Spielman, a German, who established one in 1588, at Dartford*, for which the honour of knighthood was afterwards conferred upon him by Queen Elizabeth, who was also pleased to grant him a license ' for the sole gathering, for ten years, of all rags, etc., necessary for the making of such paper.' It is, however, quite certain that paper mills were in existence here

[1] The editor of the Paper-Mills Directory, in his *Art of Paper-making*, (1874), says distinctly that the first paper mill in England "appeared in 1498; the second, Spielman's, *sixty years later*," 1558; a third at Fen Ditton, near Cambridge, " if it was not erected just before."

long before Spielman's time.[1] *Shakespeare*, in *2 Henry VI.* (the plot of which is laid at least a century previously), refers to a paper-mill. In fact, he introduces it as an additional weight to the charge which Jack Cade brings against Lord Saye. 'Thou hast,' says he, 'most traitorously corrupted the youth of the realm, in erecting a grammar school, and whereas, before, our fathers had no other books but the score and tally, thou hast caused printing to be used, and, contrary to the King, his crown and dignity, *thou hast built a paper-mill.*' An earlier trace of the manufacture in this country occurs in a book[2] printed by Caxton, about the year 1490, in which it is said of John Tate :

> " 'Which late hathe in England doo make thya paper thynne
> That now in our Englyssh thys booke is printed inne.'

" His mill was situate at or near Stevenage, in Hertfordshire ; and that it was considered worthy of notice is evident from an entry made in Henry the Seventh's Household Book, on the 25th of May, 1498: 'For a reward given at the paper mylne 16s. 3d.' And again in 1499: 'Geven in rewarde to Tate of the mylne, 6s. 3d.'[3]

" Still, it appears far less probable that Shakespeare alluded to Tate's mill (although established at a period corresponding in many respects with that of occurrences referred to in connection) than to that of Sir John Spielman.

" Standing, as it did, in the immediate neighborhood of the scene of Jack Cade's rebellion, and being so important as to call forth at the time the marked patronage of Queen Elizabeth, the extent of the operations carried on there was calculated to arouse, and no doubt did arouse, considerable national interest; and one can hardly help thinking, from the prominence which Shakespeare assigns to the existence of a paper-mill (coupled, as such allusion is, with an acknowledged liberty, inherent in him, of transposing events to add force to his style, and the very considerable doubt as to the exact year in which the play was written), that *the reference made was to none other*

---

[1] The writer of an article on paper in the *Encyclopædia Britannica* argues, with reason, that the cheap rate at which paper was sold, even in the inland towns of England, in the fifteenth century, affords ground for assuming that there was at this time a native industry in paper, and that it was not all imported.

[2] *De Proprietatibus Rerum*, Wynken do Wordes, edition 1493.

[3] "The water-mark used by Tate was an eight-pointed star within a double circle. A print of it is given in Herbert's *Typis Antiquit.*, i. 200. Tate died 1514."—J. Munsell.

than Sir John Spielman's establishment of 1588, concerning which we find it said :

> " 'Six hundred men are set to work by him.
>   That else might starve or seek abroad their bread,
> Who now live well, and go full brave and trim,
>   And who may boast they are *with paper fed.*'" [1]

What Shakespeare lover is there who will not recall the echo of the last words in Nathaniel's answer to his fellow pedant's strictures upon the ignorance of Dull, the constable :

Holofernes. Twice-sod simplicity, *bis coctus!*

O, thou monster Ignorance, how deformed dost thou look !

Nathaniel. Sir; he hath never *fed of the dainties that are bred in a book;* he hath not *eat paper*, as it were; he hath not drunk ink: his intellect is not replenished, etc. [2]

The supposed date of *Love's Labour's Lost* is 1588-9, precisely the date of the establishment of our first great mill. Can the poet, we wonder, have been *en rapport* with the inditer of the lines quoted by Herring (who, by the way, omits to say whence he quotes them) — and which of the two poets, if there were two, originated the notion of men being *fed with paper?*

The omissions of Richard Herring, quite as much as his statements, raise in our mind various misgivings and suspicions concerning him and the information which he gives. Does this writer know more than he " professes " to know? Are these remarks, in which he draws in *Shakespeare*, hints to the initiated reader as to the true facts of the case? Like the Rosicrucians, *we cannot tell;* but recent research leads us more and more to discredit the notion that particulars such as these about the establishment of the first English paper-mill are unknown ' to those whom they chiefly concern; or that shifting, shadowy, contradictory statements, of the kind quoted above, would pass unchallenged, were it not that an excellent mutual understanding exists between the writer and his expert readers.

---

[1] Herring, pp. 41-44. See also *A Chronology of Paper and Paper-making,* by Joel Munsell, fourth edition, 1870.

[2] Love's Labour's Lost, iv. 2.

If, speaking from without the charmed circle, we are expected to declare an express opinion regarding these things, it must be after this kind: Whatever paper-mills may have existed in England before the erection of Sir John Spielman's at Dartford, they must have been small, private (perhaps attached to religious houses), employed only in the manufacture of *writing paper*, and at all events quite inadequate to Bacon's purposes when he " was for volumes in folio," when he " feared to glut the world with his writings," and when the " Reformation of the whole wide world" was to be attempted by means of the press. The erection of the first great paper-mill in England is almost coincident with the establishment of the great printing-houses, whose first and noblest work was the printing and publication of the Bible in nearly every language of the globe.

" It is certain that printing was the great instrument of the Reformation in Germany, and of spreading it throughout Europe ; it is equally certain that the making of paper, by means of the cotton or flaxen fibre, supplied the only material which has been found available for printing. Whether this coincidence was simply accidental, or was the effect of that high arrangement for high purposes which we so often find in the history of Providence, may be left to the consideration of the Christian. But it is evident that if printing had been invented in any of the earlier ages, it would have been comparatively thrown away. . . . But at the exact period when printing was given to the world, the fabric was also given which was to meet the broadest exigency of that most illustrious invention." [1]

And who in those days had reason to know these things better than Francis Bacon? Who more likely than he to have inspired the enterprise of erecting the great paper-mill which was to serve as an " instance of the wit or hands of man," and to be ranked by him amongst " Helps to the Understanding in the Interpretation of Nature "?

Bacon never uttered opinions on subjects which he had not studied. Neither did he exhort others to undertake works which he had in no way attempted. When, therefore, we find him

---

[1] Dr. Croly's introduction to *Paper and Paper-making*, p. xii.

saying that *all mechanical arts should be sought out and thoroughly inspected,* and when, within a few lines, he associates these remarks with the masterpieces and *mysteries of the art of paper-making,* no shadow of doubt remains on our mind as to his own intimate knowledge and observation of the processes in the recently established paper-mill.

Going forward into the regions of speculation or anticipation, we can quite conceive that when Mr. Donnelly's cipher system shall be brought to bear on the second part of the play of *Henry VI.,* it will be found that the erection of this mill is recorded in cipher. This seems to be the more probable because it appears that, five-and-thirty or forty years ago, it was asserted by the then occupier of North Newton Mill, near Banbury, in Oxfordshire, that *this* was the first paper-mill erected in England, and that it was to this mill that *Shakespeare* referred in the passage just quoted ; and further (take note, my readers) — this Banbury mill *was the property of Lord Saye and Sele.*

Now, although the late Lord Saye and Sele distinctly discredited the story of this mill taking precedence of Sir John Spielman's, by showing that the first nobleman succeeding to that title who had property in Oxfordshire was *the son of the first Lord Saye,* [1] yet it is a coincidence not to be overlooked, that the Lord Saye and Sele of modern times should possess a paper-mill with the tradition attached to it of its being the mythical mill alluded to by *Shakespeare.*

The perplexity involved in these statements seems to be disentangled if we may venture to surmise that the cryptographer had to introduce into his play a sketch of the history of England's first great mills, erected in 1588, for the manufacture of *paper for printed books.* [2] The other small mills (which, for our own part, we think, *did* previously exist) were probably private establishments, producing paper for the special use of religious

---

[1] Shakespeare's reference is to *the first Lord Saye ;* there is no hint or suspicion that *his son* had anything to do with a paper-mill.

[2] Note Cade's words: "Whereas, before, our forefathers had no other *books* but the score and the tally, thou hast caused *printing* to be used." (*2 Hen. VI.,* iv. 7.)

houses, for state papers, or for the letters and other documents of important personages. In short, the earlier paper was, so far as we may yet judge, *writing* paper, too expensive to be used for books, but, as a rule, substituted, in important documents, for the costly parchment and vellum of earlier times.

It strikes us as a curious thing that, when our expert instructor comes to the point at which he affords some "*general observations*[1] *on what are termed water-marks,*" he should, for the second time, be drawn to illustrate his subject by circumstances connected with *Shakespeare.* Having briefly commented upon the use which has sometimes been made of watermarks in the detection of frauds, monkish or legal, he continues in a long passage, which we abridge:

"A further illustration of the kind occurs in a work entitled, *Ireland's Confessions*, respecting his fabrication of the Shakespeare manuscripts, — a literary forgery even more remarkable than that which is said to have been perpetrated by Chatterton, as 'Rowley's Poems.' . . . This gentleman tells us that the sheet of paper which he used was the outside of several others, on some of which accounts had been kept in the reign of Charles the First; and '*being at the time wholly unacquainted with the water-marks used in the time of Elizabeth,* I carefully selected two half sheets, not having any mark whatever, on which I penned my first effusion.'"

After relating, with a naiveté which borders on the comical, the way in which, by a payment of five shillings to a bookseller named Verey, the narrator obtained permission to take from all the folio and quarto volumes in his shop the fly-leaves which they contained, "by which means I was stored with that commodity," Ireland goes on to say that the quiet, unsuspecting disposition of the bookseller would, he was convinced, never lead him to make the transaction public.

"As I was fully aware, from the variety of water-marks which are in existence at the present day, that *they must have constantly been altered since the time of Elizabeth,* and being for some time wholly unacquainted with the water-marks of that

---

[1] They are rightly described as *general.*

age, I very carefully produced my first specimens of the writing on such sheets of old paper as had no marks whatever. Having heard it frequently stated that the appearance of such marks on the papers would have greatly tended to establish their va-lidity, I listened attentively to every remark which was made upon the subject, and from thence *I at length gleaned the intelli-gence that a jug was the prevalent water-mark of the reign of Elizabeth*, [1] in consequence of which I inspected all the sheets of old paper then in my possession, and, *having selected such as had the jug upon them*, I produced the succeeding manuscripts upon these, being careful, however, to mingle with them a certain number of blank leaves, that the production on a sudden of so many water-marks might not excite suspicion in the breasts of those persons who were most conversant with the manuscripts."

" Thus," continues our guide, " this notorious literary forgery, through the cunning ingenuity of the perpetrator, ultimately proved so successful as to deceive many learned and able critics of the age. Indeed, on one occasion, a kind of certificate was drawn up, stating that the undersigned names were affixed by gentlemen who entertained no doubt whatever as to the valid-ity of the Shakspearian production, and that they voluntarily gave such public testimony of their convictions upon the sub-ject. To this document several names were appended by per-sons as conspicuous for their erudition as they were pertinacious in their opinions." [2]

And so the little accurate information which is vouchsafed to us poor "*profani*," standing in the outer courts, the few acorns which are dropped for our nourishment from the wide-spreading tree of knowledge, begin and end in *Shakespeare*. In *Shake-speare* we read of the erection of the first great paper-mill — an anachronism being perpetrated to facilitate the record. In the *forged Shakespeare manuscripts*, the workings of that same paper-mill, and the handing down of Bacon's lamp of tradition, are even now to be seen. These signs are so sure as to have gulled the learned, " as conspicuous for their erudition as for their pertinacity."

---

1 Readers are invited to bear in mind this sentence in italics.

1 *Paper and Paper-making*, p. iii.

What further need have we of arguments to show that the true history of our paper-marks, and their especial value and importance, was perfectly well-known to the learned of two generations ago? Are we prepared to believe that such accurate knowledge is now lost? Surely not. The Freemasons, and more particularly the Rosicrucians, could tell us all about it. But, though they *could* if they might, they *may not*. Therefore, let us persevere, and seek for ourselves to trace, classify, and interpret the multitudinous paper-marks which are to be found onward from the date at which Mr. Sotheby has thought fit to cut off our supplies.

As to other works, we have given the names of a few from which, out of an infinite deal of nothing, we have picked a few grains of valuable matter hidden in a bushel of chaff. But, indeed, the reader, if he " turns to the library, will wonder at the immense variety of books which he sees there on our subjects, and, after observing their endless repetitions, and how men are ever saying what has been said before, he will pass from admiration of the variety to astonishment at the poverty and scantiness of the subjects; " and he will agree that " it is nowise strange if opinion of plenty has been the cause of want; . . . for by the crafts and artifices of those who have handled and transmitted sciences, these have been set forth with such parade, and brought them into the world so fashioned and masked as if they were complete in all parts, and finished. . . . The divisions seem to embrace and comprise everything which can belong to the subject. And although these divisions are ill-filled and empty cases, still, to the common mind they present the form of a perfect science." Bacon goes on to show how the most ancient seekers after truth set to work in a different way by storing up short opinions and scattered observations which did not profess to embrace the whole art. " But as the matter now is, it is nothing strange if men do not seek to advance in things delivered to them as long since perfect and complete." [1]

The early paper-marks were very rude and irregular. They

---

[1] Nov. Org. I. lxxxvi.

did not greatly improve until the time of the Bacons and the *Renaissance.* Still, they were common in all the manuscripts (whether books, letters, or other documents) which issued from religious houses, and as soon as printing began, then also began to appear these marks in printed books published on the continent, and on foreign paper imported into England.

But, rough as the early paper-marks are, *from the very first they had a meaning;* and so distinctly are they symbolic, so indubitably is their symbolism religious, that it would seem strange and incongruous to meet with them equally in the various editions of the Bible, and in the early editions of the masques and plays of the Elizabethan period, were there not strong evidence that these, and scores of other secular works, were brought out by a society established with a high religious purpose, and which, guided by Bacon's " great heart" and vast intellect, was bent upon ameliorating the condition of the world to its lowest depths, and by the simplest and least obtrusive methods.

Bacon drew no hard and fast line between religious and secular, or between good and evil, in things, in individuals, or in ideas. He thought that Nature, and pre-eminently human nature, were " biform, " a mixture of the earthy and the spiritual. Man, he said, is of all creatures the most compounded; and, knowing this, he appealed by turns, in the multifarious works which he wrote for man's instruction or recreation, to the many sides of the human mind, and of nature; to the dull animal who could take in ideas only through the eye and the ear, in dumb shows, masques, or stage plays, as to the bright, keen intellect of the man whose brain he compares to a diamond cut with many facets.

Everywhere, and by all means, he would endeavour to raise " man, who by his body is akin to the brute," to the higher and more spiritual level, where he would be, in some degree, " akin to the image of God. "

So, when we find within the pages of *Every Man in His Humour* and *Bartholomew Fair* the sacred symbols of the vine, and the pot of manna, we may reflect that this is no mere accident, no advertisement of the firm who manufactured the paper. These are some of the many records handed down by good Baconians of their " great master's " desire to draw together the most opposite ends of human society, and human thought, and to mingle with the coarsest earthy matter some bright and imperishable grains of the heavenly gold of truth and knowledge.

Let us turn to the plates of illustrations, of which a complete catalogue will be found appended to this volume.

There we see, first, a reduced mark from Jansen's *Essai sur l'Origine de la Gravure*, etc. Jansen records that this is the earliest mark known; it occurs, says Mr. Sotheby, " in an account book dated 1301 ; a circle or a globe surmounted with a cross ! A mark that is capable of suggesting much to the mind of a Christian." [1]

Probably the scarabeus forms (of which several may be seen on the plate) are not so capable of suggestion to most minds as the former symbol, but their deep signification is interesting, and should lead us to search into the origin of these mystical marks, admiring the wonderful way in which the wisdom of the earliest antiquity endeavoured to inform and teach, whilst the minds of men were too childish and uncultivated to receive truths except in the form of a picture or of a story.

That the matters to be instilled were in many cases eternal truths, thoughts and doctrines of the most sublime description, is seen in that these very same symbols, with a deeper intensity of meaning, and with further light shed upon them, have been, in various forms, passed on from one nation to another, from generation to generation; adopted and modified to suit the requirements of religious expression in many different forms of worship. However the external appearance may shadow or disguise the true substance, there are found in these symbols the same fundamental ideas, the same great universal doctrines and con-

[1] *Principia*, iii. 10.

ceptions of the one God — all-knowing, all-powerful, ever present — of His divine humanity, or manifestation in the flesh, of His Holy Spirit, comforting, sustaining, inspiring. The mystical teaching of the universal church of Christ was shown first as in a shadow or from behind a curtain, then with increasing clearness, until it reached its full development in the light of Christianity. Now with regard to the Egyptian beetle or elliptical form, introduced into the secret water-marks of Christian books. The beetle or scarabeus, like the peacock, or the iris, was, on account of its burnished splendour and varied colours, a symbol of the Heavenly Messenger. In many cases it was synonymous with the mystic Phœnix and Phanes, or Pan — another name for the Messenger or Holy Spirit. The Phœnix was supposed to return every six hundred years, upon the death of the parent bird, and thus it exemplified the perpetual destruction and reproduction of the world. The scarabeus, like the Phœnix, was the symbol of both a messenger and *of a regenerated soul.* It was the most frequent impression upon seals and rings in ancient Egypt, and hence the insignia of the Apocalyptic Messenger, the " *Seal-opener.* "

With such hints as these, it is easy to see, not only why the old religious writers and secret societies used this scarabeus, mixed with the cross and other Christian symbols, but, also, the cause and meaning of the extensive adoption of elliptical forms in engraved portraits in the mural tablets, monuments, and frames to memorial busts, on the tombs of the Rosicrucians and their friends. These memorials, when in black with gold lettering (typifying *light out of darkness*), reproduce absolutely the ancient idea adopted and assimilated by the Rosicrucians, of the perfect regenerate soul, destined by God to show forth His praises, who had called him out of darkness into His glorious light! [1]

Where the orb or globe and the ellipse are united with the cross, or where the undulating water-line on an ill-drawn circle

---

[1] Pet. ii. 9. The ellipse bore in ancient symbolism the same interpretation as the beetle.

represents the Spirit of God, as waters upon the face of the earth, Bacon's idea is before us of the "mingling earth with heaven," which was his dream, and his perpetual endeavour.

The few specimens which are given of the various and frequent unicorns and panthers, or dogs, as ecclesiastical symbols, are curious not only from their quaintness, and the persistent manner in which, by one device or another, they exhibit the emblems of the church, but also because here in the anchors we see spots which should incite inquiry. These have been explained as caused by the crossing or junction of wires in the paper-mark, but this explanation seems to be unsatisfactory, considering the position of the spots. They are usually in places where wires do not cross; and what is to be said of the unicorn (Plate II., fig. 1) with a line through his head? Do not these dots suggest to the cryptographic expert some of the many systems by which words can be spelt out, or information conveyed, by means of counting, or by the relative position of dots?

The nearest approach to the figure of a dog which we have found in Baconian times is the nondescript creature in Plate II., fig. 8. This is in some letters in Anthony Bacon's correspondence.[1] It seems to be intended to delude the eye as a serpent, but to be really the sacred horn, combined with the head of the dog or hound, in Hindu symbolism a type of the messenger of truth.

Serpents or serpentine lines are very frequent in early paper-marks, usually in combination with a cross, an anchor, or a Mercury's rod; they are conspicuous in the large collection of bull's-head water-marks which fill a folio volume in the British Museum.[2]

Bulls' heads in every conceivable variety of size and arrangement, in every degree of good and bad drawing, prevail throughout most of the MS. Bibles of the fourteenth and fifteenth centuries. Bulls with two eyes, or with one or none,

---

1 Tenison MSS., Lambeth Palace.

2 Press-mark 318 C. vol. vii.

with horns flat or exalted; curved like the crescent moon, or
rounded like leaves. Bulls with bland expressions and regular
features, formed by the adroit arrangement of a *fleur-de-lis* for
eyes, nose and mouth. Bulls with a Greek cross growing out at
the tops of their heads, or a Mercury's rod entwined with a serpent descending from their chins, and terminated by various
symbols, as the triangle, the figure 4, the rose or five-petaled
flower, the *fleur-de-lis*, or the so-called Templar's or Maltese
cross. Ubiquitous as this mark is in the old paper of the continent before the days of printing, and although fine specimens
may be seen of it in letters from foreign ecclesiastics and statesmen, in Cotton's collection of Baconian MSS., we have not yet
found one specimen in an English printed book. Special attention is, however, drawn to it because we are sure that this bull's
head, more and more disguised, was, in England especially,
changed into the *mock shields* which pervade Baconian literature, and which, as we will presently show, are used in the
present day by the same society which introduced them three
hundred years ago. [1]

This paper-mark is peculiarly interesting, and to the present
purpose as a forcible witness to the fact that the origin and
meaning of these marks is distinctly *religious*, and *the symbolism*
of the mediæval and modern churches in direct and legitimate
descent from that of the most ancient forms of worship, when
men, groping after truth, sought for means by which they
might make visible, to those who were more dull and dark than
themselves, thoughts and aspirations which they had hardly
words to express, or their hearers intelligence to comprehend.

The bull was one of the most ancient Indian and Egyptian
emblems of God; a symbol of patience, strength, and persistency
in effort. It is said to be in consequence of these attributes of
the bull that *Taurus* became the appointed zodiacal sign
at the vernal equinox; and under that sign God was adored as
The Sun, or the Bull.

---

[1] The bull is considered by Jansen to distinguish books by Fust. The single
head belongs to Germany.

We read in the Bible how the Jews, despairing of the return of Moses from the mount, wished to make for themselves the image of a god who should lead them through the desert, and cast out the ungodly from before them. To this end they melted down their golden ornaments, and made the shape of a calf or bull. [1]

The bull's head, although not reproduced in England in its original form, was and is, as has been said, preserved in disguise. Plates IV. and V. show a few of the many patterns of these disguised heads in mock shields. They are exceedingly various and frequent in Baconian works, and in editions of the Bible of which Bacon, we think, superintended the revision and publication. A comparison of the specimens given from the 1632 edition of *Shakespeare*, the works of " *Joseph Mede,* " 1677, and the modern-contemporary water-mark used by L. Van Gelder (Plate V.) will explain our meaning. In Van Gelder's paper the bull's head is clearly discernible, and so is the mutual connection between this and the earlier marks. In the specimens from the " Diodati " Bible, 1648, there is the same general effect as in those from the *Shakespeare* of 1623, and Bacon's works 1638. Certain particulars are never failing — indications of horns, eyes, and in some cases protuberant ears. Doubtless these mock shields were intended to pass with the profane vulgar for coats of arms of some great personage, as Jansen and Sotheby would lead us to think them. But a pennyworth of observation will correct this notion. The sacred symbols of the *fleur-de-lis*, the trefoil, cross, horns, pearls, and diamonds, with the sacred monograms, numbers, and mystic or cabalistic marks, show plainly whence the old paper-maker derived them.

---

1 It is said by some learned authorities that there seems to have been confusion in words, and that the Greeks put into Greek characters the Egyptian Ma-v-ocin, which means the place of light, or the sun. (See commentary on the Apocalypse, iii. 317.) But even this error, if it exists, only serves to show more clearly the close connection in the minds of the translators of Holy Writ between the most ancient religious symbols and those which they themselves employed. Bacon shows, in his Essay of Pan, the connection in parabolic language between horns and rays.

In the Bible horns are frequently used as emblems of pushing and conquest. They are, as we see on the Nineveh marbles at the British Museum, signs of prophet, priest, and king. In many emblem pictures the idea of omnipotence is so mixed up with the further god-like attributes of omniscience, omnipresence, and universal beneficence, that it is often difficult to decide whether the design is most suggestive of the horns of power, the rays of spiritual and intellectual light, or the cornucopiæ of Abundance. Sometimes serpents or serpentine lines found in connection with the bull, the cross, and the anchor are (especially in connection with wood-cuts) so rendered as to suggest the same mixed symbolism.

To the mystics in India and Greece, as well as to the ecclesiastics of the middle ages, and the philosophers of the sixteenth and seventeenth centuries, the serpent of eternity was the sign of God, the Holy Spirit. The symbol is retained in the stained glass of our church windows, and in emblematic designs from the Apocalypse, where St. John the Divine is distinguished by the chalice whence issues the serpent, typifying wisdom, or reason and speech, the gifts of the Spirit.

In the caduceus of Mercury, whilst the symbolism is somewhat changed, the idea is similar. The rod is said formerly to have been a *scroll* or ancient *book*, and the two serpents entwined round it typify everlasting wisdom. It is likewise the emblem of peace; for Mercury (according to pagan mythology), finding two serpents fighting, reconciled them by a touch of his wand, and thenceforward bore this symbol of reconciliation. This is held to figure the harmonising force of religion, which can tame even the venomous and cold-blooded snakes. The same line of thought may be followed up in Bacon's *Essay of Orpheus*, and in other places where he expounded his own views of the best methods for "tuning discords to a concord."

The old bugle mark, of which innumerable instances are found in old letters and MS. books, and which is in use at the present day, seems to have been originally derived from the bull and his horns. In the first instance, associated with the conception of the Su-

1

preme Being and His universal power, wisdom, and goodness, it
became, after a time, the bugle or trumpet which was to call
forth men to their duties — the Ecclesia — called out to do
especial service for God and for Humanity. [1]

Bacon and his friends adopted this bugle or trumpet, and, giving it an additional or secondary significance, assimilated it in
their hieroglyphic pictures and their parabolic phraseology.
Bacon is about to treat of the " *Division of the Doctrine concerning Man into* the Philosophy of Humanity *and* Philosophy
Civil." He shows throughout this chapter, as elsewhere, that

" The proper study of mankind is man,"

and this is his prologue:

" If any one should aim a blow at me (excellent King) for
anything I have said, or shall hereafter say in this matter (besides that I am within the protection of your Majesty), let me
tell him that he is acting contrary to the rules and practices of
warfare; for *I am a trumpeter, not a combatant;* one, perhaps,
of those of whom Homer speaks:

' *Hail, heralds, messengers of Jove and men!* ' [2]

and such men might go to and fro everywhere unhurt, between the fiercest and bitterest enemies. Nor is mine a trumpet
which summons and excites men to cut each other to pieces
with mutual contradictions, or to quarrel and fight with one another ; but, rather, to make peace between themselves, and, turning with united forces against the nature of things, to storm and
occupy her castles and strongholds, and extend the bounds of
human empire as far as God Almighty in his goodness may
permit." [3]

In the 1658 edition of the *History of Life and Death*, you may
see a fine example of the bugle with the SS in a shield-frame of
olive, surmounted by the usual crown, with pearls, horns, and
fleur-de-lis. [4] The olive, commoner, even, in the hieroglyphic

---

[1] Until recently, when the assizes were being held in country towns in England, the judges and council (barristers, etc.) were thus, when the court was to
begin business, *called out* from their lodgings by the sound of a bugle or horn.

[2] Hom. i. 334.

[3] De Aug. iv. 1.

[4] Observe also the distinct form of a pot in the outline of the shield or
wreath.

wood-cuts than in the paper-marks, is an evergreen, figuring
eternity. This tree was sacred to Minerva, wisdom. From it
was distilled the ambrosia, drink of the gods, "divinest olive
oil," with which Achilles was anointed in order to make him
invulnerable. "My friends, chew upon this." Try to realise
the deep symbolism of that pretty water-mark. See how, by a
few well-chosen outlines, within two square inches of paper, it
calls up the thought of one specially endowed for the benefit and
service of the whole human race, of winning for it all provinces
of learning; winning, "not as a combatant," but with sweet,
smooth, and winning words of divinest poesy — that "oil of
gladness" with which he was anointed above his fellows.
Songs of joy and gladness are for times of peace, and "the olive
is symbolical of the joy which peace diffuses. The leaves of the
olive (as a wreath) suggest the thought of its oil, used for the
anointing of the head. *Thou anointest my head with oil*, says
David, recounting the abundant blessings which he had received from God; and the ancients were accustomed to anoint
the head with oil on all festive occasious." [1]

"Blessed are the meek, for they shall inherit the earth. Blessed are the peace-makers, for they shall be called the children
of God." [2] Gentle, conciliating, peace-making, and peace-lov-
ing; endowed with powers and knowledge beyond all other men,
yet modest, retiring, and totally free from dogmatism and intolerance; a herald, not a trumpeter of his own learning — such was
Francis Bacon. Apparently, in his own day, and with some of his
biographers, he would have been more highly esteemed, had he
asserted himself, defended himself, stood upon his rights, and
refused to be thought wrong or to confess an error even for carelessness. By nature we know that he was, according to his
own showing, hasty, impatient, disposed to be over-impetuous
in his zeal, and exhibiting, though at rare intervals, "the flash
and outbreak of a fiery mind." But before setting forth to con-

---

1 *Free Masonry*, C. I. Paton, 1873, p. 158.

2 Quoted 2 *Hen. VI.* ii. 1.

quer others, he studied to conquer himself, with what result we see. The sweetness and calm beneficence which pervaded his whole being are the perpetual theme of letters and other authentic records which remain of him. His great desire, " as much as lay in him, to live peaceably with all men," made him shrink from controversy and disputations, prefer self-effacement, misconstruction, even disgrace, to the risk of endangering the realization of his visions and schemes for the happiness of the future ages.

And truly this " celestial peace " has perpetually hovered over his work; truly may this work, begun in faith and meekness, be said to *inherit the earth.* For where is there a region, inhabited by civilised man, which is left unpossessed by it? Founded upon Eternal Truth, that work must be, as Bacon himself believed, imperishable as Truth itself, and rightly is it figured by evergreen branches of the olive, sacred to Pallas.[1]

Sometimes the mock shields sprout into wreaths of laurel and bay (figuring triumph and victory). These seem to have been used for books published after the author's death. Other shields, whether foreign or English, of later date than 1626, have *chains* or interlinked SS, representing, perhaps, "not only the *chain of nature* and the thread of the fates, which are one and the same thing, but the famous *chain of Homer, that is, the chain of natural causes,*" " a chain which is confederate and linked together, and which, when the mind of man beholdeth it, must needs fly to Providence and Deity." The chains have, as usual, a double and Masonic meaning. Love, friendship, and true " brotherhood " are also *chains* held together by many bands or links firmly soldered, and difficult to break.

Bacon moves the Queen to friendly relations with France by showing how their mutual interests should form a bond of union between them, and, by means of her Majesty's friendship, " *solder the link*[2] which religion hath broken."

---

[1] Having stumbled across a quaint coincidence which may interest some readers, we give it for what it may be worth. " Pallas (*wisdom*) takes her name from vibrating a lance " In other words *shakes a spear,* " representing heroic virtue with wisdom."—(See *The Book of God,* iii. 98.)

[2] Compare : "They are so linked in friendship."—3 *Hen. VI.* iv. 3, 116.

He is expressing much the same thought about the Queen which is in the speech of King Philip to Pandulfo, the Pope's legate, regarding his own recent alliance with the English King:

> "This royal hand and mine are newly knit,
> And the conjunction of our inward souls
> Married in league, *coupled and link'd together*
> With all religious strength of sacred vows." 1

The wise words of Ulysses, commenting upon the anger of Ajax because " Achilles hath inveigled his fool from him," come often to the mind in reading such Baconian sayings.

" *The amity that wisdom knits not, folly may easily untie.*" 2 Nestor has rejoiced and laughed over the quarrel and consequent disunion of the two rival parties.

" All the better, their *fraction* is more our wish than their *faction* — but it was strong counsel a fool could disunite! "

Bacon furnishes a reply. The wisest of princes, he tells us, choose true and wise friends " *participes curarum,*" care-sharers, *for it is that which tieth the knot.* 3 Divisions and factions weaken the state, and " the cord breaketh at last by the weakest pull. " Those are the strongest whose welfare *joineth and knitteth them* in a common cause, 4 and since religion is, after all, the chief band of human society, " it is well when church and state are alike contained within the true *band* of unity. 5 He is not so Utopian as to expect that men will ever think all alike, on any one subject — there are " certain self-pleasing and humorous minds which are so sensible of every restraint as they go near to think their girdles and garters to be bonds and shackles " — yet he gives this advice according to his " small model." " *In veste varietatis sit, scissura non sit.*" Uniformity is not the same as unity — the *bond* of peace and of all virtues — and humanity should be drawn together by the chains of sympathy and mutual dependence, not rent asunder by hatred, jealousy, and uncharitableness.

---

1 *John* iii. 1.   2 *Troilus and Cressida,* ii. 3.
3 See *Essay of Friendship.*   4 *Ess. Sedition.*   *Of Unity.* 5

Thus we interpret the chains surrounding the shields, foreign or English, to be seen amongst our drawings. These shields form links with many paper-marks, assuming the shapes by turns of mirrors or hearts, or suppressing the escutcheon in favour of the crown which should surmount it. Or the outline of the shield is marked only by a wreath, or (in works, we think, not original, but the product of many translators, editors, etc.) by the chain, which sometimes includes shells and a pendant — and which points to the order of the Golden Fleece as its origin.

The heart shields often contain or are surmounted by a cross something like Luther's seal, or hearts are introduced into the frame of a mirror-shield, as in the example taken from the posthumous edition of Bacon's *History of Henry VII.* What a parable the old paper-makers have given us here! No need for " drawing it into great variety by a witty talent or an inventive genius, delivering it of plausible meanings which it never contained."[1] The parabolic meaning stands out plain before our eyes as we hold that old sheet against the light for the sun to stream through.

This shield, modified to the form of a *mirror*, is " the glass of the understanding," the mirror of man's mind, which Bacon calls the microcosm — the little world reflecting the great world without. " To hold the mirror up to nature," was one of his chief endeavours. He would " show vice its own deformity," kindly, gravely, or laughingly, " for it is good to mingle jest with earnest,"[2] and " what forbids one to speak truth with a laughing face ?"[3]

See the *bugle* of which we have spoken, the *heart* reminding us of the whole-hearted devotion which must be brought to the work of raising fallen humanity and regaining our paradise lost. Then the *scrolls*, are they not to bring to mind the magic wand of Mercury, *once a scroll or book?* It was by books that this regeneration was to be chiefly effected. By the *pearls* of knowl-

---

1 Pref. to *Wisdom of the Ancients.*

2 *Ess. of Discourse.*

3 Horace quoted *Promus* 1041.

edge uniting the *scrolls*, the *ellipse* which surrounds the mirror, and the *fleur-de-lis* which surmounts the whole, we are again bidden to confess that every good and perfect gift of genius, wit, or knowledge comes from the great God who has created and redeemed us, and who ever comforts, helps, and inspires us, that we may glorify Him with our bodies and with our spirits, which are His.

Returning for a minute to the bugles, we must say that it appears incomprehensible how a paragraph such as the following should be allowed to find its way into a book professedly instructive, "founded upon lectures delivered at the London Institution," and thereby claiming a certain authority :

"Post paper seems to have derived its name from the post-horn, which, at one time, was its distinguishing mark. It does not appear to have been used prior to the establishment of the General Post-office (1670), when it became the custom to blow a horn, to which circumstance, no doubt, we may attribute its introduction."

The post-horn or bugle was, at the time of the establishment of the post-office, more than three hundred and fifty years old. Even supposing the writer to be speaking of the bugle or horn, as used only in *printed* books, still it seems almost incredible that an expert should be unaware of the presence of this same "post-horn" in the works of Bacon thirty years before the establishment of the post-office. As for the bugles or "post-horns" in the writing-paper of Baconian correspondence, we pass them lightly over, on account of their multitude, but some specimens are given in the plates.

One more paper-mark, common in old religious books, is the fool's-cap. There are, as usual, various forms, some resembling a mitre, others diverging into distinct rays, five or seven, which rays sometimes develop into coronets or radiant rising suns.

The book before quoted proceeds to throw another sprinkling of "puzzling dust" in our eyes by the following observations :

"The foolscap was a later device (than the jug or pot) and

does not appear to have been nearly of such long continuance as the former. *It has given place to the figure of Britannia*, or that of a lion rampant, supporting the cap of liberty on a pole. The name, however, has continued, and we still denominate paper of a particular size by the title of *foolscap*. The original figure has the cap and bells, of which we so often read in old plays and histories, as the particular head-dress of the fool who at one time formed part of every great man's establishment.

" The water-mark of a *cap* may sometimes be met with, of a much simpler form than just mentioned, resembling the jockey-caps of the present day, *with a trifling ornamentation or addition to the upper part*.[1] The first edition of ' *Shakespeare*,' printed by *Isaac Jaggard and Ed Blount*, 1623, will be found to contain this mark interspersed with several others of a different character. No doubt the general use of the term *cap* to various papers of the present day owes its origin to marks of this description. "[2]

Turning our backs for a short time upon authority, we ask counsel of experience and research. First, as to the antiquity of the fool's cap? The earliest printed book which contains it seems to be the *Golden Legend*, written in 1370, but printed by Caxton.[3] After this it is not infrequent, especially in the modified forms which sometimes suggest a coronet or crown, sometimes the rays of a rising sun.

Perhaps the thoughts which the fool's cap suggested were akin to those in " Quarles' Emblems: "

> " See'st thou this fulsome idiot: in what measure
> He seems delighted with the antic pleasure
> Of childish baubles? Canst thou but admire
> The emptiness of his full desire?
> Canst thou conceive such poor delights as these
> Can fill th' insatiate soul, or please
> The fond aspect of his deluded eye?
> Reader, such fools are you and I."[4]

---

1 The writer omits to say that this "addition" is a *fleur-de-lis*, or other sacred emblem.

2 Herring, p. 104–106.

3 The illustration given is copied from Sotheby's *Principia*.

4 Quarles' Emblems, book iii. 2.

The text which furnishes the *motif* of these lines is from Psalm lxix, 5: "O God, thou knowest my foolishness, and my sins are not hid from thee."

In the modern edition, a child with a fool's cap and bauble rides astride upon the world, which wears an ass's head.

Little as we have reason to trust any printed statements on these subjects, yet there seems to be no cause for disbelieving the uncalled-for assertion that the *fool's cap gave place to the figure of Britannia, or that of a lion rampant.* There are apparently no modern fool's caps, but "Britannias" are common in English, and lions in foreign foolscap paper. So there can be no harm, for the present at least, in registering this item of knowledge. Yet we will, a little curiously, inspect our much-esteemed ruled foolscap. Holding towards the light the sheet on which we are about to write, we see that on one half it bears the inscription, "Toogood's Superfine." This is truly its trade-mark. According to our authority, on the other half we have Britannia portrayed as on our national penny, seated, and occupied as usual in ruling the waves.

This is the first impression. But Britannia should wear a helmet, should bear in her hand a trident, and beside her a round target or wheel, with the mixed crosses of St. George, St. Patrick, and St. Andrew, in the Union Jack.

The lady of our paper-mark seems to be crowned with five pearls. In her right hand she holds a trefoil or *fleur-de-lis*, in her left a spear tipped with a diamond. By her side rests a shield of elliptical form, and on it a plain cross. Beneath her feet are the ancient marks of waters, and her image is framed by three elliptical lines surmounted with a crown of pearls, and the Maltese cross and orb. Pearls, *fleur-de-lis*, diamond, crosses, ellipses — surely again we see in the very texture of our paper a reminder of the "Sovereign Lady," Truth; the heavenly jewel of knowledge tipping the spear which "pierces to the heart of things;" the pearls, the dew of heaven, the celestial manna, which Truth affords. Then the threefold ellipse, the cross, trefoil, and waters, are they not reminders of the fact that knowledge without Faith is but vain, that of ourselves we can do nothing, but that all things are possible through the Holy Spirit that strengheneth us."[1] The trefoil which Truth holds in her extended right hand is a silent emblem of the great doctrine of the Trinity in unity, to which heaven and earth alike bear witness.

Would any one endeavour to explain away such an interpretation, and to say that this paper-mark either represents Britannia, or that it represents nobody in particular; that the symbols are imaginary, or that they have come together by chance; in short, that this is nothing but a manufacturer's work, adopted by a certain firm, from whim or fancy, but with no especial aim?

Such conjectures cannot be accepted. For trade-marks are, as it were, private property; it is even actionable to appropriate a name or device previously adopted for commercial purposes. How, then, can we pronounce this paper-mark to be a trade-mark, when, taking up a sheet from another parcel marked " Joynson's Superfine," we find in it *the same* image of " Britannia," or Truth, as that in Toogood's?[2] *The same*, that is, in all essential particulars, ellipses, pearls, diamond, cross, crown, trefoil, water — yet with differences in small details such as we hope to show in similar wood-cuts in the " Baconian " books, and such as are perceptible in paper-marks of the same design, three hundred years old.

Joynson's mark is one-tenth of an inch smaller in all directions than Toogood's. The waves are fewer, the cross on the shield of thinner proportions; the garment of Truth, which in Toogood's pattern is loose, fits tightly in Joynson's similar design. We say, then, that *this is no mere trade-mark.* It is an emblematic or hieroglyphic design, deliberately adopted and reproduced by two distinct firms of paper-makers. It bears witness to a mutual understanding, and to a traditional method

---

1 Philippians, iv. 13, Vulgate, noted in Bacon's Promus, as " against conceyt of impossibilities." Fol. 114, 1242.

2 Since writing this we have seen another mark where a man's figure, Time, we think, takes the place of Truth. Bacon says that Truth is the daughter of Time, not of Authority.

amongst them of transmitting secret information, and, as we think, cardinal points of religious doctrine.

For, examine, trace, catalogue as we may, we never get away from these chief and dominant ideas and meditations of Bacon upon the unity and diversity and universality of God, in religion as in nature — of the beauty, love, and order in creation — that love and truth are inseparable — that the Bible and nature are God's two great lights, the greater light to rule the day of spiritual life, the lesser light to rule the night of intellectual darkness — and that man himself is the little world in which the whole great world, the universe, is reflected and mirrored.

Never for an instant are we allowed to forget that every good gift, every power or faculty of soul or intellect, the reason and speech which raise man above the level of the brute, are " God's gifts," to be used to His glory, and for the benefit of His creatures, and that all mankind is bound together by chains and links of sympathy and brotherhood, as every part of knowledge is linked in a never-ending circle.

One more mark should be especially noted, for, although it is amongst the oldest, it was used all through the life of Bacon, not only in England, but in books and letters from abroad. " *The open hand* " is variously interpreted of faith and trust, or of generosity and open-handed liberality; usually these qualities in their best examples all go together. To the open hand is sometimes added the trefoil, or the key, symbol of secresy, or the figure 3, perhaps again an allusion to the Trinity. Every variety of size, proportion or disproportion, is to be seen in these hands, which diverge into other forms, puzzling to the copyist. Sometimes the five fingers spread out into rays, or a crown, at other times contract, so as to suggest a vase. The most notable alteration (the addition of a star) seems to have taken place in the time of Sir Nicholas Bacon, and it was retained long afterwards.

Mr. Sotheby says that an open hand *with a star at the top* was in use as early as 1530, and probably gave the name to the " hand " paper.

This remark again encourages the erroneous idea that these are trade-marks, rather than the secret signs of a religious, literary society, which they surely were. The addition of " the star on the top " (sometimes not a star, but a rose or a *fleur-de-lis*) was made just about the time when the other " Baconian " marks began to appear, in the time, that is, of *Sir Nicholas* Bacon. [1]

The few specimens given in Plate III. are chiefly selected from a very large number which are found in the paper of one of· Anthony Bacon's chief correspondents — Anthony Standen. These letters were written from various parts of the continent, and under various names. Sometimes they are signed La Faye, at other times Andrieu Sandal. Under the latter name Standen was cast into prison in Spain, upon suspicion of being a political spy. The charge was disproved, and his release effected, apparently by the Bacons' influence, but Standen's history has yet to be written. Other specimens given from the Harleian, Cottonian, Lansdowne, and Hatton Finch MSS., at the British Museum, are in documents concerning the Bacons and their friends. They are chiefly in letters or documents sent from abroad, or in copies.

The secresy attaching to all these matters is the strongest proof that at some time or other there was *danger* involved in the writing, printing, and disseminating of books. Now, when there is no such danger, in free England and America at least, the secrets would certainly be made public, were it not that the vows of a secret society, vows perhaps heedlessly and ignorantly taken by the large proportion of members, prevent the better educated and more fully initiated amongst them from revealing things which must, one would think, be, at the present hour, matters chiefly of history or of antiquarian curiosity —

---

1 Joel Munsell specifies 1539 as the "era" of the "ancient water-mark of the hand with a star at the fingers' ends." ·He does not mention that *the star was then a new addition.* By 1559 this sign must have become sufficiently familiar to excite no inquiry, for in that year Richard Tottel printed " in Flete Strete, at the signe of the Hand and Starro," a translation of Seneca's *Troas*, made by Jasper Haywood.

immense aids to the study of " Elizabethan" and " Jacobean" literature, but hurtful to no one.

" It is much to be regretted that in tracing so curious an art as that of the manufacture of modern paper, any definite conclusion as to the precise time or period of its adoption *should hitherto have proved altogether unattainable.* The Royal Society of Sciences at Gottingen, in 1735 and 1763, offered considerable premiums for that especial object, but, unfortunately, all researches, however directed, were utterly fruitless." [1]

So says our guide. But is it credible that in the history of mechanical arts paper-making and printing are the only such mechanical arts which have no record of their own origin?

We cannot believe it. Some day, when the secret brotherhoods, especially the higher grades, shall have persuaded themselves that " the time is ripe," or when narrow protectionist systems shall, liberally and *pro bono publico*, give way to free trade in knowledge (as they have given way to Francis Bacon's other great *desiderata* — freedom of thought and freedom of the press) — then it will, we are convinced, be easy for those who hold the keys to unlock this closed door in the palace of Truth, and to let us know the rights about these precious and inoffensive arts and crafts.

——

The following is a list of the water-marks which we have found in books previous to the Baconian period, or in MSS. or other documents. The paper seems to be all foreign, from mills chiefly in Holland or Germany. Some of these figures were retained in the end of the sixteenth century and developed into other forms. Each figure seems to have been varied almost indefinitely. In our limited research we have seldom found two precisely alike, and there seem to be about sixty figures, not reckoning " nondescripts" and doubtful forms or variations:

1. ANIMALS. *Quadrupeds*—Ape or Monkey, Bull, Cat (or Panther?), Dog (Hound or Talbot), Goat, Horse, Lamb (some-

---

[1] Herring, *Paper and Paper-making*, 34.

times with flag), Lion (rampant or *passant*), Panther, Pig, Hog, Swine, Stag (head or *passant*), Wolf. *Birds.*—Cock, Duck (or Goose ?), Eagle (sometimes *spread,* or with 2 heads or 4 legs), Goose, Pelican, Swan. *Fish.*—Carp, Dolphin, Porpoise or Dolphin. *Reptiles.*—Lizard, Newt, Serpent. *Mythical.*—Dragon or Griffin, Mermaid, Phœnix, Unicorn.

2. *Flowers.*—Bell-flower, Fleur-de-lis or Trefoil, Lily, Rose (five-petaled, or nondescript, four-petaled). *Fruits.*—Cherries, Fig, Grapes, Pear, Pomegranate.

3. *Miscellaneous.*—Anchor (sometimes in a circle), Angel or Acolyte, Anvil, Ark, Bars with names, letters, etc., Battle-axe, Bell, Bow and Arrows, Cross Bow, Bugle or Trumpet or Horn, Cap (see Fool's Cap), Cardinal's Hat, Cask or Water-butt, Castle or Tower, ¹ Chalice, Circle (sometimes with cabalistic figures), Compasses, Cords or Knot, Cornucopiæ (or Horns), Crescent, Cross (Greek or Maltese), Crown, Fool's Cap, Globe, Golden Fleece, Hambuer, Hand, Heart, Horn, Bugle, Trumpet, Cornucopia, Key, Crossed Keys, etc., Ladder, Lamp, Lance or Spear, Letters (chiefly when alone, P and Y), Lotus (?), Mitre, Moon, Moose's Head, Mounts (3 or 7), Orb, Pope Seated, Reliquary (for Pot?), Scales on Balance, Shears or Scissors, Shell (or Fan?), Shield, Ship, Spear, Spiral line or Mercury's Rod, Star, Sun or flaming disk, Sword, Triangle with cross, etc., Trumpet (see Horn), Vine (see Grapes), Water-butt (see Cask), Waves or Water, Wheel (sometimes toothed).

---

¹ N. B.—This seems to be a modification of the Mounts and to end in becoming candlesticks.

CHAPTER XI

THE paper-marks which have hitherto been noticed were all used in manuscripts or printed books before Bacon began to publish, and chiefly on the continent. Many of them were retained or adopted by the members of his society. But their use became immensely expanded and diversified, and it will be seen that the Baconian literature contains these paper-marks so mixed (even within the covers of one volume) as to dispose of the idea that a certain quantity of paper of one kind, or with the mark of one maker, was apportioned for the printing of a particular book. On the contrary, it seems to have been almost the rule to use in one volume paper with three different marks, and each of these marks varied three or five times. This system of mixture, or of ringing the changes upon a certain set of patterns, makes it easy to establish a complete chain of connection between the books belonging to the society. Several of the marks are used as well by foreign as by English printers.

There are three paper-marks which we have learnt especially to associate with Francis Bacon and his brother Anthony. They are to be seen throughout the printed books which we ascribe to Francis, and one in particular is in the paper in which he and Anthony, and their most confidential friends, corresponded, whether in England or abroad. These marks are:

1. The bunch of grapes.
2. The pot, or jug.
3. The double candlesticks.

The grapes and the pots appear, in somewhat rude forms, as early as the fourteenth century. The candlesticks seem in their earlier stages to have been towers or pillars. As candlesticks, even *single*, we have failed to find one earlier than 1580, and then in a MS. document. (Plate VIII. 1.) Even this example is rather suggestive of a castle than of a candlestick, and as castles and towers of unmistakable forms (and sometimes showing an affinity to the mounts spoken of in the last chapter) appear in books published in Italy as early as the fourteenth century, it is possible that here we have some of the many scattered links in the chain of continuity in designs as well as ideas.[1]

These three marks we associate with Francis Bacon: (1) Because few of his letters are without the pot, and none of his acknowledged books without one or more in the paper-marked editions. (2) Because in works whose matter, language, and other signs, internal and external, point to him as their author, one or more of these marks runs through the book. (3) Because when the book is of the kind which Bacon "collected," by the aid of others, or revised and improved upon for other writers, one at least of these three patterns (used, perhaps, once or twice only in the whole book, or in the fly-leaves) acknowledges the touch of his hand. In such cases, the paper-marks in the body of the book are quite different, or there are none. To begin with the candlesticks, of which patterns may be seen on Plate VIII. These, we believe, were the latest and least frequent of the three, being used in the double form only in editions of Bacon's works published after his death. They are placed first because their meaning is, perhaps, the deepest of any, and the most far-reaching, being intimately connected with many of Bacon's greatest thoughts and "fixed ideas;" consequently, with a large section of his philosophy, to which the opening verses of the Bible are the text and the key-note:

" In the beginning God created the heavens and the earth. And the earth was without *form and void, and darkness was upon the face of the deep. And the Spirit of God moved upon the face of the waters. And God said, Let there be light, and there was light.*"

---

1 Sotheby says that grapes occur in books printed at Mentz, Strasburg, Nuremberg, Basle, and Cologne, and that they were produced by Caxton, but are not in any book printed in the Netherlands.

These words are also the key-note to Rosicrucianism. In the *Fama Fraternitatis* we read :

" Our axiomata shall immovably remain unto the world's end, and also the world in her highest and last age shall not attain to see anything else; for our ROTA takes her beginning from that day when God spake FIAT, and shall end when he shall speak PEREAT."

Another Rosicrucian work thus expresses the same ideas: " In respect that God Almighty is the only immediate agent which actuates the matter (of the world), it will not be amiss to speak something of Him, that we may know the cause by His creatures, and the creatures by their cause." Then follow some verses in which the poet compares his soul to a mole, " imprisoned in black entrenchments, . . . heaving the earth to take in air," and " mewed from the light of day." He prays:

> " Lord, guide her out of this sad night,
> And say once more, *Let there be light*."

The same writer says, in another place:

" We read that darknesse was upon the face of the deep, and the Spirit of God moved upon the face of the waters. Here you are to observe that, notwithstanding this processe of the Third Person, yet there was no light, but darknesse on the face of the deepe, illumination being the office of the Second (Person). Wherefore God also, when the matter was prepared by love for light, gives out his FIAT LUX, which was no creation, as most think, but an Emanation of the Word, in whom was life, and that life is the light of men. This is the light whereof St. John speaks, that *it shines in the darknesse, and the darknesse comprehendeth it not.*" [1]

That he " may not be singular on this point," the author quotes Pimandrus, who, in the *Book of the Creation*, informs Trismegistus: " I am that Light, the Pure Intelligence, thy God." In another work the same Eugenius argues that, " to come to the point, these invisible, central artists are lights,

---

[1] *Anthroposophia Theomagica.* " Eugenius Philalethes." Published later as the work of Thomas Vaughan. See "Vaughan's Magical Writings," reprinted and edited by E. A. Waite, 1888. Redway (Kegan, Paul, Trubner & Co.)

seeded by the First Light in that primitive emanation, or SIT LUX — Let there be light — which some falsely render FIAT LUX — Let light be made. For nature is the voice of God, not a mere sound or command, but a substantial, active breath, proceeding from the Creator, and penetrating all things." [1] In the *Lumen di Lumine* the same author describes " The New Magical [2] Light Discovered and Communicated to the World." Here we read of " a phantastic circle, within which stands a lamp typifying the light of nature, the secret candle of God, which he hath tinned in the elements. It burns but is not seen, shining in a dark place. Every naturall body is a kind of black lanthorne; it carries this candle within it : but the light appears not; it is eclipsed by the grossness of the matter. The effect of this light is apparent in all things, but the light itself is denied, or else not followed. The great world hath the sun for his life and caudle. According to the absence or presence of this fire, all things in the world flourish or wither."

In the " *Fasciculus Chemicus,* or Chymical Collections made English by James Hasolle," [3] there is a prayer for the Intellectual

---

[1] *Anima Magica Abscondita.* Eugenius Philalethes. Ed. A. E. Waite. Redway.

[2] We must not allow ourselves to be puzzled or misled by the use of language purposely adopted by the professors of the New Philosophy in order outwardly to accord in some degree with the jargon of the alchemists. Bacon explains very clearly his view of magic in the true sense. "The chief business of the Persian magic (so much celebrated) was to watch the correspondences between the architectures and fabrics of things natural and things civil. . . . Neither are these all *similitudes,* but plainly the footsteps of nature treading or printing upon different subjects and matters. . . . A thing of excellent use *for displaying the unity of nature,* which is supposed to be the office of Primitive Philosophy." — (*De Aug.* iii. 1.)
"I must stipulate that magic, which has long been used in a bad sense, be again restored to its ancient and honourable meaning. For among the Persians magic was taken for a sublime wisdom, and the knowledge of the *universal consents of things,* and so the three kings who came from the East to worship Christ were called by the names of the Magi. I, however, understand it as the science of hidden forms (*inherent natures*) to the production of wonderful operations; and by uniting (as they say) actives with passives, displays the wonderful works of nature." — (*Ib.* iii. 5). Natural magic, in short, displays not only the *unity of nature,* but also the *universal harmony of things ;* the mingling of heaven and earth — Bacon's prime object.

[3] An anagram for the name of Elias Ashmole, the celebrated Freemason and Rosicrucian antiquarian and historian, born, Lichfield, 1617.

Light strongly resembling well-known prayers of Bacon, and on the hieroglyphical frontispiece to this curious book is another allusion to the mole as a type of the soul struggling towards Light and Freedom.[1]   Amongst many other emblems there is an ash-tree, from which rises a scroll, surmounted by a square (or " Templar ") cross, a sun and a moon.   On the scroll is written : " *Quod est superior est sicut inferius.* "   Beneath the tree is seen a mole digging, and the motto : " *Fraximus in Silvis pulcherima, Talpa in Terris operissima.* "

In the lower margin of the picture the device is thus expounded :

> " These Hieroglyphics vaile the vigorous Beames
> *Of an unbounded Soul :* The Scrowle & Schemes
> The full Interpreter: But now's conceald,
> Who through Œnigmas lookes, is so reveald."

In the *New Atlantis* (which so-called *fragment* of Bacon's is the same as the *Journey to the Land of the Rosicrucians*),[2] we read of a great pillar of light rising from the sea a great way towards heaven ; and on the top of it, a large cross of light, which was regarded as a heavenly sign.   " One of the wise men (of the society of the Rosicrucians), after offering up prayer to God for his grace in showing him this miracle, causes his boat to be softly rowed towards the pillar, but ere he came near, the pillar and cross of light brake up, and cast itself abroad into a firmament of many stars, which also soon vanished. "   The wise man presently informs the travellers to his land : " You see we maintain a trade, not for gold, silver or jewels, nor for any commodity of matter, but only *for God's first creature, which was light,* to have light, I say, of the growth of all parts of the world."

---

[1] Frequent allusions of this sort remind us of Hamlet comparing the Ghost (or Soul) of his father to " an old mole " working in the grouud (*Hamlet,* i. 5), and of the " blind mole casting copped hills to heaven " in his efforts toward air and light.   (See *Pericles,* i. 1, 98–102.)

[2] This last, though published twenty years later than the *New Atlantis,* appears from its language to be the first editiou.   The *Atlantis* was, by Bacon's order, published after his death by his secretary, Dr. Rawley.   It is inserted without date, though with separate title page, between the *Sylva Sylvarum,* 1640, and the *Hist. Life and Death.*

The merchants whom the Atlanteans or Rosicrucians send forth they call " Merchants of Light," and in " certain hymns and services of laud and thanks to God for his marvellous works," there are, they say, forms of prayers invoking His aid and blessing "*for the illumination of our labours*, and the turning them into good and holy uses."

Can we read these words without recalling one of Bacon's most beautiful prayers, part of which concludes the " Plan " of the *Novum Organum?* [1]

" Thou, O Father! who gavest the visible light as the first-born of Thy creatures, and didst pour into man the intellectual light as the top and consummation of Thy workmanship, be pleased to protect and govern this work, which, coming from Thy goodness, returneth to Thy glory."

In another prayer, we find the great student earnestly entreating that

" Human things may not prejudice such as are divine ; neither that from the unlocking of the gates of sense, and *the kindling of a greater natural light*, anything *of incredulity or intellectual night* may arise in our minds towards the divine mysteries." [2]

Bacon is never weary of finding analogies between the brightness of heaven and the light of truth, knowledge, heavenly thoughts, " heaven-born poesy." In the dullest minds some spark, some glimmer of intelligence may, he thinks, be kindled, and the faintest rays will penetrate into darkest places.

> " How far that little candle sheds its beams !
> So shines a good deed in a naughty world."

It would be a grand thing, he said, " if a man could· succeed in kindling a light in nature — a light that should, by its very rising, touch and illuminate knowledge;" and he describes the ancient churches as " torches in the dark." In the *Wisdom of the Ancients*, suggestive metaphors are used, or fables expounded of Vulcan and the efficacy of fire, and of the *games of the torch*

---

1 Published after his death in *Baconiana*, by his friend, Dr. Tenison, and by him entitled " The Writer's Prayer." See Spedding, Works, vii. p. 259.

2 "The Student's Prayer." Ib.

instituted to Prometheus, in which the object is *to keep the torch alight and in motion.* The torch is like the candlestick, the means by which the light is maintained and transmitted; it usually symbolises the mind of man, his " pure intelligence." " Solomon," Bacon says, " was one of the clearest burning lamps whereof he himself speaketh . . . when he saith, *the spirit of man is the lamp of God wherewith He searcheth all inwardness.*"

There are men whom fortune has " set on a hill;" they have position, perhaps, as well as powers of mind; wealth as well as ability. These must act as beacons,[1] to guide the traveller from afar; others may perform the humbler but still useful offices of lamps, lanterns, tapers, candles. The slightest efforts, well directed, should not be despised, and we cannot dispense with even the soft radiance of the " watch candle," or the shy, retiring helper, who never will assert himself, and prefers to work unrecognised —

> " Like the glowworm in the night,
> The which hath fire in darkness, none in light." [2]

There are those who, though incapable of emitting the light of original thought from themselves, can yet afford mechanical help to others. Such lowly but willing spirits are compared to " candle-holders," or torch-bearers, who do not merely look on whilst others labour, but who shed light from the torch which has been put into their hand. There were and are a multitude of such candle-holders in the society of which we speak.

In collating the Baconian and Rosicrucian works, no one can fail to observe the noble spirit of self-sacrifice, and disregard of personal interest, which pervades them.

" Be not as a lamp that shineth to others, and yet seeth not itself, but as the Eye of the World, that both carrieth and useth

---

1 It is worthy of notice that the Bacon family in early times spelt their name Becon or *Beacon.* Some of them seem to have written under this name, and there is a work by Thomas Becon, 1563–4, in which, on the title page of the second volume, his name changes from Becon to Beacon. Francis Bacon, who "could not pass by a jest," cannot have failed to see this opportunity for a quibble.

2 *Pericles,* ii. 3.

light." [1] "For," says Bacon, in another place, "the sense is God's lamp," [2] and he gives the King credit for being that which he desired him to be, "a clear-burning lamp." [3]

In the *Novum Organum,* unwise experiments are compared to a "mere groping in the dark," but the true method of experience first lights a candle, and then, by means of the candle, shows the way." [4] The communication of knowledge is described as that "of one candle with another, which lights up at once." [5] This is somewhat the same as Bacon's other figure of "handing down the lamp of tradition." He urges men to unite in one great effort, rather than to fritter away their powers in small detached experiments and weak works. "Were it not better for a man in a fair room to set up one great light or branching candlestick of lights, than to go about with a small watch-candle in every corner?" [6]

"For mere contemplation, which should be finished in itself without casting beams of light and heat upon society, assuredly divinity knows it not." [7]

> "*Heaven doth with us as we with torches do,*
> *Not light them for ourselves: for if our virtues*
> *Did not go forth of us, 'twere all alike*
> *As if we had them not. Spirits are not finely touch'd*
> *But to fine issues.*" [8]

The first twenty-six *Shakespeare* sonnets repeat these sentiments. The poet reproaches his friend,

> "That thou, contracted to thine own bright eyes,
> Feed'st thy life's flame with *self-substantial* fire;" [9]

and, although he continually changes the figure, the same idea is worked out in many different ways. He speaks of the enthusiasm which gives fire to our nation, [10] and which set men's hearts on fire; of the fires of love, hatred, zeal, or sedition, which glow, burn, smoulder, are blown up into flame, or smothered and extinguished; [11] sparks which fly abroad lighting upon free and no-

---

1 *Gesta Grayorum.* Comp. Part ii. *Tamburlaine the Great,* iv. 3; 1. 88; v. 3, l. 3, 158. 2 *Nat. Hist.* x. Pref. 3 Speech. 4 *Nov. Org.* i. 82. 5 Ess. of Sphinx. 6 *Advt. of L.* i. 1. Comp. with the above. 7 *De Aug.* vii. 1. 8 See *M. M.* i. 1, 29–40. 9 Son. i. 10 Of Calling Parl. 1615. 11 *Hist. Hen. VII.*

ble minds and spirits apt to be kindled; sparks of affection, of grace, " liberty, spirit, and edge." [1] " *My heart,*" he says, in one of his prayers, " hath been an unquenched coal on thine altar."

" Have a care," says one of the councillors in Bacon's device, " The Order of the Helmet," " that the light of your state do not go out, or burn dim or obscure." Bacon was continually trying to urge upon the sovereign for the time being, her or his duties and responsibilities in regard to the handing on of the lamp. He received little encouragement from Elizabeth, but by dint of impressing upon the mind of the King, not only that he ought to assist learning, but that he *was learned,* and capable of doing what he pleased in the fields of literature and science, he seems to have succeeded in making that dull monarch appear, and believe himself to be, something like the bright creature which Bacon so earnestly desires that he should become. There " are joined in your Majesty *the light of nature, the light of learning,* and *the light of God's holy spirit* (and that) *fourth light, the light* of a most wise and well-compounded counsel." [2]

A *watch-candle* is the emblem of " *care and observation.*" In a letter to King James (May 31, 1612) Bacon says: " My good old mistress was pleased to call me her watch-candle, because it pleased her to say I did continually burn (and yet she suffered me to waste almost to nothing)." Elsewhere he says: " There should be a sort of night-watch set over nature, as showing herself rather by night than by day. For these may be regarded as night studies, by reason of the smallness of the candle and its continual burning." [3]

Amongst our candlesticks is one (Plate VIII.) from the *Observations on Cæsar's Commentaries* of 1609. This volume has on its title-page a medallion portrait of a young man, sixteen or seventeen years of age, who bears a striking likeness to the juvenile portraits of Francis Bacon. These *Observations* on " those most excellent Commentaries that Cæsar writ " [4] are published

---

[1] *Advt.* ii., *De Aug.* viii. 2, etc.   [2] *Pacification of the Church.*   [3] *Nov. Org.* ii. 4.   [4] *2 Hen. VI.* iv. 7.

with the name of " Clement Edmundes, Remembrancer of the Cittie of London." To occupy such a position Edmundes must have been a man of some standing; his, therefore, cannot be the boyish portrait which figures at the top of this title-page. May we not rather believe it to be that of the youth who for seven years devoted himself, heart and soul, to the study of the ancient authors, and who thus speaks of these very Commentaries, with which we see that he was more than ordinarily acquainted ? [1]

" As for Julius Cæsar, the excellency of his learning needeth not to be argued from his education, or his company, or his speeches; but in a farther degree doth declare itself in his writings and works; whereof some are extant and permanent, and some have unfortunately perished. For first . . . there is left unto us *that excellent history of his own wars, which he entitled only a Commentary, . . . wherein* all succeeding times have admired the solid weight of matter, and the real passages and lively images of actions and persons, expressed in the greatest propriety of words and perspicacity of narration that ever was." [2]

The one little candlestick referred to is the only one of the kind which as yet we have met with ; it may, however, be expected that other examples will be found in early editions of some of the boyish works published by his friends; for we suppose this figure to represent some utterance or aspiration of the youthful student, that he might himself be a humble light, or candle-holder, for others. This conjecture is not unreasonable, seeing that immediately after his death, and for fifty years subsequently, his immediate friends and followers developed and made conspicuous use of this symbol in editions of his acknowledged works, and in others which we ascribe to him.

And would any one find it easy to devise an emblematic water-mark more suitable for works such as Francis Bacon engaged in than this of the double candlesticks, with their varied, " bifold " meanings? Once perhaps the mounts of knowledge, then rocks, castles, towers difficult to scale or

---

1 Again we insert a saving clause in regard to " Anthonie," the " deare brother," fellow-student in youth, twin in mind and face, who may prove to have been the translator or inditer of these " Commentaries." 2 See a long criticism, from which the above is condensed.—*Advancement of Learning*, i. I.

surmount — pillars of Hercules, bounding and obstructing human knowledge and aspiration — they are now converted into pillars of light, beacons for guidance and encouragement to distressed and weary travellers. They are lights of truth and beauty. The divine light of the Holy Spirit and the light of the human intellect. The light of God's word and the light of nature. God's "two witnesses, . . . the two candlesticks standing before the God of the Earth." [1]

In combination with the candlesticks are *fleur-de-lis*, trefoil, pearls, and other symbols of the Holy Spirit; sometimes an R C or C R; almost invariably grapes piled in a pyramid or diamond. The bunch of grapes, alone, or in combination with other figures, is the second great mark in Bacon's books; he has explained their symbolism:

"As wines which flow gently from the first treading of the grape are sweeter than those that are squeezed out by the wine-press, because these last have some taste of the stones and skin of the grape; so those doctrines are very sweet and healthy which flow from a gentle pressure of the Scripture, and are not wrested to controversies and commonplaces." [2]

Again: "I find the wisdom of the ancients to be like grapes ill-trodden: something is squeezed out; but the best parts are left behind;" [3] and he likens the laws to "the grapes that, being too much pressed, yield an hard and unwholesome wine." His own "method, as wholesome as sweet," [4] tolerant of other men's opinions, whilst firm in his own, appears in these words:

"I may say, then, of myself (since it marks the distinction so truly), *it cannot be that we should think alike, when one drinks water and the other wine*. . . . Now, other men have, in the matter of sciences, drunk a crude liquor like water, either flowing spontaneously from the understanding, or drawn up by logic, as by wheels from a well. Whereas I pledge mankind in a liquor pressed from countless grapes — from grapes ripe and fully seasoned, collected in clusters, and gathered, and then squeezed in the press, and then, finally, purified and clarified in the vat." [5]

---

1 *Revelations*, xi. 3, 4.   2 *De Aug.* ix. 1.   3 *Controversies of the Church.*
4 *Ham.* ii. 2.   5 *Nov. Org.* i. 123.

And here, in his books, are the grapes in clusters or " collections " ready for the " first vintage." Books of all kinds, and in all degrees of " crudity," will be found to contain these famous symbolic paper-marks, of which only a few examples can here be given. Pray, my readers, heed them, note them, and add to the list appended to this chapter. If not in one edition, yet in another, of every work of Bacon, writ by the light of God's two candlesticks, these grapes will be found. He was at first treading the wine-press alone, and his efforts were those pioneer labours often so painful, and so unrewarded to the performer, but which " smooth successors their way."

" Since truth," he says, " will sooner come out from error than from confusion, I think it expedient that the understanding should be permitted" (*after " a due presentation of instances,"* or collection of facts on the subject in hand) " to make a kind of essay, which I call the *Indulgence of the Understanding*, or the *Commencement of Interpretation*, or the *First Vintage.*" Then he proceeds to press, out of the few facts which he has been able to collect, " a first vintage," on the nature of heat.

Perhaps we may gain hints as to the degree of completion which Bacon considered that certain of his works had attained, by the number of the grapes, or the perfection of the diamond shape in which many of the bunches are arranged. In this diamond we are reminded of the " heavenly jewel " of knowledge, the reason and speech which Bacon says is especially the divine gift to man. Where there is not this form, a *fleur-de-lis* or the letters R C have been almost invariably found. The latter, often combined with another letter, are conjectured to be a signature of the Rosicrucian brother by whose aid the work was produced; as, for instance, in *Cynthia's Revels*, two distinct forms of I R C are found, which *may* mean " Ionson, Rosy Cross." [1] The same letters are in a bar in the last page of *Shakespeare*, 1623, but they are differently arranged — R C I, and a reversed C, as may be seen in

---

[1] Often the letters are very confused or inverted, or written so that they can only bo read in a mirror. This complicates matters. We do not pretend to give positive opinions about these things.

Plate XI. 7, Plate XII. 46, 52. It is well known how Ben Jonson laboured in the production of that famous folio. But, with regard to the oft-repeated *fleur-de-lis,* again we are reminded that the truth which we *express* is itself divine; that it is of the nature of the Holy Spirit, who Himself guides us unto all truth. " To one is given *by the Spirit* the word of wisdom; to another, the word of knowledge, *by the same Spirit;* to another, faith; . . . to another, the gifts of healing; . . . to another, prophecy; to another, divers kinds of tongues; to another, the interpretation of tongues, but *all these worketh that self-same Spirit,* dividing to every man severally as he will." [1]

The grape, more than any other fruit, furnished Bacon's bright imagination with images by which to explain his ideas of the cheering and stimulating effects of true knowledge; its tendency as a vine to spread and ramify, and in its fruits to *cluster.* As in many places he shows that all sciences hang together like links in one great chain, so here he finds that though *"* chance discovereth new inventions by one and one, science finds them *by clusters,"* [2] and " axioms rightly discovered . . . produce works, not here or there one, but *in clusters."* [3] True to himself in his longing after truth, and his aversion to controversy, he exclaims: " God grant that we may contend with other churches, as *the vine with the olive,* which of us shall bear best fruit; and not as the briar with the thistle, which of us is most unprofitable." [4]

When we come to a consideration of title-pages and their hieroglyphic illustrations, we shall again see the vine in full bearing, supported by pillars or props, the powerful or wealthy authorities in church and state, or the munificent " benefactors" of private life, who, though they could, perhaps, not contribute to the clusters or the growth of the vine, could help to protect and maintain it. For, Bacon again explains, " the sympathy of preservation is as . . . *the vine which will creep towards a stake or prop* that stands near it." [5]

---

1 *Cor.* xii. 8–11.   2 *Instn. Nat.* 11.   3 *Gt. Instn. Plan,* rep. *Nov. Org.* i. 70.
4 *Controversies of the Church.*   5 *Apologia,* 1603.

Like almost all of Bacon's chosen or adopted symbols, the vine, as the emblem of truth, is very ancient. Indian mythology represents Osiris (the Grecian Bacchus) as a wonderful conqueror who travelled over the face of the whole earth, winning territories wherever he came, yet to the advantage of those whom he subdued. Here is Bacon's figure of "*taking all knowledge to be his province*," for the benefit of humanity.

Osiris is said to be the son of Rhea (*the Holy Spirit*), and his chief attendants were Pan, Nature; a dog, Experience; Maro, *a great planter of the vine (of knowledge);* and Triptolemus, *much skilled in husbandry.* He is described with the Nine Muses and the Sciences in his train. It is needless to follow the mythical Osiris into his various connections with Apollo, music, songs, dancing, and with the arts of speech and healing. All these spring from truth, nature, and *cultivation* of the mind and soul — *(husbandry);* and that the vine was from the earliest times the symbol of truth, is certain from many passages of the Holy Scripture, where Jesus Christ even speaks of himself under this figure. " I am the true vine, and my Father is the husbandman. Every branch in me that beareth not fruit, he purgeth it, that it may bring forth more fruit." [1]

The poet philosopher has collected his clusters, and it remains to express them, and to store up the precious juice so that in due season it may be poured into other men's vessels.

In the *Promus* he condenses into two words an adage of Erasmus, " *Vasis — Fons.*" [2] The man who can originate nothing, but who draws all from others is the vase; the source whence he draws is the fountain. Bacon adopts this notion, and expands it in all directions, humbly appropriating to himself the functions of the cistern, bucket, vase, pot, or pitcher. " I am, as I formerly said, but *a bucket and cistern* to that fountain," and so he wrote in a Latin letter to Trinity College, Cambridge :

---

1 John, xv. 1. And see Ezekiel, xvii. 5–10. Psl. lxxx. 14, 15. Canticles, i. 16; vi. 11; vii. 12; viii. 11–12. Jer. ii. 21. Rev. xiv. 18. Matt. xx. 1–7, etc.
2 *Promus*, 698, from *Eras: Adagia*, 292.

" All things, and all the growths thereof, are due to their beginnings. And, therefore, seeing that *I drew my beginnings of
knowledge from your fountains,* I have thought it right to return
to you the increase of the same."

Elsewhere he says that " the mind of man is not a *vessel*
sufficiently capacious to comprehend knowledge without helps,"
and that the " Divine water of knowledge is first forced up into
a *cistern* and thence fetched and drawn for use, or else it is received in *buckets and vessels* immediately where it springeth."
" Divinity," he adds, " hath been reduced to an art, as into a cistern, and the streams of doctrine fetched and derived from
thence." [1]

The *means* for the advancement of learning, he says, include
three things :

" The *places* of learning, the *books* of learning, and the *persons* of the learned. For as water, whether it be the dew of
heaven, or the springs of the earth, easily scatters and loses
itself in the ground, except it be collected into some receptacle,
where it may, by union, consort, comfort, and sustain itself (and
for that cause the industry of man has devised aqueducts, cisterns, and pools), . . . so this excellent liquor of knowledge,
whether it descend from divine inspiration, or spring from
human sense, would soon perish and vanish into oblivion, if it
were not preserved in books, traditions, and conferences, and
specially in places appointed for such matters."

These passages are sufficient to show the drift of Bacon's
ideas with regard to the vase or pitcher symbol. It is to remind
us that the heavenly liquor of knowledge must not be wasted,
but stored up and poured forth for the use and delight of others.
This pitcher or pot is impressed not only on the private letters
of Francis and Anthony Bacon — or perhaps it is safer to say,
of the Bacon family — and their confidential correspondents, but
on the pages of nearly every English edition of works acknowledged as " Bacon's," published before the eighteenth century.

---

[1] Observe the frequency of the vase as a decoration in the architecture of our
great buildings dedicated to art, science, or literature. Although often, in modern edifices, private houses, etc., this symbol is used ignorantly and as a mere
ornament, it was not so two or three hundred years ago, nor is it always so at
the present day.

There are certain accessories to the Baconian pitchers, one at least being always present: (1) A rising sun, formed by the cover or round top of the pot; (2) five rays; (3) pearls; (4) *fleur-de-lis;* (5) a four-petaled flower, or a Maltese cross; (6) a moon or crescent; (7) the bull's horns in a crown; (8) grapes; (9) a diamond, triangle, ellipse, or heart. Sometimes there are two handles distinctly formed, as SS; often on the body of the pot are letters — they may be initials, as A B, and F B, often found in the correspondence of the brothers; or S S, *Sanctum Sanctorum,* etc.; R C, Rosy Cross; F or F F, *Frater* or *Fratres;* G G, Grand Geometrician — God, according to Freemason books.

> *Resp.* In the midst of Solomon's Temple there stands a G,
> A letter for all to read and see;
> But few there be that understand
> What means the letter G.
> *Ex.* My friend, if you pretend to be of this Fraternity
> You can forthwith and rightly tell what means that letter G.

This letter was associated with the third sacred name of God in Hebrew — Ghadol, *Magnus;* but also the *Masonic Cyclopædia* refers it to the Syriac *Gad,* the German *Gott,* the English *God,* all derived from the Persian Goda, signifying *Himself.* The reference to Geometry is to be seen in the concluding lines of the above doggerel, which, says the encyclopædist, may go for what it is worth:

> " By letters four and science five,
> This G aright doth stand,
> In a due art and proportion;
> You have your answer, friend."

The pot was one of the earliest paper-marks; in examples as old as 1352 we find it extremely rude in outline, like an ill-drawn pint-pot of the present day, or of the same proportions, round-bodied.[1] Perhaps the original mark alluded to the pot of manna said to have been laid up in the Ark of the Covenant by Aaron. This pot of manna is mentioned in the " Royal Arch

[1] See " *Etudes sur les Filigraves des Papiers,*" E. Midioux et A. Mattou, 1868.

Degree" in Masonry, but the author of the *Royal Masonic Cyclopædia* rejects it, saying that it has no significance. In later specimens than Caxton's the pot becomes usually more graceful, and more like the sacramental chalice, yet without having any of the accessories enumerated above.

If Francis Bacon or his father, Sir Nicholas, helped to devise new or to develop old symbolic water-marks, this idea of a pot of manna would commend itself to them, lending itself easily to the further development of pots and jugs whence issue bunches of grapes — the fruits of knowledge ; pearls, the dew of heaven — Wisdom ; manna, the spiritual food, all symbols of the Holy Spirit, Truth, the gifts of reason and sweet speech, which link themselves together in such passages as the following from the *Natural History,* or *Sylva Sylvarum :* [1]

" There be three things for sweetness : sugar, honey, *manna.* . . . I have heard from one that was industrious in husbandry that the labour of the bee is about the wax, and that he hath known in the beginning of May honeycombs empty of honey, and within a fortnight, when *the sweet dews fall,* filled like a cellar."

A note in Spedding's edition of the Works says here : " *Bacon's informant took the same view of the matter as Aristotle, and probably was directly or indirectly influenced by his opinion. According to Aristotle, the bees manufacture the wax from flowers, but simply collect the honey which falls from the sky.*"

The "informant," we think, was probably Aristotle himself, and Bacon was here thinking of his own husbandry and of the hive in which he made the frame or comb, wherein the labour *consisted, whilst his busy working bees merely collected the dew of knowledge* without any great exertion to themselves, but thus enabling him rapidly to store up and methodise it for the advancement of learning.

" It is reported by some of the ancients that there is a *tree* called Occhus in the valleys of Hyrcania that distilleth *honey* in the mornings. It is not unlike that the saps and tears of some

---

[1] This work, as has been said, is considered by the present writer to be a masterpiece of ambiguous writing — a study in metaphor and simile from beginning to end. These extracts concerning manna are thus interpreted. See *Emblems,* etc.

trees may be sweet.   It may also be that some sweet juices may
be concocted out of *fruits* to the thickness of *sugar*.   The like-
liest are the raisins of the sun [*i. e., grapes*].   The *manna* of
Calabria . . . is gathered from the *leaf* of the mulberry tree, *but
not upon such mulberry trees as grow in the valleys.   Manna falleth upon the leaves by night*, as other dews do. . . . Certainly it
were not amiss to observe a little *the dews that fall upon trees or
herbs* growing upon *mountains ;* for it may be many dews
fall that spend before they come to the *valleys ;* and I suppose
that he that would gather the best May-*dew for medicine* should
gather it from the *hills.* "[1]

Here, as in the preceding passage, Bacon had in his mind the
collecting of manna and other of the sweetest things *which fall
chiefly from heaven*, and the " distilling " and " concocting "
them into poetry — " sugared sonnets," " honeyed words,"
with the dew of heaven, filled with thoughts and words sweeter
than manna.

What is the idea connected with all those crescent moons?
It is, we think, a very deep and comprehensive thought, and to
illustrate it we must turn to books of Hindu mythology, to the
Rabbinical writings, and to the Masonic symbolism drawn, it
would seem, from those ancient springs of mysticism.[2]

In the second Book of Kings, xxiii. 5, it is said that Josiah
put down them that burnt incense unto Baal (*the Sun*) and to
the *Moon*, and *Mazaloth*.   This word signifies, literally, the
flowing or distillations which emanated from the spirit of waters.
And again, in Isaiah lxv. 11, we read, " Ye are they that prepare a table for God, and that furnish an offering for Meni,"
that is, for the Holy Spirit, called plurally the dispensers or dis-
tributers of the manna or bread from Heaven.[3]

Here, then, the moon and the dew, pearls, or heavenly food,
are associated.   " Meni," the Holy Spirit, was adored by the
Arabians under the name of Ma Nah ; and this adds great interest to the symbolic miracle of the supernatural feeding of the

---

[1] *Sylva Sylvarum*, 612, 781.   [2] See for detailed particulars "The Book of
God," Vol. i. 9–68; ii. 102, 260, iii. 31, 35, 205, 316, 324, 559.
[3] This is the reading in the margin.   Old editions print *troop* for " God," and
" *that number* " for " Meni," thus obscuring the sense.   The marginal readings
of modern Bibles give the version of our text above.

Israelites during their stay in the wilderness. The *manna* with which they were supported was symbolic of the Ma Nah — the nourisher, the comforter, *the Holy Spirit of God.* Surely, living as they were in Arabia (the very country where Ma Nah was adored) the Israelites must have been well aware of the symbolic or mystical meaning of the heavenly food which was for many months their daily bread.

Then again we read in the Bible that the Ark of the Covenant (the sacred chest or coffer which was deposited in the most holy place of the Tabernacle and the Temple) was made the receptacle of the original tables of the law, of *a quantity of manna in a golden pot,* and of Aaron's rod that had budded. Here is, therefore, a connection between manna and a pot. The manna was found by the Israelites in the early morning, after the dew had evaporated, and before the sun had sufficiently risen to melt it. *Manna, the dew,* and the *rise of the sun* are thus connected. An omer of the manna was preserved as a memorial in the sanctuary, testifying to God's power and willingness to give food for the subsistence of his people, in the most apparently destitute circumstances.

The names Meni and Mazaloth, used by Isaiah,[1] both mean the " Holy Spirit of God," the " Bread Dispensers." Meni was also Mona, and Mon (Welsh), the Sacred Mountain of Paradise; she was Mens, the Everlasting Mind, the *Logos* of the Gentiles.

Now observe the highly-figurative nature of the passage lately quoted from the *Sylva Sylvarum.* The manna, the sweet dews which fall in the stillness of the night, are not found upon *such mulberry trees as grow in the valleys,* but upon trees and herbs growing upon the *mountains,* the sacred hills and mounts of knowledge, the Mountain of Paradise, the Everlasting Mind. Here, indeed, we see the apparently dry notes of a commonplace book gilded by the beams of heaven-born poesy, and converted into " gold potable," a parable " deep and rich," truly " drawn from the centre of the sciences."

---

1 Isaiah, lxv.

Observe, further, how often the pearls and rays of our pots arrange themselves in fives.

Five is the central figure in the mystical square of the Hindus, used by them as an amulet, designed to represent the whole world.

The even numbers (by a mystic symbolism which cannot here be explained) designate the *earthy*, and the uneven numbers the *heavenly* bodies. The numbers, as arranged in this cube, form in every direction the sum of fifteen, this number consisting of the sacred 3, emblem of the Supreme Being, and of 12, the number of the " Messengers" in Hindu theology.

6	7	2
1	5	9
8	3	4

The number 5 thus occupies the middle station, and designates *the Soul of the World*. This *anima mundi*, soul of the world, is a central idea in the doctrine of the microcosm — man, a little world in himself. Upon this a large portion of Bacon's philosophy hinges. It is also of fundamental importance in the philosophy and mysticism of the Rosicrucians, which cannot be properly understood without some knowledge of its meaning. The Hermetic books are, as has been shown, full of allusions to it, as the Holy *Light*, the Holy Spirit — " air shining with ethereal light." Just so Bacon describes the soul, as " of *an airy and flamy nature,"* and thus this goddess of the Hindus and the Egyptians[1] is described as " The Soul of the World."

In the mystical square of 15, the Hindus draw a figure of a man with his hands and feet extended to the four corners. He is the image of the world, a real *microcosm ;* as Bacon says, *" an ancient emblem that man was a microcosm or epitome of the world."*[2] In a work which the present writer believes to be Bacon's — written or dictated by him about the year 1600 — we read:

" Man in the beginning (I mean the substantiall inward man), both in and after his creation for some short time, was a pure Intellectual Essence, free from all fleshly, sensuall affections. In this state the *Anima,* or Sensitive Nature, did not prevail over the spirituall as it doth now in us. For the superior mentall part of man was united to God by an essentiall contact, and the Divine Light, being received in and conveyed to the inferiour parts of the Soul, did mortifie all carnal desires. . . . The sensuall, cœlestial, æthereal part of a man is that whereby we move, see, feel, taste, and smell, and have commerce with all material objects whatsoever. . . . In plain terms, it is part of the Soul of the World."

The writer explains at some length the nature of " this medial soul or ethereal nature," and how by its means man's mind is tuned to the cœlestial harmonies. He repeats, though in different words, many Baconian ideas of the vital spirits which are in all nature — " in man, in beasts, in vegetables, in minerals, and in everything this spirit is the mediate cause of composition and multiplication; " adding remarks which echo precisely the ideas in the *De Augmentis* of the *biform figure of nature* — the sensual nature of man as contrasted or allied with the rational spririt, — the *Mens,* or concealed intelligence. (Here we have the *Meni, the Moon,* explained before.) " Now, as the divine light flowing into the *Mens* (or intellect) did assimilate and convert the inferior portions of the soul to God, so, on the contrary,

---

[1] The Egyptians, though describing her as a *Mother,* yet use the masculine pronoun in speaking of her. See *The Book of God,* i. 147.

[2] The Microcosm will be fully explained when we come to speak of the *Symbolic Language* of Bacon's Secret Society.

the tree of knowledge did darken and obscure the superior portions, but awaked and stirred up the sinful nature. *The sum of this is* — man." [1]

The writer winds up his treatise by " saluting the memory of Cornelius Agrippa." " He is indeed my author, and next to God I owe all that I have to him." The Poet-philosopher then concludes with some verses to this " great, glorious penman ! "

> " The spirits of his lines infuse a fire
> *Like the World's Soul,* which makes me thus aspire."

In another Rosicrucian document, or treatise (which we also attribute directly to Bacon), the same thoughts are returned to, in different language. It is not enough, says the writer, to call the inward principle of life " a form, and so bury up the riches of nature in this narrow and most absurd formality. . . . To be plain, then, this principle (*of rational intelligence*) is the *soul of the world,* or the universall spirit of nature." [2]

In *Timon of Athens* there is a satirical allusion to the sad fall of man from the first " pure intellectual essence in which he was created," free from all fleshly and sensual affections. Noting the ingratitude, the " monstrousness of man," in days " when men must learn to dispense with pity, *for policy sits above conscience,*" the *First Stranger* exclaims :

> " *Why, this is the World's Soul ;* and just of the same piece
> Is every flatterer's sport."

The pitcher, destined to receive and then pour forth the heavenly liquor, must be of rare and precious materials, finely wrought, and made in just proportions.

The dew or manna must be gathered before the full rising of the sun, lest it should be melted and dissipated by too great

---

[1] See *Anthroposophia Theomagica,* "Magical Writings of Thos. Vaughan," edited in English by Arthur E. Waite, p. 26–33 (Redway, Kegan, Paul, Trubner & Co., 1688. It is not a difficult work, as the alarming title might lead us to suppose; on the contrary, highly interesting with a view to the present subject.

[2] See *Anima Magica Abscondita,* also edited by A. E. Waite — in the same vol. as *Anthroposophia.* Published under the title of "The Magical Writings of Thos. Vaughan."

heat. The revival of learning was indeed the rising of the sun, the dawn of a new day to the world lying in darkness; yet the dew should be collected quietly, almost secretly, and safely stored, before the blaze of a fiery zeal should injure and perhaps destroy it.

The five rays, with their five pearls (or groups of pearls), typify the soul of the world, the " divine intellectual spirit, " " awakened, " " uproused " by the sunrise. This soul of the world has been with the spirits that are in prison—" cabinned, cribbed, confined, " like the soul of Hamlet or of the poet of the *Anthroposophia*, who concludes one chapter with verses in which are these lines:

> " My sweetest Jesus! 'twas thy voice: 'If I
> Be lifted up, I'll draw all to the sky.'
> Yet I am here! *I'm stifled in this clay,*
> *Shut up from Thee and the fresh east of day.*"

The ejaculation in the third line suggests a further allusion to clay in the hands of the potter, which must surely have presented itself to poetic Bible-students such as the Bacon family certainly were. They must have thought of the pot of clay as an image of human life, a very " compounded " but a most brittle and perishable thing.

" Or ever the silver cord be loosed, or the *golden bowl be broken, or the pitcher be broken at the fountain, or the wheel broken at the cistern, then shall the dust return to the earth as it was ; and the spirit shall return unto God that gave it.* " [1]

The clay is but the poor earthy material into which all the vital spirits of nature are " infused and mixed up with the clay, for it is most true that of all things in the universe, man is the most composite. " [2]

Falstaff is made to use almost identical words where he speaks of " This *foolish compounded clay — man.* " [3]

---

[1] Ecclesiastes, xii. Bacon was very partial to these twelve chapters and brings in allusions to their teaching throughout his works and notes. Compare his essay or treatise of *Youth and Age* with *As You Like It*, ii. 7, and then with Eccles. xii. 3–5. The first word, *Remember*, seems to be a pass-word in the old Rosicrucian books.

[2] Essay of Prometheus.

[3] 2 Henry IV. i 2. " Men are but gilded loam and painted clay." Rich. II. i. 1.

" Vanity of vanities, saith the Preacher; all is vanity; but, because the Preacher was wise, he still taught the people knowledge; yea, he gave good heed, and sought out and set in order many proverbs.[1] The Preacher sought to find out many acceptable words,[2] and that which was written was upright, words of truth. The words of the wise are as goads,[3] and as nails fastened by the Masters of Assemblies, which are given from one shepherd. And further by these, my son, be admonished; of making many books there is no end, and much study is a weariness of the flesh. Let us hear the conclusion of the whole matter. Fear God and keep His commandments, for this is the whole duty of man. For God shall bring every work into judgment with every secret thing, whether it be good or whether it be evil. "

Here is the model of a charge from a " Master of Assemblies" to his " Sons, " the *Sons of Science*, the Brethren in love and religious union. In their youth they must *Remember* their Creator, in mature years labour in the cause of truth, till the time comes when the frail pitcher is broken, even in the act of drawing fresh supplies from the heavenly fountain; its contents or its emptiness will be seen, and every secret thing made known and judged in the broad light of day.

This digression is intended to illustrate the manner in which these Baconian ideas are linked together in one great chain, each symbol or image merging into or mixing itself up with another.

To return once more to the pitcher or pot — Bacon's special mark, the humble vessels which his friends raised to honour.

Who is so dull and unimaginative as to be incapable of fitting together the scraps of erudition here disjointedly scattered before him? Who will check and refuse to see in this water-mark Bacon's well-conceived emblem of himself and his disciples as

---

[1] See the *De Aug.* viii. ii. in which, when discoursing of *The Doctrine Concerning Scattered Occasions*, Bacon extols the use of proverbs like the aphorisms of Solomon, " to which there is nothing comparable," and which he expounds and comments upon through twenty octavo pages.

[2] See Bacon's record of the necessity for doing this *(De Aug.* vi. i) and a few of his immense contributions to language in jottings amongst his private notes *(Promus*, 116–159, 272–326, 1370–1439, etc.)

[3] Quoted in the *Promus*, fol. 88, 239, and again in *Advt. of L.* i. and the *Wisd. of the Ancients*, xxviii., from the Vulgate *Eccl.* xii. 11,

mere "vases," "receptacles" for the heavenly manna, the dew, "the flowing and distillations which emanated from the Spirit of the Waters "?

The pot has never the appearance of being made of earthenware, for it was *a golden pot* in which Aaron preserved the manna. "We read in Genesis that God made man out of the earth. This is a great mystery. For it was not the common pot-clay, but another, and that of a far better nature." [1] "As the potter hath his clay, or the limner his colours, so the Spirit that worketh in Nature, in the outward lineaments or symmetry of that which he forms, proves himself nothing but a divine, intellectual spirit." [2]

THOSE who would aid in following up these researches into the history of Bacon and his Secret Society will render efficient service if in the course of their reading (in books more particularly of dates between 1580 and 1680) they will give attention to the paper-marks of the volumes which they study, noting accurately the title, date, and edition of the book, and even the number of the page on which marks are found. Copies or tracings of these should be made and duly registered. Such an examination, undertaken by some dozens of pairs of observant eyes, would be extremely useful in solving doubtful questions. For many points are still very doubtful, and probably some remain altogether undisclosed, so that hitherto only these few general statements can be considered as definitely proved :

1. That in the sixteenth and seventeenth centuries papermarks were used throughout the works which were the products of the "Renaissance."

2. That these paper-marks are not mere manufacturers' signs, but that they have a mutual relation and connection, and that they were and are means of conveying secret information to the members of some widely-spread society.

3. That the society was not a mere trade-guild, but that it was moved by motives of religion, and, in its highest branches

---

[1] *Anthroposophia*, 22.   [2] *Anima Magica*, 54.

at least, was a Christian philosophical society, or a society for promoting Christian knowledge.

4. That the subject-matter of the books does not necessarily affect the paper-marks.

5. That the three marks, the double candlesticks, the grapes, and the pitcher or pot, are notably " Baconian," the pot especially being found in all Bacon's acknowledged works, and throughout the correspondence of Anthony and Francis, especially when their correspondent was of the Reformed Church.

6. That, where any one pattern is varied many times in the same book, there is usually no other mark except in the fly-leaves.

7. The extraordinary but not unaccountable habit of tearing out the fly-leaves at the beginning and end of valuable books of the sixteenth and seventeenth centuries often makes it impossible to declare that the book in hand possessed no other mark besides those which we see.

8. The fly-leaves were wont, in many of our " Baconian " books, to be very numerous : five or eight are common numbers for the sheets. They were probably intended for the making of notes, a practice which Bacon enjoins and so highly commends. In old, untouched libraries there are usually some books where the fly-leaves have been thus utilised. Perhaps, when filled with notes, they were to be taken out, and forwarded to some central point of study, either to an individual or to a committee, who should by their means add to the value of any subsequent edition or " collection " which might be published. It is certain that fly-leaves have been stolen for the sake of the old paper, for etching or for forged reprints; but this does not account for the fact that certain books, when sent, without any special orders, to be repaired by a Freemason binder, have returned with this large number of fly-leaves restored; in many of our public libraries such extra leaves in books rebound have paper-marks.

9. In Bacon's acknowledged works the changes are rung upon the three paper-marks, the pot, the grapes, and the can-

dlesticks, the latter being apparently the rarest of the three. Usually one or two of these patterns are combined with one extra mark. With time enough and help to examine every edition of every book concerned in this inquiry, it is hardly to be doubted that a real scheme could be drawn up to demonstrate the precise method of the use of paper-marks. The following table may be sufficient to illustrate our meaning. The " moons " to which allusion will be made are not made, like the other paper-marks, by wires. They give the idea of having been produced by the impression of a thumb on the soft pulp in the process of paper-making. These moon-marks are of too frequent occurrence, in certain books and during a certain period, for any doubt to remain as to their being the result of intention and not of accident or chance. They are, therefore, included amongst the extras in our list. The chronological arrangement enables us to observe several particulars. First, that the pots seem to be in one edition at least of every work produced by Francis or Anthony Bacon, or published under their auspices. Two handles to the pot seem to mean that two persons helped in the construction of the book. Next, we notice that, in republications, compilations, or " collections " of any kind, grapes prevail, and that the candlesticks only appear when the volume which includes them is to be considered complete. Then, as to dates. The Baconian pots have been found first in a book 1579–80, and not later than 1680 — a period of one hundred years. They, like the rest of the marks, increase in size from about one inch to seven inches. The use of the Baconian grapes seems to have begun about 1600, and to have continued only in France after 1680. The double candlesticks appeared later still, after the death of Francis Bacon, and remained in use for about fifty years. The three marks all disappeared in England about 1680.

DATE	TITLE	POT.	GRAPES	CANDLESTICKS.	KETTLES.
1579	North's Plutarke	Pot (on fly-leaves)	—	—	—
1590	Book of Com. Prayer	Pots, various	—		—
1596	The Faerie Queene	Pots, various, some two-handled, with letters A B, F B, B I, R, R C			
1598	Chapman's Works	Pots, various	—	—	—
1603	North's Plutarke	Pots, various	—	—	—
1603	Montaigne's Essays.	Pots, various, some two-handled	—	—	—
1605	Advt. of Learning	Pots, various	Grapes	—	Twisted horns
1609	Book of Com. Prayer	Pots, various	Grapes	—	Crowns, shields
1609	Observas. on Cæsar's Commentaries.	—	—	Candlestick, single	(Fly-leaves gone)
1611	Bible	Pots, various	Grapes	—	Twisted horns
1611	Florio's Dictionary	Pots, various	Grapes	—	Bugle
1616	Ben Jonson's Works	Pots, various	—	—	Moons
1618	Selden's History of Tithes	Pots, various, some two-handled	—	—	Shields
1622	Shakespeare	—	Grapes	—	Crowns
1631	Love's Labour's Lost	Pots, various	—	—	
1633	"Fulke's" Bible	Pots, various	Grapes	—	Shields
1634	Jeremy Taylor's "Holy State"	Pots, various	Grapes	—	Shields
1638	Bacon Opera	Pots, various	Grapes	Candlesticks	Shields, bugles
1639	Quarles' Emblems	Pots, various	Grapes	Candlesticks	Shields, bugles
1640	De Augmentis	Pots, various	—	Candlesticks	Shields
1640	Ben Jonson's Works	—	Grapes	Candlesticks	Shields
1645	Comus & other poems	Pots, various	—	Candlesticks	Fool's cap
1646	"The Art of Making Devices," Ciphers, &c.	Pots, various	Grapes	Candlesticks	—
1647	Fuller's "Holy Warre"	Pots, various	Grapes	Candlesticks	—
1648	Hieroglyphics, Symbols, Ciphers, &c.	Pots, various	Grapes	Candlesticks	—
1648	"Diodati" Bible	Pots (enormous)	—	—	Shields
1651	Sylva Sylvarum	Pots, various	Grapes	Candlesticks	Shields
1651	Comus, &c.	Pots, various	—	—	—
1652	Comus, &c.	Pots, various	—	Candlesticks	—
1655	Comus, &c.	Pots, various, and cut in half	—	—	Shields
1655	Fuller's Ch. History	Pots, various	—	—	Shields & double-headed eagle
1658	Sylva Sylvarum	Pots, various	Grapes	—	Shields, bugle
1664	Shakespeare	Pots, various	Grapes	—	Shields, hearts, crowns, &c.
1668	Paradise Lost	Pots, various	Grapes	—	Shield
1669	Paradise Regained	Pots, various	Grapes	—	Shield
1669	Sir K. Digby's Treatises	Pots, various	—	Candlesticks	Crescent & R C
1669	Cowley's Works.	Pots, various	Grapes	—	Fool's cap
1671	Resuscitatio, 3d edn.	Pots, various, very large	—	—	—
1674	De Augmentis	Pots, various, very large	—	—	—

7. Not only is the nature of the paper-mark thus varied in each book, but the forms of each figure are varied to a surprising extent. No two volumes, often no two parts of the same volume, treatise, poem, or play, contain marks which are identical. For instance, in *Ben Jonson*, 1616, there are at least fifteen different forms of the pot, two of which are sometimes in one

play. In *Selden's History of Tithes*, 1618, the variations are as frequent. In *Burton's Anatomy of Melancholy*, 1621, there are at least thirty half-pitchers, no two of which seem to be alike. Again, we have not succeeded in finding any form of mark precisely repeated in books of different titles, editions, or dates.

In the writing-paper of the Bacon family and their friends, there is almost as striking a variety in the representation of the same figure or pattern. It is certain that these marks were not of the same kind as the ornaments, etc., on letter-paper of the present day, in which crests, monograms, etc., are adopted by certain individuals and retained by them for some time at least. In letters in Baconian correspondence, written in rapid succession by the same person, the marks are found different, and on the other hand, different persons writing, the one from England and the other from abroad, occasionally used paper with precisely similar marks. It would seem that, in such cases, paper had been furnished to these correspondents from some private mill.

8. There are, in combination with some designs, or apart from them, " bars " on which appear names, sometimes of paper-makers, as " Ricard," " Rapin," " Conard," " Nicolas," etc. These seem to be chiefly in the foreign paper, as nowadays we have " Whatman," " Joynson," etc.[1]   But often these bars are as cabalistic as the rest of the designs, or they seem to contain the initials of the " producer " of the book, not, we think, of its true author. The pots have no bars in connection with them; perhaps the letters upon them render further additions unnecessary. Observe, in the plates of pots, the large number which occur inscribed A B, F B, B, B I, R, R C, C R, the letters being sometimes inverted, sometimes placed sideways, or otherwise disguised.[2]

---

[1] The practice of inserting the full names of the makers is said to have come into fashion in the sixteenth century. See *The Manufacture of Paper*, C. T. Davis, 1886.

[2] We would draw especial attention to a bar taken from the first edition of *Ben Jonson's Works*. At the first glance the markings on this bar appear to be meaningless, or cabalistic, but if the reader will take a card in each hand and cover up or screen each portion by turns, he may agree with the present writer that the marks resolve themselves into a name, and perhaps a double repetition of the letters R C. Thus, to the left extremity C followed by R reversed. Then

9. The *system* of paper-marks still exists, though under modified conditions. Books are now printed too cheaply to admit of the old use of "water-marked" paper. Where, however, these marks are absent, we find a series of other marks, less beautiful, and far less conspicuous, but equally significant and curious, and which, in due season, we hope to explain by the aid of photography and the microscope.

On the other hand, "deficiencies" in this department of knowledge are unhappily numerous. Let it therefore be inquired:

1. Which were the very earliest paper-mills in England? To whom did they belong? What were the water-marks on the paper produced there?

2. Which was the first *printed* book for which the paper was made in England?

3. From what foreign mills did our English printers import paper?

4. At what date did the papers with the hand and the pot receive the distinctive additions which, for want of a better name, we have termed Baconian?

5. In what books may we see the very latest examples of the candlesticks, the grapes, and the pot in the paper?

6. When and why was the use of paper-marks in printed books discontinued? Was the discontinuance simultaneous and universal? Was there truly a discontinuance of the *system* of secret marks, or, rather, did a change or modification take place, in order to adapt these secret marks to the exigencies of modern requirements in printing and book-making?

7. When Sir Nicholas Bacon, in his youth, resided for three or four years in Holland, did he visit and study the manufactories of paper? Does any record show him mixed up in any business relations with paper manufacturers?

---

begins the name, A, of which the right side forms part of the sloping letter N; an upright with cross-piece, T; the same upright, connected half way down with a curved stroke, H; at the end of the curved stroke, a small but distinct O, followed by an N, sloping greatly to the left, and from which proceeds, to the right, a smaller Y — ANTHONY. In the H and its curved line there is an irregularity suggestive of a monogram of R C. But these are only suggestions; other eyes and imaginations may interpret them differently.

8. What part did the old printers and publishers play in the secret society? For instance, John Norton (Lady Anne Bacon's cousin) and the Spottisworths (both families in which these trades have in an eminent degree flourished ever since).

9. Did the "Baconian" water-marks remain in use until *circa* 1680,—in fact, for just one hundred years from the time when the first document of the Rosicrucian society was published?

10. Was it intended that, by the end of the period of one hundred years, all the posthumous works of Francis Bacon, "*My cabinet and presses full of papers,*" should have been published by his followers? and did the system of water-marks in printed books cease at that period?

11. Are printers and paper-makers, as a rule, Freemasons? Do they mutually co-operate and understand each other's marks?

12. If not, what reasons do they adduce for the mystery which is still cast over simple matters connected with their useful and beneficent crafts, and for the unusual difficulties which are met with in obtaining any good books or any trustworthy information upon the subjects which we have been considering?

13. Is there any period at which modern Freemasonry and Rosicrucianism propose to clear up and reveal these apparently useless and obstructive "secrets"?

14. Or, what is supposed to be the advantage, either to the public or to individuals, in keeping up these or other mystifications, historical or mechanical? Once, doubtless, helpful and protective, guides as well as guardians, they now seem to be mere stumbling-blocks in the way of knowledge.

Further on we shall have to inquire, who are they who have the right and the power so to manipulate the printed catalogues of our public libraries as to enable them to convey hints to the initiated of books specially to their purpose; and to repress open references to certain books or documents which would tell the uninitiated too much? For the present we merely throw out these hints to encourage observers to *note very precisely every instance in which such aberrations occur.* In matters connected with these subjects they are not infrequent, and the student need not despair of getting an important book *because it is not in the printed catalogue* of a great library.

Perhaps it may not be amiss to give a few hints to observers unaccustomed to the technical matters involved in making a book. Let them take notice that in *folio* editions the paper-marks are to be found about the centre of the page; but in small *quartos*, where the paper is folded so as to form four sheets, in *octavos*, where another fold produced eight sheets, and in *duodecimos*, where the folds are again multiplied, the paper-marks will often be found divided into two or four parts. Usually, the sheet having been bent in the middle where the paper-mark is, the halves of the marks will be seen at the binding, say, half on pages 1 and 2, and the other half on pages 7 and 8. But in smaller books, the water-marks are still more divided, and sometimes appear in pieces in the outer margins. The eye soon becomes accustomed to distinguish these arrangements, although the division of the design makes the work more troublesome.

Even in the large and undivided marks, the letter-press and engravings often obscure the design. Many specimens must be compared, and many drawings made, before the exact character of the mark can be ascertained.

This is the excuse, pleaded beforehand, for any errors or misconceptions in the drawings which accompany this book. It is also the cause why these illustrations have been taken from such a limited circle of books. Those in our own library, or belonging to friends, can be traced against the light with red ink, and then carefully retraced. But this is impossible in books belonging to public libraries, where the difficulty of measuring and copying is much increased by the little aid which the all-cheering sun deigns to bestow, and by the impracticability of holding up large folios towards his veiled face. He seems to be in league with the paper-makers and printers, and the electric light is kinder in this respect.

For the present, to avoid fruitless controversy, and to enclose

the range of observation within a manageable area, we withhold
any notice of paper-marks in books produced by "authors"
living only *after* Bacon's time. Yet it is right to caution observers that they should by no means discontinue their notes
and researches in books published, even for the first time, after
1626.

Startling disclosures are made by collating these paper-marks,
and other technical particulars, in books which, from internal
evidence, are judged to have been written or aided by Francis
or Anthony Bacon, and which, by these external and demon-
strable signs, are "hall-marked" by the paper-maker and the
printer. To any one sufficiently possessed by the spirit of inquiry or love of truth, to labour after it, and personally to test
and follow up the statements and suggestions made above, it
will, we think, be difficult to resist the conclusions to which we
have been drawn. They will perceive that, if indeed Anthony
Bacon was not (as we think) a considerable author, poet, and
playwright, yet that, for more than twenty-five years, he ener-
getically collaborated with the beloved younger brother, *whom
he equalled in wit*, though not in profound learning; the style of
writing of the brothers, twins in heart and soul, being in these
lighter works almost indistinguishable.

It must also, we think, be ere long made manifest that the
works hitherto attributed to Francis Bacon are *samples* only,
tastes of his quality; giving, as they were intended to give, excellent hints and indications of the manifold works of all kinds
and (as Ben Jonson declared) in "all numbers," actually written,
dictated, or directed by him; constructed and published by his
"*Method.*"

Which of Bacon's works is in the true sense *complete?* Perfect in its kind it may be (as, for instance, any single essay).
But can any of these works be considered finished and exhaustive? Does any one of them "fill up" its own subject? On the
contrary, almost all are in some sort fragmentary; [1] and, for our

---

[1] Perhaps the *History of Henry VII.* should be excepted. Yet even this
begins as though it were the end or concluding portion of a *History of Richard
III.*, and not as would be expected in a separate and complete history.

own part, in the acknowledged works of Francis Bacon we see but a collection of masterly sketches—vast maps in outline, magnificent designs, whose every detail he had elsewhere studied and attempted to trace out, so that the next ages should have but to copy, fill in, enlarge, diminish, colour, or elaborate. " Will you make this man a monster, with powers abnormal and supernatural?" The question has been asked more than once, and the reply is as before. No man could have read, imagined, cogitated, and devised as Francis Bacon did, if at the same time he had to conduct the mechanical business requisite in the production of great works on a vast variety of subjects. Though we have it on the authority of Dr. Sprat, that the powers of mind of Bacon were equal to those of twenty, *if not* (as some seem to have said) of a thousand men; yet neither his bodily strength nor length of days would have sufficed for such a work. He must have had help in the most tedious particulars, and the method has already been explained by which, according to the present view, the Freemasons and Rosicrucians became engines or machines for the execution of all mechanical work.

And for a *monster in mind*, who has ever matched Francis Bacon? Truly, like Cæsar, he

> " Did get the start of the majestic world,
> And bear the palm alone."

Is it not true that still

> " He doth bestride the narrow world
> Like a Colossus; and that petty men
> Walk under his huge legs, and peep about
> To find themselves dishonourable graves "?

A monster?—Yes, that is the very name which his friend Sir Tobie Matthew claims for him. He challenges any one " to muster out of any age four men who, in many respects, should excel four such as we are able to show—Cardinal Wolsey, Sir Thomas More, Sir Philip Sydney, and Sir Francis Bacon, for they were all a kind of *monsters* in their several ways." After extolling the first three, he continues:

" The fourth was a creature of *incomparable abilities of mind,* of sharp and catching apprehension, large and faithful memory, plentiful and sprouting invention, deep and solid judgment; . . . a man so rare in knowledge of so many several kinds, indeed with the facility of expressing it in so elegant, significant, so abundant, and yet so choice and ravishing a way of words, of metaphors, and allusions, as perhaps the world has not seen since it was a world."

So, of all intellectual *monsters* who had appeared until the time of Sir Tobie Matthew, incomparably the greatest was Francis Bacon. Sir Tobie was well aware that detraction would not suffer his eulogy to pass unchallenged, but he throws down the gauntlet which no man has yet ventured to pick up:

" I know," he continues, " that this may seem a great hyperbole and strange kind of riotous excess of speech ; but the best means of putting me to shame will be for you to place any man of yours by this of mine. And in the meantime even this little makes a shift to shew that the genius of England is still not only eminent, but predominant, *for the assembling great variety of those rare parts, in some single man,* which *may be incompatible anywhere else.*"

Bacon's works are sometimes described or alluded to as being of so stupendous a kind that it is impossible to conceive his having time, even had he the ability or inclination, for other compositions. But, in fact, the whole of his written compositions, excluding letters but including the law tracts and charges, would fill only four of the fourteen volumes which appear on our shelves as Spedding's *Life, Letters, and Works of Bacon.* The rest consist of letters, transactions, variorum editions, and comments by the editors.

Compare with this the voluminous productions of some of his contemporaries. Coke " wrote thirty-one volumes with his own hand " (yet he was a busy public man like Bacon). Richard Baxter is " said to have produced " 145 distinct works, as he himself says, " in the crowd of other employments." Thomas Heywood, the actor, is " said to have written " 220 or 240 plays, " *A Life of Merlin,*" a " *Life of Elizabeth,*" " *The Lives of the*

24

Nine Worthies, etc.," the last item admitting of many possibilities.

Montaigne "feared to glut the world with his works " (a surprising statement if nothing is claimed for him excepting one volume of essays). As to Jaspar Barthius, though his contemporaries do not bestow upon him any particular notice, yet Bayle tells us that his works on many various subjects "make so prodigious a mass that one has difficulty in conceiving how a single man could suffice for such things."

When, at some future time, we are able to discuss at leisure particulars which have been collected, and which link together the friends, correspondents, and colleagues of Francis and Anthony Bacon, we will endeavour to satisfy inquirers as to the methods of these and other "voluminous writers" of the sixteenth and seventeenth centuries. For the present let it be noted that Francis Bacon's acknowledged works were neither voluminous nor stupendous; that, on the contrary, three or four modest volumes are all that were published under his name. Other authors, who are ranked amongst the giant minds of Bacon's time by the critics, commentators, and biographers of the nineteenth century, are *not so much as named* by their prototypes of the sixteenth and seventeenth centuries. Neither Sir Tobie Matthew, Sir Henry Wotton, nor Ben Jonson include them in their lists of great writers or thinkers.

There is indeed no weight or value in the argument that Francis Bacon had not the time, even if he had the ability, to write the works which we attribute to him; he had time, knowledge, and genius enough for it all; nor is there any great difficulty in conceiving the method by which he achieved his great enterprise. Neither does he leave it to our imagination, but explains clearly that it is only by the combination of many minds to one general end, and by the division of labour in particulars, that any real advance can be made, and that it is by examination and experiment, not by talk and argument, that the work can be accomplished.

" This road [of practical experience and demonstration] has an issue in the open ground not far off; the other has no issue at all, but endless entanglement. . . . Moreover, I think that men may take some hope from my own example. And this I say, not by way of boasting, but because it is useful to say it. If there be any that despond, let them look at me, that, being of all men of my time the most busied in affairs of state, and a man of health not very strong (whereby much time is lost), and in this course altogether a pioneer, . . . have, nevertheless, by resolutely entering on the true road, and submitting my mind to things, advanced these matters, as I suppose, some little way. And then let them consider what may be expected (after the way has been thus indicated) from men abounding in leisure, and *from association of labours in successive ages:* the rather because *it is not a way over which only one man can pass at a time* (as is the case with the way of reasoning), *but one in which the labours and industries of men, especially as regards the collecting of experience, may with the best effect be distributed, and then combined. For then only will men begin to know their strength, when, instead of great numbers doing all the same things, one shall take charge of one thing, and another of another.*[1]

Observe that he puts *distribution* first. This assumes a distributor, a head or chief moving spirit, who shall apportion to his subordinates the work which he considers them to be capable of performing. Moreover, look at the phrase in brackets. Here Bacon hints that he did the *reasoning* part of the work himself. That could be deputed to none other. In days when language was halt and lame, when men's powers of observation were dimmed, and all other faculties for resolving high and deep thoughts into beautiful language were ranked among the deficients, how was it possible that ordinary men combine in their writings or their speeches the most extensive learning, the finest reasoning, and the clearest, most cogent, or charming method of delivery?

Bacon warns[2] " those who take upon them to lay down the law as to the bounds of knowledge — as to what is possible and what impossible to know or achieve," that they " have done great injury. For, whether they have spoken in simple assur-

---

[1] *Nov. Org.* i. cxiii. [2] *Nov. Org.* Pref.

ance or professional affectation, they have been equally suc-
sessful in quenching and stopping inquiry, and have done more
harm by stopping other men's efforts than good by their own."
Was there ever a time when these words were truer than now,
and in relation to his own works, and the investigations connected with them?   Can we too strongly grapple to our hearts
his advice that we should "take up, with better judgment, a
position between these two extremes — between the presumption
of pronouncing on everything and the despair of comprehending
anything; that, though frequently and bitterly complaining of
the difficulty of inquiry and the obscurity of things, yet, none
the less, we should follow up our own object, thinking that this
very question — whether or no anything can be known — is to
be settled, *not by arguing, but by trying* "?   He "draws an
argument of hope from this, that some of the inventions already
known are such as, before they were discovered, could hardly
have entered any man's head to think of; for, in conjecturing
what may be, men set before them the example of *what has been*,
and divine of the New, with imagination preoccupied and coloured by the Old."

Having illustrated his meaning by examples from the inventions of gunpowder, silk, and the magnet, he continues: "We
have discoveries to show of another kind, which prove that
noble inventions may be lying at our very feet, and yet mankind may step over without seeing them. For, however the
discovery of gunpowder, of silk, of the magnet, of sugar, of
paper " (*which, observe, he did not mention before*) "may seem
to depend on certain properties of things themselves and
nature, there is, at any rate, nothing in the art of printing
which is not plain and obvious.[1] . . . This most beautiful discovery, which is of so much service in the propagation of knowledge," he attributes to the observation of simple facts, arguing
that such is the infelicity and unhappy disposition of the human
mind in this course of discovery or invention that it first dis-

---

[1] Though so plain and obvious, the art of printing is amongst the subjects,
enumerated by Bacon, which required, *and which still requires*, a separate " History." See the Catalogue of Histories, No. 110, at the end of the Parasceve.

trusts and then despises itself; first, will not believe that any such thing can be found out, and, when it is found out, cannot understand how the world should have missed it so long." Far from being discouraged, he repeats that he takes all this as a ground for hope, and there is yet another. " Let men but think of their infinite expenditure of understanding, time, and means, or matters of pursuit of much less value, whereof, if but a small part were directed to sound and solid studies, there is no difficulty that might not be overcome."

Does any one suggest that the interpretations of the paper-marks are " arbitrary " or " speculative," the attempted explanations of doubtful matters erroneous or incomplete? Let him turn to the beginning of this book and see again that these things are offered, not as perfect fruits, but as some of the best which we have been able to reach or pick up. They are, for the most part, a humble " collection," such as Francis Bacon instructed his disciples to make for examination and considera-tion; though some are the products of real research and exami-nation, and of a simple but effective process of " putting two and two together."

Should more accurate information be forthcoming, better sug-gestions be offered, we shall heartily greet them from whatever quarter they may come, rejoicing if we may in any degree have cleared the way for the advance of truth, or inspired others to better work than we are capable of doing. All that is asked, and this earnestly, is that these things may be fairly discussed, pressed home, and thoroughly looked into. It is in vain " to wave them courteously aside " in the prescribed Freemason fashion, or to thrust them churlishly out of sight as trivialities, matters of course, mere curiosities for the book-worm or the " crank."

It is surely wrong as well as vain to attempt to quench the true spirit of inquiry by endeavouring to make the inquirer ap-pear contemptible, and his researches childish and silly. Such devices must in the end return upon the heads of those who practice them, and, although they may delay and harass the advance of knowledge, they cannot stop it; for " nothing is subtle when it be conceived," and we know now that, though we have not, as Bacon says, "found an issue into open ground," yet we have got out of the "entanglement," and see daylight.

The questions asked, and the problems propounded, are neither trivial nor absurd, nor matter for pedantic dogmatism and argumentative controversy. Rather they are questions to be weighed and considered — and more. If it be true that "cogitation resides not in the man who does not *think*," so, surely, it resides but as smoke and fumes in the man who does not *examine.*

"Orpheus was torn to pieces by the Furies, and the River Helicon, in sorrow, hid its waters underground, and rose again in other places." So with the great religious, literary, and scientific society which Francis Bacon did so much to glorify and render permanent. It hid its waters in England during the time of the civil wars and their attendant miseries. But those waters rose again with renewed freshness. Can we not trace them bubbling up in France, Spain, and Italy, but still more in Germany and Holland, which seem for a while to have been their largest reservoir? The Rosicross Brethren never ceased their beneficent efforts in England, but they worked like the "old mole," underground, and in silence. Bacon and his wonderful work are better known and understood in Germany than in England. "His fame," says Dr. Rawley, "is greater, and sounds louder in foreign parts abroad, than at home in his own nation, thereby verifying that divine sentence, '*A prophet is not without honour, save in his own country and in his own house.*'" He concludes the short life of his beloved master with these words: "Howsoever his body was mortal, yet no doubt his memory and works will live, and will in all probability last as long as the world lasteth."

Plate I. from MSS.

PLATE II. FROM MSS.

Plate III.

Plate IV.

Plate V.

Plate. VI.

Plate VII

Plate VIII

Plate IX.

Plate X.

Plate XI.

Plate XII.

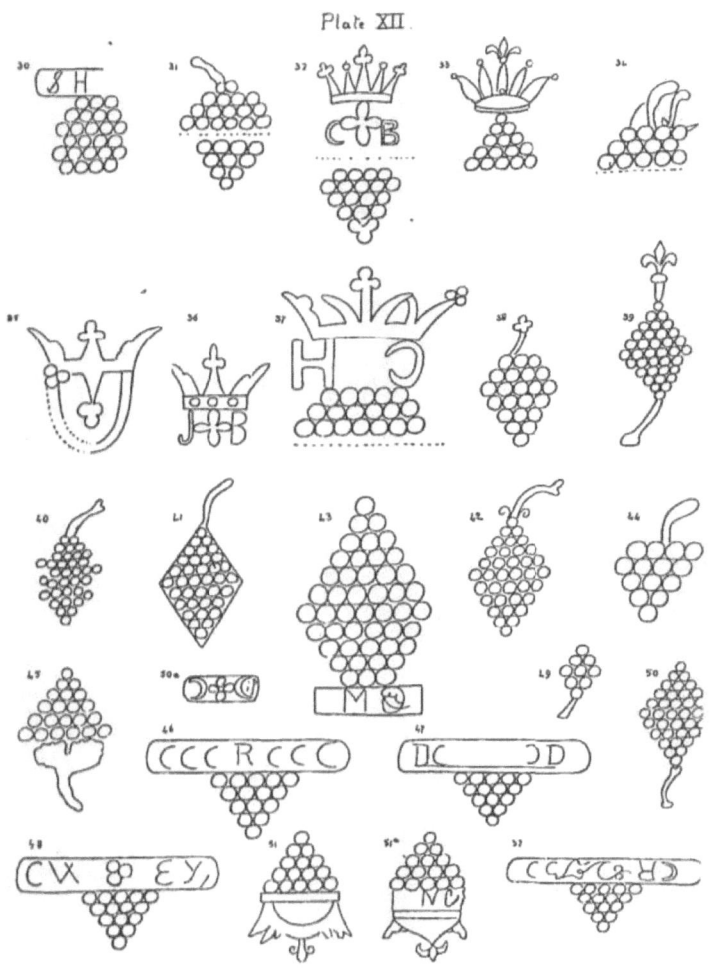

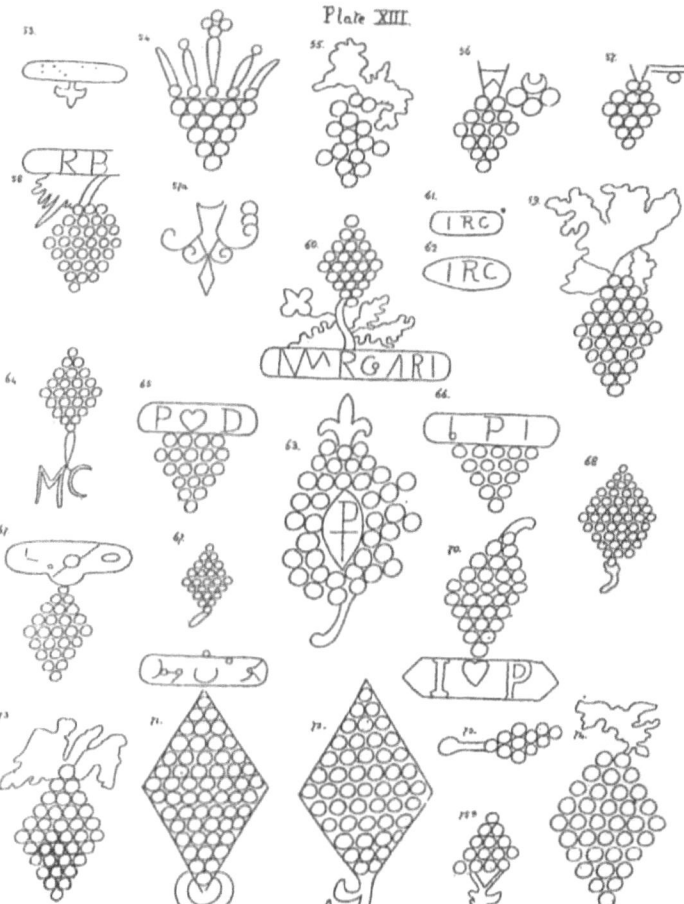

Plate XIII.

Plate XIV.

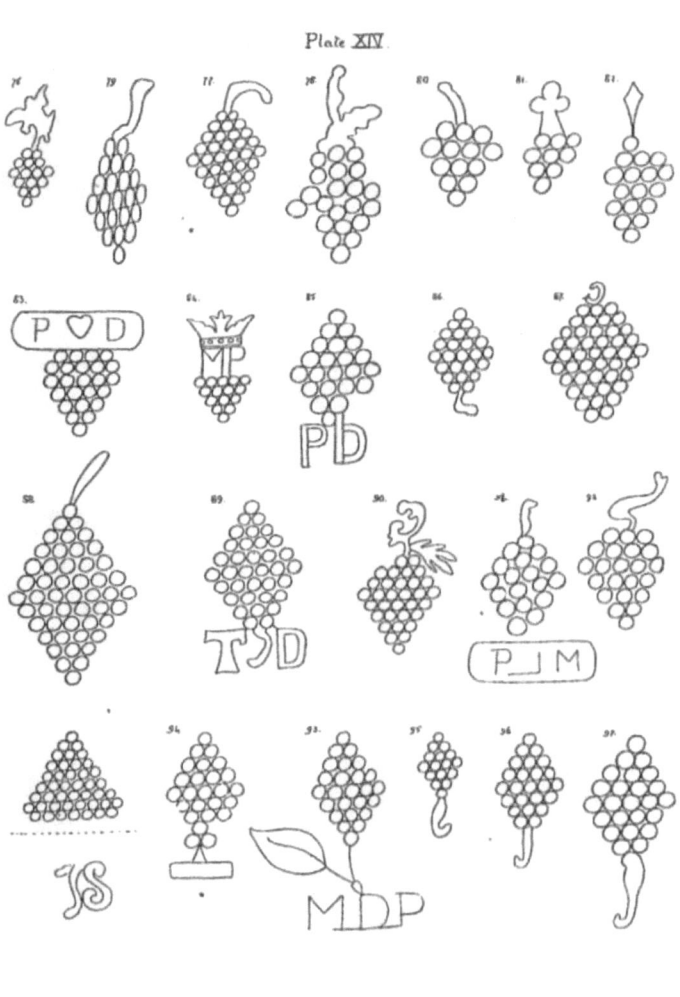

Plate XV.

Plate XVI

Plate XVII.

Plate XVIII

Plate XIX.

Plate XX.

Plate XXI.

Plate· XXII.

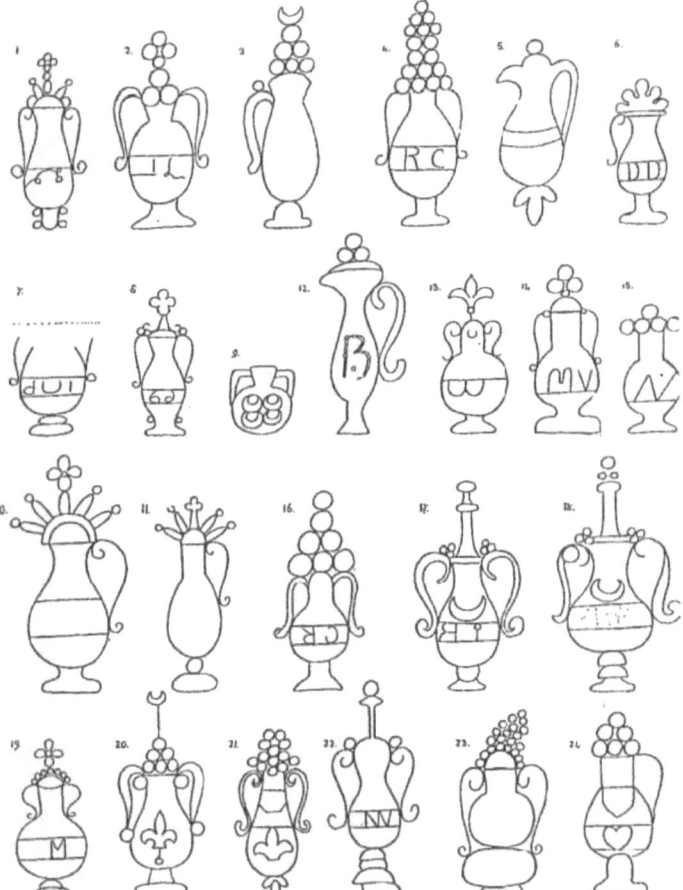

Plate XXIII

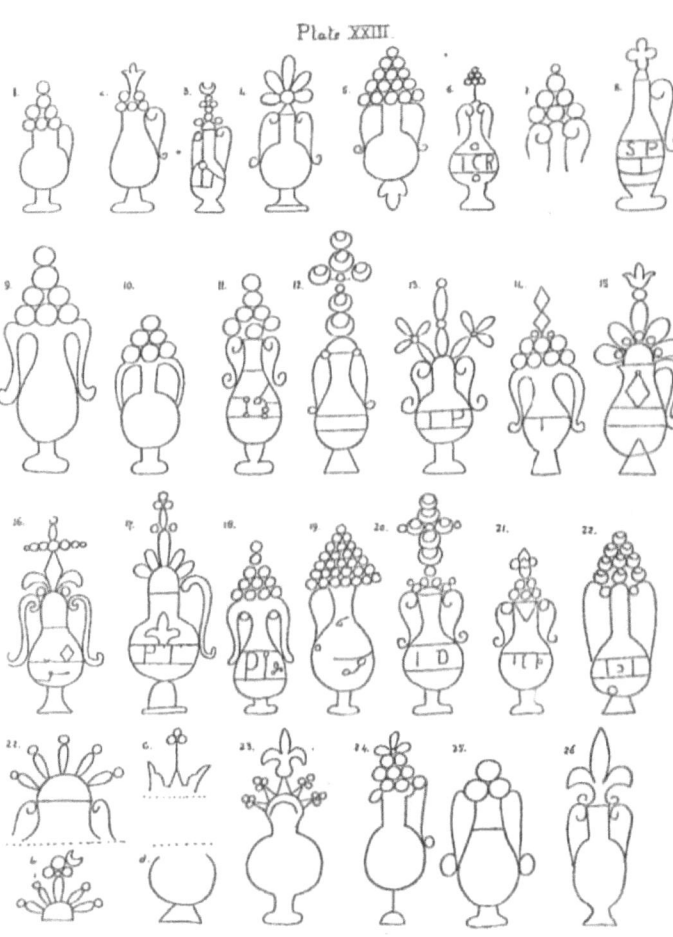

Plate XXIV

Plate XXV.

Plate XXVI.

Plate XXVII

PLATE I.

1. Sphere, surmounted by star or crosses. Account books, Hague. British Museum collection. 1301.

2, 3. Sphere, surmounted by star or crosses. Account books, Hague. British Museum collection. 1356, 1430
Another, 5½ inches high, slightly different. Cotton MSS. Nero 127.

4. Sphere, cross, scarabeus. Jansen (in Sotheby). 1315.

5, 6. Sphere, cross, scarabeus, one with water line = Holy Spirit. Jansen (in Sotheby). 1360.

7-11 Sphere, with triangle = the Trinity; ellipse = Holy Spirit. The figure 4, sacred number in " Perfect Masonry," meaning the universe, four elements, four winds, four seasons, four dimensions, as generally conceived, length, breadth, depth, height. In 9a is a figure 4, the Egyptian hierogram = Greek alpha and omega. The T, which frequently appears in these plates, signifies light. The double *tau*, a very ancient symbol of the sacred sanctuary of light and beauty, resembles H. Two I's, with a cross between, as 9b, conveys the same idea as at fig. 10. A cross in a sphere is the Druidical silver wheel, Arianrod — emblem of the Bi-une God, the alpha and omega of the Revelations. Chiefly from the collection, British Museum, 318c, vol. vii. No. 11 is five inches long. *Circa* 1400.

12. D, a mystic word expressive of the power of expanding, spreading, unfolding, laying open.[1] *Di* was a term

---

[1] *Celtic Researches*, p. 446, Davies, quoted *B. of God*, ii. 441.

for the Deity, from which we have Day (Dai), the
Disposer, the Distributor. We ask God to " give us
each day our daily bread."   *Biblia Pauperum;*
Sotheby's *Principia;* Cotton, Nero vi. 218, 230.   1590.

13, 14. Spanish letters.

15–17. The three mounts — probably Calvary or Golgotha,
Moriah, and Sinai, to which Masonic traditions are
attached. At Golgotha Adam was buried, who caused
the ruin of mankind. Here the Saviour suffered, who
came to redeem mankind. Here, too, Enoch is said to
have constructed his nine-arched vault, and concealed
from men the ineffable name of God. It is said that
the Masons discovered this vault and brought it to
Solomon. Mount‧ Moriah was the seat of Solomon's
Temple, and a story too long for insertion relates how
this mount came to be consecrated to brotherly love.[1]
Mount Sinai is said to be referred to in the twenty-
third and twenty-fourth degrees of the (Prince of the
Tabernacle) Scottish Ancient and Accepted Rite.
But Scottish Masonry is not traceable to a date earlier
than 1758, and then only in Paris. Perhaps it then
adopted the modern name of " Free Mason." British
Museum, 318c, vol. vii.

18 Five mounts (or hills of knowledge?). British Museum, 318c vii.

19. Some of many varieties of keys.   *Biblia Pauperum*

20. Anvil. True size, 3½ inches, many patterns. Haarlem
account book. 1416–1421.

21. Anvil. German MS. Fifteenth century.

22. Anvil cross. Double tau. Cotton MSS. Nero vi. 163.
1603.

23. Flaming sun. Cotton MSS. Caligula E 302. 1598.

24. St. Katherine's wheel, or disguised sun. *Ars Moriendi*
— Hibbert.

25. Scales. *Biblia Pauperum.*

---

[1] See *Royal Masonic Cyclopædia* — Moriah.

26. Scales. Many patterns, some within a circle. British Museum, 318c. *Circa* 1400.

27. Scales. British Museum, 318c.

28, 29. Anchors. Eleven varieties in account books, etc.—Holland. British Museum, 318c. 1416–1463. See, also, Nos. 21, 22, Plate II. Some have roses, *fleur-de-lis*, etc.

30. Serpent, with its tail in its mouth—emblem of eternity—$3\frac{1}{2}$ inches diameter. British Museum, 15c ii.

31. Five-pointed star in circle. Five is a mystic number, meaning the soul of the world. A star, the emblem of a heavenly messenger, or teacher. The circle = the world.

32. The ship or ark of the church. Cotton MSS. Nero vi. 108. 1529. British Museum, 318c vii. 1400.

PLATE II.

1–3. Unicorns. Symbol of the church. One marked as if for cipher. There are four other varieties, 1430, and more 1460—all German. *Ars Moriendi.* 1440. Also in *Apocalypse*, and in the *Speculum*, first edition, 1430–1465.

4, 5. Unicorns. Drayton's Poems, three patterns. Brit. Mus., 11,573. (Sotheby.) 1620.

6. Talbot or hound, symbol of hunting or experience. The Oxford Book St. Jerome. (Sotheby.) "Printed date," 1468.

7. Talbot, from a Dutch Bible, copy of the Aretin. The paper of the Bodleian copy of the Aretin, "dated" Oxford, 1479, exhibits no fewer than twenty-two different paper-marks, nearly all of which occur in the Dutch Bible of 1477. Brit. Mus., 318c. 1477.

8 A dog-headed figure merging into a horn or spire. Anthony Bacon's correspondence. Tennison MSS., Lambeth Palace.

9–11. Bulls' heads. Brit. Mus., 318c. *Circa* 1470.

12. Bull's head. The original is seven inches high. *Ars Moriendi.*

13–20. Bulls' heads. No. 20 is seven inches long. Brit. Mus., 318c. 1400.

21, 22. Anchors. See PLATE I. Brit. Mus., 318c.

22–26. Letters G, M, P, Y. See Sotheby's *Principia Xylographica*, xi., leaf 8, chap. 25. In the " Barclay " copy of the Apocalypse, the I H S are elaborately introduced in the style of the early English letters, and with crosses and flourishes. MSS. and the Apocalypse, Spenser copy. 1440, 1460.

PLATE III.

1. Open hand. Archives Haarlem, British Museum, 318c. 1432.

2. Open hand. Letter written to the Archbishop of Bath. Archives Haarlem, British Museum, 318c. 1433.

3–5. Open hand, with heart. Cotton MSS. Caligula E vii. 205. 1573.

6. Open hand, with 3. From Rome. Cotton MSS. Caligula E, vii. 205. 1521.

7. Open hand, with cross. Chapman's Works, British Museum, C 34c 11. 1598.

8. Hand, with key. Archives Haarlem. 1427–8.

9. Hand, with bunch of grapes.

10. Hand, with star. Hatton Finch MSS. Dateless.

11, 12. Hand, with star. Cotton MSS. British Museum, Nero vi. 35. Dateless.

13. Hand, with letter, signed A. Powlet. Cotton MSS. Caligula E vii. 205. 1577.

14. Hand, horn or crescent and trefoil, and A B, in pedigrees of the Bacon family. Harleian MSS. 1393, fol. 85.

15. Hand, with crescent in palm. *Shepherd's Garland*—Drayton. British Museum, C 30e 21. 1593.

16. Hand, with 3. No star. Undated document, foreign. Hatton Finch MSS. 1393.

17, 18. Bugle. Accouut book, Hague, and letter to the Bishop
of Durham. British Museum, 318c. 1421.

  19. Bugle (in heart, trefoil). *Paradise Lost;* Andrew Marvel's *Verses.* 1668.

  20. Bugle in shield. Letter of Francis Allen, or Alleyne,
to Anthony Bacon. Tennison MSS., Lambeth. 1592–
1641.

  21. Bugle in mirror, hearts, trefoil, etc. Bacon's *History of
Henry VII.*

  22. Bugle on shield, imperfect; and a bar on which is PAN.
Quarles' *Emblems.* 1639.

  23. Another. *Paradise Lost.* 1668.

  24. Another. *A Learned Discourse of Justification by
Faith* — Richard Hooker, D. D. 1631.

  25. Bugle on shield made by olive wreath and crown, horns,
trefoil. Observe the S S, and that the same shield is
a pot in disguise. From Bacon's *History Natural and
Experimental,* title page, and *History of Life and
Death,* preface. 1658.

26–30. Specimens of innumerable *fleur-de-lis,* some 2½ inches
high, scattered about in the above works and MSS.

PLATE IV.

  1. Horns of a bull. MSS. Frankfort. British Museum,
318c. 1470.

  2. Horns of a bull. Burton's *Anatomy of Melancholy;*
unique copy, presented by Burton to the Nation.
British Museum, C 45c 30. 1621.

3–5. Horns of a bull. Molière's Works. 1682.

  6. Horns of a bull, or cornucopeia, crown indistinct.
Cotton, Nero vi. 132. 1632. Another in Shakespeare,
1632, and Cotton, Nero vi. 48.

  7. Horns of a bull. Cotton, Nero vi. 368.

  8. Horn in shield, etc. Bullock pedigree. Harl. 1393,
fol. 96.

10–12. Fool's cap and fragments. Quarles' *Emblems.* Dyce
& Forster Library, S. Kensington Museum. 1676.

13. Fool's cap. Bagford collection, fol. 29.
14. Moor's head, with bandage pushed up from the eyes. (An allusion to the efforts being made to convert the Mahommedans?) *Circa* 1420.
15. Twisted horns.
16. Twisted horns. *Advancement of Learning.* 1605.
17. Triangle, hearts. Harl. MSS., 1393, 88.
18. Shield. Account book, Zuid, Holland. British Museum, 318c. 1469–1470.
19. Shield. Document, Frankfort on the Main. British Museum, 318c. 1470.
20, 21. Shield, other specimens. Dutch. 1460.
22, 23. Shields. *Apocalypse,* Haarlem. Early 15th century.
24. Shield, heart-shaped. Letter, H. Maynard to Anthony Bacon. Tennison MSS., Lambeth. 1592.
25, 26. Shield, heart-shaped. Poems of Michael Drayton. 1619.
27. Shield, heart-shaped. Letters of Sir Francis Bacon. Copies. Hatton Finch Collection.
28. Shield, heart-shaped. North's *Plutarke.* 1595.
29. Shield. Letter from Theodore Beza to Anthony Bacon. Tennison MSS., Lambeth. 1593.
30. Shield, heart-shaped. Letter unsigned. Cotton MSS. Nero, 229. 1590.
31, 34. Shield, heart-shaped, with R C. *Advancement of Learning.* 1640.
32. Shield, heart-shaped. Document. Cotton, Nero vi. 180.
33. Shield, heart-shaped. *De Augmentis.* Holland. 1652.

PLATE V.

1. Shield, with Greek omega, and eight rays within. Cotton MSS. Nero vi. 62. Dateless.
2. Shield, with B, and the name NICOLAS. Cotton MSS. 372. Dateless.
3. Shield, with C R. *Advancement of Learning.* 1640.
4. Shield, with B (almost like No. 2). Harl. MSS. 1393, fol. 118.

5, 6. Shield (note horns and eye). From the *Comedy of
Errors*, Shakespeare. 1632.

  7. Shield (note bull face). *Shakespeare.* 1632.

  8. Shield (note bull face). The Works of Joseph Mede.
1677.

  9. Shield (note bull face). Modern mark, in L. Van Gelder's paper. 1890.

10. Mock shield, lions. George Herbert — *The Temple.*
1633.

11. *History of Life and Death.* 1638.

12. *Advancement of Learning.* 1640.

14. *Fleur-de-lis. Coriolanus* — Shakespeare. 1632.

15. *Fleur-de-lis* and crown. *Apocalypse*, Haarlem. Early
fifteenth century. Large oval shields, lions, harp,
fleur-de-lis, Harl. Bagford's Collection, 5892, fol. 5;
other patterns, fols. 80, 96, 105, 122; others, with lions
rampant, one five inches high, Bagford, 5896, 6.

17, 18. Bar. I R C. *Cynthia's Revels* — Ben Jonson. (Perhaps Jonson Rosy Cross?)

Plate VI.

  1. Shield, chains, cabalistic marks. Works of J. Mede.
1652.

  2. Shield, chains. *The Rule of Conscience* — Jeremy Taylor.
1671.

  3. Shield, chains. Theophrastus Paracelsus — *Opera Om-
nia.* Geneva. 1658.

    Shield, chains and cross. *Companion to the Temple* — J.
Comber, D. D. 1684.

4–9. Mock shield and *fleur-de-lis.* "Diodati" Bible and
Commentary. 1648.

10. Bar. Shakespeare folio — *Cymbeline*, last page. C I R C.
(Jonson Rosy Cross?) 1623.

11. Bar. Ben Jonson's Works — title-page and catalogue.
1640. (Anthony? This bar surmounted by large
bunch of grapes.)

12, 13. *Fleur-de-lis* and pearls. *Vestal Virgin* (epil.) — Sir R. Howard. *Circa* 1450–1600.

14, 15. Spires rising from bulls' heads. Foreign paper.

16. *Fleur-de-lis.* Shakespeare — *Cymbeline.* 1632.

17, 18. *Fleur-de-lis. The Merchant's Book of Commerce* — Thos. Horne Cornhill. 1700.

PLATE VII.

1–4. Crowns. Shakespeare, Works. Brit. Mus. copy. 1623.

5–9. Crowns. Shakespeare, Works. Kensing. Mus. Forster copy. 1623.

10. Crowns. Philomathes — *Pleasure with Profit.* 1594.

11. Crowns. Harl. Bagford Collection, 5892, 1.

12. Crowns, with rose in pentagon. Hatton Finch MSS. 304.

13. Crowns, diamond. MS. Quintilian. Brit. Mus. 4829 iv.

14. Crowns. *Themata Varia.* Hatton Finch MSS. 304.

15. Crowns. MS.

16, 18. Crowns. Sir Walter Raleigh's *History of the World.* Several patterns. 1614.

19. Crowns. North's *Plutarke.* Brit. Mus. 10,605, i. 2. 1603.

20. Truth seated in triple ellipse, five pearls, diamond, trefoil, water, cross, crown. Joynson's foolscap paper. 1890. Another, one-tenth of an inch smaller, details different, Toogood's paper. Another in fly-leaf to book has Time as au old man instead of Truth.

PLATE VIII.

1. Tower. Nuremberg Chronicle. Jo. Ames' collection, Bodleian library.

2. Castle-like candlesticks. A. Powlett — French document. Cotton MSS. 73, 92.

3, 4. Pillars or candlesticks, drawn in Fenn's collection, pp. 8, 21.

5. Double candlesticks, with grapes, etc. Note the B. Douai Testament. 1600.

6. Single candlesticks. *Observations on Cæsar's Commentaries* — Clement Edmundes. 1609.

7. Double candlestick in *Visitation of Wiltshire.* Pedigrees signed by Wm. Camden (Clarenciens). Harl. MSS. 1111. This water-mark follows for five pages the Bacon pedigree, beginning at fol. 38. Again they occur ten times in a pedigree of the Penryddokes. The widow of John Penryddoke married John Cooke, kinsman of Lady Anne Bacon.

8. Double candlesticks. *Lectures on St. John,* " preached " by Arthur Hilderson. 1628.

9. Double candlesticks. Quarles' *Feast for Wormes.* 1631

10. Double candlesticks. Marlowe's *Jew of Malta.* British Museum, 644c 70. 1633.

11. Double candlestick. Milton's *Comus.* (Several patterns.) 1634.

12–12e. Double candlesticks. Quarles' *Emblems.* (Sixteen patterns.) 1635—1634.

13, 13a. Double candlesticks. *A Review of the Councell of Trent* — Anon. (Five patterns.) 1638.

14, 14a. Double candlesticks. *De Augmentis.* 1638.

Plate IX.

15. Double candlesticks. *History of Life and Death.* 1638.

16. Double candlesticks. *Advancement of Learning.* 1640.

17, 17a. Double candlesticks. Ben Jonson's *Poetaster.* 1640.

18, 19. Double candlesticks. *History of Henry VII.* 1641.

20. Double candlesticks. Sir Kenelm Digby's *Treatises.*

21. *The Art of Making Devises, etc.* — Anon. Various. Very large and elaborate in edition 1650. S. Ken. Forster, 87c. 1646.

22. Double candlesticks. Fuller's *History of the Holy Warre,* 3d edition, Cambridge. 1647.

23. Double candlesticks. Undescribed and dateless. Bodleian collection, 25, 837d i.

PLATE X.

24, 25. Double candlesticks. Sir Kenelm Digby *Of Man's Soul.*
1669.

26, 27. Double candlesticks. Sir Kenelm Digby *Of Bodies.*
1669.

28, 29. Double candlesticks. *De Augmentis.* 1674. Others
like these and the above, but with variations, in Clark's
Examples, 1656.

30. Double candlesticks. Undescribed and dateless. Bodleian collection.

PLATE XI.

1-3. The vine and grapes. Dutch MSS. British Museum
collection, 318c, vol. v. 1431–1445.

4. Grapes, diamond. Letter from the Ambassador of
Venice. Cotton MSS. 1600.

5. Grapes, diamond. Letter, Spanish, signed " Alonso."
Cotton MSS. 1603.

6. Grapes, diamond. Letter, Seville. Cotton MSS. 1603.

7. Grapes, diamond, C R I (or reversed?). Livorno.
Cotton MSS. 1603.

8. Grapes, diamond, B R. Heraldic and Historical Collection. Lansdowne, 205, fol. 248.

9-10. Grapes, diamond. These and a great variety of others.
Lansdowne, 187, 205, 230, etc.

11. Grapes. *Biblia Pauperum.*

12. Grapes. Bible. 1588.

13-22. Grapes. (Some fragments.) *Advancement of Learning.* 1605.

23. Grapes. Bible. 1609.

24-29. Grapes. *Book of Common Prayer.* 1609.

PLATE XII.

30-34. *Book of Common Prayer.* Continued from Plate XI.
1609.

35-39. Bible. 1610.

40-42. Florio's Italian-English Dictionary. 1611.

43. Marlowe's *Hero and Leander.* Letters M C (for C M ?). 1613.

44, 45. *Sidero Thriambos.* 1618.

46–48. (With bars.) *Shakespeare* folio. 1623.

49. D'Aubigne's *History of the Reformation.* 1626.

50, 51. (With bars.) *Shakespeare.* 1632.

52. Quarles' *Emblems.* 1635–1634.

PLATE XIII.

53. Bar in *Shakespeare.* 1632.

54. *De Sapientia Veterum.* (Five rays and pearls as crown.) 1638.

55. *Review of the Councell of Trent* — Anon. 1638.

56–58. Quarles' *Emblems.* 1639.

59–62. Ben Jonson's Works. 1640.

63. *History of the Councell of Trent* — translated Sir N. Brent. (*Vesica Piscis* and sacred monogram.) 1640.

64. Collection of pamphlets, including the *Religio Medici* — Sir Thos. Browne. 1642.

Almost the same in *Twenty-seven Songs of Sion* — Christmas Carols — W. S.

65. *Perspective Curieuse* — Père Niceron — Paris. 1652.

66. *A Priest of the Temple* — George Herbert. 1652.

67. *Chronicle of the Kings of England* — Sir Sam'l Bake. 1660.

68, 69. Sir Philip Sidney's *Arcadia.* (See Plate XIV.) 1662.

70. *Life and Death of Thomas Cromwell.* (Supposed " spurious " play of Shakespeare.) 1664.

71, 74. *Ecclesia Restaurata.* 1641.

72, 73. Philippe de Comines' *History.* 1665.

75, 75a. " Fulke's " Bible and Commentaries. 1633.

PLATE XIV.

76. *De Augmentis.* 1638.

77, 78. *Sylva Sylvarum.* (See Plate XII.) 1638.

79–82. Sir Philip Sidney's *Arcadia.* 1662.

83–89. *La Perspective Curieuse* — Niceron. 1663.

90, 91. *Paradise Lost.* 1668.

    92. *Paradise Regained.* 1668.

    93. The Works of Abraham Cowley. 1669.

    94. *The New Atlantis.* 1669.

95–97. Molière's Plays. 1682.

PLATE XV.

    1. Pot, like chalice. From book printed by Caxton, before Sotheby. 1491.

    2. Pot. From MS. British Museum, vi. 318c. 1497.

    3. Pot. Letter (or copy) from W. Latimer to M. W. Pace. Hatton Finch, 29,549. 1530.

    4. Pot. Letter, French, unsigned. Cotton MSS. Nero vi. 1596.

 5, 6. Pot. Letter, copies of English. Cotton MSS. Nero vi. 1596.

    7. Pot. Letter, signed Walsingham. Cotton MSS. Nero vi. 1577.

    8. Pot. Letter, Walsingham to Leycester. Cotton MSS. Nero vi. 1577.

    9. Pot. Letter, Nathaniel Bacon to the Lord Chancellor. Tennison MSS. 1579.

  10. Pot. Letter, H. Maynard to Anthony Bacon. Tennison MSS. 1580.

11, 12. Pot. Letter, H. Maynard to Anthony Bacon, copies. Tennison MSS. 1580.

  13. Pot. Letter, Francis Bacon to W. Doylie. Tennison MSS. 1580.

  14. Pot. Letter, Sir Amyas Powlett to A. Bacon. Cotton MSS. 1580.

15, 16. Pot. Letter, Walsingham to A. Bacon. Cotton MSS. 1587.

  17. Pot. Advertisement from Paris. Cotton MSS. 1587.

  18. Pot. *Ten Sets of Emblems in Verse* — Anon. (The verses are like Quarles'.) Tennison MSS. 1587.

  19. Pot. Mrs. Anne Bacon to her brother Anthony. Tennison MSS. 1591.

Another pot, exactly similar, Richard Barker to Anthony Bacon. Tennison MSS. 1591.

20. Pot. Lady Anne Bacon to her son Anthony. Tennison MSS. 1592.

21. Pot. Henry Maynard to Anthony Bacon. Tennison MSS. 1592.

22. Pot. M. Colman to Anthouy Bacon. Tennison MSS. 1592.

23. Pot. Alexander Bence to Anthony Bacon. Tennison MSS. 1592.

.   PLATE XVI.

1. Letter by Sheryngton to Archbishop Whitgift. Tennisou MSS., Lambeth. 1593.

   Another, but without rays, Alexander Bence to Anthony Bacon. Tennison MSS., Lambeth. 1592.

2, 3. Miscellaneous pedigrees—some of the Bacon family. (Several patterns.) Harleian MSS. 1393, fols. 31, 42, 46, etc.

4. Letter, unsigned—Of the debt of the Low Countries. Various. Hatton Finch MSS. 338. 1590.

5. Letter unsigned, undated.

6. Letters from Henry Cobham. One speaks of Daubigne being sent into Scotland. Another has the letters A B. The same in letters from Sir Amyas Powlett. Cotton MSS. Calig. E. 108, 159-161, 203, 210. 1581.

7. *Estratto da Avisi da Constantinopoli.* Cotton MSS. Nero vi. 19. After 1603.

9. Letters, dateless, unsigned. Speak of Cardinal Alobrandini. Cotton MSS. Nero vi. 17.

10. Letters, intercepted, to Signor Valete "al Conte." Signed Andrea Van Nellecouen. Cotton MSS. Nero vi. 23.

11, 12, 15, 17. Letters unsigned, undated. Cotton MSS. 235, 267, 314, 393-437.

14. Pedigrees connected with the Bacon family. Harl. 1393, 108.

16. Note: This is the only example of a two-handled pot in the British Museum collection. It is there called "Vase, from MS. Quintilian." The latter is not in the museum. (The sheet on which this "vase" is found is amongst a collection of foreign papers, 1881.) Dateless.

PLATE XVII.

1. From the Works of Thos. Becon, vol. i, or Thos. Beacon, vol. ii. 1560. (Note this mark and spelling of the name, with regard to the last pot in our collection.)
2. Francis Bacon's *Apologie*. 1604.
2–5a. *Advancement of Learning*. 1605.
6–14. *Translation of Certaine Psalms*. 1625.
   10. *War with Spain*. 1629.
   15. *Hist. Vitis et Mortis*. 1637.
16–18. *Sapientia Veterum*. 1638.
19–23. *Hist. Life and Death* (and next sheet). 1638.

PLATE XVIII.

1–3. *Hist. Life and Death*. 1638.
   4. *Hist. Experimentalis et Naturalis, De Ventis*, etc., 1638, and others in edition of 1650.
5, 6. *History of Henry VII*. 1638.
7–14. *De Augmentis*. 1638.

PLATE XIX.

1–4. *Advancement of Learning*. 1640.
   5. *De Augmentis*. 1645.
   6. Bacon's *Remaines*. Baconiana (one of three varieties). 1648.
   7. *New Atlantis* and *Sylva Sylvarum*. 1650. In the *New Atlantis*, 1669, there are five patterns.
8–10. *Sylva Sylvarum*. 1651.
   Nearly the same as No. 10 in *XXVIII Sermons by Jeremy Taylor*. 1654.
11–12. *Sylva Sylvarum*. 1658.

PLATE XX.

13. *Sylva Sylvarum.* 1658.
14. *History of Life and Death.* 1658.
15. Undescribed, in the Bodleian Collection. 1662.
16–18. *New Atlantis.* 1669.
19, 20. *Advancement of Learning.* 1674.

PLATE XXI.

1. North's *Plutarke.* Last fly leaf; otherwise foreign paper. 1579.
2, 2a. *A Handful of Gladsome Verses Given to the Queen's Maiestie.* 1592.
3 to 3y. Spenser's *Faerie Queene.* S. Ken. Mus., Forster and Dyer Library. 1596. Note the A B, F B, A F, R C, etc., and a date (1586 reversed ?).
4, 5. Homer's *Iliades* — Chapman. 1598.
6, 6d. *A Pithie Exhortation.* 1598.

PLATE XXII.

1–8. Montaigne's *Essays.* 1603.
9. North's *Plutarke.* 1603.
10, 11. *The Examination, etc., of George Sprot.* 1609.
12–15. *Observations on Cæsar's Commentaries* — Clement Edmundes. 1600.
16–22. Florio's Italian-English Dictionary. 1611.
23, 24. *London Triumphing* — T. Middleton. 1612.

PLATE XXIII.

1–3. Drayton's *Polyalbion.* 1613.
4, 5. *Civitalis Amor.* 1613.
6, 7. Marlowe's *Hero and Leander.* Brit. Mus. 1076h 6. 1613.
8. Another pot with I I.
9–21. Ben Jonson's Works. 1616.
22 *a, c* & *d.* Stowe's *Survey of London.* 1618.
22 *b.* *The World Lost at Tennis.*
23–26. Selden's *History of Tithes.* 1618. See next plate.

27

PLATE XXIV.

1-11. Selden's *History of Tithes.* See Plate XXIII. 1618.

    12. *Triumphs of Love and Antiquity* — Middleton. 1619.

    13. *The World Lost at Tennis* — Middleton. 1619.

14, 14a. Chapman's *Byron's Conspiracie.* 1625.

    15.

    16.

17-17c. *Love's Labour's Lost* (quarto). 1631.

Space does not admit of a collection found in C. Marlowe's *Troublesome Reigne of King Edward II.*, 1622 (Brit. Mus. 82c 22); *Dr. Faustus,* pot, hand and rose; *Jew of Malta,* pot with V D; others with crescent and crown. Also in *Edward II.*, 1598, other patterns with hand and star. Also in *Hero and Leander,* 1629 and 1637; *The Rich Jew of Malta,* 1633; *The Queen's Wake,* 1610; *The Order of the Solemnitie of the Creation of Prince Henrie,* 1610; *Tam Robur in Colis Arbor Jovis,* 1610; and other plays, masques, etc., of "the Elizabethan and Jacobean" dramatists, some anonymous.

PLATE XXV.

    1. Euphues' *Anatomie of Wit* — J. Lilie. 1631. Almost the same in Euphues' History of England. (British Museum, 12, 410cc 1.)

    2-9. Hooker's *Eeelesiastical Polity.* 1632.

    10. Milton's *Comus.* A masque presented at Ludlow Castle. 1634.

    11. Quarles' *Emblems.* 1639. No second half visible; other patterns in the edition of 1645, and a pot with I P in *History of Samson,* 1631.

    12. Sir Kenelm Digby, *Observations on the 22nd Stanza, &c. of the Faerie Queene.* (British Museum, 11,805aab, p. 17.)

    13. Fuller's Church History. 1648.

    14. "Diodati" Testament and Commentary. Annotations to the Book of the Revelations. 1648.

PLATE XXVI.

1-6. *The Alcoran of Mahomet* — Anon.   Six bold patterns. 1649.

   7. New Testament.   1650.

8-10. Daniel's *Collection of the History of England.*   1650.

11, 12. *Scourge for the Assyrian* — Anon.   Tract.   1652.

   13. *Designe for Plentie.*   Tract.   1652.

14, 14*a*. George Herbert's *Priest to the Temple* (and some non-descripts).   1652.

   15. Clark's *Examples.*   1657.   Some similar in *XXVIII. Sermons* — Jeremy Taylor.

PLATE XXVII.

1. *The Way of Bliss* — Elias Ashmole.   1658.

2. *The Doctrine of Original Sin* — Ashmole.   1658.

3. From *Paper and Paper Making* — Richard Herring, 3d edition.   1863.   This is reprinted from *Ure's Dictionary of Arts and Manufactures,* " with illustrations and Additions."   As is usual in all books professing to publish any account of these matters, the illustration is without any date or description as to its meaning, or the book from which it was taken.

4. Sir Robert Howard's *Four New Plays.*   1664.

5. *Shakespeare.*   1664.

6. Sir Kenelm Digby's *Powder of Sympathy.*   1669.   One of several patterns.   This book is an allegory or parable of the " Rosicrucian " sort.

7. Sir Kenelm Digby's *Treatise of Bodies.*   1669.   Several patterns.

8. Sir Kenelm Digby's *Treatise of Souls.*   1669.   Several patterns.

9. Traced on a piece in the collection of English paper-marks at the Bodleian Library.   On the paper is written: " Geneva Bible, 1561."   But the Geneva Bible of that date (*which is the date of Francis Bacon's birth*) has not this paper-mark, and a pot of this size

(nearly 5 inches) is not found till nearly one hundred
years later. The figures reversed — 1651 — would be
about the date.

10. On the same sheet as No. 9. Here the pot is not traced,
but on the paper is written in the same hand of a
well-known Professor: " From Bacon's Works," with
the date added, 1563-4. In the works of " Thomas
Becon," vol. i., or " Thomas Beacon," vol. ii., there
is no pot like this. See *ante.*

11. CR.   From Sir Kenelm Digby's *Of the Soul.*   1669.

12, 13. Cowley's Works.   1669.

Had space permitted, it was the intention to add extra and
nondescript designs to prove that it was by intention and selec-
tion that the marks specially classed as " Baconian" were introduced into a certain very comprehensive circle of books of the
sixteenth and seventeenth centuries. The curious and industrious reader should satisfy himself on this point by studying the
" extras" in these or other books of the period. He will find
shields, chains, *fleur-de-lis*, roses, bell-flowers, cardinals' hats,
shrines, lambs and flags, lions, Mercury's rods, spread eagles,
double-headed eagles, etc., with a quantity of distinct but nondescript figures, and many of the old foreign marks, varied or
modified.

It must be borne in mind that the present collection consists
only of *selections* made from the limited number of books from
which we have been able to draw.   Unfortunately, many other
books related to the subject had been examined with a view to
other particulars before we had grasped the importance of the
paper-marks as *first links* in the chain.

All the editions of books of the sixteenth and seventeenth centuries should be searched; the most elementary educational
books, as well as the sermons " preached;" masques and plays
" produced;" songs and hymns " written," " penned," " presented," " set to music;" theological, scientific and historical
works " collected," " augmented," " revised;" classical and

foreign works " translated out of the Latin," or " first printed in the English tongue."

Where the hieroglyphic pictures, next to be described, are conspicuous and abundant, the water-marks seem to have been less regarded. Yet this is not an invariable rule. On the other hand, where the name of the supposed author on the title-page, or the signature of the dedication, is printed in *mixed types* differing from the rest of the printing, we are seldom disappointed in our search after water-marks, unless the book was published abroad, or the paper made from wood and not from cotton fibre.

FRANCIS BACON

Francis Bacon, 1st Viscount St. Alban, Kt, KC, was an English author, philosopher, jurist , scientist, and statesman. He served both as Attorney General and Lord Chancellor of England. Although his political career ended in disgrace, he remained extremely influential through his works, especially as philosophical advocate and practitioner of the scientific method during the scientific revolution. Bacon has been called the creator of empiricism. His works established and popularised inductive methodologies for scientific inquiry, often called the *Baconian method,* or simply the scientific method. His demand for a planned procedure of investigating all things natural marked a new turn in the rhetorical and theoretical framework for science, much of which still surrounds conceptions of proper methodology today.

Bacon was knighted in 1603, and created both the Baron Verulam in 1618 and the Viscount St. Alban in 1621; as he died without heirs, both peerages became extinct upon his death. He famously died by contracting pneumonia while studying the effects of freezing on the preservation of meat.

Bacon was born on 22 January 1561 at York House near the Strand in London, the son of Sir Nicholas Bacon by his second wife Anne, the daughter of noted humanist Anthony Cooke. His mother's sister was married to William Cecil, 1st Baron Burghley. Biographers believe that Bacon was educated at home in his early years owing to poor health (which plagued him throughout his life), receiving tuition from John Walsall, a graduate of Oxford with a strong leaning towards Puritanism. He entered Trinity College, Cambridge, on 5 April 1573 at the age of twelve, living for three years there together with his older brother Anthony under the personal tutelage of Dr John Whitgift, future Archbishop of Canterbury. Bacon's education was conducted largely in Latin and followed the medieval curriculum. He was also educated at the University of Poitiers. It was at Cambridge that he first met Queen Elizabeth, who was impressed by his precocious intellect, and was accustomed to calling him "the young Lord Keeper".

His studies brought him to the belief that the methods and results of science as then practised were erroneous. His reverence for Aristotle conflicted with his loathing of Aristotelian philosophy, which seemed to him barren, disputatious, and wrong in its objectives. On 27 June 1576, he and Anthony entered *de societate magistrorum* at Gray's Inn. A few months later, Francis went abroad with Sir Amias Paulet, the English ambassador at Paris, while Anthony continued his studies at home. The state of government and society in France under Henry III afforded him valuable political instruction. For the next three years he visited Blois, Poitiers, Tours, Italy, and Spain. During his travels, Bacon studied language, statecraft, and civil law while performing routine diplomatic tasks. On at least one occasion he delivered diplomatic letters to England for Walsingham, Burghley, and Leicester, as well as for the queen.

The sudden death of his father in February 1579 prompted Bacon to return to England. Sir Nicholas had laid up a considerable sum of money to purchase an estate for his youngest son, but he died before doing so, and Francis was left with only a fifth of that money. Having borrowed money, Bacon got into debt. To support himself, he took up his residence in law at Gray's Inn in 1579.

Bacon had three goals: to uncover truth, to serve his country, and to serve his church. He sought to further these ends by seeking a prestigious post. In 1580, through his uncle, Lord Burghley, he applied for a post at court which might enable him to pursue a life of learning. His application failed. For two years he worked quietly at Gray's Inn, until he was admitted as an outer barrister in 1582.

His parliamentary career began when he was elected MP for Bossiney, Devon in a 1581 by-election. In 1584, he took his seat in parliament for Melcombe in Dorset, and subsequently for Taunton (1586). At this time, he began to write on the condition of parties in the church, as well as on the topic of philosophical reform in the lost tract, *Temporis Partus Maximus.* Yet he failed to gain a position he thought would lead him to success. He showed signs of sympathy to Puritanism, attending the sermons of the Puritan chaplain of Gray's Inn and accompanying his mother to the Temple Church to hear Walter Travers. This led to the publication of his earliest surviving tract, which criticised the English church's suppression of the Puritan clergy. In the Parliament of 1586, he openly urged execution for Mary, Queen of Scots.

About this time, he again approached his powerful uncle for help; this move was followed by his rapid progress at the bar. He became Bencher in 1586, and he was elected a reader in 1587, delivering his first set of lectures in Lent the following year. In 1589, he received the valuable appointment of reversion to the Clerkship of the Star Chamber, although he did not formally take office until 1608 – a post which was worth £16,000 a year.

In 1588 he became MP for Liverpool and then for Middlesex in 1593. He later sat three times for Ipswich (1597-1601-1604) and once for Cambridge University (1614).

He became known as a liberal-minded reformer, eager to amend and simplify the law. He opposed feudal privileges and dictatorial powers, though a friend of the crown. He was against religious persecution. He struck at the House of Lords in their usurpation of the Money Bills. He advocated for the union of England and Scotland, thus being one of the influences behind the consolidation of the United Kingdom; and also advocated, later on, for the integration of Ireland into the Union. Closer constitutional ties, he believed, would bring greater peace and strength to these countries.

Bacon soon became acquainted with Robert Devereux, 2nd Earl of Essex, Queen Elizabeth's favourite. By 1591, he acted as the earl's confidential adviser.

In 1592, he was commissioned to write a tract in response to the Jesuit Robert Parson's anti-government polemic, which he titled Certain observations made upon a libel, identifying England with the ideals of democratic Athens against the belligerence of Spain.

Bacon took his third parliamentary seat for Middlesex when in February 1593 Elizabeth summoned Parliament to investigate a Roman Catholic plot against her. Bacon's opposition to a bill that would levy triple subsidies in half the usual time offended many people. Opponents accused him of seeking popularity. For a time, the royal court excluded him.

When the Attorney-Generalship fell vacant in 1594, Lord Essex's influence was not enough to secure Bacon that office. Likewise, Bacon failed to secure the lesser office of Solicitor-General in 1595. To console him for these disappointments, Essex presented him with a property at Twickenham, which he sold subsequently for £1,800.

In 1596, Bacon became Queen's Counsel, but missed the appointment of Master of the Rolls. During the next few years, his financial situation remained bad. His friends could find no public office for him, and a scheme for retrieving his position by a marriage with the wealthy and young widow Lady Elizabeth Hatton failed after she broke off their relationship upon accepting marriage to a wealthier man. In 1598 Bacon was arrested for debt. Afterwards however, his standing in the Queen's eyes improved. Gradually, Bacon earned the standing of one of the learned counsels, though he had no commission or warrant and received no salary. His relationship with the Queen further improved when he severed ties with Robert Devereux, 2nd Earl of Essex, a shrewd move because Essex was executed for treason in 1601.

With others, Bacon was appointed to investigate the charges against Essex, his former friend and benefactor. A number of Essex's followers confessed that Essex had planned a rebellion against the Queen. Bacon was subsequently a part of the legal team headed by Attorney General Sir Edward Coke at Essex's treason trial. After the execution, the Queen ordered Bacon to write the official government account of the trial, which was later published as *A DECLARATION of the Practices and Treasons attempted and committed by Robert late Earle of Essex and his Complies, against her Majestie and her Kingdoms* ... after Bacon's first draft was heavily edited by the Queen and her ministers.

According to his personal secretary and chaplain, William Rawley, as judge Bacon was always tender-hearted, *"looking upon the examples with the eye of severity, but upon the person with the eye of pity and compassion"*. And also that *"he was free from malice"*, *"no revenge of injuries"*, and *"no defamer of any man"*.

The succession of James I brought Bacon into greater favour. He was knighted in 1603. In another shrewd move, Bacon wrote his *Apologie* in defence of his proceedings in the case of Essex, as Essex had favoured James to succeed to the throne.

The following year, during the course of the uneventful first parliament session, Bacon married Alice Barnham. In June 1607 he was at last rewarded with the office of Solicitor-General. The following year, he began working as the Clerkship of the Star Chamber. In spite of a generous income, old debts still couldn't be paid. He sought further promotion and wealth by supporting King James and his arbitrary policies.

In 1610 the fourth session of James' first parliament met. Despite Bacon's advice to him, James and the Commons found themselves at odds over royal prerogatives and the king's embarrassing extravagance. The House was finally dissolved in February 1611. Throughout this period Bacon managed to stay in the favour of the king while retaining the confidence of the Commons.

In 1613, Bacon was finally appointed attorney general, after advising the king to shuffle judicial appointments. As attorney general, Bacon successfully prosecuted Robert Carr, 1st Earl of Somerset and his wife, Frances Howard, Countess of Somerset for murder in 1616. The so-called "Prince's Parliament" of April 1614 objected to Bacon's presence in the seat for Cambridge and to the various royal plans which Bacon had supported. Although he was allowed to stay, parliament passed a law that forbade the attorney-general to sit in parliament. His influence over the king had evidently inspired resentment or apprehension in many of his peers. Bacon, however, continued to receive the King's favour, which led to his appointment in March 1617 as the temporary Regent of England (for a period of a month), and in 1618 as Lord Chancellor. On 12 July 1618 the king created Bacon Baron Verulam, of Verulam, in the Peerage of England. As a new peer he then styled himself as "Francis, Lord Verulam".

Bacon continued to use his influence with the king to mediate between the throne and Parliament and in this capacity he was further elevated in the same peerage, as Viscount St Alban, on 27 January 1621.

Bacon's public career ended in disgrace in 1621. After he fell into debt, a Parliamentary Committee on the administration of the law charged him with twenty-three separate counts of corruption. To the lords, who sent a committee to enquire whether a confession was really his, he replied, "My lords, it is my act, my hand, and my heart; I beseech your lordships to be merciful to a broken reed". He was sentenced to a fine of £40,000 and committed to the Tower of London during the king's pleasure; the imprisonment lasted only a few days and the fine was remitted by the king. More seriously, parliament declared Bacon incapable of holding future office or sitting in parliament. He narrowly escaped undergoing degradation, which would have stripped him of his titles of nobility. Subsequently the disgraced viscount devoted himself to study and writing.

There seems little doubt that Bacon had accepted gifts from litigants, but this was an accepted custom of the time and not necessarily evidence of deeply corrupt behaviour. While acknowledging that his conduct had been lax, he countered that he had never allowed gifts to influence his judgement and, indeed, he had on occasion given a verdict against those who had paid him. The true reason for his acknowledgement of guilt is the subject of debate, but it may have been prompted by his sickness, or by a view that through his fame and the greatness of his office he would be spared harsh punishment. He may even have been blackmailed, with a threat to charge him with sodomy, into confession.

On April 9, 1626 Bacon died of pneumonia while at Arundel mansion at Highgate outside London. An influential account of the circumstances of his death was given by John Aubrey's Brief Lives. Aubrey has been criticised for his evident credulousness in this and other works; on the other hand, he knew Thomas Hobbes, Bacon's fellow-philosopher and friend. Aubrey's vivid account, which portrays Bacon as a martyr to experimental scientific method, had him journeying to Highgate through the snow with the King's physician when he is suddenly inspired by the possibility of using the snow to preserve meat: "They were resolved they would try the experiment presently. They alighted out of the coach and went into a poor woman's house at the bottom of Highgate hill, and bought a fowl, and made the woman exenterate it".

After stuffing the fowl with snow, Bacon contracted a fatal case of pneumonia. Some people, including Aubrey, consider these two contiguous, possibly coincidental events as related and causative of his death: "The Snow so chilled him that he immediately fell so extremely ill, that he could not return to his Lodging ... but went to the Earle of Arundel's house at Highgate, where they put him into ... a damp bed that had not been lain-in ... which gave him such a cold that in 2 or 3 days as I remember Mr Hobbes told me, he died of Suffocation".

At the news of his death, over thirty great minds collected together their eulogies of him, which was then later published in Latin.

He left personal assets of about £7,000 and lands that realised £6,000 when sold. His debts amounted to more than £23,000, equivalent to more than £3m at current value.

The Baconian theory of Shakespearean authorship, first proposed in the mid-19th century, contends that Sir Francis Bacon wrote some or all the plays conventionally attributed to William Shakespeare, in opposition to the scholarly consensus that William Shakespeare of Stratford was the author.

Francis Bacon often gathered with the men at Gray's Inn to discuss politics and philosophy, and to try out various theatrical scenes that he admitted writing. Bacon's alleged connection to the Rosicrucian's and the Freemasons has been widely discussed by authors and scholars in many books. However others, including Daphne du Maurier (in her biography of Bacon), have argued there is no substantive evidence to support claims of involvement with the Rosicrucian's. Frances Yates does not make the claim that Bacon was a Rosicrucian, but presents evidence that he was nevertheless involved in some of the more closed intellectual movements of his day. She argues that Bacon's movement for the advancement of learning was closely connected with the German Rosicrucian movement, while Bacon's *New Atlantis* portrays a land ruled by Rosicrucian's. He apparently saw his own movement for the advancement of learning to be in conformity with Rosicrucian ideals.

The link between Bacon's work and the Rosicrucian's ideals which Yates allegedly found, was the conformity of the purposes expressed by the Rosicrucian Manifestos and Bacon's plan of a "Great Instauration", for the two were calling for a reformation of both "divine and human understanding", as well as both had in view the purpose of mankind's return to the "state before the Fall".

Another major link is said to be the resemblance between Bacon's *"New Atlantis"* and the German Rosicrucian Johann Valentin Andreae's *"Description of the Republic of Christianopolis"* (1619). In his book, Andreae shows an utopia island in which Christian theosophy and applied science ruled, and in which the spiritual fulfilment and intellectual activity constituted the primary goals of each individual, the scientific pursuits being the highest intellectual calling – linked to the achievement of spiritual perfection. Andreae's island also depicts a great advancement in technology, with many industries separated in different zones which supplied the population's needs – which show great resemblance to Bacon's scientific methods and purposes.

The Rosicrucian organization AMORC claims that Francis Bacon was the "Imperator" (leader) of the Rosicrucian Order in both England and the European continent, and would have directed it at that time of the Renaissance.

Francis Bacon's influence can also be seen on a variety of religious and spiritual authors, and on groups that have utilised his writings in their own belief systems.

Bacon's works:

A complete chronological list of Francis Bacon'w works:

- Notes on the State of Christendom (1582)
- Letter of Advice to the Queen (1585-6)
- An Advertisement Touching the Controversies of the Church of England (1586-9)
- Dumb show in the Gray's Inn Christmas Revels (1587-8)
- Misfortunes of Arthur (1588)
- A Conference of Pleasure: In Praise of Knowledge, In Praise of Fortitude, In Praise of Love, In Praise of Truth. (1592)
- Certain Observations made upon a Libel (1592)
- Temporis Partus Maximus ('The Greatest Birth of Time') (1593)
- A True Report of the Detestable Treason intended by Dr Roderigo Lopez (1594)
- The Device of the Indian Prince: Squire, Hermit, Soldier, Statesman. (1594)

- Gray's Inn Christmas/New Year Revels: The High and Mighty Prince Henry, Prince of Purpoole (1594-5)
- The Honourable Order of the Knights of the Helmet (1595)
- The Sussex Speech (1595)
- The Philautia Device (1595)
- Maxims of the Law (1596)
- Essays (1st edition) (1597)
- The Colours of Good and Evil (1597)
- Meditationes Sacrae (1597)
- Declaration of the Practices and Treasons attempted and Committed by the late Earl of Essex (1601)
- Valerius Terminus of the Interpretation of Nature (1603)
- A Brief Discourse touching the Happy Union of the Kingdoms of England and Scotland (1603)
- Cogitations de Natura Rerum ('Thoughts on the Nature of Things') (1604)
- Apologie concerning the late Earl of Essex (1604)
- Certain Considerations touching the better pacification and Edification of the Church of England (1604)
- The Advancement and Proficience of Learning Divine and Human (1605)
- Temporis Masculus Partus ('The Masculine Birth of Time') (1605)
- Filium Labyrinthi sive Formula Inquisitionis (1606)
- In Felicem Memoriam Elizabethae ('In Happy Memory of Queen Elizabeth') (1606)

- Cogitata et Visa de Interpetatione Naturae ('Thoughts and Conclusions on the Interpretation of Nature') (1607)
- Redargiutio Philosophiarum ('The Refutation of Philosophies') (1608)
- The Plantation of Ireland (1608-9)
- De Sapientia Veterum ('Wisdom of the Ancients') (1609)
- Descriptio Globi Intellectualis ('A Description of the Intellectual Globe') (1612)
- Thema Coeli ('Theory of the Heavens') (1612)
- Essays (2nd edition −38 essays) (1612)
- Marriage of the River Thames to the Rhine (1613)
- Charge...touching Duels (1614)
- The Masque of Flowers (1614)
- Instauratio Magna ('Great Instauration') (1620)
- Novum Organum Scientiarum ('New Method') (1620)
- Historia Naturalis ('Natural History') (1622)
- Introduction to six Natural Histories (1622)
- Historia Ventorum ('History of Winds') (1622)
- History of the Reign of King Henry VII (1622)
- Abcedarium Naturae (1622)
- De Augmentis Scientiarum (1623)
- Historia Vitae et Mortis ('History of Life and Death') (1623)
- Historia Densi et Rari ('History of Density and Rarity') (1623)
- Historia Gravis et Levis ('History of Gravity and Levity') (1623)
- History of the Sympathy and Antipathy of Things (1623)
- History of Sulphur, Salt and Mercury (1623)
- A Discourse of a War with Spain (1623)

- An Advertisement touching an Holy War (1623)
- A Digest of the Laws of England (1623)
- Cogitationes de Natura Rerum ('Thoughts on the Nature of Things') (1624)
- De Fluxu et Refluxu Maris ('Of the Ebb and Flow of the Sea') (1624)
- Essays, or Counsels Civil and Moral (3rd, final edition – 58 essays) (1625)
- Apothegms New and Old (1625)
- Translation of Certain Psalms into English Verse (1625)
- Revision of De Sapientia Veterum ('Wisdom of the Ancients') (1625)
- Inquisitio de Magnete ('Enquiries into Magnetism') (1625)
- Topica Inquisitionis de Luce et Lumine ('Topical Inquisitions into Light and Luminosity') (1625)

The following works were published after his death:
- New Atlantis (1627)
- Sylva Sylvarum, or Natural History (1627)
- Certain Miscellany Works (1629)
- Use of the Law (1629)
- Elements of the Common Laws (1629)
- Operum Moralium et Civilium (1638)
- Dialogum de Bello Sacro (1638)
- Cases of Treason (1641)
- Confession of Faith (1641)
- Speech concerning Naturalisation (1641)
- Office of Constables (1641)
- Discourse concerning Church Affairs (1641)
- An Essay of a King (1642)
- The Learned Reading of Sir Francis Bacon (to Gray's Inn) (1642)

- Ordinances (1642)
- Relation of the Poisoning of Overbury. (1651)
- Scripta in Naturali et Universali Philosophia (1653)
- Scala Intellectus sive Filum Labyrinthi (1653)
- Prodromi sive Anticipationes Philosophiae Secundae (1653)
- Cogitationes de Natura Rerum (1653)
- De Fluxu et Refluxu Maris (1653)
- The Mirror of State and Eloquence (1656)
- Opuscula Varia Posthuma, Philosophica, Civilia et Theologia (1658)
- Letter of Advice to the Duke of Buckingham (1661)
- Charge given for the Verge (1662)
- Baconiana, Or Certain Genuine Remains Of Sr. Francis Bacon (1679)
- Abcedarium Naturae, or a Metaphysical piece (1679)
- Letters and Remains (1734)
- Promus (1861)